Accumulation in Post-Colonial Capitalism

Iman Kumar Mitra · Ranabir Samaddar
Samita Sen
Editors

Accumulation in Post-Colonial Capitalism

Springer

Editors
Iman Kumar Mitra
Mahanirban Calcutta Research Group
Kolkata, West Bengal
India

Samita Sen
School of Women's Studies
Jadavpur University
Kolkata, West Bengal
India

Ranabir Samaddar
Mahanirban Calcutta Research Group
Kolkata, West Bengal
India

ISBN 978-981-10-9312-8 ISBN 978-981-10-1037-8 (eBook)
DOI 10.1007/978-981-10-1037-8

Softcover reprint of the hardcover 1st edition 2016

Printed on acid-free paper

This Springer imprint is published by Springer Nature
The registered company is Springer Science+Business Media Singapore Pte Ltd.

Acknowledgement

This volume would not have been possible without the encouragement from Rosa Luxemburg Stiftung (RLS), Germany. Some of these essays were presented in their initial forms at the Fifth Critical Studies Conference, 2014, in Kolkata, organized by the Mahanirban Calcutta Research Group (MCRG) with support from the RLS. We are grateful to Anirban Das, Arup Kumar Sen, Dipankar Sinha, Immanuel Ness, Ingo Schmidt, Kalpana Kannabiran, Mouleshri Vyas, Paula Banerjee, Sabyasachi Basu Roy Chaudhury and Sanjay Chaturvedi for their invaluable comments on these essays. We also thank the two anonymous referees for their comments. We thank Rita Banerjee for her help in preparing the manuscript. The authors, needless to say, are all indebted to each other, for this volume is not a mere collection of essays conceived and written in isolation; they are fruits of endless discussions and deliberations, fights and struggles, cajoling and collaborating, all done collectively. Our colleagues at CRG, as always, have been immensely helpful in every step of the journey.

Finally, we dedicate this volume to the memory of Rosa Luxemburg (1871–1919).

Contents

Editors and Contributors

About the Editors

Iman Kumar Mitra has studied economics and is a research associate at the Mahanirban Calcutta Research Group. His doctoral dissertation explores the history of dissemination of economic knowledge in colonial Bengal through various pedagogical and institutional networks. His research interests include history of economics, migration, urbanization and labour issues. He is currently involved in a research project on the interconnectedness between rural-urban migration, urbanization and social justice in post-liberalization India.

Ranabir Samaddar is distinguished chair in Migration and Forced Migration Studies, Mahanirban Calcutta Research Group. He has worked extensively on issues of forced migration, the theory and practices of dialogue, nationalism and post-colonial statehood in South Asia and new regimes of technological restructuring and labour control. His most recent publication in the form of a co-authored volume on new town and new forms of accumulation *Beyond Kolkata: Rajarhat and the Dystopia of Urban Imagination* (Routledge, 2013) takes forward urban studies in the context of post-colonial capitalism.

Samita Sen was the first vice-chancellor of the Women's University at Diamond Harbour. Currently she teaches at the School of Women's Studies, Jadavpur University. She has worked extensively on labour and gender issues. Her publication includes *Women and Labour in Late Colonial India: The Bengal Jute Industry* (Cambridge University Press, 1999) and the co-authored monograph *Domestic Days: Women, Work, and Politics in Contemporary Kolkata* (Oxford University Press, 2015). She is a member of the Mahanirban Calcutta Research Group.

Contributors

Ilia Antenucci Institute for Culture and Society, Western Sydney University, Richmond, Australia

Debarati Bagchi Centre for Historical Studies, Jawaharlal Nehru University, New Delhi, India

Ritajyoti Bandyopadhyay Indian Institute of Science Education and Research, Mohali, India

Byasdeb Dasgupta University of Kalyani, Kalyani, West Bengal, India

Shruti Dubey Centre for Political Studies, Jawaharlal Nehru University, New Delhi, India

Atig Ghosh Visva Bharati University, Santiniketan, West Bengal, India

Rashmi Gopi Maitreyi College, University of Delhi, Chanakyapuri, India

Mithilesh Kumar Institute for Culture and Society, Western Sydney University, Richmond, Australia; Mahanirban Calcutta Research Group, Kolkata, India

Iman Kumar Mitra Mahanirban Calcutta Research Group, Kolkata, India

Sushmita Pati Centre for Political Studies, Jawaharlal Nehru University, New Delhi, India

Sanam Roohi National Institute of Advanced Studies, Bengaluru, India; Amsterdam Institute for Social Science Research, Amsterdam, The Netherlands

Ranabir Samaddar Mahanirban Calcutta Research Group, Calcutta, India

Samita Sen School of Women's Studies, Jadavpur University, Kolkata, India

Suhit K. Sen Indian Council of Historical Research, New Delhi, India

List of Tables

Introduction: A Post-Colonial Critique of Capital Accumulation Today

Iman Kumar Mitra, Ranabir Samaddar and Samita Sen

Abstract The introduction makes three main points, which characterize this volume. (a) It looks at how accumulation under post-colonial capitalism tends to blur various geopolitical boundaries of space, institutions, forms, financial regimes, labour processes, and economic segments on the one hand and creates zones and corridors on the other. In this context, it draws our attention to the peculiar but structurally necessary coexistence of both primitive and virtual modes of accumulation in the postcolony. With increasing inflow of virtual capital in the form of offshore funds, venture business, hedge funds, Internet-based investment and banking, and forward trading, more people are forced to accept precarious work conditions in the unorganized sectors resulting in massive de-peasantization and creation of footloose labour, otherwise known as migrant or transit labour. (b) At the same time, family household becomes the new site of capitalist production and market system, which is different from what is assumed to be a site of non-capitalist production, something that is outside of capital. (c) The introduction also draws attention to what is now called affective labour that is to say labour actualized in the forms of care work and reproductive work. Affective labour leads to the conceptualization of affective value by focusing on the labouring body and subjectivity. Affective value is often mistaken to be essentially a cultural category, and not an economic category, in spite of its vulnerability to exploitation, thus becoming an element in the dynamics of capitalist accumulation. These three aspects taken together reflect on one of the principal features post-colonial capitalism, namely the overwhelming existence of informal conditions of production. These new forms of accumulation result in new discursive and political terrains of struggle. The chapters of the volume reflect from different discursive, analytical, and conceptual perspectives on these new forms of accumulation and unique modes of struggle.

I.K. Mitra · R. Samaddar (✉)
Mahanirban Calcutta Research Group, Kolkata, West Bengal, India
e-mail: ranabir@mcrg.ac.in

S. Sen
School of Women's Studies, Jadavpur University, Kolkata, West Bengal, India

I.K. Mitra et al. (eds.), *Accumulation in Post-Colonial Capitalism*,
DOI 10.1007/978-981-10-1037-8_1

Keywords Accumulation · Post-colonial capitalism · Virtual accumulation · Affective labour · Primitive accumulation

The conditions for the accumulation of capital are precisely those which rule its original production and reproduction in general: these conditions being that one part of the money buys labour and the other commodities (raw materials, machinery, etc.).... Accumulation of new capital can only proceed therefore under the same conditions under which already existing capital is reproduced. (italics by Marx, cited by Luxemburg 2014a/1915)

> In fact, he (Marx) made the solution even more difficult by assuming the capitalist mode of production to prevail universally. (Luxemburg 2014a/1915)

In this introduction, we view the debates and discussions on the question of accumulation from a postcolonial perspective vis-à-vis a critical theory of post-colonial capitalism. We do not, however, directly comment on the historical debates on the question of accumulation, because much of this debate will today appear primarily of scholarly interest unless we situate the question of accumulation against the perspective of imperialism, or what can be called its *other scene*, the post-colonial capitalist reality of today's world. From this standpoint, we attempt to elucidate its features because such an attempt will help us develop new insights relating to the enigma of accumulation. We also have another goal—more ambitious—and thus our vacillation and possible ineffectiveness in articulating it. Maybe at the end of this introduction, we can ask: what are the philosophical implications of a post-colonial critique of the contemporary dynamics of accumulation, given the fact that such a critique can originate only from within, that is from within the post-colonial regime of accumulation? If so, what are the inside and the outside of the dynamics of capitalist accumulation? How do we negotiate the perennial duality of the inside and outside? This question will impel us to recall the classic tradition of revolutionary dialectics, and that will be a fitting tribute to the legacy of Rosa Luxemburg and the centenary of her classic, *The Accumulation of Capital*, in its English translation.

Boundaries of Accumulation

The process of separation of labourers from the means of production so that they become free wage-labourers for the purposes of capitalist exploitation is not a natural development, but rather the result of violent confrontations. Not only this process speaks of a past (the process of initial transition from the precapitalist to the capitalist mode of production), but also it continues to this day on a great scale in the post-colonial world. In developed capitalist countries as in the post-colonial capitalist countries, the workers erect social and political barriers to the extension of the length of the working day, and therefore, capital introduces machinery as a counterelement against the working class. Yet, while capital tries to reduce the number of workers, it also seeks to bring in new workers under its command as an exploitable human resource. The so-called human factor of production is thus always present, and capitalist accumulation must depend on the continuous separation of the labourer from the means of production.

We can say then that primitive accumulation is the separation which we have referred to whenever it occurs, and accumulation of capital proper includes besides this separation expansion through the mode of economy. This may be taken as a historical companion, symbolizing the separation happening continuously, of proper accumulation when the latter is the order of the capitalist economy. At yet another level, we can say that accumulation is transition (transiting the borders of production and circulation), while primitive accumulation is the specific mark of this transition, reminding us that the transition from say feudalism to capitalism did not happen as a natural process. We cannot take transition for granted, merely because history happened that way. The 'extra-economic' factors are always present in the economic, and only in this way, an adequate understanding of capitalism becomes possible. It is not without reason that war has been always the occasion for discussion on accumulation. Think of the two wars and the colonial and neo-colonial wars continuing up to our time of neoliberal restructuring of global economy. Massive post-colonial experiences only reinforce this point.

A post-colonial critique of the accumulation process is built on a fundamental understanding that capitalism demands all geographical limits to capital accumulation to be overcome, though in different ways, which leads to the characteristic penchant for space. At the same time, while production entails geographical concentration of money, means of production (thus proximity to means of production including natural resources), labour power, and consumer markets (all these for higher profits and lower costs), the circulation of capital requires circumventing various boundaries—of space, institutions, forms, financial regimes, labour processes, economic segments, etc.—thus requiring the construction of different zones and corridors. Capital accumulation begins in this contradictory mode: whenever and wherever some money is deployed to make more money by exploiting wage labour, with the important proviso that this will require specific conditions to make money in this way and in a sustainable manner. This makes border perhaps the most important institution for capital to circumvent—national political borders, natural boundaries, borders of markets, boundaries of production sites and circulation, boundaries of cities, borders of norms and violence, and most importantly the border between necessary labour and surplus labour, and thus necessary work hours and surplus work hours. We can see how a post-colonial critique of the capitalist accumulation process requires treating border as method, because a border-centric study necessitates a dialectical handling of a situation.

Sometimes, one can take this to an extreme extent (the danger of all logic) and say that the idea of accumulation of capital is enough, there is no need for an adjective 'primitive', since capital has always included force and violence in achieving the aim of separation of labourers from their means of production, and that capital has always presupposed transition, and thus, there is no need to invoke a 'primitive' to acknowledge the reality of accumulation. This kind of logic is absurd because it is non-dialectical. It forgets the duality of the inside and the outside of a process.

Lenin, always a practical revolutionary, was cautious on this point. He said:

> New and important in the highest degree is Marx's analysis of the accumulation of capital, i.e. the transformation of a part of surplus value into capital, and its use, not for satisfying the personal needs or whims of the capitalist, but for new production… From the accumulation of capital under capitalism we should distinguish what is known as primitive accumulation: the forcible divorcement of the worker from the means of production, the driving of the peasants off the land, the stealing of communal land, the system of colonies and national debts, protective tariffs, and the like. 'Primitive accumulation' creates the 'free' proletarian at one pole, and the owner of money, the capitalist, at the other. (Lenin 1964a/1915, p. 64)

Many of today's Marxists take Lenin to task for being 'doctrinaire' and sticking to the letters of Marx. In our understanding, Rosa Luxemburg also, notwithstanding her complicated expositions on this issue, was careful in final formulations, while she debated with Marx's writings on the origins of accumulation and stressed what can be called 'the ground outside' in understanding the process of accumulation.

It also means that we cannot do away with logic and think that historical narrations will give us a clear analysis of capitalism. While determining the reproduction of aggregate social (total) capital, we have to keep aside the issue of singularities. In the *Grundrisse*, Marx says that the concrete is 'the concentration of many determinations' (Marx 2014b/1939). This is the way in which we can define singularity. Singularity is the concrete. Yet, as Marx tells us, the concrete is the point of departure in reality, not in thought. Thus, we arrive at the concrete through a process of abstraction, which means starting from the abstract. In its immediacy, the concrete gives us only what Marx calls a 'chaotic conception'. And when Marx adds that the concrete is the 'unity of the diverse', what is significant is not the words 'unity' and 'diverse', but the indication by Marx of the dialectical relation of the two: the unity and the diverse. We can approach the issue of accumulation in that spirit without getting bogged down into the endless and sterile debate whether while pursuing a logic Marx is right in clearing the analysis of historical impurities that mark any analysis of the concrete. We shall then see that the unity of the process of reproduction of capital through the process of reproduction of surplus value is the abstraction of many concrete determinations of the process of realization (including the violent process). Furthermore, this unity yields also to a mode of production of an essential difference. To continue, unity, if we come to think of it deeply, is a transition of singularities to an abstraction. We have now reached the link between transition and accumulation.

Marx in the second and third volumes of *Capital* showed how markets become crucial for accumulation. Thus, global and local capitalists, as well as non-capitalist enterprises, are interconnected today through global (i.e. where exchange happens between entities across national boundaries) and local (i.e. where exchange happens between intranational entities) markets. This is the materialization of a value chain. Neoliberal capitalism through the supply chains (consisting of various modes such as outsourcing, subcontracting, and offshoring) gives rise to new circuits of global capital. Connected to these circuits are new practices and relationships that produce new subjects and a new hegemonic social reality that aims to foreclose the language of class precisely by retaining and underscoring the presence of the so-called informal, agricultural, and the household sectors. Yet, Marx showed at the same time how capitalist crisis becomes one of the accumulations through the reinforcement of the social in the productive process; thus, the resistance of the worker (and the society) does not allow beyond a point the operation of the so-called remorseless laws of accumulation. The state whose singular importance in the accumulation process was brought out by Lenin again and again becomes the crucial site where politics negotiates the inevitable binds that accumulation as a process continuously throws up. There is thus perhaps as some have called

> … an elective affinity between capitalism and passive revolution: the decentralised nature of the accumulation process, driven by competition among capitals, is evidently compatible with a wide range of political forms, giving scope for individual states to restructure the process. (Callinicos 2010, p. 491)

Accumulation and Transition

As indicated at the outset, one of the salient aspects of the post-colonial situation then is the near-permanent condition of primitive accumulation as the other of the most modern form of capital, which one may term as virtual capital. Developmental and conflict-induced migration (known as forced migration) within the country and to other countries takes place under primitive and precarious conditions, and female labour forms a substantial chunk of this scenario. Keeping this in mind, two perceptive observers describe migration as the 'multiplication of labour' (Mezzadra and Neilson 2013). As more and more virtual capital in the form of offshore funds, venture business, hedge funds, sovereign wealth funds, Internet-based investment and banking, forward trading-based wealth, etc., reach the post-colonial shores and result in massive property boom, skyrocketing land prices, construction upsurge, a new surge in the prices of raw material like iron ore, etc., and at times foodstuff, the more people are pushed towards accepting precarious and unorganized work conditions, and as a consequence, there is more de-peasantization, and appearance of unorganized labour, which can with some qualification be called as 'immaterial labour'. Flexibilization here appears not so much in the form of what is called in the West 'post-Fordism', which is based on microcomputerization, flexible technologies, and the domination of process industries, but much more in the shape of uncertain work profiles and conditions of reproduction of labour, catering to the backward linkages of new capital which is based on various automated technologies and flows.

We can ask two questions here:

First, does this scenario in any way contradict Marx's analysis? The answer is no, because once again this scenario shows how the social is inserted in an economic process and the economic and the extra-economic are intertwined. Not only the domination of finance over industry and the production process needs political and administrative restructuring of supply, investment, banking, and credit norms, but also it signals something more fundamental. It points to the dialectical way in which the limits to capital's expansion function in latter's life as a continuous process of aggrandizement. Probably, Rosa Luxemburg got Marx wrong when she commented, 'In fact, he [Marx] made the solution even more difficult by assuming the capitalist mode of production to prevail universally' (Luxemburg 2014a/1915). This is because we often disregard how Marx inserted the social in the economic. Not only he thought that the definite social relation between men becomes the fantastic form of relation between things through the domination of the commodity form, but also he added that each commodity represented a 'phantom-like objectivity' (Marx 2014a/1867) when a congealed quantity of homogenous human labour has been abstracted from any concrete determination. As 'crystals of this social substance, common to them all', capitalism foregrounds money as the 'universal equivalent', 'the social action of all commodities' (ibid). The unity of the world is made possible precisely because money is the sovereign. As the philosopher will say, money rewrites the social contract as it emerges as a universal and representative power from a process of mutual recognition of various commodities (Marx 2014a/1867). Money has evolved today into virtual forms such as of finance, credit, and promise. In this virtual form, it will now link the two ends of accumulation. Primitive accumulation will be spurred by construction boom, land grab, urban expansion, and rampant mining and other kinds of virulent extraction of underground and surface, while virtual accumulation will be spurred by trading in money and finance as commodity in an unbridled manner.

Second, in what way does this condition constitute a predicament for the postcolony? On the one hand, the postcolony must depend on the state to come out of this scissor attack taking place in the form of a combined appearance of primitive accumulation and virtual accumulation. On the other hand, the state is in a poor situation today and we do not have yet any other substantive form of national autonomy. Therefore, we must work our way through carefully. This sense of caution will help the postcolony retain flexibility and prise its way through the bind of primitive work conditions and the reproduction of the advanced form of accumulation—a bind that leaves almost nothing as social surplus for the postcolony to develop. Precisely, for this reason, the postcolony will need the most advanced form of politics, whose core will be formed through the appearance of multitude (workers, peasants, and mass of petty producers) on the political scene. In that sense, the significance of the term, *multitude*, goes far beyond their current expositions.

The heterogeneity of labour produced out of the specifics of the accumulation process forces us to grapple with the dialectical significance of transition. The post-colonial dilemma is around the issue of transition—transition from semi-colonialism and neo-colonial conditions to new democracy, retarded agriculture to agricultural reforms, and land reforms—and further on to cooperatives, foreign and corporate-led industrialization to a balanced industrial growth, and the transition of rule from compradors and corporate class to a national popular alliances. However, as Tse Tung on the basis of the experiences of socialist construction in the Soviet Union had argued in *On the Ten Major Relationships*, this transition is not towards a predetermined socialism; it does not lead to any precharted socialist path; the transition will lead to its own future, to its socialism, the sketches of whose future can be seen only by those engaged in a patient search for that (Tse Tung 1956). This is what is meant by the word *praxis*.

Accumulation and the Reordering of Space

The reality of contradiction is of course greater than the science of it. As of now, the science is developed in the North, while the reality of contradiction in the South surpasses its scientific analysis. The reality of this situation reconstitutes the respective worlds of theory and reality, universal and the determination of historical developments, the continuous search for the realization of potential, and the knowledge that reality makes new grounds, where reality becomes its own constitutive experience. Just as in the West where in the last 50 years there were desperate attempts among the Left intellectuals to escape the world of contradictions, in the postcolony too, there have been attempts to argue that the postcolony forms an outside to the world of capital and that the postcolony can escape the features of modern capitalism, such as financial crises, crises of overproduction, existence of a reserve army of the labour consisting of unemployed human resources, and various forms of bourgeois wealth—features that are integral to production and accumulation of surplus value. Here too, attempts have been made to discredit Marx's method. Yet, precisely these attempts show that material relations are clue to ideological understanding, from the branch of political economy to say politics.

The post-colonial predicament thus needs to be explored in terms of knowledge production, global logistics, economic specifics, and political subjectivity. The angle of predicament also gives us the advantage of looking at the global scenario of transformation in a new way. Let us recall in this context the decades of the 1950s to the 1970s when the word 'ex-colony' was used by anticolonial Left movement all over Asia and Africa in place of today's 'postcolony'. There were fierce debates in the communist parties and among communists as to the path of transformation. Questions were asked: what is new democracy? What is national democracy? What is people's democracy? Perhaps this change of name is a minor question. But in any case, debates like these, more than the theoretical quarrels on transition, have to be revisited. We referred to Mao's lecture on ten major relationships in that context.

The experiences of India, South Africa, Brazil, Chile, and several other countries demonstrate how post-colonial capitalism through this combination of the low and the high forms of accumulation reorders the spaces of accumulation. Reordering of spaces becomes crucial in phenomena such as the return of the land question, resurgence of commodity prices, and the reinforcement of the extractive nature of capital (extraction of biological power, nature, subsoil resources, or cognitive abilities of human beings). It results in new practices of zoning and creating corridors as circulating modes through which accumulation will take place. There are thus continuities as well as discontinuities and new features in the working of the logic of the reordering of space. These continuities and discontinuities show how old forms or configurations of space are remoulded under the conditions of post-colonial capitalism. There are great stakes in this game of zoning and spacing. These stakes concern the biopolitical organization of post-colonial societies (for instance, in India, there are coastal regulation zones to save the coast and some say to save the fishermen besides the coast; there are disaster zones and flood-prone zones wherefrom human beings are removed to save them and to put in place protection measures such as dykes; there are earthquake zones where new norms of construction of buildings are introduced. There are even suicide zones which are often dry areas and where farmers, it is said, habitually commit suicide to end miseries of life and debt). All these compel new legislations, policies, and regulations marking the particularities of respective zones and the protective measures for endangered life. These zones thus show how features of nature and of life are getting intermeshed more than ever; the two separate registers—of nature (with all its vagaries) and life—are getting tied into a new form of existence, which borrowing Michel Foucault's phrase we may call a distinct *bio-political mode of existence*. We all know of his controversial genealogy of modern biopolitics. By insisting on *life* as the key referent of power in the modern age, he argued that politics grounded society in war, specifically race war, in ways that threatened the very human existence it had pledged to promote. He also drew correlations between sovereign and biopower and examined the relations of *bios, nomos,* and race in the context of the conduct of life and death in modern conditions (Dillon and Neal 2008). The dynamics of post-colonial accumulation suggest that this life is marked by new regulations for zoning and spacing. At its heart is the logic of economy.

The practice of zoning has assumed heightened importance in the background of post-colonial developmental urges. Highways are to be constructed; mines are to be opened up tearing the secrecy of the forests; airports are to be built; new economic zones like the free trade zones to be set up and agro-industries including fruit-processing units to be established in special areas; likewise, power grids are to be set up, and marine product processing units are to dot the coastal regions, besides the ports commanding once again distinct zones. The country looks like an ensemble of zones representing different logics—at times complementary, but often overlapping and conflicting. All these zones require corridors to function—corridors of information, freight or cargo, money, credit, oil, gas, etc., the medium being somewhere the cable, the ship, intermodal train service, the pipeline, van, truck, highway, or as in today's time containers as the most long-haul cargo transport, and finally financial corridors. These corridors can be in the form of certain forms of labour linking the zones, or certain forms of transmission of information and finance, or even certain forms of circulation and processing of commodities such as roads, pipelines, optical fibres, information highways, or special freight corridors. While analysts often concentrate on the social life of a commodity (which is indeed one of the entry points in understanding the emergence of zones, thus plantation zones, tea zones, life of tea as a commodity, etc.), the need now is to look into the life of labour in its transit forms to make sense of what makes a zone and what links one zone with another. Clearly, we are looking here beyond the factory form and trying to understand the newer forms of assembly and chain. This is also the way to make sense of the biopolitical organization of capital and its logistical form.

How will these emerging zones be spaced? The citizen-worker may be a minor figure to populate such a zone, and whole populations may have to be trained to become the denizens of such an anomalous universe. Dispossessed peasants, construction workers from villages, tea shop owners and other street vendors from nearby districts, and snooty IT workers all become parts of a heterogeneous scenario of labour. They all will demand rights, some couched in the language of citizenship, some in bare life terms, and again some couched in gross economic terms of flexibility and money. While we know that these heterogeneous forms of labour will be evened out in the form of a commodity, we cannot say immediately how the new subjectivity of these newly zoned spaces will develop. But it is very much of a possibility that labour in this heterogeneous form may not want to behave like the massed or garrisoned foot soldiers of a disciplined imperial army stationed in a zone waiting for the final battle. We must be ready for a messy picture. Therefore, a zoning exercise today may be a precarious one. Because while the governmental and administrative history of zoning may be a long one, the more virtual the capital becomes, the more a zoning exercise can be subject to the unpredictable nature of fluctuations of capital (primarily capital in the form of money and credit), and thus, a zoning exercise may be self-defeating. It will be as precarious and self-defeating as has been the creation of a Euro zone, as unpredictable as the crash of 2008–2009, or the fall of Greece. Within capital, there is this immanent contradiction of zoning and flow. Finance capital requires both governmental strategies—zoning and flow—functioning at their utmost efficiency and thus its insoluble paradox and dilemma, namely how to return to a balance of the two and how to sanctify and protect the corridor that links the zones and makes flows possible. Is the corridor then *the weakest link in the chain*? Obviously, we have the task of reimagining the Leninist idea. We can now see how the post-colonial experiences of reordering of spaces (think of the special economic zones in India in the last two decades) enrich the Marxist understanding of circuits of capital. The circuits of capital are always overdetermined.

Given the fragility of the neoliberal reconstruction of economy and society in the post-colonial world, the question then will be: does the strategy of creating zones, corridors, and circuits make the neoliberal programme of making capital fluid and resilient to shocks? One of the lessons of Marx's analysis of capital is its attention to circulation, which has now become the ordering principle of life under neoliberal economy. When corridors meant to ensure the circulation of commodities and capital, particularly in their final form, *money*, fails in their tasks, the purpose of zoning fails. In capitalist production, while zoning is resorted to as part of division of labour, the productive nature of zoning depends on a successful strategy of maintaining corridors. Corridors guarantee circulation, and the quality of commodity including its organic composition determines the nature of a corridor in question.

Of course we notice to an unprecedented degree the fact that labour engaged in circulation and in production is getting intermeshed more than ever, so that the hidden process of producing surplus value is becoming more mysterious. Labour is assuming transit forms more than ever due to this reason. In this situation, money begetting more money (which Marx pointed out as the feature of merchants' capital) is determining the fate of corridors, including financial corridors. We must remember that zones in the last quarter of the twentieth century have been created less for production of ordinary commodities or even means of production as commodities, but more for production of money as commodity (typical of these spaces would be Hong Kong, Shanghai, Dubai, Doha, Singapore, and Mumbai), that is to say, an environ where production and circulation of a commodity like money merge. Thus, we are not dealing with a situation where there is an overproduction of goods requiring new channels of circulation via public reforms programmes including fiscal reforms to widen the base of consumption (famously, the New Deal and various Keynesian programmes), but the consequences of the expansion of the credit system resulting in the accumulation of money capital in increasingly abstract, surreal, and virtual or fictitious forms. The basic principle of all such forms has been capitalization of revenue-based on future production of surplus value as well as capitalization of various forms of credit, such as banking capital or stock transactions in public debt.

The 'real' and 'financial' spheres remain different, yet they become virtually one. Capital in the form of goods and capital in the form of money are different, yet they become inseparable in economy. The difficulties in realizing profit in the industrial sector are sought to be allayed in the financial sector through emphasis on profits through credit operations, which finally tell back on the economy itself. We are thus facing here the question of several competing circuits endangering the corridors of supply and circulation, impacting especially on zones. Even though one is the virtual and the other real, yet, in a sense both are real; also to be true, one is working as the virtual to the other. Therefore, the collapse of the virtual creates new wastelands of capital in the wake of its departure.

Given this background of financial insecurity that has gripped the world, the question then to be asked is, how will it affect the pattern of zoning and linking them? If true to its origin the strategy of zones, corridors, and circuits must have the dimension of security, how would the present development (the crash of 2008) upset the efficiency and maximization calculus? What will happen to the large insurance infrastructure against sudden losses of all kinds? What will secure the zones against volatile capital flows and the sudden emergence of wastelands, breakdown of circuits due to conflicts, competition, and war, and the neoliberal way of organizing the economy, which is precisely the way of combining the virtual mode and the primitive mode of accumulation? All these inquiries require two changes in our pattern of thinking. First, it means that we increasingly view circuit as a chain (with its weak links). Second, it means viewing more than ever economic relationships as essentially social relationships on which productivity (in other words, the productive power of the present economy and its accumulation capacity) depends. These relationships variously mentioned in this paper are between agriculture and industry, industry and services, capital goods and consumer goods, the overall economy and the unorganized or informal or the 'need' (a concept used extensively by the late Indian economist Sanyal (2013)) sector, growth and infrastructure, economic infrastructure and social infrastructure (such as education and health and skill formation), state and its subregions, river basins and dry areas, valley and the hill, capital region and the distant regions, and finally zones of capital investment and the zones of social investment. Transit labour emerges in this context.

Let us review our arguments made till now on the theme of a post-colonial analytic of the accumulation process before we proceed further.

First, Marx's method of analysing accumulation is both historical and trans-historical, sticking to historical singularities as well as pursuing a logical argument in dissecting the category of capital. We are aware of the theoretical and academic controversies around this question. Yet we cannot escape the fact that Marx brings in the issue of primitive accumulation and calls this the story of 'original sin' in theology that is political economy. In other words, political economy does not become science after this. Political economy remains theology. The theology continues, along with the science, as an account of the original sin. It is original, not because from this capitalism as a system originated and then the narrative of the birth of capital becomes a matter of the past, but because it is a theological story, where in the interest of the structure of the story we need an account of the original sin. This then is a double critique: critique of theology and also critique of the argument of self-reproduction of capital without the overall social mechanism that will facilitate this reproduction.

Second, in the account of the economic life of the capital, the state is important as a category. Is budget an economic instrument to dispossess people, to pauperize them, or an administrative method? The budget and the legislations (Marx calls them 'bloody') connect to the state and speak of sovereign power needed to create the space by continuously clearing it up for the dynamics of capital to operate. Therefore, the agency and the figure of the state that facilitates and effects 'expropriation' are the great shadows hovering over the entire account of capital. We are referring here to Part 8 of Marx's *Capital* (Volume 1). People speak of the role of the state in accounting for reforms. In this account, we must include the myriad of coercive ways deployed by the state in order for capital to function as a mechanism, as a process, and as a machine. We must include the state also as the facilitator of the social conditions of accumulation (by laying down policies, guiding principles, and the legal framework, providing incentives and disincentives, facilitating internal and international trade, etc.). The significance of this point is that once we bring in the question of sovereignty, much of the quarrels over interpretation of the theory of primitive accumulation pale into insignificance and irrelevance. Where a national state is absent, the role is played by colonial state or the international political sovereign in the form of imperialism. The repeated robbery of Africa is a case in point. Include colonialism in this account, and we shall see that the ostensibly free-floating account of primitive accumulation undergoes a process of displacement. Consequently, we shall have a post-colonial view of capitalism, to wit post-colonial capitalism, which will help us in viewing primitive accumulation as something not of hoary past, but of our time.

Third, to understand all these, we have to make the issue of post-colonial capitalism the essential gradient in any analysis of the dynamics of accumulation today. Not surprisingly, Lenin stresses the question of colonies and the birth of finance capital; Rosa Luxemburg too situates her analysis of accumulation in the context of imperialism. The angle of post-colonial capitalism implies (i) a combination of the virtual and the most primitive forms of accumulation, (ii) return of the land and other resources question to the central place in political economy as the role of extraction assumes increasing significance in the expansion of capitalism suffering from its own internal contradiction, (iii) new but precarious strategy of zoning and creating corridors for a reconfiguration of the spaces of capital, (iv) the salience of transit labour (simplistically called the migrant labour), and (v) the persisting significance of the state as the facilitator of the conditions of accumulation. For all these reasons, post-colonial capitalism will be the stake on which the life of capital as accumulation will depend.

Fourth, from this angle, any discussion on accumulation of capital must involve then the significant question of the *other* of the category of capital (recall Lenin's emphasis on colonies or Rosa Luxemburg's emphasis on what Marx called the 'others' in the capitalist society, that is, population groups besides the workers and the capitalists, such as hangers on, parasites, bureaucracy, and petty producers). The *other* stares at the process of accumulation, which must now subjugate the former to complete its own life. Circulation increasingly becomes the stake on which the continuity of accumulation will depend.

Reproduction and Accumulation

Rosa Luxemburg began *Accumulation of Capital* by considering the problem of *enlarged reproduction* to argue that accumulation was more than an internal relationship between the branches of capitalist economy and that the presence of outside consumers as other than capitalists was necessary for enlarged reproduction and thus accumulation. The duality of the outside and inside remains critical in consideration of the post-colonial condition and is increasingly implicated in new forms of reproductive labour emerging in these economies.

In Luxemburg's analysis, the search for constant capital drives capital to imperialisms characterized by plunder and theft. The outside, however, remains the outside: the external environment is not internalized into capitalism. The non-capitalists in such formulations are territorially defined—mostly the colonies. One may have argued, however, that within capitalist countries, there were domains that were not incorporated within capitalism, i.e. non-capitalist domains/relations, for example the domain of familial reproduction (and its workers). After loss of colonies, and from the middle of the twentieth century, swathes of reproductive activity were drawn into the market, incorporated into capitalism. How does this inflect questions of accumulation?

Marxist feminists had taken as their point of departure the implication in Marx's theory that reproductive labour was, by definition, 'outside' of capitalism; it was not abstracted labour. It did not relate to commodity production because it was not separable from the act of production. It remained locked in use value and outside the domain of exchange. This was critical to understanding women's work that it was not only unpaid but also devalued and largely unrewarded. Moreover, it created associations around 'women's work' which helped to undervalue almost all work that women did, including productive remunerative work. Thus, the binary of family/household and market was a crucial axis for understanding women workers. The underlying premise—production and reproduction remained linked within the household economy until industrial capitalism wrought their separation—the one entering the market and the other remaining non-market and within the locus of the family household. There have been sustained debates about the applicability of such theories to colonial and post-colonial societies or to treating them as exceptions to theories of capitalism (Chibber 2013). There has not been the same disarticulation of production and reproduction in colonial and post-colonial societies such as India in its 200-year history of capitalism.

There remains a need to retheorize the relationship between capital and reproduction and the trajectory it is taking in post-colonial societies, which takes into account the relationships of inequality in which they are embedded. Indeed, the variations in the modes of incorporation of reproductive activities into exploitative global processes have major implications for the constitution of labour markets in the postcolony. How may we address the relationship between the 'inside' and the 'outside' of capital and distinct modes of subsumption?

The commodification of reproductive work and wage labour such as in domestic work was a critical element in the history of early capitalism and of class formation and has eluded schematization in the dual-system approach. The history of this exception is now becoming increasingly relevant, especially in post-colonial economies, where reproduction is in perennial crisis. The agrarian economy, which remained a critical site of reproduction despite the expansion of urban economies until recently, appears now to be in terminal decline. Unlike in the West, there has been no sustained capitalization of reproduction; it is as yet a new phenomenon whose implications are unclear. Notwithstanding a few murmurs, there have been no wages for housework/housewives campaign seeking to extend the wage relationship into the familial. There have been many efforts to disentangle these issues in the context of post-colonial capitalism, but these have been repeatedly overtaken by readjustments in the domain of social reproduction. Domestic work, however, remains central—or rather, it is acquiring a new centrality—in tandem with globalization and with the burgeoning of service economies around reproductive activities. In the 1990s, Evelyn Nakano Glenn wrote of an 'international division of reproductive labour' to indicate the transnational character of the relational net of inequalities in paid domestic work (Glenn 1992). Some now call it the 'global care chain'. At the start of the twenty-first century, there is once again a blurring of production and reproduction—both now in the domain of the market. This marks a radical shift in the dynamic relationship between material production and social reproduction in many Asian countries, including those of South Asia.

The crisis in social reproduction has rendered some of the old binaries irrelevant. Thus, one major element of immaterial labour is affective labour (or care work in another register) which is implicated in earlier notions of reproductive work. Labour, which requires human contact or care or labour in the bodily mode, i.e. affective labour, is not amenable to standard measurements of labour (because it is not bound to production time) or to classical rules of exchange value. In affective labour—which operates by what we may call the creation and manipulation of affect—labour becomes affect or finds its value in affect. The erosion of the singular signification of 'production' as the operational site of abstract labour helps to blur (though not dissolve) two binaries of classical Marxism: between labour and the labourer, and between production and reproduction. In case of both intellectual and affective labours, there is a renewed focus on the labouring body and thus on the labourer in her/his singularity rather than as a unit of a homogeneous mass. Conceptually, then, affective labour is linked to but is not only reproductive labour—it arises from a convergence of productive and reproductive labour—although one has to realize that in empirical terms the two are difficult to distinguish. Besides, there is also another strand of argument that speaks of 'affective value' (Spivak 1985), which presumably is neither quite use nor exchange value but a third category of value, entangled in emotions and corporeality, cultural rather than economic but also vulnerable to exploitation by capital.

These developments have led us in South Asia to new frontiers of capitalism incorporation, such as surrogacy. These new forms of labour are messing up not only the old categories but also possibilities and trajectories of a politics centred on labour. These are doubtless new forms of affective labour but also commodity production, and in one sense, the product of this labour is life itself, but in another, it is the physical human body. Shulamith Firestone, writing about the 'relations of reproduction' (1979), predicted that reproductive technology would liberate women from a foundational condition of their subordination, i.e. childbirth. The outsourcing of procreation to poor women in the postcolony has become a reality in a bare 30 years. The terminological shift from prostitution to sex work signalled the commodification of the sexual body. The idea of care work signals the commodification of femininity itself, especially motherhood. Sangari (2015) draws a parallel between surrogacy and natural resources, linking the cyclic reproduction associated with 'nature' with the generational use of natural resources. The corporate and market control of seeds in agriculture parallels, she argues, the new market for ova, sperm and tissues, and spare parts for the production of humans in the new medical–industrial complex. Has the female body then become the site of a new reproductive common, a site for extraction, and a manipulatable, marketable biogenetic resource? Is this a new frontier of accumulation? If women's bodies are not confined to generational reproduction and can be farmed for capital gains, are we looking at new tussles for the control of women's reproductive bodies? Further, how do we conceptualize accumulation in relation to reproduction in our time of aggressive capitalization of that sphere?

Reproduction is a new and significant site of capitalist labour. Unlike in the case of colonialism (à la Luxemburg), however, reproduction may not remain the outside. By the same logic, proletarianization—the acquisition of variable capital—implies the expansionist and imperialist nature of capital. If the progressive proletarianization of non-capitalist environment is a form of primitive accumulation, what may be the consequences of this capitalist incorporation? Feminist interventions, emphasizing 'personal' relationships, challenging patriarchal discipline, has raised the social value of women's work with its high content of affective and caring labour that centres on services necessary for social reproduction. This has broken down rigidities of gendered labour markets, incorporating men into sites of reproduction in new ways and challenging constructions of femininities and masculinities. In new regimes of biocapital, production and reproduction are simultaneous, and it entangles all aspects of social life, including body and mind in discourses of health. The displacement of the factory worker from his privileged position in the capitalist economy has signalled changes in the family, especially the working-class family. The model of the male breadwinner and non-working wives and children no longer holds. If, as Hardt and Negri (2000) suggest, the figure of immaterial, and within it affective, labour power has begun to occupy an important position in both the schema of capitalist relations of production and the composition of the proletariat, what implication does it have for politics? The progressive 'legalization of the informal' (see Chap. 2 in this volume) is calling forth new forms of organizational efforts among categories such as sanitation and domestic workers and *Anganwadi* workers (or more expansively 'scheme' workers employed contractually by the state). Equally some, such as aesthetic labour (or beauty workers), resist conventional forms of unionization, either because they resist incorporation into such disciplinary regimes or because of irreconcilable conflict of interests arising from the valorization of such forms of labour. The post-colonial situation, marked as it is by a nearly permanent condition of accumulation, proliferates and extends labour informality. The conditions of accumulation within global capitalism determine also the political possibilities of labour—historically ascribed a critical role in future transitions from capitalism.

The state is increasingly more amorphous in terms of maintaining, protecting, or underwriting workers' rights. The development of new models of governance and enterprise, the grey zones in between have produced legal ambiguities within which to create new disciplinary regimes of labour.

Implications

The accumulation debate raging for more than a century raises certain curiosities. We can take note how issues of colonialism, imperialism, production of super profit, competition and monopolies, reorganization of space, different forms of capital, above all wars, etc., had their long shadows over the debate, and there was perhaps no way it could be anything else. And it was not the case that all these intervening issues were properly integrated in the accumulation arguments. Thus, one may ask in what way does a scientific question become an ideological one? Clearly, a scientific question does not remain 'scientific' in the sense that contemporary social and political milieu interjects in our discussion. Or one can say, only by negotiating rigorously with the contemporary social and political milieu a scientific question can remain scientific.

In this context, we can take note of one discussion. It is a sensitive point, but perhaps not out of context. Amidst the war, Rosa Luxemburg wrote in the *Junius Pamphlet*:

> The modern proletariat comes out of historical tests differently. Its tasks and its errors are both gigantic: no prescription, no schema valid for every case, no infallible leader to show it the path to follow. Historical experience is its only school mistress. Its thorny way to self-emancipation is paved not only with immeasurable suffering but also with countless errors. The aim of its journey – its emancipation depends on this – is whether the proletariat can learn from its own errors. Self-criticism, remorseless, cruel, and going to the core of things is the life's breath and light of the proletarian movement. The fall of the socialist proletariat in the present (first) world war is unprecedented. It is a misfortune for humanity. But socialism will be lost only if the international proletariat fails to measure the depth of this fall (and) if it refuses to learn from it'. (Luxemburg 2014b/1915)

She mentioned in this context the mistakes of the German working-class movement. While appreciating and admiring the internationalist character of the pamphlet, Lenin wrote:

> The first of Junius's erroneous propositions is embodied in the fifth thesis of the *Internationale* group, 'National wars are no longer possible in the epoch (era) of this unbridled imperialism. National interests serve only as an instrument of deception, in order to place the working masses at the service of their mortal enemy, imperialism.' The beginning of the fifth thesis, which concludes with the above statement, discusses the nature of the *present* war as an imperialist war. It may be that this negation of national wars generally is either an oversight, or an accidental overstatement in emphasising the perfectly correct idea that the *present* war is an imperialist war, not a national war. This is a mistake that must be examined, for various Social-Democrats, in view of the false assertions that the *present war* is a national war, have likewise mistakenly denied the possibility of *any* national war. (Lenin 1964b/1916, p. 308)

Lenin then went onto a discussion on the dialectical relation between national war and imperialist war and critiqued Luxemburg's treatment of the chronology of the national wars, as if the national wars collectively formed the preceding stage of imperialist war and now with the advent of the interimperialist war national wars had become impossible. Lenin's observation is significant because in his analysis of the dynamics of accumulation under imperialist condition colonial plunders and, therefore national wars, become inevitable inasmuch as inter-imperialist wars are. The acute awareness to contemporary situation led Lenin to mention the possibility of national wars even in an era of interimperialist wars.

Lenin further wrote in his commentary on the *Junius Pamphlet*:

> We have dwelt in detail on the erroneous proposition that 'national wars are no longer possible' not only because it is patently erroneous from the theoretical point of view – it

> would certainly be very lamentable if the 'Left' were to reveal a light-hearted attitude to Marxist theory at a time when the establishment of the Third International is possible only on the basis of un-vulgarised Marxism. But the mistake is very harmful also from the standpoint of practical politics, for it gives rise to the absurd propaganda of 'disarmament', since it is alleged that there can be no wars except reactionary wars. It also gives rise to the even more ludicrous and downright reactionary attitude of indifference to national movements. And such an attitude becomes chauvinism when members of the 'great' European nations, that is, the nations which oppress the mass of small and colonial peoples, declare with a pseudo-scientific air: 'national wars are no longer possible'! National wars *against* the imperialist powers are not only possible and probable; they are inevitable, *progressive* and *revolutionary though* of course, to be *successful*, they require either the concerted effort of huge numbers of people in the oppressed countries (hundreds of millions in our example of India and China), or a *particularly* favourable conjuncture of international conditions (e.g., the fact that the imperialist powers cannot interfere, being paralysed by exhaustion, by war, by their antagonism, etc.), or the *simultaneous* uprising of the proletariat against the bourgeoisie in one of the big powers (this latter eventuality holds first place as the most desirable and favourable for the victory of the proletariat). It would be unfair, however, to accuse Junius of indifference to national movements. At any rate, (s)he remarks that among the sins of the Social-Democratic parliamentary group was its silence on the death sentence passed on a native leader in the Cameroons on charges of 'treason' (evidently he attempted to organise an uprising against the war). (Lenin 1964b/1916, p. 310)

The war brought to the revolutionary leaders of the European working-class movements new awareness of the need for dialectical judgement. Like Lenin, Luxemburg also attempted to treat the national question dialectically, even though Lenin found her short of the exacting standards that he set for theoretical argument. We have to remember that this was also the moment when Lenin immersed himself in the library in Zurich in daily study of Hegel's writings, particularly *Science of Logic*, the time when he developed the theory of revolutionary defeatism as the policy of Marxists towards their respective belligerent states and governments. This was also the time when he broke with the type of 'scientific materialism' with which the Second International had framed its national chauvinist policies.

The Lenin–Luxemburg debate was not over political tactics only. It involved as we know broader questions involving their respective views of imperialism, national revolutionary wars, etc.

Moving on to other phases in the debate over the accumulation question, we can recall how the connection between war and accumulation became a thorny issue, just as the notion of crisis became integrally linked to the debate. This also raised the question, how do we perceive the crisis? Was war a crisis? Were social welfare and recovery measures, planned in war time, such as the William Beveridge Report on Social Insurance and Allied Services (1942) and the post-war European Recovery Plan known as the Marshall Plan (1948) linked to the accumulation question? When the war in Iraq began many Marxists in the post-colonial world spoke of a crisis of the finance-driven late twentieth-century and early twenty-first century capitalism, though Marxist writings in the Western capitalist countries were playing with completely different issues, such as of culture, citizenship, democracy, and European Union. War never figured in these writings.

We also know that in the Marxist writings, security and the development of the capitalist economy have been seen less as intertwined factors. Thus, in Giovanni Arrighi's mirror of the long twentieth century (2010), the story of money, power, and the origins of our time is one of continuous accumulation and expansion of the capitalist economy with wars occasionally disturbing the path. *The long twentieth century* traces the relationship between capital accumulation and state formation (over a 700-year period) and argues that capitalism unfolds as a succession of 'long centuries' (long trends), each of which has produced a new world power that has secured control over an expanding world economic space. Examining the changing fortunes of Florentine, Venetian, Genovese, Dutch, English, and finally American capitalism, the book concludes with an examination of the forces that have shaped and are now poised to undermine America's world dominance (Arrighi 2010). This is the view from the top. The period of 'long peace' (phrase used by John Lewis Gaddis (1989)) is also the period of long accumulation. Yet, this picture cannot explain the self-working of the accumulation process. Indeed, both civil and national wars have cleared the grounds for fresh accumulation in various parts of the world. A view from below, which also informs to a great measure the post-colonial argument, tells us to take wars and conflicts seriously, as they clear the grounds for accumulation, exactly as the Marshall Plan had done more than 65 years back.

To put all these briefly then, the accumulation question that is at the centre of capitalism is never at the centre. The centre is always to one side. Capitalism is real, but also the theatre of the world of politics, religion, morality, and of course economic theories, in short of myths and opiates that make capitalism decentred because our own consciousness of the world is framed with illusion, and that is wherefrom our journey begins. Therefore, the complete demystification of the accumulation question is always deferred, always beyond, and always advancing from illusion towards the real. Philosophical battles are therefore parts of the perpetual war that the bourgeoisie has always wanted to put an end to. Yet no philosophy, least of all materialist philosophy, can exist without this theoretical relationship to force. They bear the marks of a generalized state of war.

We may ask: is a turn towards the national question justified in a discussion on the accumulation question? Apart from whatever has said till now in this introduction, there is one more thing in defence of this turn. In Volume 2 of *Capital*, Marx moves from production to circulation and once again in its most abstract form (reminding us of the first volume of *Capital*), as if in a dialectical play of logical forms. Circulation becomes an abstract process through which capital will shed its old form (the industrial form) and assume new one as it will seek to secure its realization and self-expansion. Thus, as Marx demonstrated, money capital will undergo metamorphosis within this sphere of circulation. Thus, the movement from money to commodity and then increased commodity production to increased money earning is a not a result of buying cheap and selling dear, but a consequence of surplus production. Production becomes the mediating moment—the moment of producing surplus value, more accurately the moment of realizing surplus value. Production of surplus value becomes the dynamic means, at the same time logically a disjunctive leap, to move into the sphere of circulation and back to the exploitative world of industrial production. In the accumulation question, then we are continuously crossing borders and boundaries, and phases and dynamics, to find that we are witnessing an interrupted series of crises. That is what the post-colonial method suggests. Remember what Marx wrote while concluding the 'Illustrations of the General Law of Capitalist Accumulation':

> Like all good things in this bad world, this profitable method has its drawbacks. With the accumulation of rents in Ireland, the accumulation of the Irish in America keeps pace. The Irishman, banished by sheep and ox, re-appears on the other side of the ocean as a Fenian, and face to face with the old queen of the seas rises, threatening and more threatening, the young giant Republic:
>
> A cruel fate torments the Romans,
>
> And the crime of the fratricide (Marx 2014a/1867).

Overview of Chapters

This volume is divided into two sections. The first section is titled 'New Dynamics of Accumulation', and the second is named 'Caste, Gender, Race: Axes of Accumulation'. Readers are requested to read these two sections in the light of the foregoing discussion on post-colonial accumulation. It will be needless to say that the sections have overlapping thematic and conceptual orientations. The first section, as evident from the title itself, seeks to capture the changing modalities of accumulation in our time—a theme which we have discussed in some detail in the previous pages of this introduction. The second, on the other hand, has a number of chapters on three specific axes of accumulation in India: caste, gender, and race. However, these are the only axes around which accumulation happens in a post-colonial nation state; nor are these simply some 'old' institutions and networks that had once facilitated the working of accumulative forces and are now reduced to mere vestiges of the past and hence replaced by certain new mechanisms marking the (be)coming of the present. The new dynamics, at the same time, are not 'new' in a chronological sense; rather, they refer to the comparatively recent awakening of the academic communities to the fact of their existence and the criticality of their partaking in the continual processes of accumulation. By dividing the chapters into two parts, therefore, we seek to initiate a conversation between two apparently disparate, although politically and conceptually interlinked, aspects of accumulation—the emerging frontiers and the continually evolving processes and structures.

The first set of chapters addresses diverse issues and entangled processes related to accumulation in post-colonial capitalism. On the one hand, it excavates a crucial facet of accumulation in contemporary times—the urban site of extraction of resources and exploitation of labour where the spatial question appears as though to accommodate the processes of accumulation through some 'special' measures like creating boundaries and zones seemingly in contradistinction with the disbordering of labour and capital under the regime of globalization. As some of the chapters in this volume suggest, the contradiction between fixity of boundaries and suspension of the laws of the land within the 'zones' and mobility of resources including human capital is not always resolved peacefully. The new urbanism that envelops the accumulative processes in our time thus becomes one of the sites of new conflicts and new kinds of violence that facilitate production of new subjectivities and define the hegemonic social reality of the time.

On the other hand, flexibility of the labour market and the hegemonization of financial capital have opened possibilities of accumulation by rendering the working class as the main risk-bearer in times of global crises. Thus, in the first chapter in Part I, Byasdeb Dasgupta (Chap. 2) shows that a flexible labour regime seeks to resolve the capitalist problem of accumulation by dismantling regulatory mechanisms created in the first decade of independence, which was underwritten by the state and protected by trade unions until the 1990s. The encroachment of discourses of flexibility now affects the formal as well as informal labour markets, through growing deregulations of 'rigid' labour rules and further shrinking the bargaining power of labour. The disempowering of labour is a strategy fundamental to the operations of global finance capital. In the postcolony, this means the stagnation of wage income (in real term) through continuous change in functional distribution of national income in favour of rentier and profit-earning classes.

These issues crop up in other chapters in manifold forms. In Chap. 3, Mithilesh Kumar examines the case of a demand made by contract workers against authorities rendered legally ambiguous since they operated under a public–private partnership (PPP) model. These new forms of enterprise are another means of gaining 'flexibility'. Indeed, the PPP is distinguished by its lack of a legal definition, which facilitates its primary purpose of importing the logic and discipline of the market into the functioning of public bodies. It is generally agreed that the PPP is an attempt at a combination of state and capital in which each retains their characteristics while competing or collaborating with each other. In many ways, PPP is symbolic of the general argument posed by Dasgupta: it marks the transition from the 'command and control mode of governance' with strong regulatory mechanisms to some 'new mode of regulatory governance' privileging private sector participation and the values of the market. These transitions involve force and a desire to secure the apparatuses of accumulation from the risks of structural damage. Ilia Antenucci, in Chap. 4, picks up this thread and explains how, in this process, securitization itself becomes a means of accumulation. She speaks about an enormous range of workers from those employed in multinational corporations, with reasonably good wages and working conditions to family-retained personnel, who function like and are perceived as 'servants'. The entire workforce is in the informal sector, with any kind of associational activity being rather forcefully discouraged. This industry does not, however, simply follow the demands of global enterprises but produces its own market for force. The security business is an expanding industry and at the same time a strategy for managing the social problems created by accumulation, such as dispossession and disruption. While the rising middle and upper classes demand sophisticated facilities and lifestyle, the mass of working population are marginalized by those very requirements, resulting in sharp and visible inequality and resulting conflicts. Thus, security and accumulation are the twin siblings of globalization.

In the next two chapters, the questions related to accumulation in the context of urbanization and migration become more vital. Sushmita Pati's study (Chap. 5) of accumulation through rent-seeking practices in Delhi reveals quite succinctly the connections between emergence of new interest groups and networks which contribute to the reorganization of social and economic orders, although not in a straightforward manner and not without possibilities of conflicts. In the case of Munirka in Delhi, Pati argues violence is always kept at the level of liminality, especially towards tenants from North-east India. There are small conflicts, but no all-out confrontation. In Shahpur Jat, by contrast, villagers have accepted the presence of men and women from the fashion industry, alien though they may be, to the cultures of the village. The peaceful coexistence of two culturally diverse universes depends, however, on maintaining the dominance of the landlords, and the instrument here too is fear. These local hierarchies and animosities reinforce the process of accumulation, aided by institutional means that include both traditional and modern forms of associations. Shruti Dubey's chapter (Chap. 6) explores another form of violence intrinsic to the idea of development itself—the essential unevenness of its paraphernalia that underplays the needs of one section of the population to aggravate those of the other. In her study of the transformation of a small village named Khora at the border of Delhi, Noida, and Ghaziabad into a huge labour colony serving the industrial complexes in the new urban centres around it, Dubey shows various forms of accumulation by different classes of people, especially the rentier section of the population. What stands out in these two narratives is the recognition that the rent-seeking aspect of accumulation is a necessary condition of capitalist development. They also throw light on the link between urbanization, migration, ascendancy of rent-seeking economy, and accumulation.

The last chapter in this part by Suhit Sen (Chap. 7) raises a crucial question by describing an important event in the history of post-colonial India—the nationalization of Indian banks in the late 1960s. Sen's chapter is instrumental in underscoring the contours of accumulation in India, as it links the questions of social policy, financialization of the economy, internal politics of the Indian National Congress, and augmentation of private capital through misuse of credit during one of the most interesting times in the first 30 years after Independence in 1947. In many ways, this chapter is pivotal for the rest of the chapters which deal with the successes and failures of the economic machine that post-colonial India desired to develop by incorporating various pre-existing structures and networks.

Speaking of pre-existing structures, Section II of the volume contains five chapters which critically intercept three essential signs of accumulation in India: caste, gender, and race. A caveat is necessary in this case: by 'pre-existing', we do not mean that these signs fit comfortably in the self-explanatory chronology of the nation's autobiography and continue to 'exist' through the transitions in power without any change or reorientation. In fact, the arguments proposed in this section suggest exactly the opposite. These signs did make an impact on the colonial rulers and they chose to address the related issues in various manners. This section explores how these apparently 'timeless' markers of accumulation reflect on the emerging frontiers of the same in a time, which is marked by a weakening of several distinctions in economy (such as formal/informal, city/village) in the wake of neoliberal developmentalism. Even though the chapters do not always tend to historicize the dynamism of caste, gender, and race in a postcolony, they, however, end up challenging some of the presumptions that a linear narrative of progression wants us to believe.

In Chap. 8 by Debarati Bagchi and Iman Kumar Mitra, the questions of gender and caste intermingle with issues of spatialization of the economy in an urban context. In this chapter, they speak about the workers in the waste management sector in Kolkata—the ones employed by the city municipal authority and the homeless waste pickers who live under the flyovers in the city—and how they contribute to an ongoing process of recycling of urban space. The authors explore the notion of recycling in two senses of the term. The first deals with the discourses of waste recycling which tends to leave no space outside of capital and expropriate even the so-called disutilities within the system; the second has a more metaphorical charge, referring to the constant reordering of urban space in accordance with gentrification of the city. At the end, it seems that the two senses are indistinguishable as they both operate at the level of producing and delineating social life based on an exclusionary structure of accumulative mechanisms. The contradictions between life and social life that tend to emerge in this context may lead to an explosion which will politically concretize the overdetermination of material and immaterial labour. In Chap. 9 by Rashmi Gopi, the biopolitics of accumulation once again takes on the axis of gender to create and blur the interfaces between the state and private capital in the name of development. By focusing on the self-projection of the state of Kerala as a home of authentic 'Ayurveda' experience, Gopi reflects on the homogenization of the Ayurveda practices under an accumulative nexus of the state, the market, and other agents of development. Touching upon debates around modernity and tradition in Ayurveda tourism, she develops the insights about the care economy in the dynamics of accumulation and in the process shows that the dominant idea of men as active and women as passive is shaped by the discourse of upper caste Hindus and colonial modernity and this binary is further strengthened by the growth-centric idea of development undertaken by the Kerala government.

In Chap. 10, Ritajyoti Bandyopadhyay and Ranabir Samaddar study the small- and medium-scale engineering industry in one district in West Bengal. Their paper is an intervention in two usually unattached fields—caste and labour. By connecting issues of caste and capital accumulation, Bandyopadhyay and Samaddar seek to address a question long overlooked in the standard historiography of Bengal: how instrumental are the caste dynamics in formation and accumulation of capital? In their study of the engineering industry in Howrah between the 1940s and 1970s in the context of the participation of a particular middle-caste group—the Mahisyas—in the production processes and factory organization, the authors argue that the caste question in West Bengal has been overshadowed by the 'larger issues of class and communalism that accounts for the continued hegemony of the upper caste *bhadralok* [gentleman] in society, polity and culture'. The 'caste optic' located at the crux of their 'organizational' approach allows the authors to define the 'frontiers of post-colonial accumulation' as a 'dynamic process of interface between the colonial and post-colonial society and the immanent logic of political economy'. Chapter 11 by Sanam Roohi similarly explores the concept of 'transnational Kamma philanthropy' in the light of the consolidation of the Kamma identity as an anti-Brahminical landowning caste group in coastal Andhra Pradesh (in Southern India), who, by availing higher education and through established networks, have been able to settle in the USA and contributed in a chain of philanthropic endeavours acknowledged and endorsed by the government. Roohi's chapter shows how the 'governmentalization' of these philanthropic circuits and activities has added to capital accumulation in the region.

In the last chapter of the volume, Atig Ghosh (Chap. 12) relates the incidents of violence to the people from the Northeast India in the National Capital Region of Delhi with questions of race and accumulation. From his account, one may come back to the concepts of frontier and margin where the decentring of the race question in the Northeast through and after 'autonomy movements' itself becomes conducive to subsumption of its dynamics under a global capitalist regime. All the chapters in Part II and Part I, therefore, point to the various intersections between identities and structures, processes and networks, and subjects and subjectivities that are produced and reproduced to facilitate the brazen advents of capitalist accumulation. The story, however, does not end here. There are spates of resistance and endless battles that continue to contradict and interrupt these circular narratives and self-fulfilling prophecies. The writings in this volume bear marks of resistance to the onward march of capitalism in the post-colonial world.

These chapters do not exhaust the theme, but they reflect through their own specific analyses and mutual conversation the general lessons of studying the dynamics of post-colonial accumulation. But more work remains to be done, particularly in the context of debates referred to in this introduction. Hopefully, this volume will initiate studies from new angles on this crucial theme. However, there is no doubt that the dynamics of accumulation in a post-colonial context do create ground for arguing for a theory of post-colonial capitalism. These essays collectively indicate the necessity for working towards such a theory of post-colonial accumulation—if not a full-fledged theory of post-colonial capitalism. Research towards such a theory will be a fitting tribute to legacy of Rosa Luxemburg on the issue of accumulation of capital.

References

Arrighi, G. (2010). *The long twentieth century: Money, power, and the origins of our times*. London: Verso.

Callinicos, A. (2010). The limits of passive revolution. *Capital and Class, 34*(3), 491–507.

Chibber, V. (2013). *Postcolonial theory and the spectre of capital*. London: Verso.
Dillon, M., & Neal, A. (2008). *Foucault on politics, security and war*. London: Palgrave Macmillan.
Gaddis, J. L. (1989). *The long peace: Inquiries into the history of the cold war*. New York: Oxford University Press.
Glenn, E. N. (1992). From servitude to service work: Historical continuities in the racial division of paid reproductive labor. *Signs* 18, no. 1 (Autumn), 1–43.
Hardt, M., & Negri, A. (2000). *Empire*. Cambridge, MA, and London: Harvard University Press.
Lenin, V. I. (1964a/1915). Karl Marx: A brief biographical sketch with an exposition of marxism. *Collected Works* (Vol. 21, pp. 43–91). Moscow: Progress Publishers.
Lenin, V. I. (1964b/1916). The Junius Pamphlet. *Collected Works*. Vol. 22,305–19 Moscow: Progress Publishers.
Luxemburg, R. (2014a/1915). *Accumulation of Capital*, Section 3, Chapter 26. Retrieved January 20, 2014, from http://www.marxists.org/archive/luxemburg/1913/accumulation-capital/ch26.htm#doc-2
Luxemburg, R. (2014b/1915). *The Junius Pamphlet*. Retrieved February 10, 2014, from http://www.marxists.org/archive/luxemburg/1915/junius/ch01.htm#n3.Accessed
Marx, K. (2014a/1867). *Capital* (Vol. 1). Retrieved February 2, 2014, from https://www.marxists.org/archive/marx/works/1867-c1/
Marx, K. (2014b/1939). *Grundrisse*. Retrieved February 2, 2014, from https://www.marxists.org/subject/dialectics/marx-engels/grundisse.htm
Mezzadra, S., & Neilson, B. (2013). *Border as method or the multiplication of labour*. Durham: Duke University Press.
Sanyal, K. (2013). *Rethinking capitalist development: Primitive accumulation, governmentality, and post-colonial capitalism*. Delhi: Routledge.
Sangari, K. (2015). *Solid: Liquid, a (Trans)national reproductive formation*. New Delhi: Tulika.
Spivak, G. C. (1985). Scattered speculations on the question of value. *Diacritics* (Winter), 73–93.
Tse Tung, M. (1956). *Selected Works* (Vol. 5). Retrieved February 6, 2014, from https://www.marxists.org/reference/archive/mao/selected-works/volume-5/mswv5_51.htm

Part I
New Dynamics of Accumulation

Flexible Labour and Capital Accumulation in a Post-Colonial Country

Byasdeb Dasgupta

Abstract This chapter links labour market flexibility with capital accumulation in the context of a post-colonial country like India. The chapter is organized in four sections starting with an understanding of neoliberal age and the nature of capital accumulation in general in the context of a post-colonial economic space. This is followed by an analysis of labour market flexibility. The liberal era which is supposedly characterized by rigid labour laws with an interventionist state in Keynesian sense is marked with growing strength of trade unions and labour organizations in the West and in post-colonial emerging economy like India. The neoliberal age is marked with a diametrically opposite tendency, namely, the weakening of these organizations by the neoliberal states all over the world, North and South alike. This too has some significant implications for both voice representations of labour as well as capital accumulation in the Marxian sense of the latter term. In the third section, the chapter delves into the issue of representation of labour in the neoliberal age. Finally, an attempt is made to decipher the connectivity of flexible labour and weakening bargaining strength of labour with the process of growing financialization and its implications for capital accumulation in post-colonial neoliberal space and time.

Keywords Labour · Neoliberalism · Labour market flexibility · Representation · Financialization

As far as the neoliberal age of global capitalism is concerned, labour market is characterized by more and more flexibility. This flexible labour market is marked by two features in general. One is growing flexibilization of formal labour market and the second is growing flexibility in all kinds of labour market taking the formal as well as informal together. The basic idea of formal labour market is related to organized factory-based manufacturing labour. In a country like India,

B. Dasgupta (✉)
University of Kalyani, Kalyani, West Bengal, India
e-mail: byasdeb@gmail.com

I.K. Mitra et al. (eds.), *Accumulation in Post-Colonial Capitalism*,
DOI 10.1007/978-981-10-1037-8_2

as in the developed capitalist world, formal labour market rules and regulations are also extended to parts of the services sector. If the immediate post–World War II era was marked with a growing tendency of enacting rules and regulations for labour in the formal sector of the economy, the neoliberal era thereafter for the past three decades has been marked with growing deregulations of rigid labour rules. This to our understanding is grossly related to the nature of capital accumulation in the neoliberal age. This chapter links labour market flexibility with capital accumulation in the context of a post-colonial country like India. It is organized in four sections starting with an understanding of neoliberal age and the nature of capital accumulation in general in the context of a post-colonial economic space. This is followed by an analysis of labour market flexibility. The liberal era which is supposedly characterized by rigid labour laws with an interventionist state in the Keynesian sense is marked with growing strength of trade unions and labour organizations in the West and in a post-colonial emerging economy like India. The neoliberal age is marked with a diametrically opposite tendency, viz. the weakening of these organizations by the neoliberal states all over the world, North and South alike. This too has some significant implications for both voice representations of labour as well as capital accumulation in Marxian sense of the latter term. Hence, in the third section, we will delve into the issue of voice representation of labour in the neoliberal age. Finally, an attempt will be made to decipher the connectivity of flexible labour and weakening bargaining strength of labour with the process of growing financialization and its implications for capital accumulation in post-colonial neoliberal space and time.

Before we begin, it is necessary for our own purpose to know what we mean by a post-colonial state. Is it just a linear temporal characterization of a state from being under colonial rule to an independent one? Yes, the meaning of *post-colonial* is definitely post-independent spatial and temporal—the independence or liberation from the oppressive colonial rule. However, in our own understanding post-colonial time and spaces are not just linear transition from colonialism to *post*-colonialism. There are three signifying aspects which merit our attention as far as post-colonial state and economy is concerned. Firstly, post-colonial state and economy may have some colonial hangover. For example, a country after independence may continue with some of the colonial legality and methods of governance. As far as India as post-colonial country is concerned, labour here is subject to the Trade Union Act framed in colonial era in 1926 under certain international compulsions. Another important instance is the continuation with the colonial land acquisition law till 2013 which was framed way back in 1894. Economic development in India after independence from the colonial rule had made use of this particular law whenever such need emerged in the post-colonial time. Thirdly, a post-colonial country may confront neo-colonial onslaught either in physical coercive manner (as is the case in Iraq and Afghanistan) or through some universal international means like structural adjustment programme (more popularly known as Washington Consensus) which ensures hegemonic presence of the global capitalists therein. In the existing literature on post-colonialism, it is described in multifarious forms, all of which in some way or other indicate control of a *post*-colonial space by the global capital. Post-colonialism as such does not imply any coherent theorization of a time and space which is liberated from oppressive colonial rule. It is marked with cultural, political and economic understanding of an independent country in the context of global capitalism. In this work, we will not disembark upon these cultural conceptualizations of a *post*-colonial time and space. Rather, our main focus will be upon economic and the political as far as labour and capital accumulation is concerned.

The chapter begins with an understanding of neoliberal logic of economy as the present post-colonial time and space is *mostly* shaped in terms of neoliberalism. We need to understand why the neoliberal turn was necessary for global capitalism and what is the connectivity of neoliberal state power, market and supra-state international institutions with the process of accumulation of capital à la Marx. Why the very process of capital accumulation at certain juncture of post-colonial history warrants neoliberalism? This is so because any exploration into present-day flexible labour regime cannot be complete without an understanding of neoliberal logic, which, on the one hand, is needed to recharge the capital accumulation process and, on the other hand, is needed to resolve the typical capitalist problem of accumulation. This is followed by an understanding of what we mean by labour market flexibility linking it with circuits of global capital. Labour market flexibility as a term has been coined during the neoliberal time as the very idea of neoliberal capitalist market rests on flexible labour market. The immediate post–World War II era, as far as the labour market is concerned, in advanced capitalist world and also to a great extent in its peripheries like India after independence from colonial rule, witnessed some collaboration between capital and labour following the Keynesian logic to save the global capitalism from an impending collapse during the Great Depression. But since the decade of 1970s that collaboration was ruptured. It was followed by complete disowning of rigid labour rules by the global capital as far as the present history of the neoliberal global capitalist order is concerned. Therefore, any understanding of the present-day labour market flexibility must be preceded by the understanding of rigid labour in the immediate post–World War II era. For this, we will touch upon certain basics of Keynesian logic on which the notion of rigid labour and welfare state was constructed. Otherwise, it is not possible to comprehend the deconstruction of such rigid labour in terms of an alternative flexible labour as a panacea of all ills of a capitalist society. But our attempt in this chapter is beyond Keynesianism as we are striving here to explore into the logic of capital accumulation in post-colonial context. So, we will at the same time make an attempt to relate flexible labour with the Marxian categories of class, exploitation, surplus value and like. If the immediate post-colonial era is marked by the strengthening of labour organizations and militant trade unionism the subsequent neoliberal post-colonial era saw their reverse, viz. weakening of labour's bargaining power as well as dwindling away of trade unionism in general, which has significant implications for process of capital accumulation and also for the problem of accumulation, as Harvey (2005) pointed out. Thus, in the third section, we will delve into the issue of making and unmaking of labour organization and the connectivity of the process with the circuits of global capital. Any discussion of post-colonial time and space remains incomplete in this neoliberal age without a discussion of new finance. Following Marx, it can be asserted that the issue of finance cannot be delinked from the issue of labour. We will try to understand the interrelationship of new finance and flexible labour in Sect. 'Flexible Labour and the Age of New Finance' of this chapter.

Neoliberal Logic of the Economic Space in Post-Colonialism

Neoliberalism has been shaping the economic spaces of both advanced capitalist world as well as the developing world including the emerging market economies like India. The initiation of neoliberal order is different in different geographical spaces. For example, in the USA and the UK, neoliberalism began as response to the capitalist crisis of the 1970s when these countries were hit severely by stagflation. The latter is an economic term coined during the early seventies when Bretton Woods arrangement ended and the dollar ceased to be reserve currency all over the world. It was a time when the countries were allowed by the supra-national institution—the International Monetary Fund (IMF)—to freely float their currencies, and the sudden hike in the international oil prices hit the world economy leading to high inflation, recession and unemployment. Stagflation as an economic terminology refers to the coexistence of high rates of both inflation and unemployment, hitherto unknown in mainstream macroeconomic theory. It was a time when Keynesian policy prescriptions of running budget deficit as an important tool for demand management was not working and monetarism started replacing Keynesianism as idea behind economic policymaking although monetarist inclination in policy stance too failed to solve the problem of high unemployment. Hence, lack of *effective demand* kept the advanced economies depressed. On the other hand, this is also the beginning of the era of new finance. The oil exporting countries' petrodollar surpluses were invested in the international commercial banks in the USA mostly and to some extent in the UK, France, (West) Germany and Japan. The banks were saddled with huge amounts of undesired excess reserve as due to deep recession in the West there was not adequate demand for loans from the industry as a whole. This compelled the banks in what is known in the literature as 'loan pushing'. This time banks extended loans at the market rate of interest to the sovereign, viz. to the governments of the Third World. This is unique in the history of international bank loans when international commercial banks of the West, instead of extending credit to the corporates and individuals, found it safe to extend loans to the sovereign debtors, mostly in Latin America. Thus began the era of what Samaddar (2015) has termed 'the era of debt profligacy'. At the same time, Harvey (2007) indicated there was continuous attack on Keynesianism and welfare state concept in the West, especially in the USA and the UK, by the media and also by the official mainstream economists. The latter, by that time, had discarded

Keynesianism and started fighting for a model economy which would be founded upon markets free from any state regulation; the state would become non-interventionist. This, they felt, would automatically guarantee individual freedom, the most cherished goal of the liberal philosophers in the West. 'The founding figures of neoliberal thought took political ideals of human dignity and individual freedom as fundamental, as the "central values of civilization"' (Harvey 2007, p. 5).

The basic idea of neoliberalism actually can be traced back to 1947 when Freidrich von Hayek, the most influential political philosopher as far as neoliberal ideas are concerned, Ludvig von Mises, the father of monetarist economic philosophy, Milton Friedman and Karl Popper with others formed the Mont Pelerin Society in reaction to threats to the capitalist order from socialist economic ideas then prevalent in the USSR, China and Eastern Europe. The founding statement of the society as cited in Harvey (2007, p. 20) is self-evident in this regard:

> The central values of civilization are in danger. Over large stretches of the earth's surface the essential conditions of human dignity and freedom have already disappeared. In others they are under constant menace from the development of current tendencies of policy.

The group was morally and financially supported by the corporate elites and rich individuals of the West, especially those from the USA. After three decades of this declaration, this group's sole objective found its real materialization through the adoption of neoliberal economic policy stances. With the dismantling of the socialist world in the early 1990s neoliberalism as political economic idea swept the world. Keynes once remarked that perhaps one day the material wants of all human beings would be satiated somehow; however, it is the 'idea'—good or bad—which would keep hitting the political and economic space in different ways. These words from Keynes hold good as far as neoliberalism as an idea of political economic worldview is concerned. In fact, Hayek too echoed the same viewpoint.

> Hayek, author of key texts such as *The Constitution of Liberty*, presciently argued that the battle for ideas was key, and that it would probably take at least a generation for the battle to be won, not only against Marxism but against socialism, state planning, and Keynesian interventionism (Harvey 2007, p. 21).

One point merits attention at this juncture. Although neoliberalism as the basic and fundamental idea behind economic policy and of state has engulfed the entire world today its journey as well as its beginning is different and uneven in different geographical space in the post-colonial time. In developed worlds like the USA and the UK, neoliberalism as the dominant political economic philosophy behind the role of the state and market grew in reaction to the recession of the 1970s and events like OPEC-induced oil price hike and initiation to flexible exchange rate regime. In the USA, it was President Ronald Reagan who along with the then Chairman of the Federal Reserve Paul Volckar led the beginning of neoliberalism's journey. In the UK, on the other hand, Prime Minister Margaret Thatcher capitalized on the growing anti-labour sentiment of the middle class and the city of London as the world's financial hub and vigorously started neoliberal economic policymaking. This changed the role of the state from all-encompassing welfarist to minimalist—a state which would only take care of law and order and would own only the means of violence to protect individual freedom and private property rights. Around 1978, neoliberalism began its journey in the then communist China. Deng Xiao Ping took the advice of Milton Friedman and rolled out one neoliberal policy after another with the state remaining in control of economy and society. In India, the inclination towards neoliberalism started during 1985–1986 when Rajiv Gandhi became the prime minister. But the formal inception of neoliberalism as opposed to planned economic development was in June 1991 at the diktat of the IMF to the debt-ridden Indian government. The debt profligacy of the Latin American countries since August 1982, with Mexico declaring short-term moratorium on repayment of debt to international commercial banks of the West, led to the beginning of the journey of neoliberalism there. In fact, in the Third World (now in Greece too) neoliberalism is a compulsion. It is the IMF which compels debt-ridden countries of the Third World to adhere to neoliberalism as the guiding principle of their economic policymaking whenever any debt-ridden sovereign country approaches the fund to rescue her from the impending collapse of her capitalist economic system. The fund rescues with the condition that the concerned country should follow the neoliberal path henceforth.

There are *four* basic and fundamental tenets of neoliberalism which are common to every attempt to neoliberalize an economy everywhere. They include:

(1) Without freedom no individual can act as a rational economic agent where rationality postulate signifies the ability of an economic agent to satisfy his/her self-interest.
(2) There should be private property rights, as without perfect private property rights no market can function with the aid of its Smithsonian *invisible hands*.[1]
(3) The market is self-regulating and, hence, there should not be any outside agency which would regulate the market and would make the economic system inefficient as far as resource allocation and other economic activities (consumption, production and distribution) are concerned.
(4) The state should be a minimal one implying that its activities should be confined to just preserving law and order in the country. Any state-intervention in the market for commodities including market for labour would make the functioning of the market inefficient and, hence, is unwarranted.

Given the above four basic postulates of neoliberal economic order, the ideal economy is one which is characterized by perfect competition and consumers' freedom in making choices. A perfectly competitive market presumes that all the agents in the market have perfect information regarding the products and also, about the economy and society in general. So, the question of getting deceived does not arise. In a competitive market no producing firm can set the price which is determined in the market by the invisible hands through the forces of demand and supply. Therefore, competition in other words means survival of the fittest.

[1]Adam Smith uses the metaphor of 'invisible hand' in both his *The Theory of Moral Sentiments* (1759) and *The Wealth of Nations* (1776) to explain how personal motivations to maximize one's own gain will automatically ensure growth of every sector in an exchange economy.

Those producers who can become efficient will survive. That competition of this type (price and non-price competition alike) leads ultimately to monopoly and/or oligarchy of few firms and the capitalism becomes monopoly are absolutely obfuscated by the neoliberal logic. Furthermore, an individual under neoliberalism is *homo-economicus* (not *homo-reciprocus*) implying that he/she is the best judge of making his/her destiny in the most efficient manner and so is individual labour. Any collectivism is envisaged as anathema to individual freedom. There is market to take care of all ills which may afflict the material world of an individual. Since welfare state is necessarily an interventionist state it must be done with for the sake of free market and individual freedom and also, to ensure individualism in the form of *homo-economicus*. Furthermore, neoliberalism does not distinguish between domestic and foreign as far as capital in the form of money is concerned, viz. financial capital. Free market's efficiency is supposedly guaranteed by the free flow of (money) capital across the national borders, and hence, neoliberalization warrants new globalization. All economies should be perfectly open so that capital (not labour) can be freely mobile all over the world following the market-based logic of its demand and supply (Sen 2007). This globalization as a process of integrating domestic with the global in terms of free cross-border flows of capital and other commodities can best be dubbed as neoliberal globalization—a new form in terms of new finance.

It is not that neoliberal regime—particularly neoliberal state—is without any contradictions. *First*, any neoliberal regime postulates and warrants the minimalist state in terms of its own logic. But at the same time, this regime desires that the state should take appropriate actions suitable for free market economy and facilitate the interests of capital—especially those of foreign capital (either in the form of foreign direct investment [FDI] or foreign portfolio investment [FPI]). So, we do not regard neoliberalism as signifying the retreat of the state; rather, we comprehend the neoliberal state as a reshaped and reconfigured one to facilitate the interest of a so-called free market (which actually signifies interests of the private entrepreneurship and of the corporate giants). *Secondly*, the very neoliberal tenet of individual freedom should go hand in hand with anti-authoritarianism at the political level, meaning democracy. However, in the neoliberal regime (even if the regime is characterized by the liberal democracy as in the USA and India) we find the power relation is highly asymmetric and is tilted towards corporates against the individual citizen. There is absolute freedom for corporate power, not for individuals—particularly for labour. In fact, the concrete real shows that it is capital which is subsidized by the neoliberal state at the cost of labour—a point which we will touch upon later. *Thirdly*, it is held that free market through its self-regulating mechanism is stable always. The reality is otherwise—particularly in this age of neoliberal globalization and new finance with sporadic crises and instability in the financial market jeopardizing the real economy and the market. *Fourthly*, neoliberal ideal economy is based upon free competition because that can only, at least, theoretically guarantee individual freedom and efficiency. The reality is otherwise. The last 30 years of 'free competition' have led to concentration of economic power (and political power too) in the hands of a few corporate giants all over the world. The oligarchy of the few is now ruling the market, not otherwise. *Finally,* the reality of the neoliberal order in terms of its individual-centric consumerism has led to domination of negative freedoms ruling over the positive freedoms. It is actually freedom of private enterprises, not freedom of individual. Therefore, neoliberalism is not without its own contradictions. A real ideal neoliberal state and society is diametrically opposite to its own conceived ideal.

Writing on capital accumulation is absurd if it is not related to what is happening with what Marx described as 'living labour' (Marx 1976). We, therefore, at this juncture strive to see the implications of neoliberalism on labour in general. There are variants of economic policies in different geographical spaces as far as neoliberal political economic regime is concerned. In some countries, privatization of public sector and public properties were given the main thrust. In some other, opening up the domestic economy to global capital dominated over the other neoliberal changes in fundamental economic policy stance while for some national governments deregulation of financial market and bent towards monetarism played the major role. This does not mean there is no common agenda. The basic philosophy behind all these changes in policy stances is attributable to neoliberalism. There are *four common elements* which are most fundamental as far as neoliberalism and its uneven development in different geographical spaces are concerned. They include the following:

(i) Establishment of free market economy replacing state-driven economy and leaving the market to be regulated in its own terms by itself.
(ii) Reshaping the role of the state from non-interventionist one to facilitating one, viz. making state power conducive to the interest of capital, big business and private enterprises.
(iii) Containing fiscal deficit which ultimately implies doing away with all kinds of social public expenditures and rendering social sector to be exploited for churning profit by the private enterprises, mainly by the large corporate (even MNC) business entities.
(iv) Subsidizing capital (at any cost) when *in general* containment of fiscal deficit would do away with subsidies like food subsidies in a poverty-stricken space and thus making labour the risk-bearing factor of production (Johnson 1978).

In fact, all of these have certain definite and adverse implications for labour in general. With neoliberal globalization, the structure of the post-colonial economies underwent sweeping changes and at the heart of these changes remained the basic instinct of accumulating as much as surplus labour (value) as possible (Sen and Dasgupta 2009). We are using the term surplus labour in Marxian sense and not in the sense of mainstream Development Economics discourse on Third World duality. As far as surplus labour performance and thereby the process of capital accumulation is concerned, there are two aspects of living labour which merit our attention:

(a) What is happening to job-related status of labour which concerns their means of livelihood? (Sen and Dasgupta 2006).
(b) What is happening to the reserve army of labour (unemployment in mainstream economic terminology)? (Marx 1976, pp. 781–794).

One of the several subsidies or concessions which have been given to capital by the post-colonial neoliberal state is the guarantee that within its geographical boundaries its labour would be made relatively cheaper which would be also cheaper than other geographical spaces globally. This has significant implications (i) for necessary equivalent of surplus performed and (ii) for surplus labour performed (both in absolute and relative sense simultaneously). In recent times, there has been a concern, in particular, for the erosion of the Fordist notion of stable job and related labour security as has come with labour flexibility or deregulated labour regime (Standing 1999, 2002). This point will be elaborated later in this chapter. The very idea of an economy driven by competitive market with efficiency in allocation and production at the onset requires low cost of production. The market for various commodities is today characterized by cost-effectiveness and labour is the soft target in this regard. The greater the competition, the more the cal for cost-effectiveness by lowering labour costs as far as possible. As we have mentioned already, the competition in the market for commodities has ultimately produced oligarchy of few firms in most of the commodity markets in last three decades, if not monopoly. In fact, this is against the neoliberal orthodoxy which at least in theory demands competitive market as its ideal. However, the oligarchy of a few firms or private enterprises signifies weakening bargaining strength of labour and, hence, further lowering of labour costs of production. Research has found that the real wage in USA registered continuous stagnation at a time when labour productivity increased manifold (Wolff N.D.). Secondly, reshaping of the state to facilitate the interests of capital and big business signifies once again containment of labour cost of production. The same argument holds good when concession is provided to the capital. It is labour which emerges as the risk-bearing factor in capitalist production processes. Finally, slashing down fiscal deficit by the neoliberal state is tantamount of doing away with the welfare state and all its programmes for poverty reduction and employment generation and other social expenses. Then too labour suffers as most of labouring masses in the Third World are also the poor and unemployed. Here, by unemployment we imply the Keynesian notion of involuntary unemployment meaning the non-availability of job to a person who is ready to work at any wage rate. To a neoliberal economist unemployment is voluntary and can be dubbed as search unemployment which implies jobs are available but an individual is still searching for a job as he/she is not satisfied with the job offers given his/her preference. This in other words signifies that in the labour market the supplier of labour power has the capacity and freedom to make choice! The concrete reality in the Third World is otherwise. Workers or working class as a whole do not have the freedom of making any choice. This holds good for neoliberal age as well as the pre-neoliberal age. Then, what distinguishes the neoliberal space and time from the pre-neoliberal space and time is the fact that job status of a worker is getting continuously weakened and technology-induced increase in labour productivity has increased the risk and uncertainty in a worker's life which was to some extent guaranteed in the pre-neoliberal post-colonial time at least in some developing economies like India. This is happening at a time when countries such as

India, Mexico, China and Argentina are in the process of creating *nouveau riche* classes (popularly known as billionaires) and at the same time widening the gap between the haves and have-nots. Accumulation of wealth by the rich cannot be possible unless there is super-exploitation in the standard Marxian sense. In a capitalist class process, the Marxian definition of exploitation is the ratio of surplus value generated to the variable capital, where the latter is the necessary equivalent for direct producers—the performers of surplus value—s/v where s denotes the surplus value generated in a quantitative sense and v stands for variable capital, i.e. wage component or payment for necessary labour. The working hours or time which a worker takes to produce his/her means of subsistence which is necessary to reproduce his/her labour power socially is the necessary labour time. For example, if a worker or direct producer works for 12 h a day, then suppose he/she requires at least 5 h to produce his/her means of subsistence. It should be borne in mind that these 5 h of work in value term are equivalent to the value of his/her subsistence basket. Hence, they require final commodity exchange in the market so that he/she obtains his/her necessary equivalent in money form, which is his/her wage. Note that here we have not talked about the production process where piece rate wage is the norm. Also, we have restricted our analysis keeping in mind a typical capitalist production process which involves commodity exchanges both for labour power and the final commodity (C). We are not considering here the non-capitalist processes of production which exist simultaneously in a society that is predominantly capitalist and is monetized. The discussion of these other, viz. non-capitalist, processes will be taken up later. The capitalist process, which we are considering, follows the M-C-M' circuit. The initial M is the money capital invested to procure means of production (MP) in commodity form from the market and also labour power (LP) as commodity from the market for labour. The surplus value thus produced is the difference between the final M' (the money that the productive capitalist gets by selling the product in the market) and the initial M (the money capital invested to procure MP and LP from the respective market), viz. M-$M' =$ the quantity of surplus value. This surplus value is the result of non-payment to the direct producers for a portion of their working hours. For instance, the productive capitalist makes the contract with a direct producer that the latter will work for 12 h a day and the wage (variable capital in money form) will be Rs. 500. Then suppose 5 h is sufficient for the direct producer to produce commodities worth Rs. 500, which is his/her wage. So, the 5 h specify his/her necessary labour time. Now, he/she does not work for 5 h only. Rather, as per the contract with the productive capitalist the direct producer works for 12 h a day. And this extra 7 h of work goes totally unpaid. Rather, the value of these extra hours over his/her necessary labour time is robbed by the productive capitalist as the *surplus value*. Note that here non-performer of the surplus value, viz. the productive capitalist, appropriates the surplus value performed by the direct producers. Hence, the capitalist production process entails exploitation, the rate of which is determined by surplus value generated per unit of variable capital.

Therefore, $e = s/v$ where e stands for the degree of exploitation. There are four possibilities through which one can attain super-exploitation as follows:

(1) One can increase e by increasing s, given v.

This is possible in either of the two forms. Given v, one can increase surplus value by lengthening the working time presuming that there is no change in technology of production. This in Marxian sense is absolute surplus value. One can increase s, given v, by technological innovation, i.e. by increasing labour productivity with their wages remaining unchanged. Now, the same v is produced in less time than before and the total working hours do not alter. This is what Marx has dubbed relative surplus value. So, either by increasing absolute surplus value or by increasing relative surplus value a productive capitalist can increase the quantity of surplus value (s), given the variable capital (v) at the same level.

(2) One can increase e by decreasing v, given s.

This can happen only by lowering the necessary equivalent and this warrants the necessary political climate which would continuously reproduce such an exploitative process by slashing the necessary equivalent, viz. wage of the labour. It is also possible through technological innovation. Technological innovation may reduce the necessary labour time and given the final exchange value of the commodity produced, the productive capitalist may now create such socio-political condition that wage (v) can be reduced. For example, through technological innovation the necessary labour time may be brought down to 3 h from 5 h and through the necessary changes in labour laws the productive capitalist may bring down the wage. This signifies the situation of growing wage-productivity gap as it has happened in certain manufacturing sectors in India, as the Annual Survey of Industries (ASI) data for the year 2013–14 indicate.[2] This signifies increase in relative surplus value.

(3) One can increase e by increasing s and decreasing v at the same time.

This case stands for increase in both absolute and relative surplus value. The lengthening of the working day as well as technological innovation may lead to rise in s and fall in v simultaneously. Technological innovation is always labour-saving, viz. with improvement in technology less labour is needed to produce the same output in less time. So, in this sense it signifies increase in relative surplus value. But lengthening of working hours may also happen if the capitalist class remains successful—as they are generally under a neoliberal regime—to create a socio-political climate conducive to such changes. This then signifies increase in absolute surplus value. Commodity production in the new economy under neoliberalism, like IT sector, is good example of this case.

[2]http://mospi.nic.in/Mospi_New/upload/asi/ASI_main.htm?status=1&menu_id=88. Accessed on 16 March 2016.

(4) One can increase e by increasing s proportionately more than increase in v.

This is the case which hints at the structural change which is happening at the enterprise level of late. One can measure s and v in per capita term. An interesting case is more proportionate rise in s per unit of worker than the proportionate rise in v per unit of worker. Symbolically, $(\Delta s/s) > (\Delta v/v)$ so that $(\Delta e/e) > 1$. This is happening in many private enterprises which are shedding off which they call surplus workers while allowing some increment in v for the retained workers. This also requires a type of technological innovation (contrary to the Fordist or Taylorist type of technology of assembly line production) which would increase what Marx has defined as *intensity of labour* in the production process. This new type of technological innovation warrants that an individual worker must possess multiple skills whereas the assembly line of large-scale production warranted specialization and technical division of labour in the factory à la Smith and also Marx. Take the instance of automobile production. The number of workers required for a standard private car producing factory has gone down compared to that in the 1950s or 1960s. A much smaller workforce is required to produce more cars now in the same time compared to before. Anyway, this implies (despite proportionate increase in per capita v) falling wage share in a capitalist enterprise which signifies rising share of surplus value and, hence, increase in profit share (where profit is a part of the total surplus value generated).

The capital accumulation in a post-colonial neoliberal space may have all of these four tendencies for super-exploitation. The implications for these on living labour are obvious. On the one hand, neoliberalism wants to repress necessary equivalent in production process and on the other, it tends to increase the reserve army of labour, viz. unemployment. Both these signs are visible in emerging post-colonial spaces like India. And neoliberal flexible labour regime involves changes in social relations of labour in production process to effect these twofold implications for labour as delineated above, viz. adverse change in the conditions of labour as far as their job status is concerned and also increase in the unemployed labour. The latter is to be absorbed by the informal sector in the post-colonial space where informality is characterized by the absence of any labour-related security including minimum wage norm which are supposedly enjoyed by the formal sector labour. Let us now take a look at the flexible labour regime as unleashed by neoliberal political economic regime in the post-colonial Third World.

Flexible Labour Regime

Living labour plays a vital role in surplus value (product) generation in the real economy. Post-colonial economic space is no exception. The accumulation of surplus hinges on the magnitude of the appropriation of the surplus value by the non-performers of such surplus in a capitalist economy. By the latter we mean an economy which is predominantly characterized by capitalist class processes. A class process is capitalist if the commodity produced is sold in the market for monetary revenue and the surplus value is appropriated by the non-performer of such surplus, viz. the productive capitalists. There may be two different kinds of class process based on the Marxian notion of exploitation: (a) exploitative class process where the surplus product (value) is appropriated by the non-performer(s) of such surplus; and (b) non-exploitative class process where the surplus product (value) is appropriated by the performer(s) of such surplus in the production process. This distinction between exploitative and non-exploitative class process is significant for us because those who appropriate the surplus product (value) also take the decision to distribute the surplus product (value) in the society including its allocation in the concerned production process. In an exploitative class process, the distribution will be towards those who provide the necessary conditions of existence and reproduction of the exploitative class processes in the society including in a post-colonial society. Under neoliberalism, we find a pattern of distribution of the surplus product (value) generated in different production processes towards the rich, *nouveau riche* and rentier class.

This section dwells on the emerging nature of labour (which we term as flexible labour) in this age of age of neoliberal globalization in any post-colonial economic space with India being no exception. This is labour in transit as opposed to labour in situ. Flexibility of labour warrants labour to be in transit always with a significant portion of living labour always remaining in the reserve army of labour, viz. unemployed. However, in our understanding it has a closed link with the new finance which shapes the global capital today. Neoliberalism with all its characteristic features desire that labour would always remain footloose in the interests of huge capital accumulation. The very question of *labour in transit* appears today as a never-ending process of evolution of this transition of labour to render labour as much cheap as possible and feasible. If one adheres to the class-focused Marxist approach (Resnick and Wolff 1987), then this journey of living labour needs to be understood in terms of the transition of several coexisting heterogeneous class processes as per the dictate of global capital in a post-colonial space. This journey is something like what can be called post-colonial destiny of labour which capital wants for generating capital accumulation in all its circuits. This journey in the name of flexible labour regime concerns both what are known as in the mainstream economic literature as formal and informal labour. The inception of neoliberal journey of a post-colonial economic space in general marks also the inception of flexible labour regime where formality is continuously transformed into informality and informality de facto finds the ethico-legal sanction of the neoliberal state *a la* Washington Consensus or the Fund-Bank stabilization and structural adjustment programme. Capitalism as a hegemonic construct of the economic space always dehumanizes living labour which imply treatment of labour power just like any other commodity in the market and neoliberal regime of global capitalism further dehumanize living labour by shedding off all sorts of hard earned labour rights and securities in the immediate post–World War II era in the advanced as well as the Third World economic spaces. The question of transition, if analysed in terms of class process transition vis-à-vis (global) capital, foregrounds different evolving labour processes as they are emerging simultaneously in post-colonial time with the single point agendum of capital accumulation at a superlative scale.

The traditional post-colonial notion of living labour is the image of such labour which is put into use in large-scale manufacturing activity. Note that this does not mean all production processes traditionally are large-scale ones and factory-based. Rather, the traditional imagery of labour as it was made to evolve in the aftermath of the colonial era foreclosed the various imageries of labour outside four abode of factories. It is not that non-factory labour did not exist then. Today, even the radical discourse on labour perceives the traditional imagery of labour as if here was no informal then. No, it is not the truth. Informality was very much part and parcel of global capitalist regime before the augmentation of neoliberalism. What then marks the departure from the past? The present time is characterized by the arduous attempt of the global capitalism in every economic space including the post-colonial ones to legalize the informality so as to cripple the voices and resistances of labour against capital and so that labour turns out to be cheaper. The cheapening of labour is a continuous process in the guise of flexible labour regime where capital negotiates with an individual owner of labour power case by case, not with the collectives of such owner, viz. with the trade unions.

The entry point of our analysis is the Marxian concept of surplus labour. Production is a process of making goods and services using labour power and the means of production bought with the initial money capital in the typical *M-C-M′* circuit of any capitalist class process. The process of manufacturing goods and services employing labour power over the means of production (constant capital in Marxian sense) is what is known as labour process, which involves the muscles, nerves and emotions of the owner of labour power. The labour process in any capitalist production process is the source of generation of surplus value and, hence, for capital accumulation. Given this notion of labour process, class is also a process. It is a complete process of performance, appropriation, distribution and receipt of surplus labour—the labour left after paying the necessary labour to the owners of labour power in any production process. Through commodity exchange in a capitalist society this surplus labour (unpaid labour following Marx) gets transformed into surplus value, i.e. it takes the monetary form. A part of this earned money through commodity exchange is again used to purchase new means of production and labour power so as to generate same surplus value and/or to enhance the earlier surplus value. This goes on and on till a crisis hits the global capitalist structure. Neoliberal regime is also not without any crisis. However, culmination of crisis under neoliberalism calls for austerity programmes and hence, tightening the belts of the living labour further so as to ensure capital accumulation again and again. The crises which the capitalist world order has witnessed since the decade of 1980s with the outbreak of Third World debt crisis made capital dominate over living labour more and more stringently and not otherwise. Voices of labour get choked every time a crisis strikes a capitalist economic and political order. The recent global economic crisis and also the crisis of Greece are no exception in this regard.

As we have already mentioned above, the received notion of labour viewed from the class-focused disaggregated and decentered economic space is one of labour in transition always at the dictate of global capital. And as far as neoliberal globalization is concerned this may take liberal democratic form politically, or it may mean drastic neocolonialism at the dictate of new finance capital, or it may take the form of using brutal military force in a post-colonial space. In all these forms of neoliberal globalizations, capital moves freely across the national border and so too labour, but its movement is dictated by the global capital. Capital does not flow to serve the interests of labour. It is other way round. Movement of labour from space to space, from form to form, from one class process to another class process so far under neoliberal political order remained constrained by the wishes of global capital. There are instances of huge spatial (forced) migration of labour which is never ending. There is continuous bondage of labour to capital even under capitalist order, instances of which are easily found in Indian economy. We can term this bondage as neoliberal bonded labour. There is continuous movement of living labour from one production process to another production process. There is continuous movement of living labour from the reserve army of labour to some production process and back and forth. It goes on and on with newer and newer technological innovation and outsourcing of works outside what is known as formal space of labour. The movements of labour are secured by flexible labour regime described below.

We need to keep in mind at this stage the Marxian conceptualization of productive and unproductive labour. Productive labour (whom Marx dubbed as direct producers) is the direct performer of surplus labour (surplus value in capitalist class process). And hence, they belong to the fundamental class process consisting of performance and appropriation of surplus labour (value). On the other hand, an unproductive labour does not directly produce the aforementioned surplus. They provide the necessary fundamental conditions of sustaining the very fundamental class process and thereby, they belong to what Marx called subsumed class process consisting of distribution and receipt of surplus labour (value). Both fundamental class process and subsumed class process over-determine each other in Althusserian sense of the term over-determination. So, both processes are equally important. What is unique about neoliberal globalization is the following:

(a) Depressing necessary equivalent of the direct producers to make value of such labour (variable capital in Marxian terminology) as far as possible;
(b) Depressing also the market value of the work performed by the unproductive labour too so that the distribution of surplus gets more and more tilted towards productive and unproductive capitalist class, especially the rentier clan; and,
(c) Enhancing at the same time the productivity of both types of labour so as to continuously swell the reserve army of labour to make labour cheaper and cheaper.

The economic risks confronting an individual worker (either as a productive labour or as an unproductive labour described above) who is always in transit under neoliberal order stem primarily from the ever-expanding network of global circuits of capital. The never-ending persisting expansion of this global circuit is dispossessing many in post-colonial space from their means of subsistence or livelihood. This is what Harvey (2005) dubbed as accumulation by dispossession, the concept which is borrowed from the Marxian notion of original or primitive accumulation. This dispossession is further expanding the scope of flexible labour and hence, of greater capital accumulation. There are four processes at least which are triggering the movement of labour from one form to another, from one livelihood to another and from one geographical space to another. They are as follows:

(1) Processes of industrialization, especially creation of Special Economic Zones (SEZs).
(2) Processes of urbanization at greater scale.
(3) Linked with the two above processes of informalization which put labour under more and more livelihood risk.
(4) Lastly, natural or environmental process which to a large extent is the outcome of capitalist greed for accumulating more and more (money) capital.

The economic risks concerning labour may be ascribed to an individual's livelihood risks. Industrialization, urbanization and environmental degradation have put an individual (who has nothing but to sell his/her labour power) more and more under livelihood risks. It signifies the physical sustainability of an individual labour. And with each crisis this risk intensifies as crisis means income deflation for a worker in simple monetary term. It is typical for low-income earning groups of a post-colonial country to occupy several class positions when class is envisaged as a process of performance, appropriation, distribution and receipt of surplus labour (value). One may occupy a place in the fundamental class process and the subsumed class process in the same production process. For instance, one may be a direct producer and labour contractor in the same manufacturing activity. One may occupy more than one fundamental class position. For instance, one may work at a factory as a productive labour and also, in another production process in the same category. One may occupy the fundamental class position in a production process as direct producer and also, the subsumed class position in another production process. For example, one may work at a factory as a direct producer and as labour contractor for the other factory. It is also possible that one may work as a direct producer in a capitalist production process and as owner of farming land as an appropriator. The last case is typical of many agrarian spaces of India today. The list is not exhaustive. There are other instances of an individual occupying more than one class positions. This tendency has grown with the upsurge of neoliberal globalization as the economic risk, viz. the risk of livelihood, got intensified. The more an individual's principal or main work is being rendered temporary, casual, irregular, mobile and seasonal along with the increasing rate of privatization of the economic space under flexible labour regime, the more is such tendency of an individual performing several income generating tasks to eke out the socially bare minimum standard of living. It actually foregrounds the basic question whether a person works to live or lives to work? Is it not the curbing of individual freedom (of having leisure), the very freedom which neoliberal worldview cherishes today all over the world!

Before we end this section, let us see how flexible labour works to make living labour cheaper. In commonplace parlance, labour flexibility means ‘easy hire and exit policy’ for labour. The flexibility of labour norms today works in four ways as described below following Sen and Dasgupta (2009):

(1) **Numerical flexibility** This basically signifies easy adjustments in the number of workers to meet the varying levels of demand as well as technological innovation. It requires that the production firms have the legal sanction of easy shedding of those workers whose need given the demand and/or new technological innovation is not there anymore. Also, at the same time it implies that a firm can easily hire new workers on contractual or temporary basis (mostly sans any written contract) so that they can be easily laid off when such situations arise. This is the most popular notion of flexibility which is generally now preached by the neoliberal advocates and also, practised by the business firms with or without any de jure change in rigid labour rules.

(2) **Functional flexibility** This stands for the ability of the business firms to reorganize its labour force without any constraint to varying levels of tasks. It basically means that today’s labour should possess multiple skills as opposed to specialized skills which were the general norm under Fordism in assembly line production. A worker without any resistance should agree to perform several tasks. Large corporate firms are increasingly adhering to this type of functional flexibility which in a way reduces per unit labour cost of production and leaves very few incentives for firms to hire new workers at increasing rate. This flexibility is intrinsically related to ever increasing productivity of labour in any production process.

(3) **Wage flexibility** Wage flexibility refers to a business firm’s capacity to adjust wages (necessary equivalents for the variable capital) at its own terms which would suit the capitalists’ need for cost-effectiveness so that they survive the capitalist competition in the commodity markets. Wage flexibility today is ensured by the attempt to do away with the minimum wage laws in different post-colonial societies. The neoliberal state power may not always succeed in that as it has not in India so far. So, it works through the route of informalization which is shaped by outsourcing, subcontracting and replacing nominal money wage by piece rate wage and like.

(4) **Temporal flexibility** This refers to adjustments in the utilization of labour hours over time according to the temporal and/or seasonal variations in product demand. It allows business firms to adapt to the practices of overtime work (i.e. work beyond stipulated working hours a day) when the demand in the market is high. At the same time, it means utilization of less labour hours a day when demand is low and hence, implying seasonal or temporal unemployment for some owners of labour power. At times therefore labour demand may be high and at times may be low. And when the labour demand is low this flexibility norm implies that the business firms can easily shed some labour at its own will.

Each one of these four forms of flexibility facilitates cheap labour regime which is actually facilitated by the neoliberal state power in post-colonial societies with or without formal changes in rigid labour laws. And this can be done only in a political climate which would speak the language of capital in a liberal democratic façade as it is happening in India since the mid-1980s. Where the liberal democracy itself may be problematic the global capitalism does not hesitate to speak in terms of brute military force so as to ensure cheap labour regime. With every migration of labouring masses (whatever may be the reason: racism, religion, terrorism, partition, economic crisis resulting abject income depletion and like) living labour became cheaper and cheaper and also remains divided as the voice representation of labour becomes more and more distant labour right. Let us now have a brief look at what has happened to voice representation, collective bargaining right of labour since the inception of neoliberal order in post-colonial context.

Voice Representation as a Labour Right

This section is about the voice representation of labour. We have chosen India as our post-colonial space in the present time characterized by the onslaughts of neoliberal globalization. Neoliberalism, as we have already discussed, in our rendition signifies liberalization of market from the holds of the state making it free and competitive in neoclassical sense. In this view of market, private initiatives in the sphere of production and resource allocation remain pivotal and they replace the direct involvement of state in the productive activities and also, state-intervention and regulations in the market. In such a view, an individual is *homo-economicus*, meaning a self-enterprising economic agent who is rational and efficient, where efficiency signifies the individual's ability to optimize his/her position either as consumer or as producer. This view of efficiency also pertains to the free *laissez faire* market which is supposedly efficient through the workings of so-called *invisible hands* in equilibrating supply and demand and at the same time ensuring maximum profit to business firms and maximum utility to consumers. Resource allocation as per the standard neoclassical microeconomic textbook is dubbed efficient if equilibrium in the market, such that above two optimal situations, is attained without generating any externality (either positive or negative) in terms of social benefit or social costs. This is a worldview which poses an entirely capital-centric view of the world. Every aspect of social and economic life is viewed from the perspective of capital which warrants a focus on profit orientation of productive agents. Viewed in the logic of neoliberalism, labour is also poised in terms of capital. There is a capitalo-centric view of labour which warrants labour to be productive all the time so as to ensure more and more surplus and hence profit. Labour market in this view is treated just like any other marker for commodity. That labour market is a social institution is totally ignored in the neoliberal rendition of labour (Solow 1990). And to make labour more productive, neoliberalism proposes the replacement of what it calls a rigid labour regime by a flexible one with easy hire and fire clauses and flexible wages and working hours. Productivity of labour is ensured also by never-ending technological advances, which are labour-displacing in nature.[3] In this setting, any organization of labour, viz. trade unions and the like, is treated as an anathema to smooth working of the labour market, and hence, the commodity market, as it is held to pose, in the neoclassical as well as neoliberal views, distortions to the functioning of the free, competitive market.

India started following the neoliberal path since 1991 which was imposed upon her by the IMF-World Bank following her severe external payment crisis at that time. And, this neoliberal reform had the sanction of the handful ruling elites of the country to which joined the Indian big capitalist class. Since then the terms like 'efficiency', so-called free market competition and profit have gained momentum in the Indian economic space. The principal objectives of the New Economic Policy (NEP) include the following: (a) replacement of direct state-initiatives in production by private (domestic as well as foreign) initiatives and doing away with state-interventions in the workings of free market; (b) supplement, if not replace, domestic capital by foreign capital; and (c) installing a growth-centric economic order. The NEP has severe implications for Indian labour. In fact, the period since 1991 has been described as a period of *job-less* growth in India (Sen and Dasgupta 2009). The most dramatic is the fall in public sector employment from 190.58 hundred thousands in 1991 to 178.62 hundred thousands in 2010. This fall is steepest in the manufacturing industries under public sector which was from 18.52 hundred thousands in 1991 to 10.66 hundred thousands in 2010. This fall in our opinion is the outcome of the disinvestment process incepted since the beginning of the NEP regime in 1991 as well as outright closure of several public sector production units. Overall (taking public and private sector together), total employment has increased during a 20-year period (1991–2010) from 267.33 hundred thousands to 287.08 hundred thousands which signifies an increase of 19.75 hundred thousands only. This means on average formal employment grew only by 0.9875 hundred thousands every year during 1991–2010. The formal employment in the private sector went up from 44.81 hundred thousands in 1991 to 51.98 hundred thousands in 2009 and then fell to 51.84 lakh in 2010. During 1991–2009, this implies that formal private sector employment increased only by 7.17 lakh or by 0.3585 lakh only per annum on average. In the private sector most of these new jobs are casual, irregular or temporary in nature and cannot be ascribed as *quality jobs*. This is the finding of our field survey which we carried out in Delhi, Uttar Pradesh, West Bengal, Haryana, Gujarat and Maharashtra during 2003–06 (Sen and Dasgupta 2009). So, this is a period of growing informalization of the economy and it has occurred in two senses: (1) burgeoning of informal activities as people who could not find any place in the formal sector had to take to informal occupations/activities which do not have any security and are mostly low paid

[3]On the technological point, see Sen and Byasdeb (2009), where the authors have empirically shown that in post-reform period in India even the high-growth industries are adopting modern labour-displacing technologies which have, on the one hand, increased labour productivity in these industries manifold and, on the other hand, contracted new jobs.

and also uncertain in terms of regular and sustained generation of earnings; and (2) growing informalization of the formal space, as is evident in increasing casualization and contractualization of formal jobs. There is also farming out of work from the formal sector to the informal sector in terms of subcontracting and outsourcing to reduce the costs of production.

Globalization, narrowly defined, implies the opening up of the economy to the global economy. It is a never-ending process of integration of the domestic economy with the global economy. It is occurring in the context of India in terms of: (a) growing linkage with the global economy through international trade flows and (b) growing linkage with the global economy through foreign capital flows. It is often claimed in the mainstream literature on Indian economy that flexible labour rules would facilitate more foreign capital flow. Indian labour rules are rigid and, hence, they pose obstacle to free flows of foreign capital in the direction of India—particularly of the FDI variety. First of all, what is desirable and warranted is a more open economy with hardly any controls on capital and exchange rate. And, secondly, the openness of the economy would be more assured and strengthened if the country has flexible labour rules replacing its so-called rigid rules. Foreign capital desires labour to be passive and within its control. So, this is a case of deregulation of capital along with re-regulation of labour, subjecting the latter to the whims and fancies of global capital.

Through neoliberalism and globalization, global capitalism has been at work in India for the last two decades. It is functioning in terms of global circuits of capital, some of which are linked even with informal economic space. What is the major implication of this neoliberal globalized onslaught of global capitalism on labour organization and voice representation of labour in India? Labour remains the main risk-bearing factor in this regime. Efficiency and competitiveness are garnered by squeezing the space of labour. Labour is denied its just share in production. At the same time, it is asked to be more and more productive. This is an era where rampant cost-cutting strategies adopted by the firms across different sectors which basically stand for slashing down labour cost as far as possible. As the ASI data show, labour costs as percentage of total costs of production in registered manufacturing factories have declined from 7.78 % in 2000–2001 to 5.63 % in 2007–2008, which is the obvious result of the cost-cutting strategy of manufacturing firms of late.[4] This means that the onus of cost-cutting has fallen on labour. Note further that the number of average workers per factory increased only marginally from 47.81 persons in 2000–2001 to 56.10 persons in 2007–2008, which signifies an increase of 8.30 persons for this 7-year period, or on average a rise by 1.19 persons per factory every year. On the other hand, contract workers' proportion in the total workers rose from 20.50 % in 2000–2001 to 30.96 % in 2007–2008.[5] This does not include casual workers in registered factories. So, including

[4]http://mospi.nic.in/Mospi_New/upload/asi/ASI_main.htm?status=1&menu_id=88. Accessed on 16 March 2016.

[5]These estimates are obtained from the statistics provided by the Labour Bureau, Government of India, available online at www.labourbureau.nic.in. Accessed on 12 November 2012.

the casual workforce, the proportion of the informal in the formal manufacturing employment would be much higher no doubt. Surely, labour in casualized, contractualized and informalized forms are much more exploited than labour in regularized conditions. Moreover, in this age even those who are in regular employment conditions are facing some flexibility in terms of undefined working hours and contraction in different non-wage benefits, including retirement benefits, medical insurance and housing benefits, which used to be the principal features of such employment. In addition, there is a large labour force engaged in informal work (a significant of proportion of them being self-employed) with low payment and without any non-wage benefits and labour security. Almost 93 % of the total labour force in India is in informal activity as many of them could not find any opportunity in the formal segment of the economy. Finally, a great number is unemployed; and some of them may be categorized as the discouraged unemployed.[6]

Against this backdrop, the question of voice representation of labour assumes greater significance as the space of labour is continuously squeezed by (global) capital. Flexible labour rules under neoliberal globalized order warrant less and less scope for voice representation of labour. Labour should not have the chance to organize itself to represent its voice against (global) capital. In the context of BPO and ITES sector, Sandhu (2006, pp. 4321–22) noted that:

> … there are real concerns about whether the unions can even organize effectively given the structural organization of BPO work. Most of the call centre employees work nights and sleep during day. They even maintain this schedule over weekends, when the only groups that they are able to socialize with are other call centre employees who keep similar schedules. This has given rise to a call centre tribe, which stays up weekend nights and socializes to get rid of the buildup of stress that comes out of the stress at work. How can one approach the workers when they are picked up from home and driven into the innards of the building where they work—and after work, are picked up and dropped outside their home? The tired workers who sleep during the day much rather catch up on sleep than spend time on any other issue.

In fact, the space of voice representations of workers of different varieties in this age of neoliberal globalization is continuously shrunk even without formal change in the existing 'rigid' labour rules towards more flexible ones. But through the back door already flexibility has engulfed the space of labour without much dissent or resistance. Otherwise, how one can justify the significant rise in the casual workforce in the formal sector?

---

[6]The discouraged unemployed have no place in the late modern neoclassical theory of unemployment search. The discouraged unemployed have given up searching for jobs after getting frustrated in doing so indefinitely. Hence, they cannot be classified as unemployed after searching for jobs as claimed by the search theory of unemployment (http://economistsview.typepad.com/economistsview/2006/10/the_searchmatch.html. Accessed on 16 March 2016). There is no official data on discouraged unemployment in India. However, official statistics of the USA show a significant presence of discouraged unemployed in the labour force (http://www.bls.gov/opub/ils/pdf/opbils74.pdf. Accessed on 16 March 2016). Noted French philosopher Rada Ivakovic in a discussion with the author has argued that there are not enough jobs (either in the North or in the South) under the present global capitalism to exploit even all those who are willing to offer their services, or all who are in the labour force; some are left to be exploited!.

This section deals with issues pertaining to voice representation of labour in the post-NEP period in India. The issues that we want to disembark upon are actually the challenges facing labour in the context of its voice representation. The section discusses with the help of some empirical facts the status of voice representation in the formal and informal sectors.

Primarily, the trade unions (henceforth, TUs) remained at the centre stage of voice representation of the industrial working class in India. There are several trade unions or labour organizations in India which played crucial roles in fighting for the cause of different kinds of labour in India. In fact, there is a long history of trade union movement in India which dates back to the pre-independence days (Dutt 2008). As an organized movement, trade unions began to take shape in India in the years immediately following the end of the World War I. Trade unions are essentially the product of modern large-scale industry. Indian trade unions did not grow out of any existing institutions in the society. They developed as a new institution. So far as the question of formation and development of TUs in India is concerned, its necessity was realized from 1875 onwards by philanthropists, social workers such as Soirabji Shapaji Bengalle and N.M. Lokhandey (Vargeese 2010). As a result of their concrete efforts, there was awakening among the workers and they had formed a few unions such as The Printers' Union, Calcutta (1905) and the Bombay Postal Union (1907). Yet the necessity of having workers organization on a large scale was realized only after the World War I when there was an outburst of industrial strike. The first union started in Madras at the initiative of B.P. Wadia in 1918 which was known as the Madras Textile Union. In 1921, the law was made use of against it by employers who obtained an order from the Madras High Court restraining the union activities. The event focused the attention of the public on the need for trade union legislation which did not exist till then in the country (Chatterjee 2008).

Leaders like Gandhi had given due impetus to the organization of workers. He advised the working class 'to combine themselves in the form of unions but not for political motives but for bettering their social or economic positions' (Gandhi 1946, p. 229). Besides Gandhi, the Whitley Commission on Labour in India (1929–1931) had also pointed out that '[m]odern industrialism is itself of western importation and the difficulties which it creates for labour in India are similar to the difficulties it has created elsewhere' (GoI 1929, p. 322). Moreover, the Commission did not find an evidence of any alternative remedy that is likely to be effective. So it emphasized that the need of organization among Indian workers is great and it further recommended that 'nothing but a strong Trade Union movement will give the Indian working class adequate protection' (GoI 1929, p. 322). Meanwhile, in 1920, in Ahmedabad an association of workers was formed which developed into a model union known as the Ahmadabad Textile Labour Association under the guidance of Gandhi (Mukerjee 1945). The year also saw the establishment of the All India Trade Union Congress (AITUC) as a central organization of labour. The passage of the Indian Trade Union Act of 1926 conferred a legal and corporate status on registered TUs and granted them certain immunities in regard to industrial disputes. The Act makes provision for two matters: (1) the conditions governing registration; and (2) the right and privilege accorded to registered TUs. The Act also allowed the funds of the registered unions to be spent for the conduct of the industrial disputes and for the provision of benefits to its members. Under this Act, the registered unions are required to submit annual returns to the Registrar of Trade Unions. It is, however, not compulsory for all unions to be registered under the Act. 'The 1930s started with a climate which was favourable to the growth of the trade union movement. The prosecution of the communists involved in the Meerut Conspiracy case, and the failure of the Bombay Textile strike of 1929 brought a dullness in trade union activity. The serious economic depression of this period has the same effect. There was wide spread retrenchment (due to economic depression) and the strikes of this period were aimed at maintain normal wages and preventing retrenchment' (Karnik 1998). During the World War II, the government used the Defence of India Rules and prohibited strikes and lockouts and referred industries disputes to conciliation and adjudication. But the deteriorating economic conditions made workers conscious of the need for making organized efforts for securing relief. This gave a fillip to the TU movement and there was a marked increase both in the number of unions and of organized/unionized workers (Karnik 1998).

Labour and trade union movements during the pre-independence days were very much part and parcel of the broader freedom struggle against British colonial rule. In the immediate post-independence days during the planning period, trade unions were viewed by the state as an inseparable part of the country's industrial organism because they were supposed to integrate workers with their social and communal ties and responsibilities (Knowels 1952). The necessity of the existence of TUs to safeguard the interests of labour was reflected in several initial plan documents.[7] The Second Five Year Plan postulated that 'a strong union movement is necessary both for safeguarding the interests of labour and for realizing the targets of production' (GoI 1956, p. 575). Hence, to build strong unions the plan emphasized the need 'to grant them (trade unions) recognition as representative unions' and for this purpose the states were asked to enact 'some statutory provision for securing recognition of unions' (p. 575). The Indian state during the heyday of planning (early 1950s to late 1980s) considered TUs as 'an essential part of the apparatus of industrial and economic administration of the country'.[8] The subject of labour has been so important that the Government of India, to improve working conditions and to solve workers' day-to-day problems, had appointed a National Commission on Labour in 1966 which submitted its report in 1969. On the

[7]See First Five-Year Plan, Planning Commission, Government of India, (1950–1951), p. 581; Second Five-Year Plan, Planning Commission, Government of India (1956), p. 575; Third Five-Year Plan, Planning Commission, Government of India; Fourth Five-Year Plan, Planning Commission, Government of India; and Fifth Five-Year Plan, Planning Commission, Government of India. All Five-Year Plans are available at http://planningcommission.nic.in/plans/planrel/fiveyr/welcome.html. Accessed on 16 March 2016.

[8]Planning Commission, Government of India, Third Five-Year Plan (http://planningcommission.nic.in/plans/planrel/fiveyr/3rd/welcome.html. Accessed on 16 March 2016).

question of inevitability of TUs the Commission opined that the unions must have a share in the success of the national plans for economic development, since these are formulated and implemented as much for maximizing production as for distributing the product in an equitable manner (GoI 1963, p. 287; Crouch 1966).

Major Indian TUs remained attached with some political parties. In fact, they are one of the mass (labour) organs of mainstream and non-mainstream political parties/outfits.[9] In the post-Independent period, TUs in India were mostly confined to narrow economic issues like wage hikes and improvement in labour conditions. TUs in India were never part of any broader social movements or spearheaded any such movement. They remained characterized by narrow economism. This is not to suggest that such economic issues are not significant for Indian labour. Probably, without such issues organizing labour would have been difficult. TUs in general hardly looked beyond that. Neither were labour movements taken to the level of general political movements in India (except, of course, with some exceptions), nor were they instrumental in any social mobilization. Even between the sectors and/or the industries, cohesion or coordination absent as far as labour movements and organizations were concerned. Even within industries, the isolation among firm-specific TUs did not allow broad-based growth of the TU movement. And now, in this age of neoliberal globalization the TUs are continuously under attack and the voice representation of labour is day-by-day shrinking. This is happening at a time when there is greater need of representation of the voice of labour.

The space of labour in Indian context is broadly divided into formal and informal. So we have one kind of labour organization and movements for formal or organized labour, and another kind for the informal or unorganized segment. Informal labour implies that labour laws of the country are not applicable. Hence, it is expected that labour is more exploited in informal than in the formal sector. As such, data on TUs and other labour organizations in the informal sector are not readily available at the secondary level. Whatever information we have regarding TUs pertains to the formal sector. Table 1 indicates how the number of TUs in the formal sector of the economy has changed during the post-reform period. It is interesting to note that since 2004 the number has been fluctuating, which was quite intensive during 2007 and 2008. On the other hand, the number of unions submitting returns has been constantly falling. In 1991, only 15.72 % of the TUs submitted returns, whereas in 2008 only 11.47 % of the total unions did so. Given the magnitude of labour force in this country we find that union density is not very high where union density is defined as the number of unions divided by the total number of workers. On the other hand, we find that the growth in the number of TUs is fluctuating of late. Note that the formal sector comprises both public and private sectors. Almost all the public sector units in this country have Tus, which is not the case with private formal sector units. There are different types of TUs in this country. Some are industry specific and affiliated to a political party.

[9]For details, see Kennedy (1966).

Table 1 Number of trade unions in the formal sector (1991–2008)

Year	Number of registered unions	Number of unions submitting returns
1991	53,535	8418
1992	55,680	9165
1993	55,784	6806
1994	56,872	6277
1995	57,952	8162
1996	58,988	7242
1997	60,660	8872
1998	61,992	7403
1999	64,817	8152
2000	66,056	7253
2001	66,624	6531
2002	68,544	7812
2003	68,544	7258
2004	74,649	5242
2005	74,403	8317
2006	78,465	8471
2007	95,783	7408
2008	84,642	9709

Source Trade Unions in India, Labour Bureau, Government of India (2008), pp. 14–57

Five of the central trade union organizations have been accorded recognition of being national centres of trade unions. They are, in descending order of membership: the Bharatiya Majdoor Sangh (BMS), affiliated to the Bharatiya Janata Party (BJP); the Indian National Trade Union Congress (INTUC), affiliated to the Indian National Congress (INC); the Centre for Indian Trade Unions (CITU), affiliated to the Communist Party of India Marxist (CPI-M); and the Hind Majdoor Sabha (HMS) and All India Trade Union Congress (AITUC), affiliated to the Communist Party of India (CPI). Some are unit specific, which may or may not be affiliated to a political party. Of late, there is some growth in independent unions, meaning unions not affiliated to a particular political party. Also, there are unions which are specific to a particular economic activity—not firm specific, e.g. fishermen's unions, bank employees' unions. However, at the secondary level we have data and information of only those unions that submit returns every year. There are other forms of workers' organizations such as *morcha*s (protest platforms), labour cooperatives, NGOs, etc., performing the role of promoting workers' welfare. This means that the total number of unions as indicated in Table 1 is much greater than what is officially reported.

Table 2 indicates that in a span of 18 years from 1991 to 2008 the total membership of all the TUs in the formal sector has increased from 6,101,000 to 9,574,000, which means a rise of 3,473,000. On an average this means an increase in membership by 192,944 only. Note that in terms of the male–female divide

Table 2 Membership of trade unions* (1991–2008) (in thousands)

Year	Men	Women	Total
1991	5507	594	6101
1992	5148	598	5746
1993	2636	498	3134
1994	3239	856	4095
1995	5675	863	6538
1996	4250	1351	5601
1997	6504	905	7409
1998	6104	1145	7249
1999	5190	1218	6408
2000	4510	910	5420
2001	4392	1481	5873
2002	5102	1871	6973
2003	4854	1423	6277
2004	2954	443	3397
2005	6334	2385	8719
2006	7754	1206	8960
2007	5751	2126	7877
2008	7420	2154	9574

Note *Membership of TUs refers to the membership of TUs submitting returns. We have no data about the membership of TUs not submitting the returns and also about the union membership in the informal/unorganized sector. However, we can safely presume the TUs, submitting the returns are the TUs which have large members in the formal sector

Source Trade Unions in India, Labour Bureau, Government of India (2008), pp. 14–57

women are still lagging behind men. In 2008, only 2,154,000 women were unionized against the male membership of 7,420,000. However, if we consider the percentage share of female membership in the total membership, we find that the percentage share of women has increased from 9.74 % in 1991 to 22.50 % in 2008. But the number is fluctuating more than the male membership, as is evident in terms of the coefficient of variation in the number of female membership (48.41) vis-à-vis that in the number of male membership (27.08). In 1991, per 1000 male members there were only 108 female members, which increased to 290 in 2008. During the period under consideration the total increase in male membership was 1,913,000 and the increase in female membership was 1,560,000. In absolute terms, the gross increase in female membership is more significant than that in male membership. Yet, women members are still few in numbers compared to the men members. We have observed during our field survey in Delhi, Gujarat, Haryana, Maharashtra, Uttar Pradesh and West Bengal during 2003–2006 women workers are comparatively shy of being members of TUs.[10] On an average, every

[10]The outcome of this survey is provided in Sen and Dasgupta (2009).

Table 3 Average membership of trade unions

Year	Men	Women	Total
1991	654	71	725
1992	562	65	627
1993	387	73	460
1994	516	136	652
1995	695	106	801
1996	587	187	773
1997	733	102	835
1998	825	155	979
1999	637	149	786
2000	622	125	747
2001	672	227	899
2002	653	240	893
2003	669	196	865
2004	564	85	648
2005	762	287	1048
2006	915	142	1058
2007	776	287	1063
2008	764	222	986

Source Trade Unions in India, Labour Bureau, Government of India (2008), pp. 14–57

year during 1991–2008 male membership went up by 106,278 whereas female membership by 86,667, which means per 1,000 increase in male membership female membership went up by 815 persons every year.

Table 3 in Chap. 3 indicates the average membership of a TU in the formal sector in India. It is to be noted that although average male membership has increased from 1991 to 2008 in recent time it is subject to fall. The average female membership compared to the male membership is low and is subject to greater fluctuation than the male membership. The average membership of TU in general is subject to great year-to-year fluctuation as is evident from Table 3. The coefficient of variation of average membership is 20 % and for female membership it is as high as 45 % (for male membership it is 18 %). This may signify continuous entry and exit of workers in TUs. The pertinent questions in this context are as follows: (1) whether the TUs are failing to attract new members; (2) whether the significance of TUs in collective bargaining is getting blurred day by day; and (3) whether contraction in formal regular employment has significant impact on the very existence of TUs?

The focus of the trade union movement remained the workers in the formal or organized sector and more so those employed in the government-owned enterprises:

> … the mass of workforce engaged in the unorganized sector remained not covered by the trade union movement. Consequently, over 90 % of the workforce remained not unaware

> of their rights as workers and as such were being exploited by their employers. Most of the times the worker is not even aware of the employer's excesses. Long working hours, under payment, sexual abuse, physical confinements are day-to-day affairs. The workers take these actions of their employer as fate (Sinha 2013).

> Trade Unions are a major component of the system of modern industrial relations in any country, each having, in their constitution, their own set of objectives or goals to achieve. Change in the political, social and educational environment has seen them rechristened as a forum that protects and furthers workers' interests and improves the quality of life of workers, enlarging their traditional roles of establishing terms and conditions of employment (Ghosh et al. 2009).

In developing countries, the right to form a union and bargain collectively supposedly protects workers from exploitative and abusive conditions at work and puts pressure on employers to share productivity gains with their employees. Protection of basic worker and human and democratic rights in developing countries thus necessitates unionization so that the workers can reap the benefits of economic growth and development (Ghosh and Geetika 2007). This is not the case in post-reform India which is characterized by jobless growth and rising income and wealth inequality, where the benefits of economic growth have not reached the working population at large. This is happening at a time when the stance of the Indian state has changed from labour-friendly, planned capitalist development to (global) capital-friendly, market-based economic development. In the changed scenario, the attitude of the state towards labour has undergone drastic change, with the Indian state viewing trade unionism as a deterrent to free market-led growth and development which is reflected in many occasions in the media, judiciary and also in administration in their anti-strike stance and attempt to restrict the powers and functions of trade unions. It is a clear aberration to the right to organize as laid down in the Constitution of India.

Flexible Labour and the Age of New Finance

Flexible labour regime thus helps depress labour costs in a pure economic sense of the term. In so doing it requires repression of the voice of labour, as we have analysed in the preceding section. The current neoliberal global order is shaped by what is known in the literature today as 'financialization', which as a process signifies the hegemonic presence of the interests of finance in every sphere of economic and social life. A post-colonial space too is shaped continuously by this process. The classical role of finance to intermediate between financially surplus units and deficit units is completely negated by the overarching financialization process. Finance today has created its own circuit. Surplus from the real circuit enters financial circuit not to return to the real circuit again. Financial surplus of the real serves as the initial money capital of the financial sector (M). It recharges again and again the M-M' circuit (where $M' > M$) but not the other way round. The theoretical explication of this financial circuit is made in Sen (2003). The relation between the real and the financial is asymmetric in nature. While there is no positive feedback upon labour when the financial sector is in upswing, there is adverse impact on labour when there is asset devaluation at the time of financial crisis. Through flexible labour regime, labour has become the main risk-bearing element of financial crises (or for that matter, any crisis). What happens at the macroeconomic space of a post-colonial society is stagnation of wage income (in real terms) through continuous change in functional distribution of national income in favour of a rentier class as well as a profit earning class. Wage share in national income falls implying a persistent rise in capital's share. With crisis, wage share falls more sharply (which actually negates the profit squeeze hypothesis regarding the crisis of capitalism) and, therefore, the capital share as the remaining obviously rises. The fall in wage share is facilitated by flexible labour regime which every Fund-Bank structural adjustment programme in the name of economic liberalization attempts. This is not the end of the story.

Wage share is distributed between workers (productive as well as unproductive labour excluding high income earning managers) and managers, especially those in the financial sector. The stagnation in wage is further entrenched at any time as the managers' share keeps on rising when the total wage share is stagnating.

Capital's share is distributed as interest income and, also, as profit income. Profit is further distributed as profit of financial sector in the M-M' circuit and also as profit of the real sector in the M-C-M' circuit.

Financialization as a process ensures a rising trend in the shares of interest income, financial sector's profit and financial managers' share in total national income. Now the question is, what is the link between flexible labour regimes and financialization as an economic process in a post-colonial society the world over? A flexible labour regime facilitates the adaptation of the (cheap) labour regime, which is conducive to the interest of global capital in general and global finance in particular. Each of the four flexibility norms, viz. numerical flexibility, functional flexibility, wage flexibility and temporal flexibility, has positive bearings for capital accumulation in post-colonial space and time. The implications of the flexible labour regime are as follows:

1. Financialization is intrinsically related to labour processes, as it causes an increased distribution of surplus value towards the financial sector. The financial circuit is continuously fuelled by the surplus generated in the real sector, which is getting accumulated in various exploitative class processes through the circuits of global capital. This accumulation of capital (including the accumulation by dispossession) in post-colonial society's is increasingly channelized towards the new finance to sustain its M-M' circuit with $M' > M$. A financial crisis in general implies stagnating M' whose resolution neoliberal global order tries to find in the public finances of the post-colonial societies through what is termed as austerity programme (austerity for labour while profligacy for capital) and also, in more flexibilization of labour.
2. The global circuit of financial capital as opposed to industrial capital is based upon a social structure in any post-colonial space of the different capital

accumulation processes derived from multifarious exploitative class processes. This is more and more made feasible through flexible labour regime since without flexible labour continuous availability of cheap labour cannot be assured.

3. The degree of financialization is proportionately linked to the rate of exploitation in the real sector and also, to accumulation by dispossession in post-colonial societies today.
4. All that global capital wants today is cheap labour. This is furthered by the process of financialization. And flexible labour regime facilitates to accomplish that.

Conclusion

Summing up our arguments in this chapter, it can be said that the capital accumulation in post-colonial country like India is occurring through flexible labour regime whose ultimate aim is to make labour as cheap as possible. In so doing, it is deteriorating the job-related status of workers, increasing the reserve army of labour and, also, repressing the organized voice of the labour. The process of financialization as witnessed the world over demands cheap labour so that the financial circuit can be reproduced again and again and labour be made to bear risk in times of crisis.

References

Chatterjee, S. K. (2008). *Personal management and industrial relations*. Delhi: Surjeet Publications.

Crouch, H. (1966). *Trade unions and politics in India*. Bombay: Manaktals.

Dutt, R. (2008, May 3). Emerging trends in trade union movement. *Mainstream, 46*(20).

Ghosh, P., & Geetika. (2007). Unionisation: A feasibility study for the indian software industry. *Russian Management Journal, 2*, 45–56.

Ghosh, P., Shefali, N., & Ashish, G. (2009). The changing roles of trade unions in India: A case study of national thermal power corporation (NTPC), Unchahar. *Asian Academy of Management Journal, 14*(1), 37–57.

Government of India. (1929, September 30). *Report of the royal commission on labour in India*.

Government of India Planning Commission. (1956). *Second five year plan*. Retrieved March 16, 2016, from http://planningcommission.nic.in/plans/planrel/fiveyr/index2.html

Government of India. (1963). *Report of national commission on labour*. Retrieved March 16, 2016, from https://casi.sas.upenn.edu/sites/casi.sas.upenn.edu/files/iit/National%20Commission%20on%20Labour%20Report.pdf

Gandhi, M. K. (1946). Untitled. *Harijan*, 21 July: 229.

Harvey, D. (2005). *The new imperialism* (Paperback ed.). New York: Oxford University Press.

Harvey, D. (2007). *A brief history of neoliberalism* (Paperback ed.). Oxford University Press: New York.

Johnson, E. (1978). Labour as risk-bearer. *Cambridge Journal of Economics, 2*, 373–380.

Karnik, V. B. (1998). *Indian trade unions: A survey*. Bombay: P.C. Manekalal & Sons.

Kennedy, V. D. (1966). *Unions, employers and government*. Bombay: Manaktals.

Knowels, K. G. J. C. (1952). *Strikes*. Oxford: Basil Blackwell.
Marx, K. (1976). *Capital* (Vol. 1). London: Penguin Classics in association with New Left Review.
Mukerjee, R. (1945). *Indian working class*. Bombay: Asia Public House.
Samaddar, R. (2015). *The postcolonial bind of Greece*. Retrieved September 9, 2015, from https://viewpointmag.com/2015/08/20/the-postcolonial-bind-of-greece/
Sandhu, A. (2006). Why unions fail in organising India's BPO-ITES Industry? *Economic and Political Weekly, 41*(41), 4319–4322.
Sen, S. (2003). *Global Finance at Risk: On Real Stagnation and Instability*. New York: Palgrave-Macmillan.
Sen, S. (2007). *Globalisation and development*. New Delhi: National Book Trust.
Sen, S., & Dasgupta, B. (2006). Labour in India's manufacturing sector. *Indian Journal of Labour Economics, 49*(1), 79–101.
Sen, S., & Dasgupta, B. (2009). *Unfreedom and waged work—Labour in India's manufacturing industry*. New Delhi: Sage.
Sinha, P. (2013). *Issues before the Indian Trade Union Movement*. India: Friedrich Ebert Stiftung. Retrieved September 9, 2015, from http://www.google.co.in/url?sa=t&rct=j&q=&esrc=s&source=web&cd=2&sqi=2&ved=0CDkQFjAB&url=http%3A%2F%2Flibrary.fes.de%2Fpdf-files%2Fiez%2F01963.pdf&ei=US_CUOKBIMrUrQeZyYGYAw&usg=AFQjCNEOnBOq7zrG6aFs02R0o1ufzFla8g&sig2=OQ429fu9ScsA0mnEBOp0mw
Solow, R. M. (1990). *Labour market as social institution*. Oxford: Basil Blackwell.
Standing, G. (1999). *Global labour flexibility—Seeking distributive justice*. London: Macmillan Press Limited.
Standing, G. (2002). *Beyond new paternalism—Basic security as equality*. New York: Verso.
Vargeese, M. (2010). *Historical background of trade unionism in India*. Retrieved September 9, 2015, from http://www.google.co.in/url?sa=t&rct=j&q=&esrc=s&source=web&cd=22&ved=0CDYQFjABOBQ&url=http%3A%2F%2Fshodhganga.inflibnet.ac.in%2Fbitstream%2F10603%2F610%2F11%2F11_chapter3.pdf&ei=nxTCUNsnxPetB6q3gIgO&usg=AFQjCNHsrVE8EaGV76WYZFBA27mkVh8aYA&sig2=hddDrVshF2gUEJ3Q_cZdgg
Wolff, R. (N.D.) *Capitalism hits the fan*. Retrieved September 9, 2015, from http://www.rdwolff.net/sites/default/files/attachment/4/03Wolff.pdf
Wolff, R. D., & Resnick, S. A. (1987). *Economics: Marxian versus neoclassical*. Baltimore, London: The John Hopkins University Press.

Law, Statistics, Public–Private Partnership and the Emergence of a New Subject

Mithilesh Kumar

Abstract The objective of the chapter is to understand the new form of government that has come into being. The questions to be asked in this context are the following: What is being governed in the first place—the population or the circuits of capital? What is the relationship between the two? Circuits of capital are generated through forms of infrastructure consolidation (the Indira Gandhi Airport in New Delhi, for example). What makes the monopoly of infrastructure distinct is the emergence of public–private partnerships (PPP). This chapter examines these PPP endeavours, their efficiencies, successes, failures and effects on labour politics and social struggles. There are PPS of the institutional nature and PPPs of the legal nature; this calls for political and legal innovation. Though scholars argue that PPPs are used to break the model of state activity in social sphere and curb its manipulation of social relations, the author argues that PPPs allow the state to restructure itself. The 'population' is modelled as a composite of consumers of goods in a profit-base. The PPPs are more than the sum of its public and private parts; they give rise to a distinct mode which operates through a distinct relationship of space, politics and people that influence the market.

Keywords Governance · Circuits of capital · Logistics · Public–Private partnership · Labour politics

> As for the question of 'the system of government', this is a matter of how political power is organized, the form in which one social class or another chooses to arrange its apparatus of political power to oppose its enemies and protect itself. There is no state which does not have an appropriate apparatus of political power to represent it.
>
> Mao (1965, p. 352)

M. Kumar (✉)
Institute for Culture and Society, Western Sydney University, Richmond, Australia
e-mail: kmithilesh@hotmail.com

I.K. Mitra et al. (eds.), *Accumulation in Post-Colonial Capitalism*,
DOI 10.1007/978-981-10-1037-8_3

In a document of the Planning Commission which seeks to come up with a framework for the regulation of infrastructure there is an attempt made also to define the nature of state (Planning Commission 2008). It is a reflexive exercise. It is evident that the Commission is aware of the transition in the characteristics of the state as a result of the changes in the economy. The question of the state is positioned vis-à-vis law, judiciary and most importantly the 'people at large'. It is within this matrix that the state seeks to define itself as well as its functions.

The document makes a clear distinction between the 'command and control mode of governance' which was based on state ownership and a 'new mode of regulatory governance' based on public–private partnerships and private sector participation. In between these two periods and modes of organizing the economy and corresponding structure of power lies the dilemma of governance in contemporary times. The rupture between the two is not easily achieved and the document readily admits that this 'transformation…remains an inadequately understood process' (Planning Commission 2008, p. 1). This inadequacy is brought about as a result of the contradiction between legal mechanisms already in place and a need to find new mechanisms that is suitable for the transformation under way. It is in this process of change and continuity that the problem of governance lies.

In the bid to transform itself into a 'regulatory state', the question is what kind of legal and other state apparatuses like statistics are unleashed and how does it affect labour. The legal ambiguities that are created as a result of this transformation provide a space for innovation in governance and redefining the relation of state with the workers. It is not a coincidence that in such a transformative process, public–private partnership (PPP) has played a key role and the question of how to build and govern infrastructure through this model has acquired a new urgency in state discourse. Mezzadra and Neilson (2014) have poignantly pointed out that 'the repressive work of states, which is classically considered part of their core business, is outsourced to private interests or pursued through the *perverse logic of the public-private partnership*' (emphasis added). The perversity of this logic needs to be dissected as it is in the details of the functioning of PPP that one can unravel the mechanics of the new 'regulatory state' as well as the logic behind the creation of such a state.

PPP and infrastructure are closely linked, almost synonymous, in the case of India. The Indira Gandhi International Airport, New Delhi, was the first experiment in India with the PPP model which was then followed by airports in Mumbai, Hyderabad and others. This model is now being actively pursued, and there is a consensus within the government that infrastructure can be rolled out effectively only through this particular model. This nexus between new form of political and economic arrangement, i.e. PPP and infrastructure allow us to study the latter in terms of political theory in addition to geographical and technical studies. There is now a large volume of literature which studies infrastructure in terms of production and redistribution of spaces, the most celebrated being *Splintering Urbanism* by Graham and Marvin (2001). Graham and Marvin have traced the development of infrastructure from the state-controlled monopoly phase to the contemporary phase of private sector-led development with or without various forms of combination with the public sector. They have termed this phenomenon 'unbundling' of infrastructure which results in the creation of privileged networked infrastructures and is exclusionary in practice.

Monopoly in infrastructure is still the main characteristic in India. Amrita Datta has pointed out that 'since many infrastructure projects are naturally monopolistic, it calls for regulations when markets are not competitive' (Datta 2009, pp. 73–78).

It is important here to explain why the question of infrastructure is posited through the question of state, popular politics and governmental mechanism, i.e. PPP. It is my contention here that infrastructure, its creation and management have allowed the state to reconfigure and redirect the question of politics and political subject. The theoretical tools to understand this new phenomenon are heavily borrowed from the works of Ranabir Samaddar, and Mezzadra and Neilson. Samaddar in his book *Emergence of the Political Subject* (2010) brings out the problem of state and the political subject in the post-colonial condition. Samaddar demonstrates that since the anti-colonial struggle was against the colonial state the problem of classical political philosophy of a state-centric political subject never weighed heavily on the former. State as 'the crux of politics and political philosophy' was displaced 'when politics came to be associated not so much with state or rule, but with war' (Samaddar 2010, p. XXVI). The most important insight that Samaddar gives, in my opinion, is that the question of political subject instead looked at from a 'state-centric' point of view can be located in the practices of political struggle that makes a subject. This can be extended to another proposition. It can be claimed that the state loses its primacy in the arena of politics because of the political struggles that subjects make. The state can govern or conduct only in its attempt to create proper political subjects. In a different context, Mezzadra and Neilson (2014) make a similar point. In the article 'The State of Capitalist Globalization', they observe that the state 'emerges as an economic actor that holds particular relations with specific fractions of capital… as one capitalist among others, although it may be in a stronger or weaker position with respect to the interests and agencies with which it interacts'.

If we take the formulation of Mezzadra and Neilson, one has to point out the changes that would firmly establish and identify the state as an economic actor that is also capitalist. The question is as follows: What should be the indicators of that transformation?

It is in the attempt to answering the above question that PPP becomes important. PPP firmly puts the nature of relationship between one capitalist (the state) and another (private corporation) in the realm of legal and political contract. The state no longer only acts as a facilitator or obstructer of capital but is legally and economically bound to the process of accumulation. In that sense, the state does not have to evoke exceptional laws or public good to legitimize accumulation but that accumulation itself becomes the basis of legitimacy.

The new relationship has brought out a different set of analytical problems where all categories of political theory have to be examined in new ways. The problem is put acutely in Mezzadra and Neilson's *Border as Method* (2013). They point out that:

> …for Foucault the people corresponds to the 'legal' logic of sovereignty and citizenship (and the language of rights), he posits population as the target of biopolitical government. To be governed, the population has to be known, and since it is an elusive, statistically unstable entity, it has to be continually traced in its movements and dissected into discrete groups. The more unstable and mobile the population to be governed becomes, the more finely tuned and sophisticated the knowledge devices deployed must become (Mezzadra and Neilson 2013, p. 173).

To this particular observation, I want to add that when the knowledge devices are being made more sophisticated and stable, the knowing of the population and the attempt of making discrete groups become ever more difficult. This process is actually what produces knowledge. The desire to produce a statistically stable, discrete group as political subjects who could be then governed is the frontier of governmentality, not its centre. In fact, to govern the statistically un-producible subject is how the art of governmentality tries to solve the problem. The art of governmentality then tries to ensconce itself in producing a normative phenomenon and at the heart of this new art is the question how to govern conditions of production without producing a subject. We will give the example of a legal judgment in the case of airport workers to illustrate this phenomenon.

Mezzadra and Neilson also provide the concept of 'sovereign machine of governmentality' to examine the dynamics of sovereignty and governmentality:

> …(The) sovereignty we are talking about is at the same time immanent to governmentality—because it tends to be subjected to its rationality—and transcendent to its devices—because it retains its autonomy, otherwise it would not be possible for it to act as a supplement of governmentality (Mezzadra and Neilson 2013, pp. 203–204).

There is still an unresolved tension between sovereignty and governmentality in this formulation. The autonomy of sovereignty which allows it to supplement governmentality still, to an extent, retains the understanding that the sovereign can and is one who decides on the exception. The formulation I want to put forward is that sovereignty and governmentality in the contemporary age should be seen as acting not in a bipolar way but in a relational way. There is no threshold where sovereignty ends and governmentality begins or vice versa or when one is supplemented with the other. Samaddar points out that 'postcolonial researches… demonstrate the link between sovereignty and governmentality, juridical power and molecular power, mass and body and normalcy and exceptionality' not as a disjunction but as an interface (Samaddar 2013, p. 40). In this case, the moment of exception is not the moment of the sovereign but is an over-determined moment when state, governmentality and the political subject that has formed itself through political struggles collide together.

A Short and Turbulent History of Delhi International Authority Limited (DIAL)

In this section, we will analyse the fusion of the state with private capital. Since Indira Gandhi International Airport was the first venture under the PPP model, it gives us a unique opportunity of transition of the state from the command and control position to the regulatory characteristic which it wants to achieve. The contradictions and tussles in this fusion are laid bare, and the interaction between state capital and various forms of private capital can be dissected in this process. It also shows how different state authorities negotiate with each other as well as some new authorities are created in order to streamline the process in which state decides to act as a capitalist. Finally, it shows how the Planning Commission which was the symbol of the state in the welfare regime intervenes and slowly disappears when it is realized that if the state has to be capitalist, it has to discard the baggage of welfare planning.

The route to the adoption of the PPP as a model for the development of Delhi airport and subsequently Mumbai airport was an uneven one. In fact, it was not even a preferred model of development. According to the report of the Comptroller and Auditor General of India (CAG), 'In January 2000 the cabinet approved the restructuring of airports through the long term leasing route' (CAG 2012, p. V). It was only in September 2003 that the cabinet approved the restructuring of Delhi and Mumbai airport through the joint venture mode.

As the CAG report mentions:

> In pursuance of this decision, after selection of the JV partner, AAI (Airport Authority of India) incorporated a subsidiary company viz. M/S Delhi International Airport Pvt. Ltd (DIAL), and subsequently sold 74% of the shares of DIAL to the JV consortium. On 4 April 2006, in the capacity of the state promoter, AAI signed an Operation Management Development Agreement (OMDA) with DIAL. The AAI handed over IGI airport, Delhi to DIAL on 'as is where is' basis and granted DIAL the exclusive right to undertake functions of operations, maintenance, development, design, construction, modernization, finance and management of the Airport. On 26 April 2006 Government of India signed another agreement with DIAL viz. State Support Agreement (SSA). The agreement laid down conditions and nature of support to be provided by Government of India, along with the mutual responsibilities and obligations between Government and DIAL (CAG 2012, p. V).

A further complication occurred with the establishment of an independent Airport Economic Regulatory Authority (AERA). When OMDA and SSA were being thought of, there was no independent regulator in place. The AERA Act was passed in December 2008 and came into force on 1 January 2009 (CAG 2012, p. vi). The CAG report noted conflicts between provisions in OMDA and SSA on the one hand and the AERA Act on the other and as the report notes 'which will have long term repercussions on the Regulator's role on tariff fixation in Delhi and Mumbai airports'. The conflict is related to the definition of aeronautical and non-aeronautical services. The CAG report gives the example of ground handling service which, according to the OMDA, is a non-aeronautical service but is an aeronautical service according to the AERA Act. AERA notes that services like ground handling and cargo handling are less capital intensive and more profitable. The CAG notes that

> … treatment of services such as Ground handling, Cargo handling or parking as non-aeronautical services in OMDA provided undue financial advantage to DIAL, as in terms of SSA, the Targeted Revenue for the purpose of tariff fixation takes into account only 30 per cent of the revenue generated from non-aeronautical services. (CAG 2012, p. VII)

This difference between aeronautical and non-aeronautical services apart from the juridical problem of fixing and distribution of revenue has an important impact on the constitution of labour force and processes at the airport. It is much easier to informalize the labour process and labour force in non-aeronautical services than it is in the aeronautical services. This is so because once an economic activity is classified as aeronautical services, the legal regime, under which it functions, changes. It becomes much more restrictive and stringent as it will fall under various laws which have to do with security, safety and surveillance.

A reading of Schedule 5 and Schedule 6 of the OMDA which deals with aeronautical and non-aeronautical services, respectively, will make this amply clear. Also, businesses such as ground handling and cargo handling which are parts of the non-aeronautical services have had a long relationship with the villages surrounding the Delhi airport. For example, the village of Nangal Dewat which was displaced as part of the expansion of the airport was a major supplier of labour force in ground and cargo handling at the Delhi airport before DIAL came into existence. Similarly, Mehram Nagar which is close to the domestic terminal of the airport specialized in the movement of cargo at the airport.

Non-aeronautical services in some ways expand the operation of the airport outside the boundaries of the airport. The airport through its economic activities, thus, becomes embedded in the larger urban economic process bringing into its fold labour processes and labour force in what we can call ‘differential proximity’. In some ways, the airport then follows the model of just-in-time or lean production where the process of production is fragmented at various spaces and then integrated through a supply chain. This creates its own logistical chain and airport and then becomes the node from where all these economic activities and labour processes are controlled.

We now come back to the issue of OMDA, PPP and the discussion it generated. The claim that I am making is that the ambiguity and conflict in the making of law and legal contract are not results of incompetence, oversight or trial and error. The new art of government lies in the construction of legal ambiguity and conflict. Amrita Datta in her study mentions that ‘PPPs…have been emerging out of an unstructured process almost as a trial and error’ (Datta 2009, p. 74). This statement has a lot of truth in it but it needs to be extended further to understand the full implication of this unstructured process. The legal and governmental spaces that are created because of this conflict and ambiguity are where the state as capitalist lodges itself in its interaction and fusion with various forms and fractions of capital. It can also be seen as the condition of creating a quasi-market situation in which the infrastructure monopolies operate through the route of PPP. Thus, the stable monopolies of the welfare state have given way to a contentious monopoly in the contemporary era which operates and accumulates through the legal ambiguities and conflicts between and within state agencies and private capital. The elusiveness and the instability which Mezzadra and Neilson have noted for identifying population which is mobile is also true in the case of legal mechanisms. There are spaces of mobility for capital to operate, and it cannot be otherwise if the state has to act as a capitalist in partnership with private capital.

The lack of a legal definition in PPPs has not escaped scholars, and they find this lack of definition in the legal tradition. In the case of European Union (EU), Christina Tvarno has pointed out that if a legal definition was set up, 'it would open itself up to a long list of projects that would not be covered by this definition and the EC public procurement rules' (Tvarno 2011, p. 219). This should not be seen as an attempt to escape or preclude law and jurisprudence but to make it contingent, to open a space for perpetual conflict and negotiation. It is a call for perpetual legal and political innovations. Tvarno also points to two kinds of PPPs: 'PPPs of a purely contractual nature and PPPs of an institutional nature, in which the public and private parties establish a joint public limited company'. (Tvarno 2011, p. 219). It is important to discuss PPPs of an institutional nature which is the case with DIAL as it provides important insight about the transformation of state and capital.

Scholars are almost unanimous in suggesting that the PPP model is used to bring the logic and discipline of the market in the functioning of public bodies. Roger Wettenhall (Wettenhall 2011, p. 17) suggests that 'public-private mixing has existed since the beginnings of organized government'. It 'retreated as nation states became stronger in the 1700s and 1800s…but it has flourished again…as the evolution of governance systems has required…they share significant power and influence with market institutions and civil society'. He sees the evolution of PPP as admittance by the state that it no longer has the monopoly of governance. Tony Bovaird, tracing the intellectual history of PPP, cites several works and interpretations of the model. In one interpretation, PPP is seen as 'a mode of governance through which the state attempts to restructure itself and, indirectly, class relations, by transforming the social relations of service and infrastructure provision and subordinating them to the discipline of the market' (Bovaird 2011, p. 53). Yet others, according to Bovaird, see PPP as a method of coordinating the forces of capitalist development. Matthew Flinders (2011) makes a similar argument that the logic of PPPs is based on accepting the supremacy of market relationships and focus on efficiency and outputs as the primary indicator of performances. He, however, makes a more important point that what this logic of PPPs leads to is the possibility of interpreting and modelling the public as consumers or customers in a political marketplace rather than as citizens.

The refrain in all these studies is that PPP are combination of state and capital in various measures but they each retain their characteristics while competing or collaborating with each other in a market place or a similarly simulated place in the case of contentious monopolies. The point that I am trying to make is that it is true that PPPs are one of the modes in which the state is restructuring itself vis-à-vis capital and labour. However, this does not automatically mean that the state enters in competition with capital and has to cede its function to the latter. Consequently, it is also not a corollary of PPP that capital acquires the nature of state. If anything, these should be considered as the limits of state and capital on the political graph. In the first instance, it will produce totalitarianism under monopoly state capital and in the second the liberal dream of free competition. However, what can be said of the current transformation is that instead of competing with each other, state and capital are in the process of fusing with each other. This is not an assemblage of distinct categories or simply a network but an altogether different entity which is producing new forms of economic and political processes.

It is quite evident that the legal ambiguities which came up during the bidding process for Delhi and Mumbai airports were also an attempt to give form to the as yet state capital alloy. The joint venture which was sought to be created and did finally emerge as DIAL is at once a profit-making company and a tool of governmentality. They are intertwined but not discrete.

The bidding process for Delhi and Mumbai airports was a controversial one, and it laid bare the limits of the rule of experts. It also allowed the Planning Commission to reinvent and reinforce itself, momentarily, in the new regime which was being forged. To oversee and monitor the bidding and award process, an Empowered Group of Ministers (EGoM) was constituted. An Inter-Ministerial Group (IMG) of officers was set up as well for assisting the EGoM. ABN Amro was appointed as the financial consultant and transaction advisor, and expression of interest was invited on 17 February 2004. However, in May 2004, there was a change in government and the EGoM was reconstituted. Air Plan, Australia, was appointed as the global technical advisor (GTA), and Amarchand and Mangaldas and Suresh A. Shroff and Company (AMSS) was appointed as the legal consultant. The bid documents, including the Lease Deed (LD), the Shareholders Agreement (SHA), the State Support Agreement (SSA), the State Government Support Agreement (SGSA), the Substitution Agreement (SA) and the proposed Operation, Management and Development Agreement (OMDA), were issued to the bidder.

A dissenting voice from the Planning Commission on the provisions of the OMDA halted the bidding process, sent it to the courts and irreversibly changed the nature of the Airport City which was envisaged for Delhi. The OMDA contained provisions that allowed the use of 230 acres and 190 acres of land at the Delhi and Mumbai airports, respectively, for commercial purposes such as shopping malls, office complexes, commercial plazas and IT parks. The representative of Planning Commission maintained that the law did not allow the airport land to be used for commercial purposes unconnected to airports. The issue was referred first to the Solicitor General of India (SGI) whose opinion was thought to be not free from ambiguity and then to the Attorney General of India (AGI) who agreed with the objection of the Planning Commission. The advice of AGI was endorsed by the EGoM.

The ambiguity was a result of the provisions of Schedule 19 of the draft OMDA on which the SGI had given his advice and was interpreted differently by the Planning Commission and the Ministry of Civil Aviation. The Planning Commission interpreted the advice to mean that commercial activities independent of the airport would have to be excluded while the Ministry of Civil Aviation interpreted it to mean that commercial exploitation of unutilized and under-utilized land for generating revenues in the best commercial interest of AAI was permissible. Schedule 19 was then 'intentionally omitted' from the OMDA. Since the advice of the AGI prevailed, this decision made DLF and Hiranandani, real estate developers, pull out of their respective consortia.[1] The bid for Delhi airport finally went to the consortium comprising of GMR, AAI, Fraport and Malaysia Airport Holdings Berhad. This tussle on the legal nuances of the OMDA might be the reason why Delhi as an airport city turned out to be a botched idea. The stand of the AGI and Planning Commission ensured that the non-aeronautical commercial service got fragmented and did not appear commercially very attractive to the developers who were eyeing the land to develop a self-contained airport city. For example, according to the Schedule 6 of the OMDA, a business centre and conference centres were to be part of the terminal complex and the hotel and motels were separated. Thus, instead of the airport city, we have the stillborn Aerocity with half-finished hotels and the dream for business parks, golf courses, commercial offices, convention centres, etc. all but over.

The optimism of the case study on the bidding process of Delhi and Mumbai airports by the Planning Commission suggested that the capability of institutions to transform themselves in the light of experiences of the PPP was only partially true. It has been recently announced by the current Prime Minister of India that the Planning Commission will be abolished as it has outlived its utility since it was an institution that was built around the Nehruvian consensus. One should also keep in mind that the current government is putting a huge emphasis on infrastructure development and PPP is the favourable route. One can say, thus, that PPP and the new mechanisms of governance and law it has unleashed have finally been successful in dismantling one of the strongest symbols of the welfare state. The correlation is too strong to be merely incidental.

The dismantling of the Planning Commission and the emergence of PPP in infrastructure can be linked, and it can very well be argued that this dismantling is possible precisely because state and capital can form themselves as an alloy and their discreteness is being slowly eroded. In his study of the history of planning in India and South Korea, Chibber (2006) delineates the friction and negotiation between the state and capital. Chibber sees the Planning Commission as a form of disciplining private capitalists and bringing them in alignment with the planning

[1]The information on the bidding process and commercial use of land is taken from two case studies of Planning Commission (Secretariat for Infrastructure). Prateek Kuhad, *Bidding Process for the Delhi and Mumbai Airports*, August 2010; Divya Chawla, *Commercial Use of Land at Delhi and Mumbai Airports*, August 2010.

goals of the state. He points to the handicaps that the state and capitalists faced which severely compromised the Planning Commission as well as the Industries (Development and Regulation) Act (IDRA). However, Chibber draws the conclusion that the state wanted to appease the capitalists, and hence, both the institution and the legislation were compromised during implementation. There is a possibility, though, to derive a different conclusion from the facts illustrated by Chibber.

Planning Commission has been primarily looked at from the angle of capital and not labour. It must be remembered that Planning Commission was operating when land reforms were being implemented in India. This particular political and economic situation created a huge problem of landless agricultural labour and migration. The state, thus, was not only saddled with the responsibility of disciplining capital but more crucially in the governing of this new mass of labour force. It is this tripartite division which would be at the heart of the problem of governance. In this era, it was not possible for the state and capital to fuse together as is evident from the history recounted by Chibber. The state, thus, had a differential relationship with both capital and labour and in this sense was 'autonomous' from both. I claim that the emergence of infrastructure and the concomitant development of PPP is the moment when the triangular relationship of state, capital and labour undergoes a change. The fusion of state and capital through PPP and the convoluted process to achieve it has already been discussed above. We now come to the section where we will analyse how this alloy of state capital started to interact with labour and legal regimes surrounding labour. It was the same process of creating a space through producing legal ambiguities and statistical fallacies, but this time, the tussle was not only for spaces of accumulation but for spaces where it can do away with the worker as a political subject.

The Problem of 'Appropriate Government' for the Worker

The first repercussions of the new state capital alloy were felt by labour at the Indira Gandhi International Airport in the case that was related to the trolley retriever workers. This was not unprecedented, and it was an indication that there was a definite shift in the ways labour was to be governed after the liberalization of Indian economy in the early 1990s. The first landmark judgment from the Supreme Court of India came in what became popularly known as the SAIL (Steel Authority of India Limited) case of 2001.[2]

The case was related to the absorption of contract labour in SAIL. The judgment was a landmark one because in the judgment, the Supreme Court quashed the 1976 notification of the central government that prohibited the use of contract labour by state-owned companies for jobs such as cleaning and guarding

[2]Steel Authority of India Limited (SAIL) is a state-owned steel company. The case was Steel Authority of India Ltd. versus National Union Water Front on 30 August 2001.

buildings. The issue had come up because around 350 contract labourers who worked at SAIL's stockyards demanded absorption with the 'Principal Employer'. The court in its judgment said that on abolition of the contract system, the workers had no right to be absorbed automatically. The judgment also, significantly, made the point that it was the industrial adjudicator that would decide if a contract was genuine or a camouflage to deprive workers of the benefits that they were entitled to. Another interesting aspect of the case was the debate around the 'appropriate government' in the dispute with labour at SAIL within the meaning of the Contract Labour (Regulation and Abolition) Act, 1970 (CLRAA)—the central government or the state government. Since, SAIL was a state-owned company, the question of 'appropriate government' was not as complicated as it would be with DIAL, a PPP. This particular fact would have important repercussions on how labour, contract and labour rights would come to be defined as we shall see here.

The DIAL case is related to workers employed as trolley retrievers at the Delhi airport who were under a contracting company called TDI International Private Limited (hereafter TDI). They were employed in 1992. The contract of the company expired in 2003, and a new contractor, Sindhu Holdings, got the contract for the work. The workers had already approached the Central Advisory Contract Labour Board (CACLB) in 1999 for absorption in service as regular employees. The CACLB, in their order, declined to abolish the contract labour system at the Delhi airport, and the Government of India passed an order to that effect in 2002. The workers then filed a writ petition to the Delhi High Court in 2003.

It is interesting to note that the workers had not approached the court as a union.[3] It is also quite relevant to note that in this particular judgment, the number of workers was said to be 127 (115 trolley retrievers and 12 supervisors). In the judgment of 2006 of the High Court, which we will come to later, the number of workers mentioned was 'around 136'.[4] This was when the workers filed the writ petition as a union. In the Supreme Court judgment mentioned above the number of workers was finalized at 136. The discrepancy in the number of workers points out to the difficulty, almost impossibility, of enumerating the workers who were working under the contract system. The lacuna is inherent in the way the CLRAA has been formulated, which is the source of identifying the number of contract workers working in an establishment. This is so because the onus of providing information on workers lies with the contractor. In fact, as the Supreme Court judgment notes, the CLRAA 'does not create any machinery or forum for the adjudication of any dispute arsing between the contract labour and the principal employer of the contractor'. What the Supreme Court judgment fails to mention is that there is no machinery for the adjudication of disputes between the contractor and the workers. Their relationship within this law remains undefined and out of

[3]Raj Kumar and Others versus Union of India and Others on 5 November 2003, Delhi High Court.

[4]Indira Gandhi Airport TDI versus Union of India and others on 28 November 2006, Delhi High Court.

the purview of any legal mechanism. This is the space which creates informality in the relationship between the worker and the contractor and is a source of power of the latter over the former. There are only two legal actors and subjects—the principal employer and the contractor—while the workers remain undefined or inadequately defined. We will come to this point later in the narrative with regard to the Industrial Disputes Act, 1947 (IDA), which tries to define the worker in the contract labour system as a legal subject but falls short of the task.

We continue with the story of the first writ petition. The first writ petition was filed against the 1999 order of CACLB and 2002 order of the Government of India declining to abolish the contract labour system at the Delhi airport. The 2003 judgment notes that the reason provided by the CACLB for the decision is that trolley retrieval is not 'essential or incidental' to the operation of the AAI. The most interesting aspect of the CACLB decision is how it comes up with what is 'essential or incidental'. This has implications on how an airport and work related to it is understood through security. The CACLB made a comparison with the passenger baggage conveyor system. The board considered it as an operation that is perennial, and passengers cannot be excluded from access to it, but more importantly that this operation is 'within the security zone'. Thus, the workers have to submit themselves through a definite regime of security to be identified as workers. In a sense, what the CACLB was saying is that securitized work is 'essential' work. It is the calibrated nature of security that defines work and hence the worker. In any case, the Government of India endorsed the decision of the CACLB without giving any specific reason, the judgment noted. The court quashed the order of the CACLB and the Government of India and directed the former to reconsider its decision. In 2004, the central government issued a notification abolishing the contract labour system.[5]

The AAI approached the High Court against this order. The court in 2005 directed the AAI to appear before a high-power Committee that was to consider the grievance of the parties and pass an appropriate order recommending whether the AAI was permitted to challenge the notification. The Committee noted that the restructuring of the Delhi airport was under active consideration of the Government of India. Interestingly, DIAL responded to the court that it was

> … neither a State nor the instrumentality of State and was not amenable to writ jurisdiction. The constitution of joint venture would show that the government shares in the joint venture were only 26% and rest of the shares were held by either Indian Companies or foreign companies.[6]

Clearly, DIAL was trying to make the case that it was a corporate body autonomous of the legal regime of the state. This is what led to the question of the 'appropriate government'. According to DIAL, by virtue of being a corporate

[5]M/S Delhi International Airport versus Union of India and Others on 15 September 2011, Supreme Court of India.

[6]Indira Gandhi Airport, T.D.I. versus Union of India and Others on 28 November 2006, Delhi High Court.

body, it was free of any labour laws which were incumbent on it because it was a workplace. The 2006 judgment noted that the CLRAA was equally applicable for all kinds of undertakings, establishments/industries whether in the public, private or public/private ownership or management. It should be also taken into account that the workers' union had claimed that the contract was a sham and a camouflage and the case was pending with the industrial adjudicator. (This was clearly in the wake of the SAIL case judgment.) However, the court decided that the grounds for such a claim did not hold and dismissed the petition of the union on the ground that the airport had been privatized and new notification would have to be issued by the 'appropriate government'. The High Court in its decision did not make a difference between a corporate body that comes into being through outright privatization and one which comes through the mode of PPP. There is no law that the High Court could have adduced to differentiate between the two, and it had to rely on interpretations mainly emanating from the SAIL judgment. However, the higher division of the court would tackle this question, and finally, the Supreme Court would make observations that would delineate that PPP is not merely privatization.

The higher bench of the High Court came up with a twofold formulation of the question. First, whether the central government was indeed the 'appropriate government' for DIAL and whether the workers engaged by the contractors of DIAL could be said to be contract labourers.[7] It is quite clear that in this formulation, the question of the nature of DIAL (PPP) and the question of labour are not separate. The nature of DIAL would substantially define or should define the nature of 'contract labour'. The central government submitted to the court that DIAL was operating under its authority. The court observed that the authority of DIAL was 'not merely by the OMDA but by statute' and that OMDA makes an express reference to the AAI Act and it is the latter through which the function and powers of DIAL could be traced. Thus, in the last analysis, DIAL or a PPP, does come under the jurisdiction and control of the legal state. Hence, the 'appropriate government' is the Government of India. DIAL contended that it was 'not a mere contractor or agent of AAI' and it was carrying on 'its own industry in its own establishment'. The court observed that the establishment 'is that of the AAI which has been leased out to the DIAL'. This has implication on the airport as the legal object. As the court observed, a PPP through the OMDA 'not only transfers the powers and functions but also the corresponding statutory obligations of the AAI'.

It is then quite clear that the airport because of the PPP model cannot be similar to a special economic zone (SEZ). This is an important point. Aihwa Ong (2006) identifies these zones as zones of exception, of extraordinary policies. In contrast, Neilson (2014) provides a more complex analysis of zones and his analysis needs a closer look. According to Neilson, if the centralization of legal, political and economic function has historically made the nation state the essential political unity

[7]Indira Gandhi Airport TDI versus Union of India and Others on 18 December 2009, Delhi High Court.

globally, the zone registers the partial undoing of these processes and the emergence of a new political topography of territory, strongly connected to the spaces of global flows of capital, goods, information and people.

The operative word in this analysis of zones is 'partial'. The emergence of the new is dependent on 'partial undoing' of the centralization of the nation state. The trick of governance is to keep it 'partial' and that is at the heart of the problem of governmentality in contemporary era. In his further analysis, Neilson (2014) evokes the phenomenon of PPP:

> The establishment of a zone definitely involves a sovereign gesture; it is an act that is increasingly separated from state power. This is not only because zones are increasingly established at the prerogative of private–public partnerships—a common arrangement, for instance, in India. There are also multiple non-state actors and legal orders that operate in zones, configuring infrastructural arrangements and labour relations as well as organizing the spatial and temporal relations between zones and other territorial formations.

The conclusion that Neilson draws from this is that 'the zone is a space saturated by competing norms and calculations that overlap and conflict'. The question, now, is whether these 'competing norms and calculations' are in 'free competition' with each other. How is it that the balance of power would be maintained, because it is almost certain that not all competing norms and calculations are repositories of equal power? While it is true that there is an increasing separation from state power, the problem facing the sovereign is how to manage this separation so that it does not reach the extreme of secession. It is here that PPP evolves as a definite mechanism to prevent such secession. Also, infrastructure (in this case the airport) becomes a site, a zone different and as an alternative model of governance from that of SEZ which in the extreme are 'fully exempt from civil law and government control' (Neilson 2014). We will come back to this point when analysing the Supreme Court judgment. It is important to complete the narrative of the 2006 judgment of the High Court.

The 2006 judgment rejected DIAL's contention with regard to trolley retrievers observing that if 'every time a fresh agreement is entered into, the entire process of getting a notification issued by the appropriate government in relation to the same work … would defeat the rights of the workmen which are meant to be protected by the CLRAA'. This was so precisely because PPP is as much a transfer of power as it is of obligations. It ensures that secession between state as a capitalist and private capital is never attained. The precise nature of PPP and the mechanism of this new form of power were materially conceptualized in the judgment delivered by the Supreme Court.

The Supreme Court observed that 'DIAL only has "*incomplete* control" over the airport and that only a "*portion*" of AAI's work' had been leased to it (emphasis mine). This also defined the nature of the work of trolley retrieving. The question was if the trolley retrieval services performed by DIAL are done for the 'transport by air of persons, mail or any other thing'. The Supreme Court observed that 'trolleys at airports relate to air transportation—just as they relate to a single or a series of flights'. This meant that the IDA and the CLRAA are not only restricted in their application to 'pilots, stewardesses and others engaged in the actual, physical transport of people and objects'. The judgment said that the workers were liable to be regularized as regular employees by DIAL, but since that would not be possible in the current circumstances DIAL was to pay Rs. 500,000 as compensation to the workers of TDI.

The interesting observation was regarding the nature of PPP. The final judgment made it clear that a PPP would not be equivalent to privatization and complete autonomy of private capital even if it is the majority stakeholder. The discreteness with which the Supreme Court defines the PPP as 'incomplete' and portioned is slightly misleading. It is so because in the judgment, DIAL is a single entity with AAI as one of the constituents. It is this organic embedding of the entity which gives up its portion that makes the PPP unique and an alloy of state capital. It is this which allows the central government to be the 'appropriate government'. An independent AAI, I am quite sure, would have created a different outcome. It would have created distinct spaces of authorities and the workers' petitions would have been directed to AAI while DIAL would have functioned as a totally different unit, which would have completely escaped the legal net.

Conclusion

The politics of the 'regulatory state' depends on the concept of new governmentality which is not Foucauldian. It is like the PPP, or state capital alloy. It is the cusp where life and non-life coexist. Governance is not totally predicated on the body or the quality of being alive. It is in a sense being increasingly separated from the living body which is capable of work or, to put it differently, one who has to sell labour-power. What is now being attempted is to derive a quality which can then be inscribed on the body so that a subject comes into being. In other words, the problematique of governmentality is no longer the knowledge of population but producing the knowledge of an abstract, normative category. This is where the emancipatory politics has to be conceived. As Samaddar reminded us (2010), it is in the struggle that the political subject is formed. In the situation described above, it is quite possible to think of an alternative in which the new political subject would not only conceive itself through struggle against the state but, because in the abandonment of statecraft in producing its proper subject, an autonomous political subject can indeed come into being.

References

Bovaird, T. (2011). A brief intellectual history of the public-private partnership movement. In Hodge et al. (Eds.), *International handbook on public private partnerships* (pp. 43–67).

Chibber, V. (2006). *Locked in Place: State-building and late industrialization in India*. Princeton: Princeton University Press.

CAG. (2012). *Report of the Comptroller and Auditor General of India for the year ended March 2012 on Implementation of Public Private Partnership Indira Gandhi International Airport, Delhi* (Report No. 5 of 2012–13). Retrieved March 16, 2016 from http://www.cag.gov.in/sites/default/files/audit_report_files/Union_Performance_Commercial_Implementation_Public_Private_Partnership_Ministry_Civil_Aviation_5_2012.pdf

Datta, A. (2009). Public-private partnership in India: A case for reform? *Economic and Political Weekly, 44*(33), 73–78.

Flinders, M. (2011). Splintered logic and political debate. In Hodge et al (Eds.), *International handbook on public private partnerships* (pp. 115–131).

Graham, S., & Marvin, Simon. (2001). *Splintering urbanism: networked infrastructures, technological mobilities and the Urban Condition*. London: Routledge.

Mao, T.-T. (1965). "On new democracy". *Selected Works* (pp. 339–3384, vol. 2). Peking: Foreign Language.

Mezzadra, S., & Neilson, B. (2013). *Border as method, or, the multiplication of labor*. Durham: Duke University Press.

Mezzadra, S., & Neilson, B. (2014). The state of capitalist globalization. *Viewpoint Magazine*, 4 September. Retrieved November 10, 2014 from https://viewpointmag.com/2014/09/04/the-state-of-capitalist-globalization

Neilson, B. (2014). Zones: Beyond the logic of exception? *Concentric: Literary and Cultural Studies, 40*(2), 11–28.

Ong, A. (2006). *Neoliberalism as exception: Mutations in citizenship and sovereignty*. Durham: Duke University Press.

Planning, C. (2008). *Approach to regulation of infrastructure*. New Delhi: Planning Commission.

Samaddar, R. (2010). *Emergence of the political subject*. New Delhi: Sage.

Samȧddar, R. (2013). Michel foucault and our postcolonial time. In S. Mezzadra, J. Reid, & R. Samaddar (Eds.), *The biopolitics of development: Reading Michel foucault in the postcolonial present* (pp. 25–44). Dordrecht: Springer.

Tvarno, C. (2011). Law and regulatory aspects of public-private partnerships: contract law and public procurement law. In G. A. Hodge, C. Greve, & A. E. Boardman (Eds.), *International handbook on public private partnerships* (pp. 216–236). Cheltenham: Edward Elgar.

Wettenhall, R. (2011). Mixes and partnerships through time. In Hodge et al. (Eds.), *International handbook on public private partnerships* (pp. 17–42).

Security and the City: Post-Colonial Accumulation, Securitization, and Urban Development in Kolkata

Ilia Antenucci

Abstract The chapter explores the interconnected issues of accumulation, securitization, and governmentality in the context of transformation of the city of Kolkata into a 'world-class' metropolis. In both academic and common languages, securitization has rapidly embraced a wider meaning; this includes the increasing emphasis on security in the political debate and the growth of a global security apparatus. In this chapter, the author discusses securitization in relation to what have recently been described as 'operations of capital', which include the functions of extraction, logistics, and finance that are crucial in understanding how global capital works. The author investigates the security industry and urban changes in Kolkata and explores urban securitization as a global capitalistic process. Based on interviews with the relevant actors, both in the security industry including workers, managers, and advisors, and in the urban transformation sector that included developers, residents, and local authorities, and archival research and discourse analysis of relevant documents, the author argues that securitization, besides supporting and complementing the processes of accumulation over cities, constitutes a space of intense accumulation itself. But simultaneously, it becomes crucial for governance of a contradictory and contended urban space. The market-oriented interventions on the city have allowed for an impressive growth of the security business. Yet, the process of securitization has exceeded the pattern of urban development. It has become a powerful industry, as well as a strategy for management of at least two principal effects of accumulation: dispossession and disruption.

Keywords Securitization · Governmentality · Operations of capital · Urban transformation · Dispossession

I. Antenucci (✉)
Institute for Culture and Society, Western Sydney University, Richmond, Australia
e-mail: i.antenucci@westernsydney.edu.au

I.K. Mitra et al. (eds.), *Accumulation in Post-Colonial Capitalism*,
DOI 10.1007/978-981-10-1037-8_4

Accumulation, securitization, and governmentality are all at work to transform the city of Kolkata into a 'world-class' metropolis. Recent discussions on post-colonial capitalism offer material and theoretical context within which to examine such transformation, the disruptions that go with it, and the heterogeneous modes of production that characterize such urban settings.[1] Both the academic areas of security studies and urban studies also come into play in this analysis, with a focus on studies that explore the capitalistic dynamics connected to securitization (Neocleous 2008; Policante 2012; White 2012) and urban development (Harvey 2006; Robinson 2013; Sassen 1991).

The word securitization was originally introduced by Ole Weaver and Barry Buzan to describe the discursive processes that are capable of transforming any issue to a matter of security (Buzan et al. 1998). Still, in both academic and common language, securitization has rapidly embraced a wider meaning; this includes the increasing emphasis on security in the political debate and the growth of a global security apparatus. In my work, I put securitization in relation to what Sandro Mezzadra and Brett Neilson have recently described as 'operations of capital', which include the functions of extraction, logistics, and finance that are crucial in understanding how global capital 'hits the ground' (Mezzadra and Neilson 2015).

Security, I suggest, is an essential part of any operation of capital. From armed intervention to facility management, from accident prevention to intelligence, practices of extraction, logistics, and even finance all rely on some modalities of security provision. A growing global industry caters to each of these needs. In most academic quarters though, security is still commonly considered either as a side effect of the capitalist processes, or merely as a social issue, with scarce appreciation of its material and economic rationale.

Both these perspectives fail to grasp the core quality of securitization: that it forms a junction between the dynamics of capitalist expansion and practices of governmentality. Indeed, security today is, at the same time, a set of policies and procedures, a major political assertion, and a globally expanding industry. Importantly, authors such as Leander (2005) and Neocleous (2008) have observed how the private security industry does not simply follow the demands of global enterprises, but produce its own market—the market for force.

I have investigated the security industry and urban changes in Kolkata as part of my Ph.D. project, which explores urban securitization as a global capitalistic process. My study included many interviews with the relevant actors, both in the security industry including workers, managers, and advisors, and in the urban transformation sector that included developers, residents, and local authorities; I also carried out archival research and discourse analysis of relevant documents.

My findings in Kolkata suggest the following argument: securitization, besides supporting and complementing the processes of accumulation over

[1]Among the rich debate on post-colonial capitalism, I particularly refer to Sanyal (2007), Mezzadra (2011), Samaddar (2012).

cities, constitutes a space of intense accumulation itself. But simultaneously, it becomes crucial for governance of a contradictory and contended urban space. The market-oriented interventions on the city have allowed for an impressive growth of the security business. Yet, the process of securitization has exceeded the pattern of urban development. It has become a powerful industry, as well as a strategy for management of at least two principal effects of accumulation: dispossession and disruption. In this chapter, I will try explaining the intertwining of governance and accumulation through security within the controversial transformation of the city.

World-Class and Class War

The city of Kolkata, once the capital of the British Empire (as Calcutta), later sadly famed as the capital of poverty and urban disaster, is now changing dramatically. The landscape of the 'developing' city is scattered with construction sites of all sorts, such as flyovers and subway stations, high-rise gated communities, luxury hotels and shopping malls, and corporate headquarters that have come up by ripping out the space of old neighbourhoods, *bastis* (slums), and farmlands. At the same time, this scenery shows another regular feature: the presence of thousands and thousands of men and women in uniform who man the landmarks of urban change. This is the silent army of private security guards.

The process of development and renewal of the India's main cities—Delhi, Mumbai, and Kolkata—and the intense growth of the business of private security in the country have a common time path as well as common political ground, namely the process of neoliberalization that started in India in the early 1990s. The consequences of this political turn, which implied the downsizing of the public sector, the large-scale privatizations of industries and services, and the dismantling of large state-run industries as well as policies of assistance and poverty relief, are polarized.

On the one hand, the formation of new elite of billionaires, as well as a middle-class professionals and small entrepreneurs, has occurred; but on the other, there is an escalation of mass poverty. The ratio between the two is dramatically unbalanced on the side of the latter. Mass poverty has dramatically increased, especially in rural areas, due to the state policies of land grabbing and forced displacement of the inhabitants, for the purpose of establishing special economic zones (Banerjee-Guha 2013; Levian 2012). The already congested megacities, including Kolkata, have become the destination for millions of forced migrants, who make up what is defined as the 'informal', 'need', 'parallel', or 'peripheral' economy (Sanyal 2007; Dey et al. 2013).

At the same time, big cities are the places where global capital concentrates its headquarters and the rising middle and upper classes demand up-market facilities and lifestyle. This context of sharp inequality and resulting conflicts was described by an acute observer as a proper 'class war'. It is where the world-class city and securitization projects are taking place. Drawing on the case of Kolkata,

I will try to explain how these two capitalistic operations are joined by practices of accumulation.

Much has been written on 'neoliberal urbanism', or the ways in which cities under neoliberal conditions are reshaped into hubs in the circulation of global capital. In this perspective, Indian metropolises have undergone massive interventions of renewal and development, to meet international standards of productivity and liveability. This included the transformation of Kolkata into a 'world-class' city.

Most popular in the media and commercial languages, the term 'world-class' describes a set of state-of-the-art infrastructures, up-market services, and aesthetic requirements capable of attracting a global community of wealthy businesspeople and tourists. It is, in short, the ideal capitalistic city, connected to a corporate, hierarchical worldview—no coincidence that several rankings of the 'world-class' cities are released every year by magazines such as *Forbes* and *The Economist*, in an attempt to measure the commercial and touristic appeal of established or emerging urban hubs. The concept has been criticized for reproducing a colonial bias (Robinson 2013), as well as for bringing along practices of accumulation and dispossession over cities (Harvey 2006).

As the capital of West Bengal and one of the principal urban areas in India, Kolkata was naturally included in the Jawaharlal Nehru National Urban Renewal Mission (JNNURM).[2] Started in 2005, JNNURM represents the framework for urban renewal in India, based on the creation of new infrastructures including roads, urban transport, sewerage, water sanitation, waste management, and the provision of services to the urban poor.

While claiming relief to urban poverty and life quality improvement as its main goals, the programme clearly reflects a market-oriented view, for example, in encouraging the public–private partnership (PPP) model for development of projects. In this respect, JNNURM brings into action core strategies of the Indian neoliberal turn, such as giving priority to private investments over public funding, favouring real estate developers through land deregulation, and weakening the democratic control over funding and administrative processes (Banerjee-Guha 2009).

Therefore, this programme was intended to reshape urban governance, much more than just the urban landscape. Interestingly, while one of the focuses of JNNURM is the provision of service to the urban poor, the implementation of the programme in Kolkata was preceded by two remarkable 'antipoor' campaigns jointly conducted by the (still leftist at the time) West Bengal government and by the Kolkata Municipal Corporation (KMC) under the aegis of 'beautification': I am referring to the 'Operation Sunshine' (1996), aimed at pushing hawkers and pavement dwellers away from central areas, although with different outcomes (Bandyopadhyay 2011), and to the series of often violent slum evictions that took place between 2001 and 2005.

---

[2]http://jnnurm.nic.in/.

Over the past 10 years, a number of projects have transformed the face of the city as well as the relations in it. Part of these projects within the JNNURM framework concerns the realization of new infrastructures such as flyovers, drainage, sewerage, and water supply systems; but what has dramatically changed the urban setting is the plethora of new residential enclaves and gated communities, shopping malls, business hubs, luxury hotels, private hospitals, and university campuses that are rising in place of farmlands, swamps, and *bastis*. It is this urbanscape of flashy buildings and construction sites that really gives a sense of the making of a 'world-class' Kolkata.

Still, the unevenness and contradictions of the urban development are stunning. Just like post-colonial capitalism, post-colonial urbanism is marked by repeating crisis[3]; the path of (presumed) development is continuously interrupted by moments and spaces of acute deprivation and peril for millions of people. The inequalities are economic and spatial and are very visible. In the first place, the geography of transformation is strongly differentiated: the new projects are mostly concentrated at the fringes of the city, such as in New Town in Rajarhat, East Township, Salt Lake, the Eastern Metropolitan Bypass, and soon Howrah, while the city centre and the old neighbourhoods of north Kolkata are only minimally touched. In this regard, the urban changes in Kolkata seem to be occurring more as expansion than gentrification and renewal. This is probably due to the acknowledged unmanageable character of both urbanization and the residents of 'old' Kolkata.

As a result, the sites of world-class Kolkata are separated by wastelands, slums, and *basti*s, not-gentrified and highly congested areas. Moreover, the luxurious buildings intended for the old and new rich are rising in symbiosis with the typical signs of urban poverty: shanties, makeshift settlements, and street dwellers. This contrast speaks of two crucial aspects of post-colonial capitalism that are reflected in the urbanization: the deep entanglement of formal and informal economy, the former broadly relying on the latter for the supply of cheap and flexible labour and services. As a result, a permanent contention over space continues. An army of cleaners, caretakers, maids, drivers, and, not the least, security guards is required to ensure the lifestyle standards of the middle and upper classes. In the absence of dedicated facilities, these workers take the space they need for their own subsistence; hence, there is a proliferation of eateries, tea shops, houses, etc., as close as possible to the workplace.

It is precisely within this complexity that the process of securitization thrives for two main reasons. First, security is required to manage this contended space, and second, the informal economy is an essential resource for the security industry. The 'class war' is, at the same time, interdependent, and as I will explain in the next sections, securitization works as a filter that regulates the modalities of contact between masters and servants.

[3]In a recent intervention, Ranabir Samaddar brilliantly illustrates how the moment of crisis connected to the recurring of the moment of accumulation lies at the core of post-colonial capitalism (Samaddar 2014).

Securing the Dystopia

Due to the dramatic contrasts I have just described, some consider the attempt to turn Kolkata into a 'world-class' city to be a hopeless one. In the words of one KMDA (Kolkata Metropolitan Development Authority) officer, 'No matter what those people say, developers and politicians, they are either liars or fools. Kolkata will never be a world-class city. We have other problems'.[4]

Such scepticism might also have roots in the dark reputation of Kolkata, which goes a long way back in the early colonial period, with the British struggling to establish their settlements. Triggered by the urge of dominating a challenging nature and unknown habits, the colonial bias—a mix of discomfort, haughtiness, and morality—became commonplace during the eighteenth century in the British accounts of the nascent city of Calcutta, soon to be the capital of the empire (Chattopadhyay 2005). In a recent work, Partha Chatterjee has explored the many ways in which, starting from the myth of the Black Hole, the horrific narratives about Calcutta became cultural and political justifications of the colonial rule (Chatterjee 2012). The bad fame though did not leave Calcutta with the British. Overwhelmed by the huge incoming migrations after the Partition of Bengal, and wrecked by the crisis in the jute industry, post-colonial Calcutta became a symbol of catastrophic urbanization. Needless to say, this obscure narrative was not without its political implications; it was part of the hierarchical representation of the First/Third World that informed global politics in the second half of the twentieth century.

To pick an example of how this representation was built and reproduced in the 'Western' discourses, in the emphatic celebration of Mother Teresa's mission,[5] we see one of the pillars sustaining the rhetoric of Kolkata as the capital of the Third World: a hopeless city marked by disease, misery, and despair. Given this background of damnation, the making of 'world-class' Kolkata looks like a catch-up even more than other post-colonial, 'normally backward' cities.

It is undeniable that so far, the world-class horizon in Kolkata appears distant, unlikely, and quite dystopian. And yet, in the developing areas of the city, the world-class rhetoric is ubiquitous. Everywhere, along the main roads and above the rooftops, huge billboards showcase lavish gated communities or futuristic

---

[4]Interview taken in June 2015.

[5]An Albanian-born Catholic Nun, Agnes Bojaxhiu, later known as Mother Teresa, founded her Order of Missionaries of Charity in 1948 in Calcutta, for the purpose of helping the poor and sick in India and other countries. Her work drew great attention to the dramatic hygienic and economic conditions of the city of Calcutta. Mother Teresa became an international symbol of charity and received numerous acknowledgements and prizes for her activities, including the Nobel Peace Prize in 1979. Yet, her figure results controversial in some respect, as she drew criticism regarding the financial resources of the Order of Missionaries, suspects of forced conversions of the sufferers, and her support of the most conservative Catholic positions against birth control and abortion. For a complete picture of the character, see Serrou (1980), Chatterjee (2002), and Hitchens (1995).

university campuses, calling for a dramatic upgrade in lifestyle for the happy few. But all around, unfinished facilities, piles of garbage, and dilapidated neighbourhoods compose the everyday setting for millions of inhabitants. As ubiquitous as the world-class adverts are the signs of the security apparatus. Not only guards in uniform, but thousands of metal detectors, X-ray screenings, and CCTVs are in place to maintain order in the dystopian space.

The word dystopia has been used to describe the present outcomes of the world-class dream in the book *Beyond Kolkata*, which provides a pivotal analysis of Kolkata's urban transformation in terms of political economy (Dey et al. 2013). It explains in depth the expansion of the city driven by industrial zoning policies, such as the establishment of SEZs in the IT hub of Sector 5, Salt Lake. In many respects, my own research starts where this book ends. Indeed, by going back to the controversial making of New Town in the area of Rajarhat, *Beyond Kolkata* casts light on the political and material violence that is part of accumulation in the urban space, wherefrom the process of securitization also spreads. In Rajarhat, the forcible acquisition of land for the benefit of private developers triggered sharp conflicts between the local population and the authorities, including intimidation, physical confrontations, and murder.

This is the context in which the opulent corporate headquarters hosting the new generation of IT workers, shopping malls, five-star hotels and a plethora of gated communities have arisen, or are still under construction. Part of the local inhabitants—mostly farmers whose lands were taken—have been 'recycled'[6] in the supply of domestic and care labour for the new residents, many as security guards. Not surprisingly, New Town is still a sensitive place. The security manager of a prominent developer in Kolkata and West Bengal openly admits to what he calls 'local hooliganism' as the principal risk factor.[7] While he claims, 'There were no problems with the local people, they all got compensation for their lands' and does not admit to the disturbed history of New Town, he describes the inhabitants as troublemakers and 'not business inductive'. As a result, the company employs around 500 security guards only for their properties in the Rajarhat area[8] and adopts strict rules of control such as separate gates and personal searching for cleaners and housekeepers.

This case provides a meaningful example of the connections between city development and the security industry in Kolkata. I have already mentioned how the two have run parallel to each other over the past two decades under favourable neoliberal conditions. In fact, the provision of private security as such is not new at all in Kolkata; on the contrary, it has close association with the evolution of the

[6]This pretty brutal word was used by one of the managers of City Centre 2, a shopping mall in New Town, precisely to describe what happened to the local people where their lands were acquired.

[7]Interview taken in June 2015.

[8]This includes the Ecospace Business Park, City Centre 2 shopping mall, and several residential enclaves.

city since British colonization. The army of the British East India Company was, after all, itself an example of a massive corporate military. Besides, it has always been customary for the most wealthy—rich merchants, high-ranking officials, and bureaucrats—to hire guards for their personal and asset protection. Some forms of private security were not new to the lower classes and 'common people', seen in the case of 'neighbourhood watch', a community-based security practice in the popular districts of North Kolkata.

However, it is only in recent times that the provision of security has spread immensely and become a massive business. This should be related to the global trend of expansion of a market for force, for both civil and military purposes, which has reached an outstanding turnover and influence. In India, this market has reached record numbers, featuring about 15,000 companies all over the country, with over 7 million employees, well outnumbering the police officers. According to the latest FICCI (Federation of Indian Chambers of Commerce and Industry) report:

> The global private security services industry is estimated to be US$132 billion in 2011 and is expected to grow at a CAGR of 7 % to reach US$220 billion by 2019. However, the Indian private security services industry is expected to grow faster, at 20 % over the next few years, and is estimated to grow from INR 365 billion in FY13 to INR 640 billion by FY18.[9]

Despite the records provided by the police and the business associations, it seems very difficult to get the exact figures on the security companies and workers active in India today. As for Kolkata, the police have a register of about 500 security firms based in West Bengal and mostly in the metropolitan area of Kolkata. But almost every expert in the sector I have had the chance to speak to agrees that the list is incomplete. The first detailed study on the security guards in Kolkata, conducted by Gooptu (2013), explains that a large part of the industry operates unofficially, often completely off the records, and yet is present in the new corporate circuits. This 'organized informality' is crucial for the rapid growth of the security sector.

More specifically, in Kolkata, I have observed how this rampant business sector is, based on the structural intertwining between the most advanced corporate practices and a totally unregulated underworld. Indeed, the renowned multinational companies, such as G4S and Securicor, dominate the market by taking advantage of a supply chain that is largely composed of a plethora of small, often unlicensed firms and casual workers. The contracts in place between the major companies and their clients are fulfilled by subcontracting out to smaller firms, which provide precarious, low-paid personnel upon request. This allows the big ones to minimize the employment costs, while ensuring the survival of a petty economy of security.

[9]'Private Security Services Industry: Securing Future Growth', report published by the Federation of Indian Chambers of Commerce and Industry: http://www.ficci.com/spdocument/20329/Private-security-services-industry-Securing-future-growth1.pdf; accessed on 10 February 2016.

If the map of the activities of security companies follows changing geography of the city, the structure of the industry reflects its blind spots. The middle- and upper-class residential areas, commercial and corporate quarters, and infrastructures and construction sites that are proliferating all along the EM Bypass, in Salt Lake and New Town, are all under constant surveillance. At this point, it is important to note that according to the official statistics, Kolkata is certainly not among the most dangerous cities of the country.[10] Apart from a normal rate of petty crime, considered as endemic to megacities, there is no evidence of any crime escalation. Murders, rapes, robberies, and kidnapping are below the average for other major Indian cities.

And yet, the most common justification that I have heard among residents and business owners for such a massive employment of private security points to the incapability of the police in keeping under control the masses of migrants, slums, and street dwellers. These 'masses' are crucial. On the one hand, they represent the point where the world-class utopia crashes and turns itself into a dystopia.

As we will see in the next section, the persistence of huge poverty, with the resulting disorder in the urban space, proves the failure or at least the radical inadequacy of development plans while feeding upper-class anxieties. On the other hand, these enormous pools of poverty offer cheap and easily exploitable labour for the fast-growing capitalist market, where the security industry has a leading role. In this respect, the reproduction of poverty is required to keep the business growing. In the end, poverty needs to be governed and disciplined, which is another major operation for the security industry.

Operations of Security

Notoriously, the moment of accumulation requires extra-economic means to achieve its end, that is, the seizing of resources and the production of an exploitable labour pool. While the essence of such extra-economic means is violence in all its possible forms, ways to govern the effects of this violence become necessary at the same time. In this respect, a comprehensive analysis of the concept of accumulation should always integrate the crucial aspect of dispossession (Harvey 2003) with a focus on the management of what follows: how the dispossessed are forced to work, or alternatively, just kept surviving at the margins of the capitalist system, or even left to die.

More specifically, as Kalyan Sanyal has brilliantly explained, in the context of post-colonial capitalism, accumulation of capital and accumulation of poverty proceed in symbiosis, the latter becoming a critical terrain for governmental strategies. Not only the state, but also transnational institutions and NGOs take care of

[10]National Crime Reports Bureau, http://ncrb.nic.in/StatPublications/CII/CII2014/Table%202.1.pdf; http://ncrb.nic.in/StatPublications/CII/CII2014/Table%202.2.pdf.

those who are not absorbed by the capitalist expansion, thus reproducing a parallel, need economy (Sanyal 2007). The concept of need economy clearly overlaps with that of informal or peripheral economies that I have largely used so far. Noteworthy here is that the process of securitization is doubly implicated with this predicament: first, as accumulation, and second, as governance. In this section, I explore this twofold nature of securitization, which entails accumulation over poverty and governance of poverty at the same time.

Accumulation

In the first place, securitization is part of the primary aspect of accumulation: the forcible separation of people from their livelihood. This includes the displacement of inhabitants and the dismantling or limitation of the local, petty economy. In the processes of urban enclosures and land grabbing, security issues are regularly invoked, while private security companies are often in charge of surveillance of the contended areas.

I have already mentioned a representative case of this scheme, concerning Rajarhat, but countless examples can be found in the metropolitan area of Kolkata. The security managers and officers describe a regular mechanism: every time a big development project is launched, issues come up in the acquisition of land. 'You always find encroachments there, people who believe they can stay and live on the plot. The police cannot cover all the sites. So the developers call us, our job is to watch and patrol and make sure these people don't come back'.[11] In addition, construction sites are considered at risk for burglaries and sabotage: the former inhabitants of the area are held responsible for this as well. A KMDA officer explained that every construction site needs security as 'those people around' would steal the materials to take revenge for being displaced, or for not being given a job. As a common policy, security companies reject association with violence. They insist on surveillance, prevention, and risk containment.

A popular argument is that the display of security apparatus, presence of guards in uniform, patrol cars, and CCTVs are sufficient to discourage potential offenders most of the time. It is important to consider that a majority of the security guards cannot carry weapons and are not prepared for physical confrontation. However, the largest and most experienced companies are able to provide gunmen for the surveillance of high-risk sites. Also, security workers are often employed to deal with trade unions and worker protests on construction sites. When I asked what exactly they were expected to do in case of confrontations with workers, the manager I was interviewing glossed over the details. Yet, the message was clear and sounded like this: 'Our clients hire guards, because they don't want issues of any nature. So, if our guards are there, troublemakers (workers, unions) cannot be there'.

[11] Interview taken in May 2015 with a manager of a security firm in Kolkata.

At the same time, the security industry takes advantage of the cheap labour pool resulting from the practices of accumulation. In a city like Kolkata, long-standing urban poverty is being constantly enlarged by migrations from the rural areas, triggered by the processes of land acquisition (Somayaji and Talwar 2011). Millions of people struggle to make a living from casual and precarious work. Many of them join the fast-growing security business.

I have observed how both the security industry and market are organized hierarchically, with the biggest multinational companies at the top on both sides. For example, G4S will provide services for high-end customers such as Siemens, Volvo, luxury hotels, and shopping malls, while smaller, local firms work for less wealthy customers. A vertical chain of contracts and subcontracts connects these layers, with precarious, super-exploited labour as a constant. At the lowest level, the firms are unregistered and unlicensed; often, they do not even have an office or an establishment.

I have been in contact with this type of security providers through the members of a Residents Association (RA) in the middle-class area of Salt Lake. Indeed, among the services offered by the RA, there is brokering for security personnel for residential and commercial establishments in the area. Most of the times, such deals are conducted informally, through personal contacts and verbal agreements. The majority of workers are migrants from the rural areas who live in *basti*s, or commuters from villages around Kolkata, and belong to the lower castes. Recruitment is based on family and community connections that go back to the villages of origin. Workers are hired on a daily basis, in the absence of any contract or protection. In fact, their situation looks like a very poor form of self-employment: not only have the workers no guarantees, no paid leave, or accident insurance, but also they need to promote themselves with business owners and middlemen and please them in order to be considered for a job. No professional training is provided. Workers do not speak English and are not prepared for tasks such as fire emergency and evacuation, use of detection systems, and gunfights.

As a result, security at this level is often merged with domestic and care labour: the same firm frequently caters for guards as well as housekeepers, drivers, and doormen. It is not unusual that all these tasks are demanded from the same person: in such cases, the intense exploitation of the worker is combined with contempt for menial labour. The Salt Lake residents were very clear on this point: the guard is not considered to be a security professional, but a servant. Accordingly, salaries are extremely low, paid in cash, under the table, and on the basis of working hours.

Although these kinds of small, informal security firms can operate independently, such as in the area of Salt Lake, through word of mouth and personal connections, they are part of a supply chain of low-cost labour that goes up to larger, up-market security companies. With their informal network of precarious workers, these are able to provide a quick labour backup for larger companies that require low-cost staff on short notice. Medium-sized companies are typically founded and run by former military or police officers. This is probably the most common typology of security firms. Their offices are typically located in the middle-class neighbourhoods of Kolkata, in the new shopping malls or corporate establishments.

They have websites and social network accounts and invest a certain amount of money in advertising. At this level, there is much emphasis on training and expertise. Managers pay much attention not only to the grooming and appearance of the staff, but also to their technical skills. The aim is to be differentiated from menial and domestic labour and be acknowledged as professionals. Customers of these companies are higher end, including luxury residential enclaves, corporate offices, shopping malls, medium-sized factories, and construction sites.

They strive to grow and expand their business and look up to the standards set by the multinational security corporations. Still, the road to success of these firms seems to rely on the intense exploitation of vulnerable labour. Very strict working conditions are imposed on their employees. Discipline and devotion are essential requirements. Shifts are usually long, 8–10 h, and can be extended without notice. A guard recalled that he was once required to stay on duty alone for 33 h non-stop, in an isolated factory. Also, workers are in fact forbidden to join trade unions, under the threat of losing their job. Most of them do not have any regular contract, but only a 'joining letter', a sort of informal agreement. They receive unpaid training and are equipped with uniforms and guns, if required; yet their employment is purely dependent on the customer's needs and satisfaction: as soon as the client is unhappy with the service, or decides to interrupt it, the worker loses the job until a new request turns up. One of the managers clearly depicted the level of docility that is expected from a security guard, 'They come from the villages, from the *basti*s, have no education. They would end up begging or pulling rickshaws. We offer them a decent job; they should only be thankful, never complain!'

The big multinational companies such as G4S or Securitas openly claim to reject the practices of fierce exploitation that are common in the industry. These companies entered the Indian market in the early 1990s, attracted by the neoliberal reforms, and retain the higher end of the market, working with top Indian and global customers. The common policy of these companies is to hire an Indian workforce—whereas the top management remains foreign (mostly white)—with a '100 % compliance' with labour and human rights. For example, all G4S workers have a contract and are entitled to leaves and accident compensation.

And yet, on a closer look, there is evidence of a significant degree of exploitation, based on emotional pressure. Although not explicitly, trade unions are banned here as well. A G4S job being extremely coveted, workers are pushed into severe competition, to do more, and better, and to go beyond their limits in terms of commitment, often with more working hours. The threat of sacking and replacement is ever present. Guards are continuously reminded by their supervisors of their humble background, against which working with a global corporation is a privilege; of their poor life perspectives, should G4S get rid of them. And in practice, a negative reference from G4S, for example, as 'troublemakers', would eliminate any chance of finding another job in the sector.

A third aspect of accumulation concerns the complex nature of security, which includes strong symbolic and emotional features. This is extremely relevant to the development of the security industry. In the contemporary processes of valorization, the incessant exchange of knowledge, practices, and feelings, which runs 'from below' through the social bodies, is immediately put at work in the creation of brands, markets, and modalities of consumption.[12] This applies to the emergence of security as a market. Through the incessant enunciation of security threats at every level—from terrorist attacks to major infrastructures and landmarks to pickpockets and petty theft—a widespread demand for generic security is generated and reproduced.

Importantly, these discourses not only circulate informally, in terms of public opinion or media campaigns, but also become political claims and, ultimately, rules and norms governing everyday life. As a result, the massive representation and visualization of security, through the pervasive presence of security guards, checkpoints, and adverts, have become an essential requirement for the establishment and functioning of any 'world-class' site, be it a university campus, a shopping mall, or a residential area. The call for security is easily marketed and transformed into a capitalistic circuit of production and consumption. Security is identified with the presence of private guards, and this kind of security, in turn, becomes synonymous with modernity, development, and civilization. This is even more interesting in a city like Kolkata where crime is not an emergency or an everyday life toll.

In her analysis, Gooptu (2013, p. 16) relates the spread of private security to the upper- and middle-class anxiety to 'the growing mass democratic mobilization of the poor and lower castes since the 1990s'. In this perspective, security appears as the politically correct version of an intense antipoor sentiment, and its actual purpose is to keep the urban poor in their place. This body of emotions, concepts, and values associated with security also plays a remarkable role in its deployment as a governmental strategy, as I will explain in the next section.

Governance

How does securitization work as a strategy of governance of urban poverty and informal economy? I have registered this taking place in two principal ways. The first, more obvious one is that the presence of private security regulates the circulation around and across sites of contrast. Up-market and deprived areas are not only contiguous, but also intertwined through a network of jobs and services, essentially the supply of domestic and care labour. Security works as a filter between these conflicting, yet interrelated spaces.

What struck me and set me thinking during my research in Kolkata is the fact that the ubiquitous security procedures seem to be not effective at all. In most cases, the kind of controls conducted at the gates of shopping malls, corporate, and

---

[12]Among the countless interventions on the increasing role of knowledge, emotions, and 'the immaterial' in the capitalistic processes, *Cognitive Capitalism* (Moulier-Boutang 2012) has been particularly useful for my research.

residential buildings would not be able to detect or prevent any real danger. The true function of security appears to be related not to crime and disaster prevention as such, but to something else. This is, I suggest, the enforcement of hierarchies in the space through specific rituals. I was enlightened about this when I read the rules of a gated residential complex, which requests domestic workers to use separate elevators and security guards to ensure this would happen. Other rules that security guards were responsible for enforcing included domestic and construction workers not to sit, sleep, or eat on the grass.

In every shopping mall I have visited, security was charged with monitoring and regulating the circulation of cleaners, who have to use separate entrances; they are searched before leaving the premises and cannot access any area in the mall except their workplace. At the gates, the guards have to stop anyone not dressed properly by the mall's standards: bare feet, dirty clothes, and *lungis*[13] are not allowed. This looks like an explicit antipoor measure, meant to differentiate the potential consumers from the undesired ones, those who cannot afford even to look like that. Such prohibition is at the same time an entitlement for those who are allowed in seamlessly, not just into the building, but into a lifestyle and social status. In this respect, security has a powerful performative function: to differentially include and allocate people in the space according to their economic and social rank.

As Dey et al. (2013) point out in their analysis, securitization is used to break bonds and solidarity between workers who often share the same background and same levels of exploitation. But in addition to this, as I have already shown, security has a strong aesthetic and cultural significance, which is continuously reproduced 'from below' in the social interaction. In the mainstream discourses, it is deeply associated with the concepts of modernization, development, and civilization. It is a matter of status and appearance: every place with some ambition must display security guards. Yet, the examples show how development of a modern and 'civilized' society creates deep-rooted hierarchies and other forms of exploitation. In his study on Delhi urbanization, Sanjay Srivastava describes how the luxury gated communities and malls in the new town of Gurgaon are places where middle-class women can experience more freedom and relaxed behaviour, compared to the rules of traditional public life. This seems to happen in Kolkata as well. The comfort of middle-class women has its counterpart in the securitization, through most rigid control and systematic humiliation of the other women, like maids, nannies, and housekeepers.

This leads to a second modality of securitization working as a governmental strategy. According to industrial associations, the key security sectors in India are manned guarding, followed by cash services, and then electronic surveillance (see Ernst Young and FICCI 2013). These data are markedly different from the European and North American security market, where the electronic and hi-tech surveillance methods largely dominate. What does this prevalence of manned

[13]Men's clothing which is a cloth wrapped around the waist and worn floor length.

guarding denote? I argue that this has to do, rather than with a technological backwardness, with the very object of post-colonial governmentality—the masses of 'surplus' people that are not absorbed by either the capitalistic market of labour or the welfare structures.

Therefore, massive employment of guards can be seen as a twofold reaction to the problem: on the one hand, to protect properties from the potential 'assault' of the poor people and on the other hand, to provide jobs to the same poor people. In her work, Gooptu (2013) explains the collusion between the security industry and government in pushing young people 'at risk' to get a job in the security industry. Governmental agencies mobilize along with NGOs and private companies in order to recruit young people from deprived areas and bring them into motivational/training programmes that prepare them for a job as security guard. This is presented as a great chance to emancipate themselves from poverty; but at the same time, at the core of the training is the cultivation of the 'qualities' of discipline and docility.

Physical grooming is also an essential part of the programme. Importantly, as Gooptu (2013) points out, these recruitment schemes specifically target vulnerable and 'at-risk' segments of the population, as a way to prevent political radicalization. A significant convergence between the rampant security industry and the state is visible here, which benefit from both, a disciplined labour to be exploited and disciplined subjects to be managed. Foucault's argument about the mutual assistance between the state and the capitalist actors within the neoliberal framework seems to be perfectly exemplified (Foucault et al. 2010).

Conclusion

In this chapter, I have presented some reflections, based on my work in Kolkata, on the entanglement of capitalistic accumulation and governmental strategies within the domain of security, in the context of intense urban transformation.

The making of world-class Kolkata has created the conditions for the opening of a new market, that of security, which caters to the needs of developers and up-market customers. The practices of accumulation include forced displacement as well as the continuous reshaping of the space for the purpose of exploitation and consumption, involving securitization.

Subsequently, securitization proceeds along with the proliferation of investments in the urban space: infrastructures, residential enclaves, corporate headquarters, and shopping malls. The interventions over the city enact the scheme of accumulation as described by Marx: people are separated from their means of subsistence—farmlands, stalls, and houses—and forced into the lowest level of the labour market. The same people negatively affected by urban development create the pool of vulnerable labour for the new security industry.

Hence, it is clear that the security companies not only allow their clients to accumulate, but also benefit from the same conditions of security in expanding a range of operations, exploiting labour, and making great profits. This explains how securitization becomes a field of accumulation itself. This is also due to the multifarious nature of security and securitization as a process, which exceeds its economic and practical rationale and holds a powerful grip on emotions and subjectivities. At the same time, securitization is crucial for the management of urban poverty and need economy, which is a crucial task of post-colonial governmentality. In fact, the implementation of security in most cases has not much to do with effective crime prevention; rather, through its practices and rituals, securitization works to regulate the tensions between conflicting spaces and to reshape them hierarchically. It also has a crucial aesthetic function: to epitomize the ideas of modernity, development, and civilization.

Finally, the massive recruitment of low-skill, low-paid labour for security jobs emerges as a strategy for preventing poor young people from political radicalization and crime, which is pursued by the state and the industry together. With the help of governmental agencies and NGOs, the security market incorporates preexisting hierarchies and patterns of subalternization that allow acute exploitation, poor work conditions, and the systematic humiliation of the workers.

The processes I have observed and described in Kolkata are part of a global trend. Security has become central to the organization of the globalized trade and production, to enable borders, mark the economic and social hierarchies, and manage the resulting conflicts. And yet, the multiplication of security practices does not seem to reduce the overall level and perception of risk and threat: evidence of this is in the continuous growth of the security industry. This is due, I argue, to an essential and intimate bond between security and violence, ensuring that the security of someone usually means exercising virtual or actual violence on someone else.

As the case of Kolkata shows, securitization restricts the possibilities and the circulation of some people—the poor—in order to encourage the possibilities and the circulation of some other people—the upper- and middle-class consumers. Securitization is, ultimately, an intensely productive process; it creates the market for services such as security provision mixed with care and domestic labour supply; it also generates a requirement for high-value goods such as CCTVs, software, and all sorts of devices including weapons, resulting in subjectivities like those who are 'secure' and those who are not. But more importantly, through material and immaterial practices, securitization produces and reproduces its own market and demand. Indeed, the stress on security results in the production of more insecure conditions—displacement and poverty—which again needs to be securitized and so on in a vicious circle that boosts the profits of the security industry. The rationale of security that emerges from this mechanism, if there is one, is certainly not the objective reduction of insecurity. It is, I suggest, the management of an irrational development, which implicates way more violence and conflicts than wellbeing. This confirms the collapse of the developmental teleology, at the core of the theories of post-colonial capitalism.

Acknowledgment I am grateful to the Calcutta Mahanirban Research Group for providing an outstanding collection of studies as well as a thought-provoking intellectual environment from which I have benefited greatly during my research in Kolkata. The work of Prof. Nandini Gooptu—the only existing one on the security industry in Kolkata at the time I engaged with the topic—has taught me much and helped me frame my investigation. Finally, my deep gratitude goes to V. Ramaswamy, for his kind support, precious advice, and wonderful tales.

References

Bandyopadhyay, R. (2011). Politics of archiving: Hawkers and pavement dwellers in Calcutta. *Dialectical Anthropology 35*(3), 295–316. Retrieved from http://www.scopus.com/inward/record.url?eid=2-s2.0-80053319302partnerID=40md5=3e3d9db51d9b4299b4b61375f7e8933a

Banerjee-Guha, S. (2009). Neoliberalising the 'urban': New geographies of power and injustice in Indian cities. *Economic and Political Weekly, 44*(22), 95–107.

Banerjee-Guha, S. (2013). Accumulation and dispossession: Contradictions of growth and development in contemporary India. *South Asia: Journal of South Asian Studies, 36*(2), 165–179. doi:10.1080/00856401.2013.804026.

Buzan, B., Weaver, O., & De Wilde, J. (1998). *Security: A new framework for analysis*. Boulder: Lynne Rienner.

Chatterjee, A. (2002). *Mother Teresa: The final verdict*. Meteor Books.

Chatterjee, P. (2012). *The black hole of empire: History of a global practice of power*. Princeton: Princeton University Press.

Chattopadhyay, S. (2005). *Representing Calcutta: Modernity, nationalism and the colonial uncanny* (Vol. 2). London and New York: Routledge.

Dey, I., Samaddar, R., & Sen, S. K. (2013). *Beyond Kolkata: Rajarhat and the dystopia of Urban imagination*. New Delhi: Routledge India.

Ernst Young and Federation of Indian Chambers of Commerce and Industry (FICCI). (2013). *Private Security Services Industry, Securing Future Growth.* Retrieved February 10, 2016 from http://www.capsi.in/files/ficci-report.pdf

Foucault, M., Senellart, M., Ewald, F., Fontana, A., & Burchell, G. (2010). *The birth of biopolitics: Lectures at the Collège de France, 1978–1979*. New York: Palgrave Macmillan.

Gooptu, N. (2013). Servile sentinels of the city: Private security guards, organized informality, and labour in interactive services in globalized India. *International Review of Social History, 58*(1), 9–38.

Harvey, D. (2003). *The new imperialism*. Oxford: Oxford University Press.

Harvey, D. (2006). *Spaces of global capitalism*. London, New York: Verso.

Hitchens, C. (1995). *The missionary position: Mother Teresa in theory and practice*. London: Verso.

Leander, A. (2005). The market for force and public security: The destabilizing consequences of private military companies. *Journal of Peace Research, 42*(5), 605–622. doi:10.1177/0022343305056237.

Levien, M. (2012). The land question: Special economic zones and the political economy of dispossession in India. *The Journal of Peasant Studies, 39*(3–4), 933–969. doi:10.1080/03066150.2012.656268.

Mezzadra, S. (2011). How many histories of labour? Towards a theory of postcolonial capitalism. *Postcolonial Studies, 14*(2), 151–170. doi:10.1080/13688790.2011.563458.

Mezzadra, S., & Neilson, B. (2015). Operations of Capital. *South Atlantic Quarterly, 114*(1), 11. doi:10.1215/00382876-2831246 y1—2015.

Moulier-Boutang, Y. (2012). *Cognitive capitalism*. Trans. E. Emery: Wiley.

Neocleous, M. (2008). *Critique of security*. Edinburgh: Edinburgh University Press.

Policante, A. (2012). *I nuovimercenari: Mercatomondiale e privatizzazionedella Guerra*. Ombrecorte.
Robinson, J. (2013). Ordinary cities: Between modernity and development. Retrieved from http://UWSAU.eblib.com.au/patron/FullRecord.aspx?p=200247
Samaddar, R. (2012). What Is postcolonial predicament? *Economic and Political Weekly, 47*(9).
Samaddar, R. (2014). A post-colonial critique of capital accumulation today. *Policies and Practices, 64*.
Sanyal, K. (2007). *Rethinking capitalist development: Primitive accumulation, governmentality and post-colonial capitalism*. New Delhi: Routledge.
Sassen, S. (1991). *The global city: New York, London, Tokyo*. Princeton, N.J: Princeton University Press.
Serrou, R. (1980). *Teresa of Calcutta*. New York: McGraw-Hill.
Somayaji, S., & Talwar, S. (Eds.). (2011). *Development-induced displacement, rehabilitation and resettlement in India: Current issues and challenges*. London and New York: Routledge.
White, A. (2012). The new political economy of private security. *Theoretical Criminology 16*(1), 85–101. Retrieved from http://www.scopus.com/inward/record.url?eid=2-s2.0-84857775244 partnerID=40md5=2dfadf6228db4812d42f72bbcd6afd8f

Accumulation by Possession: The Social Processes of Rent Seeking in Urban Delhi

Sushmita Pati

Abstract In this chapter, the author tries to show how kinship networks have come to be entwined with the networks of capital. She looks into the caste networks that were at play in the urban villages of south Delhi by focusing on how the dominant caste (the Jats) have come to establish their dominance over the real estate market. Her argument regarding the transformation of an agrarian pastoral community into an entrepreneurial community is premised on the story of the urban development of Delhi. The author brings out the oxymoronic nature of 'urban villages', as neither have they been able to remain rural, nor have they been able to become urban and it is not merely a case of transformation from one to another. Urban villages of Delhi, she opines, are thus caught in the state of exceptionality, in the state of eternal contradiction almost as a part of their very existence and this peculiarity of its nature itself has lent to the curious modes of accumulation that are operative in these villages today. She states that these processes of accumulation are largely mediated but not subsumed by the processes of accumulation taking place in the city of Delhi.

Keywords Networks of capital · Kinship network · Urban development · Rent · Urban village

---

A version of this chapter has appeared as 'The Making of the Rentier Jat: Land, Rent and Social Processes of Accumulation in South Delhi', part of a working paper series titled *Policies and Practices*: *Accumulation under Post-Colonial Capitalism IV—Mobile Labour and the New Urban*, Mahanirban Calcutta Research Group. It is reproduced here with permission. Another version of this chapter has been presented at the Centre for Modern Indian Studies, Geörg-August Universität in Göttingen on 20 June 2014. I am grateful to Rajarshi Dasgupta, Srirupa Roy, Ravi Ahuja, Debarati Bagchi, Mithilesh Kumar, Sharmin Khodaiji, Shruti Dubey and Shivani Kapoor for their comments on this chapter.

S. Pati (✉)
Centre for Political Studies, Jawaharlal Nehru University, New Delhi, India
e-mail: sushmita.pati@gmail.com

I.K. Mitra et al. (eds.), *Accumulation in Post-Colonial Capitalism*,
DOI 10.1007/978-981-10-1037-8_5

The logic of accumulation has been central to the question of urbanism analytically. Cities historically grew around firstly trade and later, industrial production. Cities, therefore, are geographically concentrated spaces of accumulation (Tilly 1989). David Harvey explains how in order to avoid the problem of 'overaccumulation' capital has to continually look for new places to be diverted to. He explains this through the concept of spatial-temporal fix (Harvey 2004). His own thesis of accumulation by dispossession is informed by this process which goes on to contextualize urban development world over. Following from the logic of primitive accumulation, Kalyan Sanyal argues that it produces more dispossession, more than what capital can subsume within itself as the reserve army of labour (Sanyal 2007). He argues that this population becomes the part of 'need economy' and, by extension, non-capital. 'Dispossession' is largely understood as the state of destitution, which transforms people into a vast indistinguishable mass of 'have-nots'. This chapter looks into how 'dispossession' can also be mapped along a graph, where some have gone on to enter local but stable logics of circulation and capital accumulation while some have not. This chapter goes on to analyse how capital accumulation acquires a specific form without necessarily needing to be carved out in the domain of 'non-capital', while being parasitic on social and cultural relations that existed prior to the onslaught of high capital. I look at urban villages in south Delhi for this purpose to see how through a unique caveat of planning, whereby the landowners were only dispossessed of their agricultural land and were not uprooted, a localized logic of accumulation could be produced. The villagers continued to live in their 'villages' which slowly were surrounded by the rich infrastructural landscape of south Delhi from all sides. I look at a set of population, whose lands were acquired to create south Delhi, mainly the Jats (the dominant caste in the village), who call themselves '*gaonwalas*' (villagers) inside the city. They might be rich, but do not necessarily identify with the middle or upper class. What also makes this case specific is that I am not looking at the textbook case of primitive accumulation. The older inhabitants, though dispossessed of their agricultural land are never really displaced and that they do not become a part of the reserve army of labour quite contrary to classical Marxist theory, are marginalized nonetheless. Their residential area, or *abadi*, demarcated by the amorphous *lal dora*,[1] which were left 'untouched' in the utopian belief that the villages would continue to live in their idyllic state of perfect 'harmony' (DDA 1957, p. 769),[2] which of course was never to happen. Without necessarily denying the global

[1]The land earmarked for village *abadi* and the agricultural land of the village were duly demarcated in the land settlement of 1908–1909 and the *abadi* site was circumscribed in the village map in red ink; therefore, the name *lal dora* (lit. red ink). It still is in use with *lal dora* as the village residential land and the extended *lal dora* land which was left outside the village as vacant land, but has now seen massive mushrooming of buildings. The borders between *lal dora* and extended *lal dora* are extremely amorphous and, therefore, a source of confusion, and it is this confusion which makes a property legal or illegal.

[2]It remains a question, however, whether one should dismiss it as a matter purely of a utopia gone wrong or as a question of economising on compensation costs as a complete displacement would have put a higher financial burden on the state for compensation.

scales of capitalism, can we also look at forms of capitalism working on subsidiary (I am intentionally not using the term micro) levels which operate on other planes, though not in isolation?

Though the focus of this chapter is on the time period after land acquisition, the latter period and the value of compensation looms large on the question that this chapter looks at. Since only Jats were 'landowners', no compensation was offered to Dalits (downtrodden and marginalized castes) who used to work as agricultural labourers on these lands. It is this monetary compensation which becomes the basis, for them to enter into different forms of entrepreneurships. These entrepreneurships and businesses grow and intensify through older kinship structure of the Jats thereby also reinventing the nature of the kinship structure. It is these networks of post-colonial forms of capitalism that I intend to trace in this piece through the case of urban villages in south Delhi. Slowly, from businesses such as transport and construction, the major thrust of investment moved towards real estate within the *lal dora* in the 1990s. As the steady stream of migrants from all over the country started pouring in, these urban villages became the very obvious choice of lower middle class for residential purposes. Land possessed in the urban village, which is exempt from any building bye-laws because the villages predate any such modern laws governing them today, became their mainstay. This form of real estate has been possible only because of a flexible and incoherent system of land revenue documents (Pati 2015). As renting out began to seem like a rather profitable venture, many villagers started breaking down their older structures, to make series of cheap 'one room sets' in their buildings in places such as Munirka and Katwaria Sarai, which were made with the sole objective of maximizing the utility of space. This real estate market too is uniquely controlled through a system of kinship networks of Jats through various forms of associations.

A Brief Overview

The village land in Munirka, according to the dominant strain of oral history, belonged to the Jats from the Tokas clan.[3] They had migrated from Behraur district in Rajasthan arguably in the eighteenth century. Later, Jats from another clan, the 'Rathis', also came to settle in the village and were given the land on the periphery so that they could offer protection to the Tokas clan from Muslims. Similarly, the Brahmins and Kumhars, Jatavs and Valmikis also settled in the village at various points in history. Once land was acquired in the late 1950s, many of them took up jobs through the sports quota, or entered some or the other kind of business. Shahpur Jat, on the other hand, despite having a much smaller expanse of land, owned much more fertile tracts. As a result, horticulture was more popular in these villages. The village is dominated by the Panwar *gotra* (clan) of the Jat community.

[3]The story of this migration is extremely sketchy and vague and beyond the scope of this research to establish.

Fifty-sixty years since land acquisition, while Munirka has mainly let out residential and smaller commercial property; Shahpur Jat has turned host to a dense, complicated garment industry. The dingy, inner parts of the village have been rented out to the *karigars* (artisans), who work on *adda* (frames meant for embroidery) and sewing machines, while the outer, more spruced up portions of the village have been taken over by the upcoming fashion designers, start-ups and lifestyle stores. The renting business in Munirka seems to have picked up momentum around early 1980s, most probably around the time of the 1982 Asian Games in Delhi. The first tenants to have arrived were mainly labourers from Rajasthan and Uttarakhand. As offices around R.K. Puram and markets started opening up, small-time clerks and young men working in these shops started renting these houses.[4] With these area becoming more developed, the socio-economic profile of people wanting to rent houses also changed, with which changed the nature of construction. The feverish competition for land also seems to have begun around this time. The traditional village which was strictly divided on caste lines could no longer remain so because of a number of reasons. Massive amount of land grab within the village led to Jats building property in visibly Dalit sections of the village. The influx of migrants too, who live cheek by jowl with their landlords because of popularity of these places for rent, has structurally changed things about the village. This led to these villages becoming extremely cramped with tall multi-storeyed houses mushrooming everywhere. In collective memory, the image of places such as Babulal Chowk in Munirka still remains as a *chowk* (open market area) till which point even a truck could get in. The lanes are so narrow today that construction material has to be loaded on to donkeys to take them to the same places.

Chaudhary Birendra Singh Tokas,[5] the then *pradhan* (village head) of Munirka, brought out a village directory around the year 1999 with house numbers, the names of proprietors and a series of maps. This was perhaps an effort to make sense of the village land ownership pattern after the late 1980s–early 1990s 'land rush' in that area when massive land grab and construction took place within the *lal dora*. Rent also started escalating around the same period. Rajbir Sharma, who helped organize the house numbers started by Birendra Singh Tokas, remarks in the directory on how the system of house numbers allocated by the government was rendered completely useless, as people who built their houses later randomly allocated numbers to their units themselves. The lanes and by-lanes seem to create an internal coherence, a lifeworld that is not accessible to outsiders. It seems to have come to acquire a distinct character of its own, with its matchbox structures, 'villagers' who are millionaires and institutions which run with their own peculiar sets of rules and regulations.

[4]A great deal of these developments were a direct result of infrastructure such as Ring Road that was right next to Munirka and The Asiad Village that started being built around early 1980s right next to Shahpur Jat.

[5]All names have been changed to protect the identities of the respondents.

This seemingly anarchic and irregular form of real estate market, however, is run by its own rules. This market is run by its own grammar of kinship structure, overtly dominated by Jats, but without being entirely insulated to other communities. This chapter outlines three sociologically disparate forms of organizations–associations: *panchayats*[6] and the resident welfare association (RWA), youth associations and the *kunba*,[7] at specific moments in their careers in these villages where they sometimes independently or sometimes in collusion with each other work towards controlling this market for housing. While the panchayat is supposed to function more like a sociocultural institution dealing with customs, the RWA and youth associations are technically modern civil society associations concerning themselves with questions of governance and such. The *kunba,* on the other hand, is a familial unit which is technically a part of one's social and cultural life. This chapter elaborates as to how these entirely distinct forms of associations and groups tend to have similar concerns regarding the real estate market and sometimes collude and sometimes compete with each other in order to establish a form of control over this market. Sometimes through legal means, many a times through illegal; sometimes guised in the form of social welfare, and sometimes through pure violence; I see how they work as informal cartels by maintaining a form of monopoly control.

From Panchayats to RWA

This section analyses how the older form of panchayat has, in the urban context, been given the name and form of resident welfare association and has been able organize the landlords in the village into a cartel. The RWA seems to exercise control over land as that becomes the only source of both economic and political clout for the villagers. In Shahpur Jat, it seems there was a decision taken at the Panchayat to not allow the private builders into the system as that would mean a loss of control over their land. In both these villages, an unsaid rule exists which prohibits property owners from selling land or property to outsiders which has considerably restricted the entry of 'outsiders' into the fold any longer. In

[6]*Panchayat* refers to an older, pre-modern system of local government which have been modified and incorporated into the modern governance system through the 73rd and 74th Amendment in the Constitution of India in 1992. The Jats of north-west India have had a caste-based panchayat, referred to as *khap panchayat*, whereby they have taken up quasi-judicial responsibilities by pronouncing harsh judgements for going against caste norms which do not have any legal or constitutional recognition. See Chowdhry (2009), Yadav (2009). However, since urban villages of Delhi do not come under the purview of the Panchayati Raj Act, nor do they exist in rural spaces where *khap panchayat*s can be made effective, these *panchayat*s inhabit a liminal space the nature of which is elaborated in this piece.

[7]*Kunba* refers to a family structure up to 2–3 generations which encapsulates the larger familial unit.

Munirka, a huge number of migrants came from the North East[8] who began to rent places there; in Shahpur Jat, it happened because of the saturation of the land market for designers in Hauz Khas Village which made Shahpur Jat a newer hub for new designers. Slowly, restaurants, cafes, bookshops and lifestyle stores have started to come up too, given that Shahpur Jat has become a hub for the Delhi upper middle and upper classes for customized shopping for clothes.

The RWA in Munirka was made around 30 years back by Birendra Singh Tokas, the then Panchayat *pradhan.* His close aide, Rajbir Sharma, had undertaken many such works with Birendra Singh before he passed away in 2012. Instituted by the then pradhan, it was probably an attempt to gain legitimacy of the state as a recognized body. Only landowning men from all castes are eligible for voting.[9] The RWA chairperson is referred to as the *pradhan* and the meetings as panchayat. The panchayat, therefore, has ended up in the flux that urban villages themselves are caught in. The Munirka RWA is, therefore, a quasi-modern institution which, on the one hand, is hinged on a semi-legal institution of that of RWA to gain legitimacy in the eyes of the state, and on the other hand, is still deeply rooted in older, institutional ways of working to hold on to their 'community' and 'traditions'. But the interesting thing about these RWAs/panchayats is that they can flip to either side as and when required. In the booklet that Birendra Singh Tokas himself got published in 1999, it had a 20-point programme charted out for the RWA. One such point states:

> …if a conflict of interest arises over a wall or anything, while constructing a house, then please try to not go to the police immediately. Please try to resolve the issue consensually with the consent of the pradhan and side with the truth. Also, do not leave in the middle of the argument, and try to impartially resolve the issue so that the innocent is caused no trouble[10] (translation mine).

The members of the committee constantly stressed the role of the *buzurg* (elders) in the village. These functions or responsibilities of the Munirka RWA clearly overstep the civic responsibilities of the RWA that are assumed in middle-class colonies.[11] It does not command the power that Panchayats have in the rural context. Social boycott does not work any longer as the kind of dependence within

[8]Here, I am using the term 'North East' as a short hand for the people from Manipur, Sikkim, Darjeeling, Nepal and other states which are in the north-eastern part of India who live in Munirka, for the lack of a better terminology. People from Manipur, Darjeeling and Nepal, however, are a majority in terms of numbers.

[9]Only in 2016 were women allowed to vote after Youth Brigade Munirka took this issue up and filed complaints with the Delhi Commission of Women and Delhi Police.

[10]Unknown Author, Anonymous (1999, pp. 8–9).

[11]Stephanie Tawa Lama-Rewal writes that RWAs have existed since the 1970s and that there are a number of RWAs which run without any registration. The Bhagidari scheme of Delhi Government which only includes RWAs in middle class and legal colonies has been trying to attain citizen participation in matters of civic infrastructure. She argues that RWAs have been largely undemocratic and seem to have no clear overall charter to adhere to which allows every RWA to formulate its own. See Tawa Lama-Rewal (2007).

which such forms of banishment used to function does not exist. There have been inter-caste marriages amongst many other things, but the current RWA either cannot take these issues up, or even if it does, it is not very effective in stopping these from happening. Most importantly, the Panchayats can never become an all Jat Panchayat in the way Khap Panchayats are. But in moments of crisis, such as the Munirka fiasco regarding the North East tenants(which I will go on to discuss later in the section), the RWA comes to play a rather central role in putting up a united front, taking decisions and representing the community.

In Shahpur Jat, there was no such conflation between the RWA and the panchayats like it has in Munirka. In fact, there is no authoritative single RWA in the village, but several defunct ones. It is, therefore, the panchayat which is the most important community body in the village. There are 21 members in all, with one or two members from the Dalit community and one or two from the *kumhar* (potter) community and that all these meetings take place in the *purana* (old) *chaupal.*

Jagjeet Panwar, a member of one of the several RWAs in Shahpur Jat, argues that it is very difficult for any such organization to work within the village. While the families with big, important *kunba* do not feel the need to join in any such endeavour, the several political factions in the village feel that any development work should take place under the aegis of one or the other political party. In Shahpur Jat, too, property developers could not really enter because the inflow of outsiders would mean the loss of say of the community itself. '*Aur pata nahi kis caste ke honge, kis dharm ke honge*', he says.[12] This only goes on to substantiate how the panchayat takes initiative in controlling land ownership within the village and tries to limit the number of owners.

Today, more than 50 % of the tenants in the village are from the North East, mostly from places such as Manipur and Nagaland (Nandi and Bhattacharya 2014). Around the mid-1990s, many of the houses were pulled down and new houses made with scores of 'one-room sets'. Many recall this period as the time when the people from the North East, mostly from Manipur, started coming to Munirka to rent apartments in hoards. Jamil, a villager, who has a small watch and mobile phone repairing shop, laughs and says, '*Pehle toh gaonwaalon ko laga ki gaon mein foreigners aa gaye hain'*.[13] The cultural differences between the Jats and the tenants from the North East have been the cause of animosity between the two groups for years now. The tension between the two communities has been palpable not simply in Munirka but in other villages too. There have been several panchayats held in order to decide on the issue of tenants from the North East and Africa. There arguably have been several moves to agree on not renting out property to them within the panchayats. However, such efforts failed because not all property in the village is equally coveted and since many of them have been built with loans, it becomes imperative for them to rent it to whoever wants it. However,

[12]'One does not know which caste or religion they would be from'.

[13]'Initially, the villagers thought that "foreigners have come to live here"'.

this has not done much to reduce the racial animosity 'outsiders' are faced with. The constant allegation against them is that they are destroying the moral fabric of the village because of the way men and women mix freely, the way they dress, the amount of drinking they do on the streets. The beginning of 2014 saw several cases of such racially charged incidents in some of the urban villages. Out of these, the most talked about was the Somnath Bharti, the then Health Minister of Delhi, led a raid without a warrant into the house of some Ugandan women in Khirki village on the charge that they were involved in prostitution and drug trafficking on 15 January 2014 (The Times of India 2014). What ensued was a high-strung drama with Delhi Chief Minister Arvind Kejriwal holding a *dharna* (protest) outside Rail Bhawan in defence of Somnath Bharti, turning it around on the Delhi Police, which is under the Central government, for being ineffective and corrupt (The Indian Express 2014). This was followed by the rape of a minor Manipuri girl in Munirka village by a landlord's son which hit the news and automatically escalated the animosity already present between the two communities (Firstpost 2014). After a few days of the rape, the village RWA called a panchayat to discuss the 'North East problem'. This caused an alarm in the North East community, which hit the headlines as how the '*khap* panchayat' in the village had decided to throw out all the tenants from the North East (Nandi and Bhattacharya 2014; Dhapola 2014). Some newspapers also reported that a decision was taken that those who stayed out till late would be evicted (Nandi and Bhattacharya 2014). It must be kept in mind that the panchayat which unanimously passed the dictum against the North East residents had villagers not all of whom were Jats. The vocal Dalits of the village, who quote Ambedkar and M.N. Srinivas while talking of Jat oppression in the same breath, argue how the '*chinki log*'[14] have no morals and also eat extremely foul-smelling things. The villagers went on a defence and argued that the meeting was not a panchayat meeting but a regular RWA meeting. They argued that being from the village, they usually refer to any community meeting as panchayat and that *khap* panchayats are caste-specific panchayats and cannot involve the entire village. It required police intervention to bring the village representatives and the people from North East to the table and to provide a reassurance from the villagers that the tenants would not be evicted from their houses.

The defence that the villagers gave with regard to this controversy was that no such decision was taken and that it was not a *khap* panchayat but an RWA meeting. On technical grounds, while this might be true that it was an RWA meeting, and that it could not have been a *khap* panchayat meeting as it had members from all castes; it also needs to be understood that there are no fixed boundaries between the two in this context. The fact that panchayats have come to become democratized in terms of participation can be attributed to members of other castes, including Dalits, becoming 'landlords'.[15] The panchayat's relevance lies in

[14]A derogatory term for people with mongoloid features.

[15]Here, of course, it needs to be understood that only certain castes within the Dalits have been able to do so. Mostly, Jatavs among the Dalits have been able to make use of opportunity.

the fact that it ends up being some form of a platform for landlords, which it cannot be if it does not open up to members from other castes.

Chaman Singh, member of a Dalit organization based in Munirka, clearly describes the RWA as a caste institution which looks after the interests of the Jats of the village. In the name of wanting to resolve issues internally, he says that they end up using the platform to maintain their own dominance despite encouraging members from other castes including Dalits. He argues how the RWA might not ostensibly come across as a Jat organization, since there are members of other communities as well. But the function of the village RWA is to squarely keep political and social privileges of the Jats of the village intact.

Some RWAs have also come up to pool in collective resources to attract more capital. Karan, a Brahmin who initiated an RWA in Shahpur Jat, has taken up several activities in the village and the RWA does everything possible legally and sometimes even beyond the purview of the legal, to get that work done. For example, a wall of the municipal park was arguably broken to allow parking inside it. The RWA members renamed two streets 'Fashion Street 1 and 2', and then had all the houses on those streets painted orange. Karan tells me this was difficult as many people were sceptical and did not want to join the endeavour. But many slowly came round by the end and also got their houses painted themselves when they realized that it might be a good idea. This RWA has come up with a clear agenda to increase the commercial value of other lanes (other than Dada Jungi Lane, which I will discuss next), by leveraging collective effort in painting buildings in one colour, and putting up new street lights to increase the infrastructural value of these specific lanes.

These two three different formations of panchayats and RWAs clearly point towards the idea that despite calling themselves panchayats or RWAs, they have decided their mandate way beyond the usual mandate available to them. From sorting out interpersonal relationships, property feuds, to improving infrastructure by both legal means and beyond, to attracting designers to start boutiques, deciding tenants, to local elections, the panchayats/RWAs have gone on to influence and take decisions on several aspects normally not considered to be of concern to either the panchayat or the RWAs. The RWA in the case of Shahpur Jat thus comes across as an association of entrepreneurs sometimes pooling their resources together to increase their commercial value; and in the case of Munirka, it comes across as an association which firmly puts down rules and conditions that would govern the market.

Landlords, Associations and Property

The Youth Brigade Munirka, formed in 2013, by a group of young men wanting to take up Munirka's concerns, invariably started off with issues that concern the landlords. These can be about shutting shops by 11 pm, or fixing gates at the entry points of Munirka, or addressing the 'menace' that the people from the North East allegedly create in the village. Here, the idea of being owners was rather central to begin with. Started by a young man, as an 'apolitical organization', the Youth Brigade Munirka (YBM) initially set off with the tenor of being an organization of Jat landlords wanting to arouse a certain urgency about the future of the village and that it needs *aapsi samajh* (understanding) and *bhaichara* (brotherhood).

The group, however, had to tone down its language of being from the Jat community because of the presence of some young Dalit landowners and some tenants in the group. The first few meetings were rife with references to being Jats which diminished rather rapidly by the fourth or fifth meeting. YBM, when it finally began with the first few campaigns, had to start with clean-up drives in the Buddh Vihar area to come across as a non-Jat, apolitical group of youth wanting to simply talk about the issues of Munirka. In one of the pamphlets by YBM, they write:

> Do we ever think of our responsibility towards the place where we are born? Have you made Munirka a better place to live? Do I have any hope from any of my Village men? The answer that you will get from most of us will be 'Do not have any hopes from me; I'm no agent of change'. Leave apart others we shy away from standing up even for our own cause. My friends, what are we afraid of? What keeps us so passive? Why are we so dead?"... We just hold on to the old order which is familiar and comfortable income through rent. But we should remember a day will come when we will not be there and our village will also cease to exist. Can you imagine Munirka not existing? The place which gave you everything! This is our motherland! Maybe we will not be able to see it today but who would answer the questions of our coming generations? The only way is to unite and work for our present and coming generations.[16]

The rhetoric of the pamphlet is clearly addressed to the landowners of the village, to the 'sons of the soil' without limiting it to the Jats of the village. The immediate reason for this would be that the identity of a 'landlord' is no longer limited to simply the Jats. The Dalits too, apart from Brahmins and Baniyas in the village, have emerged as landlords despite having much less land. Traditionally having owned only a residential space (they owned no agricultural land and were customarily employed as agricultural labourers), they too have slowly erected multi-storeyed buildings with one room sets which they rent out. Though the rent in the Dalit localities is usually much lower in terms of both rate and numbers, the identity of becoming a landowner has for many been empowering.

Rajneesh, a youth from the Nai (Other Backward Classes) community, and who identifies himself as a Dalit activist, had come to the village as a tenant. Slowly, his family acquired property in the village and have now entered the league of the landlord. He, along with some others started an association called Adhikar Darshan Manch, towards the end of 2014, without a clear agenda. It took up its first ever campaign which is called '*Jaanch padtaal jagrukta abhiyaan*' (verification awareness campaign). The pamphlet he brought out in this regard goes with two taglines: '*Kirayedaar jaanch padtaal ki chinta nahi, chintan kijiye*'[17] and '*kirayedaar rakh*

---

[16]Youth Brigade, Munirka Pamphlet, dated 13 October 2013.

[17]Do not worry about tenant verification; rather, contemplate about it.

rahein hain ya pangebaaz?'[18]As an NGO, it provides services for police verification of the tenants and also maintains a record of the various tenants who stay in each landlord's house, whoever chooses to use their services. It intends to work closely with the police and expedite the police verification process. It lists out the rights of the landlords and the number of ways in which they are troubled and the number of legally recognized situations where they can turn their tenants out. This attempt too did not really become successful because it could not generate much interest within the people. Firstly, police verification of tenants is not a difficult process to begin with and secondly, the NGO could not really figure out the logistics of maintaining the data of such a huge number of tenants which is always in flux.

The new crop of NGOs, youth associations, etc., though not very strong, and often having a short-lived existence, can be seen as attempts to new forms of surveillance and disciplining, which can be consolidated as new forms of accumulation. The strong emphasis on 'youth' is of importance here as these young men are constantly trying to make their presence felt by taking 'charge of the situation' in opposition to the elderly. The instability of these organizations owes itself to the fact that they are mostly still trying to find their feet in this network through defining their activities and have not been able to exercise the influence of panchayat, which has enjoyed historical legitimacy in these spaces. Many of them have toned themselves down on the rhetoric of Jat community and have become bodies with no clear agenda. These organizations have not been able to find this one function that makes them an important stakeholder and makes them absolutely indispensable for the real estate market.

The *Kunba*

Number 5, or Jungi Lane in Shahpur Jat, is an entire stretch of a lane with buildings on either side, all of which are numbered as various subdivisions of 5. The two ends of the roads have a gate each, with a semi-circular board saying '*Dada Jungi Lane: Yeh aam raasta nahi hai*'.[19] The transformation, or rather the creating, of Dada Jungi Lane is one of the most striking stories of change in the village. Chaudhary Hetram had built five *haveli*s (old-style mansions) for his five sons within the same compound which has now almost been refashioned to function as a niche, separate lane within the chaos of Shahpur Jat. The courtyards have disappeared, and so have the *baithaks*.[20] Tanya Sachdeva, who owns a boutique in Shahpur Jat, recalls that she used to come here in the 1990s to buy material for the

[18]Are you renting out to a tenant or to a troublemaker?

[19]'Dada Jungi Lane: This is not a thoroughfare.'

[20]A covered courtyard kind of a place in the house, where the men would traditionally meet, chat and smoke tobacco. *Baithak*s have traditionally been a marker of social and economic capital as only rich Jat farmers could have *baithak*s in their houses.

company she used to work for. Suneet Varma, the famous designer, used to have a factory in Shahpur Jat in those days, which he used to run from one of the houses there.[21] 'It wasn't like this, the houses used to be very far apart', she says. She set up her own factory/studio in 2000 in Jungi Lane and soon put up a rack to display her designs as she started noticing interested customers around. Later, she opened up a proper boutique. It was still not a garment hub at that time. She started with paying Rs. 10,000 as rent for her place in 2000. In five years' time, that rose to Rs. 25,000. She tells me that the easiest way in which the landlords doubled their income was by breaking down their commercial property and splitting them into two. Though this meant some investment, it also fetched much higher returns.

Jungi Lane commands at least twice to thrice the rent as any other showroom in Shahpur Jat. The commercialization of Shahpur Jat started with Jungi Lane. As time has progressed, Jungi Lane has come to be an extremely posh and coveted piece for retail fashion houses. Since it is managed by an extended family, is run on very different rules, which is why it could be developed as almost a separate entity from the rest of Shahpur Jat. The landlords of Jungi Lane maintain a strict control of who can access this particular lane. Sachdeva tells me that the gate and board are relatively new, but the landlords have been roughing up 'unwanted' characters for quite some time. Sneha, who is also a fashion designer working out of Jungi Lane, says that though she is paying a much higher rent there, she does not mind it because she 'feels safe'. Despite having to work till very late, and being the only woman amongst several male *karigar*s, she has never felt unsafe or threatened because of the kind of control the landlords have.

Sharad, despite being a landlord in Jungi Lane, attempts to portray himself as very different from the older generation, as someone who is educated and sophisticated. He has now assumed the responsibility for the management of the lane along with his nephew who is roughly the same age. He has been making a consistent effort to spruce up the lane and manage it 'professionally', spending Rs. 500,000 on paving the lane itself. He felt that a sense of unity was required to 'maintain everything'. Realizing that unity in his family was going down, with internal bickering and such, he started organizing family get-togethers and lunches and even drink parties among his cousins. He says they would get initially heated up because of personal issues but then he had to get them to let go of personal grudges and work together. He says he has been able to get a lot of things going in the past 2–3 months. He has issued a 20-point guideline for the tenants of the place which includes not allowing pets, not littering the place, etc. He also wants to issue a guideline about erecting hoardings. 'Erecting 20 hoardings of different sizes does not get you more customers. That is stupid marketing', he says.

The reason many say that the Jungi sons have been able to develop their own property this way is the strongly knit *kunba* that they have, all of which has economic stakes on that one chunk of land. So while it is true that the older familial ties are breaking up, they are also being reified in other ways for economic

[21]Many famous designers like Suneet Varma and Manish Arora used to have huge factories in Shahpur Jat, which have now moved to Noida.

reasons. Their old-style *haveli*s have undergone phases of changes to become what we see as Jungi Lane. He tells me he was a banker with one of the foreign banks. Around the time he got married, he did not have a job. For 6 months, he was looking after property, '*aur yehi Jaton waale kaam*',[22] he says quite disparagingly. His wife, who was interested in fashion, inspired him to open a fashion store in Jungi Lane. Lalita, his aunt, recalls that her first stay as a tenant was in a leather factory which had two rooms, a courtyard and a bathroom, next to their cowshed. Slowly, around 15–20 years ago, they created a basement to rent out to garment factory owners. At the time of her husband's death in 1998, her rent income was Rs. 11,000 per month. She started constructing and renovating her property according to the needs of the tenants to increase her income. She looks at the house and says, 'I do not even remember the number of times I have renovated this place'. After her husband's death, they moved out and started living in a smaller house and began reconstructing the house that she lives in now. The plush living room that we were sitting in was at one point of time a huge hall which was later split into two. She says she was always very creative about the construction and would keep thinking about new ways of reconstructing her three buildings to increase her rental income. Many in the family, on seeing her success and guts, decided to do the same and started emulating her. Sharad, she says, has a lot of calibre and has been able to bring the entire family onto the same page. She is full of praise for him for having worked really hard to get the family together and make possible things that have never been possible. It is not very easy to draw consensus among 100-odd family members; 'not everyone is alike', she says.

Jungi family has been able to maintain a certain prominence in Shahpur Jat by having been able to transform their own land into a separate and niche fashion lane which is gated. It has been able to get together all the stakeholders and work towards its upkeep and also rules that hang on the gates that apply to anyone accessing the lane. Not only do they offer 'protection' and 'safety' to their customers but have also been able to charge their upper middle-class customers much higher for the niche, gated existence within the urban village. They realize that the reasons they have an edge over others in Shahpur Jat is because of the fact that they have been able to channelize their familial wealth into creating Jungi Lane and that they have been able to work together as a unit, as one single entity—the Jungi Family.

Conclusion

It is also important to understand how specifically violence, in the case of Munirka, is always kept at the level of liminality, of being palpable, at least towards the tenants from the North East. There have been sporadic cases of violence, ending up in street brawls or scuffles, but all-out violence has never taken

[22]'…and the work that the Jats do.'.

place. A certain level of dominance, which can be achieved over a community by deploying tactics of racism, does not threaten their source of income, but perhaps only goes on to create scope for more extraction. Through maintaining an order of dominance by the landlords and the presence of palpable fear, accumulation is perpetuated. Unlike Munirka, in Shahpur Jat there is no sense of palpable tension between the different sections of people inhabiting together. The villagers here seem to have reconciled to the presence of men and women from the fashion industry, dressed in ways that are absolutely alien to the cultures of the village. Yet, Shahpur Jat does not see this kind of animosity that the North East community in Munirka experiences. In fact, the relationship between the tenants and the landlords is quite the opposite. Most landlords here claim, 'I am not like others here, you see. I will help people in whichever way possible'. These claims are often corroborated by several boutique owners and entrepreneurs. The reason for this being, that commercial places face the threat of flight of capital which residential spaces do not. The young landlords of Shahpur Jat strutting around in Western formals are constantly trying to portray themselves as suave and smart with sharp business acumen. This is not to imply that feelings of animosity, hatred, violence are make-believe and are deployed for instrumentalist purposes by the landowners (Jat and non-Jat). The already existing feelings of racism and hierarchy mutually reinforce the process of accumulation, by threatening or arm-twisting their tenants. The fear of violence, caste domination and the process of accumulation in cases like this are, therefore, not really adversely related. In the case of the Shahpur Jat, for a section for which big capital is new, they probably also realize how fickle the nature of money is. Flight of capital is, therefore, not something that is entirely impossible given the rate of gentrification of the city, which is converting small shopping complexes into elite shopping areas and villages into 'chic and alternative' pockets of the city. This does not seem to be a threat in residential urban villages such as Munirka, because it taps into the cheap, lower middle-class residential market in south Delhi, which is entirely a sellers' market.

These institutions and associations, some successful, some failures, take the question of autochthony, the identity of the *gaonwala* seriously, and build the institutions of RWA/panchayats, youth associations and NGOs. Straddling both modern forms of associations and older questions of autochthony and belongingness makes possible a form of violence that is almost institutionalized. The palpability of violence in these residential quarters, which are also sources of earnings and livelihood, serves the instrumental purpose of maintaining a certain domination which is institutional-, caste- and class-based and goes on to strengthen the process of capital accumulation. Therefore, the story of capital, in its social life, meanders through institutions like caste, domination and exploitation and is exercised through fear, violence and claims of autochthony.

However, I would also refrain from arguing that the questions of caste solidarity, claims of autochthony and racism are merely being exercised for instrumental purposes. What is important here is to understand how questions of autochthony and belongingness which might be pre-market in their origin, work themselves within the logic of capital. The fear of violence, which exists at the level of liminality, rarely flares into a full-blown confrontation. The curious ways in which capital and community (kinship, caste and the village) reinforce each other, as land becomes real estate, can be understood through how these three different forms of social institutions have worked themselves around the task of controlling the real estate market within the *lal dora*.

This chapter locates these various groups as a loosely based cartel which comes into being in order to protect the real estate market. The cartel allows for the land to exist as primarily in the sellers' market. Rates are fixed arbitrarily; rules are made at the level of these units and also violence perpetrated. Rent seeking, therefore, cannot happen without establishing certain kind of dominance, sometimes a threat of violence like in the case of North East for capitalist accumulation. David Harvey (1974), taking from Marx's conception of rent, attempts at theorizing the system of house rents through what he calls the 'class monopoly rent'. He looks at how urbanization creates relatively permanent, man-made resource systems which contributes to the high value of land. He talks of a class of professional landlord managers and speculator-developers. Here, he argues that the land passes to speculator-developer through landlords. Harvey takes into account how race and ethnicity play a role in this kind of spatial organization of the city as it helps to maintain exclusive, island like structures. I look at a scenario, where these two separate classes of speculator-developer and landlords collapse into one figure and how social basis of organizing a space is constantly being reformulated in its own socially coded ways. I argue that it is not simply a question of ground rent extraction we are dealing with but rather that of rent itself. It should ideally be a question of rent because it is a matter of control over a certain resource through exercising monopoly. The act of tearing down one's house to build another to accommodate more; to start an RWA to collectively use money for attracting better investments; a family which manages its property like a joint stock company does, becomes a process of productive corporate capital. Hence, the flight of capital that in Harvey's thesis is so squarely important for a spatial-temporal fix to happen at another geographical location; the space of these urban villages need to reinvent themselves so that the spatial temporal fix could be retained at the same location. This capital formation happens at the nook and crannies of big capital. This is petty capital which has its own limitations in terms of merging into big finance capital. It is for this reason that this capital cannot be allowed to flow. This capital needs to be secured, maintained and most importantly retained at the same location through a method of rent seeking.

And in order to retain this capital in a geographically contained space, a community once dispossessed has to come up with new organizations, new methods and forms of accumulation. The panchayats, RWAs, associations and *kunba* are, therefore, trying to become institutions of this loosely based cartel, trying to devise ways in which to perpetuate the spatial-temporal fix to continue that particular form of accumulation. While at many moments they might be in competition with each other, for example, the Shahpur Jat RWA of which Karan is a part is competing with the *kunba* of Dada Jungi Lane in order to reach its levels of real estate value by constantly attempting to better its own upkeep and infrastructure.

However, in times of crisis, duress or elections, they often function in unison. The fact that most of these organizations are tentative and flexible in terms of their form or their functions, because in many ways they are still attempting to figure out how to fully control the real estate market that is not only complex but also slippery and elusive.

References

Anonymous. (1999). *Munirka*. Delhi: Birandra Singh Tokas.

Chowdhry, P. (2009). *Contentious marriages, eloping couples: Gender, caste and patriarchy in Northern India*. New Delhi: Oxford University Press (paperback edition).

Delhi Development Authority (DDA). 1957. 'Work studies relating to the preparation of master plan for Delhi 1962' (vol. 3). Delhi: Government of Delhi.

Dhapola, S. (2014). Delhi: Munirka's campaign against gandey log of North East. *Firstpost*. 19 February. http://www.firstpost.com/india/delhi-munirkas-campaign-against-gandey-log-of-northeast-1396833.html?utm_source=ref_article

Firstpost. 2014. "Manipuri Minor Girl Rape by Landlord's Son, One Arrested", 8 February. Retrieved January 9, 2014, from http://www.firstpost.com/india/manipuri-minor-girl-rape-by-landlords-son-one-arrested-1380247.html

Harvey, David. (1974). Class-monopoly rent, finance capital and the urban revolution. *Regional Studies, 8*, 239–255.

Harvey, David. (2004). *The 'new' imperialism*. Socialist Register: Accumulation by Dispossession. 40.

IANS. (2014). Khirki residents' anger forcing Africans out of area. *The Times of India,* 1 February. Retrieved January 9, 2016, from http://timesofindia.indiatimes.com/city/delhi/Khirki-residents-anger-forcing-Africans-out-of-area/articleshow/29712670.cms

Nandi, J., Bhattacharya, S. (2014). Anti-North East fiat in munirka, cops step. In. *The Times of India*, 18 February. Retrieved January 9, 2016.

Pati, S. (2015). The regime of registers: Land ownership and state planning in Urban villages in South Delhi. SOAS South Asia Institute Working Papers (vol. 1, pp. 17–31).

Sanyal, Kalyan. (2007). *Rethinking capitalist development: Primitive accumulation, governmentality and post-colonial capitalism*. New Delhi: Routledge.

Tawa Lama-Rewal, S. (2007). Neighbourhood associations and local democracy: Delhi municipal elections 2007. *Economic and Political Weekly*, *24* November, 51–60.

The Indian Express. (2014). "Kejriwal, delhi police engage in high-voltage faceoff as AAP govt begins protest at raisina". 20 January. Retrieved January 9, 2016, from http://indianexpress.com/article/india/india-others/live-kejriwal-sits-on-dharna-against-police-anarchy-shinde-says-cm-must-be-patient/

Tilly, Charles. (1989). Cities and state in Europe 1000–1800. *Theory and Society, 18*(5), 563–584.

Yadav, B. (2009). Khap panchayats: Stealing freedom? *Economic and Political Weekly*, 26 December.

Accumulation at Margins: The Case of Khora Colony

Shruti Dubey

Abstract This chapter discusses the transformation of a village called Khora at the border of Delhi, Noida and Ghaziabad (both satellite towns of Delhi) to throw light on the peculiar form of capital accumulation happening over there. Khora has rapidly changed from being a sparsely populated village in 1971 with a total population of 656 to a census town in 2011 with a population of 189,410. While these are official census figures, the actual numbers living in Khora seem to be much more with newspaper and other media sources reporting around 1 million in 2013 calling it 'Asia's biggest labour colony'. Since the high-density development of Khora is essentially linked to the development of Noida, the author shows how accumulation in Khora is tied to the new town of Noida. Khora now is an intensely dense colony which is home to a labouring population ranging from factory workers, guards, domestic helps, auto-rickshaw drivers, rickshaw pullers, rag pickers, scrap dealers and collectors. One way to look at Noida, with the foreign investments and Export Processing Zones (EPZs) on one hand and places such as Khora on the other hand, is as a classic case of uneven development. The author also looks at the way in which spaces such as Khora themselves become nodes of accumulation for various classes ranging from the erstwhile owners of farm land to migrant workers and the ways in which the two modes of accumulation interact.

Keywords Labour settlement · Migration · Uneven development · Accumulation · Urban transformation

S. Dubey (✉)
Centre for Political Studies, Jawaharlal Nehru University, New Delhi, India
e-mail: dubeyshruti2006@gmail.com

I.K. Mitra et al. (eds.), *Accumulation in Post-Colonial Capitalism*,
DOI 10.1007/978-981-10-1037-8_6

Introduction

This chapter is about the transformation of a sparsely populated village called Khora at the border of three cities/districts: Delhi, and the Noida[1] and Ghaziabad districts of Uttar Pradesh, into one of the most densely populated unauthorized colonies of Asia inhabited mostly by low-income migrants from Uttar Pradesh, Uttaranchal, Bihar and Bengal. This transformation primarily took place due to the development of the satellite town of Noida, which was created in 1976 to decentralize economic activities from the capital, prevent in-migration and decongest the metropolis; to curb speculation around the land close to Delhi giving rise to unplanned growth; to provide an alternative site for absorbing non-conforming industries in Delhi and to provide affordable housing at a manageable distance from Delhi (NOIDA 1983). The model of development followed in Noida was similar to that of Delhi. An industrial authority was constituted by an act of the state government that gave the responsibility of land acquisition and development of the villages notified under them. Khora was one of the villages notified and eventually acquired by Noida. The theoretical effort in this chapter is to explore the various regimes of accumulation involved in the development of industrial new towns such as Noida in the post-liberalization economy through the case study of Khora. The fieldwork for the following chapter has been done in the months of March and April 2013 and April and May 2014.

The sequence of this chapter is as follows. In the first section, we will describe the current location of Khora village and colony and its surrounding areas in Delhi, Noida and Ghaziabad. In the second section, we will look at the plan of the Noida authority regarding the development of Khora, the 'illegal' speculation on the ground and the developments before the acquisition of the land from the farmers. This will highlight the form of capital accumulation intended by the authority on the land of Khora village that was partly jeopardized by the unauthorized plotting and occupation of land. In the third section, we will look at the actual development of Khora, the micro-economies operating there and the way in which different classes of residents are accumulating or subsisting there. We will probe why Khora colony is always expressed in terms of a 'lack', in terms of municipal services, infrastructure and a legal status as the most densely populated 'labour colony'[2] in Asia. We will see the interconnection between the formal and informal economy and housing. We will argue that accumulation is possible for not just the Yadav village landowners but also for the low-income migrants ranging from shopkeepers, auto-rickshaw drivers, factory workers, scrap dealers, lower end

[1]Initially, an acronym for New Okhla Industrial Development Authority (NOIDA), but now referring to the district itself.

[2]The term 'labour colony' is used by newspapers and a number of residents themselves. It does not refer to any administrative categorization.

government servants and school teachers in a space like Khora. In conclusion, we will try to theoretically locate the form of development happening in Khora.

Location of Khora Village and Colony

The Khora village, with its extended *abadi*[3] in the form of Khora colony, is situated between the south eastern periphery of Delhi, the south-western periphery of Ghaziabad and north-western periphery of Noida. Being located on the eastern fringe of Delhi, it is in the vicinity of a landfill site at Ghazipur, a wholesale meat market, Gharoli village and its extension, and is contiguous with Mayur Vihar Phase III, a moderately developed residential colony. The canal of the Hindon River marks the north-western boundary of Khora colony, while the National Highway 24 separating Noida and Ghaziabad forms its northern boundary. It is flanked by gated group housing societies in Indirapuram built by private developers on the side of Ghaziabad and surrounded on the Noida side by the institutional area of Sector 62 in the east, and Rajat Vihar, a posh, gated residential colony in the south. Khora has rapidly changed from being a sparsely populated village in 1971, spread over an area of 426.55 ha in the Ghaziabad *tehsil* of Meerut district[4] with 96 households and a total population of 656 (Census 1971, p. 55) to a population of 189,410 in 2011. This increase was not evenly distributed over successive decades. The progression reported in the official census was 844 in 1981 (Census 1981, p. 54), 14,751 in 1991 (Census 1991, p. 260), 99,506 in 2001 (Census 2001) and 189,410 in 2011 (Census 2011). Officially, Khora has been declared a census town in the 2011 census. While these are official census figures, the actual numbers living in Khora seem to be much more with newspaper and other media sources reporting around 1 million in 2013.

The 'Unintended' Development: Noida Master Plan and Khora

The formation of new industrial town of Noida was announced in 1976 in the vicinity of Khora village and by 1978 the Noida authority officially brought it within the development area of its Master Plan via the notification 2691-Bha-U-18/11-27/NOIDA/77 dated 18 May 1978 (NOIDA 1983). Though the land of Khora was notified in 1978, its acquisition took place only in 1989–1990. This is

[3]It is an administrative term differentiating agricultural land with settled land. There is no English counterpart.

[4]Ghaziabad used to come in Meerut District till 14.11.1976 when it was carved out as a separate district of Uttar Pradesh.

because the development of sectors in Noida had started from another direction with the land of Haraula, Chaura, Raghnathpur, Naya Bans, Jhundpura, Nithari and Atta villages to be acquired first. In fact, the first Draft Master Plan of Noida released in 1983 with a perspective of development till 2001 mentioned Khora village as an agricultural area that was to be separated from the proposed adjacent residential areas of 55–56 through a green belt. Thus, there was no plan to develop Khora till a long time after the notification of the village. But the notification only enhanced the land speculation in Khora that had already started at the borders of Delhi due to increasing land prices over there. Khora started attracting colonizers and property dealers mostly from Delhi around the same time from the late 1970s onwards. This led to a considerable unauthorized development of Khora colony before its land could be acquired by Noida. The first person to come to Khora village to cut a colony was a dealer called Khurana from Shahdara, Delhi.[5] He bought land in Khora for a pittance at Rs 70/*bigha*.[6]

Around the same time in 1981, the National Highway 24 was inaugurated that connected Ghaziabad and Noida to Delhi by road and also served as an important trade route in north India. Khurana bought land a few years before the construction of the National Highway. Sardar Singh Yadav, one of the natives of the village, believes that Khurana already knew that the National Highway was going to come up in the area and had thus bought huge portions of land at extremely cheap rates. The first colony that he constructed was called Maharishi Garden. In order to attract population over there and give the colony a settled look, he primarily cut small plots of 25 sq. yard each. Some of these plots were given on rent to his employees, others were distributed either for free to poorer people living in Delhi or for a meagre rent of Rs. 150.[7] Pramod Kumar Thakur, a migrant from Odisha, who came to the colony in 1987, pointed to an ironical situation whereby the cost of the land was as low at Rs 40/sq. yard and the registration was more expensive at Rs 100/sq. yard. No one believed at that time that there could be a settlement over her.[8]

The dealers would buy land from the farmers, make maps of the area and sell them to migrants. The registry of transfer of land used to happen under the name of the original landowner or the villager himself and the dealers would make profit in between the deal. Sometimes, when the dealer could not sell all the land, the farmer himself sold it to the outsiders. Soon the farmers learnt how to sell their land and became dealers themselves. Rishi Fauji, the pradhan of the village from

[5]It was confirmed in several interviews with Sardar Singh, Deshraj Singh, Balle Pehelwan and Balwinder Singh. Other initial developers were also from surrounding villages in Delhi such as Chilla and Khichripur (personal interview, Sardar Singh).

[6]Personal interview with Deshraj Singh Yadav on 24 May 2014. *Bigha* is a local measurement of land.

[7]Personal interview with Pramod Kumar Thakur, famous as 'Udiya' because he hails from Odisha. A number of other respondents also told me that the government was encouraging the poorer population ousted from Delhi to settle over there.

[8]Personal interview, Pramod Kumar Thakur.

2000–2005, gave me examples of how farmers themselves became dealers and started the plotting of their farms on their own. He contended that the sons of farmers became property dealers and sold their land ahead to their relatives, dealers from outside or incoming migrants. The starting price of selling of land was Rs 30 per yard in the late 1970s. The pace of selling land increased a lot after 1990 with the increase in the flow of migrants to Noida.[9]

Khora village had a huge segment of 1200 *bigha*s as Left Main Canal (LMC), or government, land.[10] The farmers sold the LMC land to the migrants as well with the collusion of the *lekhpal* (scriber), *pradhan* (village head), property dealer and the police. This was possible because the LMC land fell between farms and it was difficult to distinguish the government land from the one owned by the farmer. In fact, one piece of land was sold several times by the owners. This was because a lot of times the buyers did not take immediate possession of the land they bought. The powerful in the area used to occupy that land and sell it to someone else. Even after taking compensation from the authority in 1990, the farmers kept on selling the land to the incoming migrants.[11]

The Second Master Plan with the perspective of 2011 was released in 1989, considering the fast pace of industrial development of Noida especially after 1985. The land next to Khora village, originally comprising of residential sectors of 57 and 58, was converted from residential to industrial for small- and medium-scale industries, and additional industrial areas were carved out in its proximity (NOIDA 1989). Since institutional areas were supposed to be located along the National Highway 24, the land use of Khora village was proposed to be institutional. The authority wanted to take possession of the whole land of the village including that which was illegally occupied. Thus, they went to Khora with bulldozers in order to demolish the unauthorized occupation in 1987. There were around 1,000–2,000 houses then. Amidst chaos and gunshots, the authority demolished parts of the settlement. One of the residents of Khora died in the incident. This stalled the demolition, and the bulldozers went back. The authority did not try to demolish it again immediately because of the casualty in the last incidence. Meanwhile, the villagers started selling their land desperately to the incoming migrants at very cheap rates. Those who bought land also started constructing rapidly so that demolition would become difficult. The authority left the area on its own, and in the words of a retired town planner, it was left 'free for all'.

After a few months of demolition, N.D. Tiwari, who was the Chief Minister of Uttar Pradesh, came to Sector 11 Noida to inaugurate the Nehru Youth Centre. People of Khora reached there and *gherao*ed (lit. circled, crowded) the chief minister. N.D. Tiwari heard their grievances. He was told that the Noida authority regarded the occupation of Khora as illegal, but there were already a number of residents living in the colony who had legally registered their land transactions.

[9]Personal Interview with Rishi Fauji on 12 May 2014.

[10]P.I., Rishi Fauji.

[11]Personal Interview with Vikram Yadav, Gram Vikas Adhikari, Khora, on 12 April 2013.

They in fact demanded development from Noida as it had been done in other villages. N.D. Tiwari assured them that the colony would not be broken and there would be development of Khora.[12] Though the state did not take any steps for the development of Khora, the announcement increased the prices of land over there from Rs. 100/sq. yd. to Rs. 250/sq. yd.[13]

The authority had realized that it would not be able to demolish all the unauthorized encroachment in Khora that had spread in a huge area and acquire the whole land of the village. In 1988, the then Land Acquisition Officer ordered a survey by the government to ascertain the *khasra*s (land registers) that had been occupied by the residents and those that were free to acquire. It was found in the survey that *khasra* no. 1–537 had been occupied. The rest of the land was taken by the authority. Out of 1,400 acres around 500 acres was acquired by the authority and the compensation was awarded from 1990 to 1991.[14] All the landowners were dissatisfied with the amount of compensation awarded to them and filed cases in the court to increase the amount of compensation. In order to prevent further expansion of Khora, the CEO of the authority ordered the construction of an 8-feet wall around Khora village and colony and separated it from the planned area of Noida.

The institutional and commercial area of Sector 62 was built on the land acquired from Khora as per the Noida Master Plan 2021. Bharat Bhushan, a retired planner who was on deputation to Noida from 1997–2001 to 2005–2006, said that the residential colony of Rajat Vihar, Indus Valley School, Karl Huber School and Sabzi Mandi (vegetable market) were recent attempts to salvage whatever pockets were available and were not encroached by the residents of Khora.[15] In fact, it was Bharat Bhushan himself who expedited the change in land use from institutional to residential by appealing to the state government for the construction of Rajat Vihar and institutional to commercial for the construction of shops in Sabzi Mandi in Sector 62, Noida. He firmly believed that if it were not for the efforts of Noida authority, the residents of Khora would have encroached on all the pieces of land that were available in its vicinity. For the planners, Khora represents an encroached space that could have produced much more surplus value for the authority and contributed to the GDP of National Capital Region, but has instead acted as a source of devaluing the land in and around Khora.

Thus, Noida did not take charge of its development, and Khora was left to fend for itself to attain basic infrastructure. In 1997, the carving out of the new district of Gautam Budh Nagar from Ghaziabad and Bulandshahr districts that incorporated Noida administratively separated it from Khora, which was left in the Ghaziabad district. This gave rise to a conflict of jurisdiction whereby both

[12]Personal Interview with Deshraj Singh Yadav on 24 May 2014.

[13]Personal Interview with Sardar Singh Yadav on 20 May 2014.

[14]Personal Interview with Deshraj Singh Yadav on 24 May 2014.

[15]Interview conducted on 4 May 2014.

Ghaziabad and Noida kept on shifting the responsibility on each other for Khora's upkeep.[16] Consequently, Khora does not have access to municipal water, sanitation, health care and sewage services usually provided by the state. Interestingly, the telephone and electricity connections come from Noida, while the police station that oversees Khora is located in Indirapuram, Ghaziabad. Despite the fact that Khora village gradually transformed into an unauthorized colony, with the rise in the number of those engaged in non-agricultural activities, it is still governed by a *gram panchayat* (village government). There are two members from Zila Panchayat (top tier of village government), one *pradhan* (head) and 15 block development committee members that are elected from Khora. Although Khora represents a village which has undergone tremendous densification and become urban in character, it still does not formally come under any municipal authority. It has 150 *mohullas*, or neighbourhoods, and 1861 lanes,[17] though most of the roads are in bad condition. With narrow lanes, open drainage and bad roads, the area seems to be a stark aberration compared to its neighbouring areas in Noida and Ghaziabad, which look far more posh and upmarket.

Khora as a Dynamic Space of Accumulation

Noida has built a well-planned institutional area with schools, management institutes and multinational companies such as Barclays in Sector 62, on the land acquired from Khora that is keeping with its aspiration of being a 'futuristic city'.[18] Its attempt to build a wall around Khora seemed to be part of its desperate efforts to confine the illegal encroachment and hide the 'problematic interstice'[19] in the otherwise well-planned area.[20] In this section, we attempt to look at the socio-economic life behind the walls in Khora and outline the dynamic ways of accumulation going on in Khora.

[16]'Khora rots as Noida Ghaziabad disown colony', *The Times of India*, Noida, 28 May 2001.

[17]'Sadkon-galionkajaal: sab tootiphootibadhaal, '*Navbharat Times*, Ghaziabad, 5 May 2011. 'A network of roads and valleys: All dilapidated'.

[18]http://www.noidaauthorityonline.com/about-noida.html, accessed on 13 October 2013.

[19]Abdou Malik Simone (2007, p. 465) has written about how immediate peripheries of metropolises, usually occupied by devalued populations thrown away from central areas, are often considered as 'problematic interstices' between differentiated poles.

[20]Khora represents an undesirable space for Noida. I got extremely anxious responses from the town planners of Noida. A retired town planner asked me why I had chosen Khora as a case study as it would reflect badly on the image of Noida. He considers Khora as a clear case of state failure. The current chief town planner of Noida also got irritated on being questioned about Khora. He asked me angrily if I wanted to give solutions or increase their problems by asking about Khora.

Accumulation Through Rent: Erstwhile Villagers and Property Dealers

The land of the farmers in Khorahad is to be acquired by the Noida authority for its development, and they had to pay them compensation. This could not happen as it was desired by the authority because of the plotting done by dealers and then the farmers themselves. The pace of plotting started increasing by 1984. This was in consonance with the increase in the establishment of industries in Noida. The dealers and farmers tapped in on the demand of shelter of the initial influx of the working class and other low-income migrants who could not afford to buy housing or land for low-income groups (LIGs) and economically weaker sections (EWS) elsewhere in Noida. Thus, even before getting compensation for the land that was eventually acquired by Noida, the farmers, in this case the dominant Yadav community amongst the villagers, sold their land to dealers or migrants.

A number of people bought land during this time: dealers from nearby areas who saw an opportunity to sell land to the migrants, factory owners in Delhi and Noida who built housing for their employers, local police who in collusion with the *pradhan*, dealers who cashed in on an opportunity to make money by selling land or flats[21] and, ironically, the lower officials in the authority themselves. After the announcement by N.D. Tiwari and a considerable unauthorized development, the residents and incoming migrants were reasonably sure that the colony would not be demolished. Hence, Khora was seen as an investment opportunity where they could buy land for cheap and sell it further whenever it was profitable. Land transactions happen at a very high rate in Khora. Various welfare associations formed by the migrants wrote to authorities in the state government staking a claim to development by mentioning the fact that the state earns revenue in lakhs due to the high rate of registries happening in Khora.

Since the 1990s, a rent economy has flourished in Khora. The main partakers in this economy are the erstwhile landowners/farmers from the dominant Yadav community[22] who have invested the money gained from selling plots in constructing buildings within Khora for the working class. There are different kinds of buildings. They could be either single-storeyed row houses with a courtyard in between or multi-storeyed buildings in which rooms are built in a row. In the absence of municipal supply of water, the Yadav or Gujjar[23] landlords who live in Khora colony also sell drinking water from tankers or have installed RO and refrigeration

[21]Personal interview with Sardar Singh Yadav on 20 May 2014.

[22]It needs to be stated that all those belonging to the Yadav caste are not referred to here as the dominant class involved in colonizing. We are specifically referring to the extended kinship networks of the three Yadav families that were there in Khora, who owned the land that was acquired by the Noida authority. There are a considerable number of migrants who also belong to the Yadav community who are working in factories or running small businesses of their own.

[23]A community spread over western and northern India, particularly Rajasthan, Punjab, Haryana, Delhi and Uttar Pradesh.

plants for their renters and others in the colony. Dharma Pal Yadav, relative of Rishi Fauji, owns around 10 buildings and 10 tankers. All his sons have their own tractors and tankers. Most of the buildings that he owned were one-room flats for workers, but the most recent building that he constructed in 2011 has two bedroom flats to be rented out to more prosperous families.[24] His brother Rangpal Yadav who lives in Lalkuan, Ghaziabad, bought back a building on his ancestral land that had been sold twice by his grandfather in Khora in 2003 for 26 lakhs for a plot of 272 sq. yd. There was hardly any profit in the land when his grandfather had sold the land. But he bought it back due to the booming rent economy in Khora. The building has 32 rooms, and he earns around Rs. 2,000 from each room. He has another similar building in Chaprail, Lalkuan, but the rent is lesser there. He has around 20 plots in different parts of Ghaziabad which are lying unused. He would either sell them at bigger profit later or make more buildings or just let them lie fallow. He claimed that instead of buying farmland, he prefers to invest in plots.[25] Similar buildings are owned by dealers living outside Khora who only come to take rent once in a month.

They also sell as well as rent out land for markets. There are a number of markets inside Khora that have been constructed on the land owned by the Yadavs. Some of the shops have been bought, and some are taken up on rent by small-time businessmen in Khora. Kalu Yadav, the de facto *pradhan* of the area,[26] invests the money earned from rent of the several buildings and shops in the area in cutting colonies elsewhere. He is currently cutting colony in Chajarsi, Ghaziabad. Cutting colonies is a practice of carving out new informal colonies from the land acquired as mentioned above.

One can add to this the way a select group of migrant settlers there have tried to get rich through what can be called subsidiary entrepreneurship. In Khora, we have to remember is a dynamic space and it offers opportunities to some lower income groups to not merely subsist in a need economy but also save money to do business. Being the contact zone of three cities, it gives locative advantage to Khora of accessing three cities, thereby increasing employment opportunities. The ability to combine residence and work is one of the chief advantages of Khora. The high pace of industrialization has continuously attracted migrant labour from the relatively underdeveloped parts of UP, Uttaranchal and Bihar to Noida. The low-income housing constructed by the authority elsewhere was too expensive for poor migrants. They were also grossly inadequate in number because the authority

[24]Personal Interview with Dharmapal Yadav conducted on 7 April 2014.

[25]Personal Interview with Rangpal Yadav conducted on 8 May 2014.

[26]The *de jure pradhan* of the area is Brajpal Singh Jatav, who has been an old servant of Kalu's family. Kalu's maternal grandfather owned a lot of land in Khora. Since he had no son to inherit his property, his daughter's sons that is Kalu and his brothers claimed his property. Kalu supported him in the elections because the constituency of Khora had turned into a reserved seat in this election.

aborted the idea of construction of EWS housing by the mid-1980s. As a consequence, urban villages and slums were absorbing most of the labouring population. Khora presented itself as an affordable place for migrants where they could either buy a small plot because of the cheap land rates and earn a livelihood due to regulative flexibility to open shops, small workshops in the residence itself, or as in some centre enter as renters and save up enough to buy a plot later. Thus, a number of migrants came to Khora as renters or squatters and were able to buy their own piece of land in due course of time. The homeowners have also incrementally built rooms to be given out on rent. Those who are in lower end government service and own land in Khora have constructed rooms, the number depending on the size of the plot, on upper floors to give on rent. Different sources of income can be easily combined in Khora. Thus, a small general store within the house to supplement the family income is one of the most common phenomena. The reason for density of Khora is that it is a place where everyone finds work. Some of these economic actors have gone on to become 'little capitalists'.

In order to illustrate the way in which accumulation takes place by a select group of migrants in Khora, we will cite some concrete cases. Pramod Kumar Thakur,[27] locally known as *Udiya* (lit., someone from Odisha), has a small shop selling boring instruments. He installs and repairs borings and has hired two labourers for that purpose. He owns two private water tankers that he sends to Delhi, Noida and Ghaziabad. He also does property dealing, which is the main or side business of every second person in Khora. It is interesting to see how space is used by him. He built his residence and shop in a plot size of 50 sq. yd at the corner of the road. The ground floor had two shops and a room. The boundary of the house is formed by wall with a small gate to enter the house and two shutters of the shops that open outside on the road. The boring shop is in one corner and is separated from both the room in which they live and a smaller shop selling bread and milk that blend into each other, by a wooden wall made of the shelves containing the boring supply material of his shop. The wood wall doubles as a divider and a holder of things in the boring shop. There are two more rooms on the first floor for residential purposes. He was an ex-military person in Bhubaneshwar. He left the job in 1984 and came to Delhi where he started working as a contractor for boring and installing pipelines in Mayur Vihar in east Delhi. Pramod said that dealers were encouraging people to live there for free as they wanted to show it as a settled colony. Hence, he moved to Khora with his family in Vandana Vihar for free in 1987. There were a few houses built in the area where no one lived then. Once he was sure that the colony would not be demolished, he bought a land for himself in 1991.

Ghanshyam[28] came from the village to Delhi and stayed in Lakshmi Nagar and then in Rajbir Colony and then in Khora. He did odd jobs such as *beldari* (job of a skilled labourer) in Delhi or vending vegetables, eggs and ice candies. He used to

[27]Interview conducted on 2 May 2014.

[28]Interview conducted on 4 May 2014.

earn around Rs. 60 per day in *beldari* then, while his income increased to Rs 300 per day by vending. He was living in Rajbir Colony on rent in the adjacent village Gharoli when he got to know about a colony being made in Khora in the early 1980s. He bought land at Rs. 70 per sq. yd. in Madhu Vihar, next to Mayur Vihar Phase 3 and made a house bit by bit. He himself used to be a scrap cart puller in the vicinity in Delhi. He then took up a shop on rent and eventually bought a shop close to his house. He employs around 7 cart pullers who collect scrap from the lanes that are assigned to them and sell them to Ghanshyam in the evening. They either live in Khora or the nearby villages in Delhi such as Gharoli and Khichripur. He sells the scrap to bigger godowns in Delhi in the nearby Patparganj Industrial Area and Shahdara. Now, he owns two more plots in Noida Sector 63 of 50 sq.yard and 90 sq. yard each.

Khora has a number of small-scale industries like that of textile printing, dyeing and manufacturing food products. The garment export houses in Noida find it profitable to give orders of printing and dyeing clothes to smaller workshops in urban villages or unauthorized colonies such as Khora that take smaller orders in accordance with the needs of the export houses. They first try out a sample of clothes in the market and increase the number of orders according to the demand. Mahipal Singh Yadav[29] bought 100 sq. yard land in Khora in 1990. He used to work in a small shop in Sector 10 where he lived. His work was seen by a foreigner, and he got his first huge order. It was from the payment that he received from him with which he bought land in Khora. He opened a printing house on the ground floor and made his home on the first floor. Yadav gets his orders from established export houses of Noida such as Bani Cloth House, NY International. The export houses supply the cloth on which he prints and send the vehicles to collect the finished orders. He had employed two workers who hailed from Farrukhabad district which is famous for textile printing. The labour employed at Mahipal's workshop also live on rent in Khora. Sometimes, they live on rent at their employer's house.

Khora: A Storehouse of Devalued Labour and Economy

The lowest rung living in Khora includes those who do not own any land and are living on rent in Khora. The rent of a single room ranges from Rs. 1,500 to 3,000. They are primarily rickshaw pullers, rag pickers, scrap cart pullers, labourers in the repair or printing shops and young factory workers earning something between Rs. 7,000 and 12,000 in Noida, most of whom are employed on a contractual basis. In addition, the low end unskilled labour such as security guards, domestic help, nannies, sweepers, drivers and cooks that are required to support those with corporate jobs and lifestyles, who form, in the terminology of Saskia

[29]Interview conducted on 13 May 2014.

Sassen (2002), the 'survival circuit' of the global city, also live on rent in Khora. The high density of Khora colony and other urban villages in Noida certifies the fact that this population cannot afford to live or squat in the planned areas of the city. It is a concentration of devalued population, and the illegal status and lack of infrastructure ensure that its land value also remains low as compared to other parts of the city.

It has absorbed not just the devalued population but also the economic activities that are important for the functioning of the core cities but are shifted in margins or peripheries. For instance, Khora is used as a storehouse by many companies. Dhoom Singh Yadav, a native of the village, has rented out space to Maruti for keeping cars for repairs. A number of dealers of the paper market that has been shifted from Old Delhi to Ghazipur have kept their machinery or operating small plants in Khora. There are hardly any free plots in Khora. Most of the free plots have been rented out to be converted into open or closed godowns for collecting and sorting waste of all kinds of recyclable material ranging from plastic bottles, cartons and paper. Khora has also become a shelter for the rag pickers from Bengal who have been ousted from Noida. The larger plots have been converted into temporary shelters made up of tarpaulin sheets where the waste pickers both live and sort waste into different gunny bags and sell to the godown owners.

A number of scrap collectors as well as godown owners have come from Delhi because of the ceilings that have been in place from the last decade. Sunil has his house in Delhi in Shakkarpur and used to have a godown where he stored the waste collected and distribute in various parts of UP, Uttarakh and Haryana. Because of the fear of ceiling that was going on a large scale, he moved to Khora which falls under UP and has no threat of ceiling. His godown is on a plot of 2000 sq. yd., and the rent for it is around Rs. 6,000. He said that ceiling in Delhi is now discontinued and he could go back to Delhi. But he is on good terms with his landlord. He trusts him and hence is assured that his material would be safe at night.

Similarly Naresh[30] is a scrap collector who works for Ghanshyam. For the first 8 years, he used to work in Delhi. But he believes that the police used to nag them more in Delhi. '*Police ka chakkar wahan jyada hai. Yahan par aisa nahi hai kyunki ye UP pad jata hai*'. [It is better to work in Khora because it falls in UP where he can work freely.] They do not harass the vendors and cart pullers as much as they do in Delhi. He says that everything that is produced in Noida and Ghaziabad is also produced in Khora. There is a lot of garment export. People have machines in their houses. They produce a lot of *katran* (strips) that is put in a bundle and sold to waste collectors. The scrap is sorted and then distributed to Ghazipur from where they are sent to Muzaffarnagar in UP, Punjab and Haryana. The scrap is ultimately sold to factories that melt them and use iron to make different goods.

[30]Interview conducted on 15 April 2014.

Conclusion

The opening of the Indian markets due to liberalization have made the peri-urban areas or the new towns in the vicinity of big metropolitan cities in India the privileged sites of global financial investment due to the feasibility of land acquisition for establishing SEZs, EPZs and offices of the emergent IT/ITES sector (Kennedy 2007).This form of capital accumulation necessitates large-scale infrastructural projects via public–private partnerships causing the development of some parts of the city that appear as 'world class' and devalue others. The internal geography of these towns gets reshaped according to selective capital investments leading to 'uneven development'(Smith 2008) that gives rise to 'splintering urbanism' (Graham and Marvin 2001) and 'fragmented cities'. Swapna Banerjee-Guha (2010) looks at this process as leading to shifting cores and peripheries; the former being a part of global society and latter remaining in the form of segmented localities. The result is co-existence of gated communities and malls on one hand and slums, unauthorized colonies and urban villages, giving rise to intense urban conflicts.

The above fragmentation is true in the case of Noida as well. Noida aspires to be a future city, well integrated into the global economy, and as a hub of businessmen and professionals. The post-liberalization investment in Noida in the industrial, residential, institutional and financial sector has made it attractive for the professional class engaged in immaterial labour. At present, there are around 27 SEZs in Noida and Greater Noida, dealing with IT, ITES and electronic hardware (26) and one unit with non-conventional energy (Dupont 2011). It has also become a thriving real estate destination bringing in tremendous investment in multi-storey group housing by private developers. But this is only one half of the story. The other half of the story highlights that 70 % of the population in Noida lives in urban villages and slums in Noida. The population living here is not a part of the global economy that Noida is proud to be plugged in. This is what the current scholarship of Marxist geographers has referred to as lopsided or uneven development. While we agree with the fact that cities such as Noida are unevenly developed, the question that we are interested in probing is whether uneven development means a binary between accumulation economy and need economy? Would a space like Khora come under the rubric of need economy? We argue that Khora lies somewhere in between an exclusively accumulation and need economy.

As we have looked at in the previous section, one of the most obvious modes of capital accumulation in Khora is from the rent economy. The accumulation by the native Yadav villagers is a result of the housing gap left by the Noida authority for those who form a part of the survival circuit of Noida. The fact that the Noida authority could never acquire most of the land of Khora implied that the farmers were never really dispossessed of the land. They sold their land to the incoming migrants and kept a substantial size of land with themselves on which they built buildings to rent out rooms to be let out to them, once the population of low-income migrants increased in Noida. Thus, the theoretical frameworks of primitive accumulation or accumulation by dispossession[31] for understanding land acquisition for urbanization whereby land is taken away from the peasants, depriving them of their means of production and rendering them into wage labour does not work completely for Khora.

The density of Khora has ensured that it is not only a space of production but also a space of consumption by offering a huge market. We have shown that all those migrants who bought land in Khora when the prices were still cheap have also been able to accumulate. They could use the land innovatively, open shops, workshops and godowns within their houses and find a ready market for their products either within Khora or in other parts of Noida, Ghaziabad and Delhi. David Harvey, in his article 'Right to the City,' appealed for a democratic control over the production and use of surplus (Harvey 2010). Khora seems to be a place where the low-income migrants could own and flexibly use the land according to their needs. Close proximity of residence and work, readily available labour as well as market, ability to combine various sources of income were the reasons for incremental development. This gave them a greater control over the production and use of surplus and hence an avenue for accumulation.

The most visible economy is that of spare parts and repair shops of automobiles, scooters, electrical appliances, boring pumps and collection, sorting and distribution of scrap and waste. In other words, Khora is quintessentially a space of dirty, devalorized material production and the habitation of devalorized material labour. It can be said that the post-1990s development in Noida has tried to 'bypass the squalor' (Bhattacharya and Sanyal 2011) present in Khora, be it by shunning its responsibility as it administratively falls under Ghaziabad or by constructing a wall around it. Thus, it appears as if development has skipped Khora. We have argued that it is a product of the development that takes place in cores of the cities and is in fact extremely essential to the functioning of core as core. Though Khora is often looked at as peripheral, marginal or as skipped by development, it is in fact most crucial for the development and maintenance of the 'cores'. They are the constitutive outside of the core. If Noida can be considered to be the core, the accumulation by the authority is happening by the entry of FDI and private capital in residential, commercial and industrial sector especially post-liberalization. The densification of Noida has happened also primarily after 1990s due to the gap that is left in the housing of the huge low-income migrant population. Also, the activities concentrated in Khoraform an integral part of the economy of Noida. The household industries, shops and workshops form a part of supply chains of the small-scale industries in Delhi, Noida and Ghaziabad of food products, hosiery and garments, paper and printing, basic metal industries, repairing and other services. Thus, we have made a case for considering Khora as a dynamic space of accumulation that is core to the development of Noida.

[31]David Harvey has argued that the violence associated with the accumulation of capital in the 'primitive' stages is very much part of the contemporary urban processes operative through dispossessing people from their means of production (Harvey 2005).

Acknowledgment This research was conducted as a part of a project called "Global Suburbanisms: Governance, Land and Infrastructure in the 21st Century" housed at the CITY Institute, York University, UK.

References

Banerjee-Guha, S. (2010). Introduction. In S. Banerjee-Guha (Ed.), *Accumulation by dispossession* (pp. 1–16). Delhi: Sage.

Bhattacharya, R., & Sanyal, K. (2011). Bypassing the squalor: New towns, immaterial labour and exclusion in post-colonial urbanisation. *Economic and Political Weekly, 46*(31), 41–48.

Census. (1971). *Primary census abstract.* Series 21, Part X-B, Uttar Pradesh: District Census Handbook.

Census. (2011). http://censusindia.gov.in/2011-prov-results/paper2/data_files/India2/Table_2_PR_Cities_1Lakh_and_Above.pdf

District Census Handbook. (1981). *Village and town directory.* Series 22, Part XIII A, Uttar Pradesh.

District Census Handbook. (1991). *Primary census abstract.* Series 25, Part XII-B, Uttar Pradesh.

District Census Handbook. (2001). *Primary census abstract.* Ghaziabad district. Uttar Pradesh. Accessed from Census Data Centre, Jawaharlal Nehru University, New Delhi on 10 September 2013.

Dupont, Veronique. (2011). The dream of Delhi as a global city. *International Journal of Urban and Regional Research, 35*(3), 533–554. doi:10.1111/j.1468-2427.2010.01027.x.

Graham, S., & Marvin, S. (2001). *Splintering Urbanism. Networked Infrastructures, Technological Mobilities and the Urban Condition.* London: Routledge.

Harvey, D. (2005). *The new imperialism.* Oxford: Oxford University Press.

Harvey, D. (2010). The right to the city: From capital surplus to accumulation by dispossession. In S. Banerjee-Guha (Ed.), *Accumulation by dispossession* (pp. 17–32). Delhi: Sage.

Kennedy, L. (2007). Regional industrial policies driving peri urban dynamics in Hyderabad. *India. Cities, 24*(2), 95–109.

NOIDA. (1983). *Draft Master Plan Noida 2001.* Retrieved September 10, 2013 from http://www.noidaauthorityonline.com/MasterPlanNew/MASTER-PLAN-2001.pdf

Sassen, S. (2002). *Global cities and survival circuits* (pp. 254–274). Holt Paperbacks: Global Woman. New York.

Simone, A. M. (2007). At the frontier of the urban periphery. *Sarai Reader 07: Frontiers* (pp 462–70). Delhi: CSDS. Retrieved June 10, 2016 from http://archive.sarai.net/files/original/e3366451a06d9bbe4187fac6a550ec91.pdf

Smith, N. (2008). *Uneven development: Nature, capital and the production of space.* Georgia: University of Georgia Press.

The Politics of Bank Nationalization in India

Suhit K. Sen

Abstract This study of the politics of bank nationalization critically explores the political change in India in the post-Nehru era. Indira Gandhi announced nationalization of 14 banks in 1969. At the same time, there was also another radical social policy: abolition of the privy purses. Between 1967 and 1969, there were prolonged battles about nationalization in India which had Morarji Desai, the then finance minister, opposing it on one hand, and the radical socialist wing within the Congress Party itself supporting it on the other. Meanwhile, the ex-communist elements in Congress had embarked upon an infiltrationist policy. The entire political situation was coming to a critical point where Indira Gandhi with the help of the younger crowd got into a fierce power struggle with the Syndicate who after Nehru's regime established control over the party organization. Against this background, bank nationalization of 1969 became a focus of attention. With a detailed history of that period, the author asks and explores a series of important questions that have played an important role in construction of the post-colonial Indian economy. The issues range from the actual achievement of bank nationalization—marginal increase in lending to the priority sectors, small-scale industry, agriculture, and export and marginal decrease in lending to large-scale industry and medium-scale industry—to its failure to stop unmitigated lending to the private sector and misuse of credit.

Keywords Bank nationalization · Congress politics · Post-colonial economy · Financial capital · Social policy

Introduction: An Overview

This chapter deals with the nationalization of 14 scheduled commercial banks in 1969 by the Congress government headed by Indira Gandhi and is part of a larger study of Indian political structures and processes in the years of her first stint as

S.K. Sen (✉)
Indian Council of Historical Research, New Delhi, India
e-mail: suhitsen@gmail.com

I.K. Mitra et al. (eds.), *Accumulation in Post-Colonial Capitalism*,
DOI 10.1007/978-981-10-1037-8_7

prime minister, between January 1966 and March 1977, ending with her party's post-emergency electoral loss in that year. This qualification has the important implication that the primary focus of the study is the politics that swirled around the issue of bank nationalization and its general outcomes rather than the technical aspects of the operations of the banks after nationalization.

The issue of bank nationalization had cropped up first in 1966 in the form of an election pledge. At an informal conclave of senior Congress party leaders following a Congress Working Committee (CWC) meeting soon after the Congress's serious reverses in the general elections—its majority in the Lok Sabha was reduced from 361 seats out of 494 to 283 seats out of 520, while it was voted out of power in seven states—the issue of bank nationalization was raised, alongside a raft of other 'socialist' issues such as the imposition of urban land ceilings and collective farming. It was a matter of some significance that the latter meeting was held to discuss economic issues so that the CWC would be aware of what the government was capable of implementing while passing its economic resolution. It was felt, in context, that the government was possibly not in a position to implement the issues mentioned above, though that did not prevent the demand for the nationalization of banks from being raised.[1]

The question of the nationalization of banks gained traction in the middle of May when the Hazari committee submitted its findings. The committee's remit included a study of the industrial licensing and the banking systems.[2] Among the recommendations made by the committee was the need for careful credit planning to reinforce priorities of national economic plans and the need, too, for guidelines to apportion credit to different sectors of the economy against the backdrop of nation's overall needs, not just in the light of collateral offered. It had also said that the big industrial houses should finance their investments from their paid-up capital and not from loans, so that public funds were available to smaller firms.[3]

With the Hazari committee setting the ball rolling, sections of the political sector, most particularly in the Congress party, could not but run with it. Just a few days later, at a meeting of the CWC, the issue of nationalizing banks cropped up again. All present agreed that this election pledge had to be fulfilled, though, it appears, there was no clarity (or unanimity) on what exactly bank nationalization entailed, and what kind and degree of control would be exercised over the relevant banks. Thus, opinions ranged from the idea that social control over banks would suffice, though what that entailed remained equally unclear—we shall have

[1]*The Statesman*, 8 May 1967.

[2]The Hazari report became something of a cause célèbre. Towards the end of May, a radical Congress MP accused some ministers of being in the pay of the Birlas at a stormy meeting of the Congress Parliamentary Party. The impugned ministers were K.C. Pant and Satya Narain Sinha, with the former defending himself, arguing that he had been a Birla employee before becoming a minister, and the latter admitting to being a member of two Birla trusts. The opposition pressed for an inquiry, which was acceded to, but after having dragged on for over two years, the issue was shelved. *The Statesman*, 27/29/30/31 May 1967; 1/2 June 1967.

[3]*The Statesman*, 16 September 1967.

occasion to return to the distinction between the two later—to the idea that it meant greater powers of control for the Reserve Bank of India (RBI) for the good of the people.[4] It bears noting at this point that though there was no unanimity or clarity on how exactly banks should have been nationalized, there was a widespread feeling in the party (or at least its leadership) on the need for bank nationalization. In other words, it was not the contentious issue it was later to become.[5]

At a CWC meeting in early May, the demand for bringing banking institutions under control was raised again, along with the demands for nationalization of general insurance, a phased takeover the export–import trade and some other 'socialist' demands[6] that later became the stock-in-trade of the 'radicals' in the party against the purported conservative proclivities of the oligarchs of the party, especially the 'Syndicate'.[7] But at this time, most of these issues, as mentioned above, did not seem to have raised many hackles among the party leaders, though it was reported that Deputy Prime Minister and Finance Minister Morarji Desai disagreed with the demand raised by Atulya Ghosh, the boss of the West Bengal unit of the party and a Syndicate member, for the abolition of privy purses paid by the government to rulers of the princely states (or their descendants) that had acceded to the Indian at the time of independence.[8]

Not very many days later, it was reported that Desai had reacted swiftly to reconstitute the boards of directors of the RBI and the State Bank of India, nationalized in 1955, in reaction to ardent pro-nationalization Congress leaders' criticisms in respect of the presence of industrialists or their spokespersons on these boards.[9] A month or so later, he asked representatives of banks to reorient lending policies in six weeks as a step towards the social control of banks, defined, against outright nationalization, i.e. the expropriation by the state of the shareholders of the banks of their holdings, as the exercise of greater control over the policies of private scheduled commercial banks by the government. The two sides agreed that banks should be more sensitive to people's needs.[10] At an All India Congress Committee (AICC) meeting on 23 June 1967, it passed a 10-point programme, which included the objective of imposition of social control over banks and rejected nationalization (Frankel 1978, pp. 397–98).

---

[4]*The Statesman*, 12 May 1967.

[5]Not unexpectedly, the communist parties were also pushing for bank nationalization. In August, they were formulating a two-pronged approach: press for bank nationalization in parliament and mobilize support for a strike outside.

[6]*The Statesman*, 13 May 1967.

[7]The 'Syndicate' was a group of state party bosses, including some chief ministers, who gained control over the Congress organization some time before Jawaharlal Nehru's death. There was some amorphousness about the group, but those definitely in it were K. Kamaraj of Madras, S. Nijalingappa of Mysore, Neelam Sanjeeva Reddy of Andhra Pradesh, S.K. Patil of Maharashtra, and Atulya Ghosh of West Bengal. The first three had at various points of time been chief ministers.

[8]*The Statesman*, 13 May 1967.

[9]*The Statesman*, 17 May 1967.

[10]*The Statesman*, 19 June 1967.

But the *contretemps* facing the Congress party in the wake of the electoral debacle allied to the recommendations of the Hazari committee were forcing the government and the organization in a leftward direction, after what was perceived to be a rightward shift in the post-Nehru era both under Lal Bahadur Shastri and Mrs. Indira Gandhi, culminating in the devaluation of the rupee, seen to be under pressure from what was to prove in later days a useful bogey, the USA. We shall not go into the involved politics surrounding the decision to devalue, nor its relative merits and demerits, except to note that it imparted to the byzantine internal politics of the Congress party a new dimension. The bickering and factional politics of the party, it is important to note here, created a divided high command, with oligarch pitted against oligarch, but also, crucially, widened the rift between the government and organizational wings of the party, epitomized by the virtual sundering of relations between the party president, K. Kamaraj, and the prime minister, Mrs. Gandhi. This in itself ratcheted up the problems of political survival with a reduced majority in parliament and the Congress party's defeat in 7 states. This, not unsurprisingly, gave the rank and file and second- or third-tier leaders space not just to manoeuvre but also to exert pressure. This opportunity was gratefully accepted by the motley group of young 'radicals', connected to or members of the Congress Forum for Socialist Action (CFSA), some of whom came to be known as the Young Turks. Thus, at an meeting in New Delhi, men such as Mohan Dharia, one of the leading Young Turks, and S.N. Mishra, deputy leader of the Congress Parliamentary Party and member of the CFSA, attacked the government for not implementing the party's programme, of which the nationalization of banks should have been, by their lights, an important part. But those taking part in aiming acerbic criticism at the government were not necessarily socialist; as noted, they constituted a motley crew of old socialists, those recently converted to socialism and the not particularly socialists (EPW 1967a, b).[11]

In late August, it was reported that the union cabinet would discuss the social control of banking alongside a raft of proposals to control wages, incomes, and prices.[12] This, of course, was consequent to a Rajya Sabha debate in May 1967 on a non-official resolution tabled by Banka Behari Das, a Praja Socialist Party (PSP) member. The government accepted at the conclusion of the debate an amended resolution committing itself to measures, not excluding nationalization, to extend effective control over banking resolutions. Subsequently, after an examination of policies and practices, the policy of social control over banks was announced in parliament in December 1967 (Ghosh 1979, p. 216). We shall return to what the policy was at a later stage.

Despite this, and the fact that the proposal for immediate bank nationalization had been defeated at the New Delhi AICC mentioned above, the demand for

[11]It needs to be noted that the terms socialism, socialist, and left were highly elastic in the context of Indian politics before and after, but especially after, 1947. For the Nehruvian period, this point has been pursued in greater detail in Sen (1998).

[12]*The Statesman*, 26 August 1967.

nationalization, i.e. the acquisition of the banks, remained an issue. It is noteworthy that it was the finance minister's rigid opposition to outright nationalization that blunted the demand, with the tacit support of the prime minister (Malhotra 1989, pp. 109–111). In October 1967, when the AICC met again in Jabalpur, Desai fended off a vigorous challenge calling for outright nationalization, again with Mrs. Gandhi's support. He had secured a majority some while ago in the Congress Parliamentary Party (CPP), while under attack from the Young Turks (Malhotra 1989, p. 111).

In September, Lalit Narayan Mishra, later a union cabinet minister, had called for bank nationalization,[13] while a few days later, the finance minister, Desai, inviting foreign investment, said banks had to satisfy the credit needs of agriculture and small-scale industry.[14] The latter statement being in line with the finance ministers clearly and repeatedly stated opposition to complete nationalization.

The picture at the beginning of 1968 and through that year was fairly clear. Young Turks, socialists, and assorted radicals were pushing for bank nationalization, but the party high command was fairly united behind Desai in opposing such a move for the time being, with the prime minister herself suggesting that the policy of social control should be given a chance for two years to deliver the desired results.

Bank Nationalization as a Political Instrument

The following narration of events will I hope clearly show that the issue of nationalization of banks was a political instrument. The nationalization issue staged a comeback in the public domain with a pretty big explosion in 1969, however, as the internal divisions deepened in the Congress party, with Mrs. Gandhi's camp on one side and the Syndicate on the other. By the time the AICC convened for its annual session in Faridabad, one of her biographers notes infighting in the Congress had intensified to the point that the Congress president, S. Nijalingappa, a member of the Syndicate, launched a blistering attack on Mrs. Gandhi, focusing on economic policies, especially public sector inefficiency. While the Young Turks tabled censure motions against Nijalingappa, which were ruled out of order by him, Mrs. Gandhi spiritedly defended herself, not knowing that at a meeting of a small committee of leaders, Desai had found himself hopelessly outnumbered (Malhotra 1989, pp. 115–116).[15]

A newspaper also noted editorially that there was no point in passing a Congress Working Committee (CWC) resolution to deal with internal 'revolts' (in the context of strife-driven politics in Madhya Pradesh), nor would it succeed in achieving its

[13] *The Statesman*, 12 September 1967.

[14] *The Statesman*, 17 September 1967.

[15] The meeting was said to have been attended by Kamaraj, Subramaniam, Jagjivan Ram, and Y.B. Chavan. No evidence for this meeting has been cited.

aim when the top leadership—the notorious high command—was itself riven by divisions in outlook which caused mutual attempts at causing embarrassment. Thus, the editorial said, while dissenting opinions were necessary in the party, they should not be actuated by the desire of a minority group to impose its will. The result was that political reverses had eroded its influence in the states and ability (or desire, my comment) to promote development and nurturing democracy.[16]

In the same issue of the paper, a commentator noted much the same thing but with greater prescience and at greater length. In the context of a crisis in the party caused by allegations made against the finance minister in parliament by Chandra Shekhar, a Young Turk member of parliament, the details of which are not pertinent here; he commented that though it was tempting to see the incident and its fallout as discord and division at the top, the problem was more complex. The CWC, he argued, was united in its desire to exercise control over the government, but beyond this it was hopelessly divided, this being true both of leaders and followers. These divisions led to mutual mud-slinging and attempts to pull the rug from under each other's feet. Low intrigue was resorted to in the belief that such behaviour would not upset the applecart. Thus, while top leaders such as Mrs. Gandhi, Morarji Desai, and Y.B. Chavan, the union home minister, did enough to antagonize each other, their camp followers exacerbated matters. The followers could be disciplined, but the initiative would have to come from the top, in other words, from Mrs. Gandhi herself. But Desai's reaction to the allegations made against him (he had threatened to resign) had put paid to this fond hope. Despite the CWC's pontifications on discipline, the commentator went on to say, the prospect of taking corrective measures was problematic, especially with the CPP in turmoil, reflecting the dire straits of the entire organization, headed ineffectively by Nijalingappa. The Congress party was on a downward slope and would not be able to arrest its descent. Then, he said with prescience that the CPP turmoil could reflect the thought of a parting of ways, which could be expedited by the high probability that there would be a coalition government at the centre after the 1972 elections. Bearing this in mind, factions could choose to split earlier rather than later to line up possible partners, with S.K. Patil, one of the party bosses who comprised the Syndicate, favouring a coalition with the Jana Sangh, Swatantra Party, and PSP, and others favouring a left coalition under Mrs. Gandhi (Malhotra 1969).

A couple of months after this piece was published, it was apparent that a serious clash was in the offing over the presidential election, especially since in the interim, the AICC annual session at Faridabad had witnessed the clash between Nijalingappa and Mrs. Gandhi. All contentious issues had, however, been shelved, for consideration at later meetings of the AICC or the CWC scheduled to be held in Bangalore. A commentator pointed to the two wings within the Congress party, the organizational and parliamentary wings, and went on to say that with the possibility of hung parliament in 1972, Congress leaders such as Kamaraj and Nijalingappa would plump for a presidential candidate steeped in the Congress tradition

[16]*The Statesman*, 14 March 1969.

(whatever that meant). The Syndicate had already eliminated potential candidates such as Gajendragadkar (a former Supreme Court judge) and Jayaprakash Narayan (or JP) who could have been acceptable to Mrs. Gandhi. In wanting a young, active candidate, they had eliminated V.V. Giri, then vice-president, though he remained a possible candidate if the prime minister kept her options open. But, the commentator wrote, whatever happened, no one could take away the prime minister's right to stamp her imprimatur on the party candidate, in other words, exercise a veto. As was her usual style, Mrs. Gandhi *was* keeping her options open until at least another round of eliminations. Unlike the earlier commentator, this one opined that within the Congress, the choice of candidate could lead to jockeying for prestige and position but not a showdown. To anticipate the outcome, the commentator could not have been more grievously in error (Singh 1969).

The 'jockeying' referred to had begun by then, with groups within the Congress preparing tactical plans for the presidential poll in anticipation of scheduled meetings of the Congress Parliamentary Board (CPB) and CWC. One group had started a signature campaign for V.V. Giri, it was reported, while another felt that Neelam Sanjeeva Reddy, at that time Speaker of the Lok Sabha and a member of the Syndicate, was a 'formidable' candidate.[17]

It was perhaps coincidentally but probably not that C. Subramaniam, a cabinet minister, a member of the CWC and a close aide of the prime minister, floated a proposal to nationalize five or six banks, though his reputation was quite the reverse of a socialist. Desai shot down the proposal saying it was pointless since the social control policy had not been given a proper chance.[18] These proved to be the first direct shots across the bows.

Meanwhile, it was reported that the choice of the presidential candidate could be postponed until a meeting of the AICC, scheduled to be held in Bangalore to resolve matters shelved at Faridabad. It was thought that making the choice in the prevailing climate of acrimony would not be wise. It was also reported that Mrs. Gandhi and Nijalingappa had had talks but had failed to resolve the problem. Various combinations and formulae were doing the rounds, including a joint Sanjeeva Reddy-Giri ticket.[19]

Prior to the Bangalore AICC session, it was reported that there would be a bitter wrangle over bank nationalization. The Young Turk, Chandra Shekhar, had circulated a document on economic policy insisting on the inclusion of bank nationalization in the party programme,[20] while the party president had circulated to the CWC (meeting on the eve of the AICC session) an official draft (prepared ironically by Subramaniam) that did not mention nationalization, but said the social control policy should be given a chance.[21]

[17]*The Statesman*, 19 June 1969.

[18]*The Statesman*, 21 June 1969.

[19]*The Statesman*, 8 July 1969.

[20]Frankel refers to this note, but does not ascribe authorship to anyone. In her narrative, it was prepared by a small group of CFSA members. See, Frankel (1978, p. 416).

[21]*The Statesman*, 9 July 1969.

What happened next has been copiously documented. Mrs. Gandhi postponed her trip to Bangalore by a day, thus being unable to attend the CWC meeting. But her cabinet colleague Fakhruddin Ali Ahmed tabled at the CWC session a note by her (later coming to be known as 'stray thoughts') on agricultural, financial, and industrial issues, which incorporated a number of policies and programmes mooted in Chandra Shekhar's note, including the nationalization of financial institutions. Desai reportedly reacted saying this would shake confidence in the banking system since the social control policy announced in Parliament in December 1967 had been embodied in legislation in January 1969.[22] Three strands were intertwining themselves: the growing schism within the party, the issue of bank nationalization, and the contention over the Congress party's presidential candidate.

The next day, at the AICC session, only Desai opposed bank nationalization; others either supported it or were non-committal, among the latter Mrs. Gandhi, who left herself elbow room for the two options of outright nationalization or tighter control by government. Mrs. Gandhi's note meant that the economic policy resolution prepared by Subramaniam would have to be enlarged or modified given that the ten-point programme adopted by the Congress at Delhi in May 1967 had favoured social control over nationalization, which did not figure in the resolution. It had been assumed that the Delhi decision had settled the issue. As for the details of the 'stray thought' note, it closely followed Chandra Shekhar's, in passages verbatim; as far as nationalization of banks went, however, she followed Subramaniam's formula referred to above, which envisaged nationalizing five or six banks or forcing scheduled commercial banks to buy more government securities to the tune of Rs. 250 crore, and retiring industrialist chairpersons of private banks' boards of directors.[23]

[22]*The Statesman*, 10 July 1969. Presidential assent for the bill was reported in *The Statesman*, 3 January 1969.

[23]*The Statesman*, 11 July 1969. It would be useful to differentiate between outright nationalization of and social control over banks. The former clearly meant complete takeover of banks on payment, in this case generous, compensation. This in turn meant in logistical terms that the government through, or in consultation with, the Reserve Bank of India (RBI) would constitute the boards of directors of the nationalized banks and appoint their chairpersons; additionally, it meant, at least on paper, that the nationalized banks would have to run their operations according to the directions of the RBI in respect of opening branches, setting interest rates both for deposits and advances, providing credit and other operations. Social control, on the other hand, meant that the National Credit Council (NCC) would assess the demand for credit from various sectors and determine priorities for grant of loans and advances. The objectives were broadly the same: divert credit from large industry and business towards what came to be known as the 'priority sectors': agriculture, small-scale industry, and exports. The council would be composed of representatives from various sectors; it was envisaged that the competing pulls of various interests would ensure a rational allocation of credit; a package of legislative measures was planned to ensure that decisions taken by the RBI would be followed by the commercial banks. For a full discussion, see Ghosh (1979, pp. 216–217, 226–228). A related development was the creation of a department of banking in the finance ministry, which reversed an earlier finance minister's decision to give all banking functions to the RBI (EPW 1969a, b, c, d, e). Another report said that the RBI had been placed under the department in all matters other than foreign exchange control; a deputy governor, who had taken over as secretary, had secured larger remit than routine administration of nationalized banks, including supervision of the National Credit Council.

But by the end of the AICC session, the Congress high command had once again displayed its talent for papering over internal differences. The resolution piloted by Chavan but moved by Desai dropped reference to nationalization in favour of tighter social control; it also dropped at Desai's insistence a clause providing for an implementation report at the next AICC session, dropping the stipulation of 'next session'. Chandra Shekhar kept up the pressure with a petition in favour of nationalization signed by 146 members. The radicals were happy since further discussions on the subject would have to factor in Mrs. Gandhi's note; the prime minister was happy at catching the bosses off guard and deflecting attention from the presidential elections; and Desai was happy that his position remained the stated policy of the party and, by inference, the government.[24]

It was reported the next day that with regard to the economic policy resolution, Desai had iterated his position that the social control policy was only 6 months old and expressed reservations about Mrs. Gandhi's note, adding it held no surprises. He also said that banks could be asked to increase investment in government securities to the extent of 5 % and that the newly formed National Credit Council, which was to play a major role in implementing the social control policy, would discuss the matter. The finance minister also defended the role of industrialists as chairpersons of boards of directors of private banks, arguing they were not influenced by the private sector, though he admitted that the government would have to be alert to the possibility. But the paper with which differences were papered over proved to be very thin. Chavan, speaking after Desai, said with reference to nationalization that the direction had been set and could not be reversed.[25] At the end, the economic policy resolution was passed in its original form, with Desai saying unity was needed and that there was no rift between him and Chavan though differences could remain.[26] The high command called upon the central and state governments to act on Mrs. Gandhi's note.

I have already pointed out that the issue of bank nationalization was inextricably linked to that of the Congress party's presidential candidate and the politics surrounding it. In an amazing display of simultaneity, the CPB announced on the same day that it had nominated Sanjeeva Reddy by a division of four votes to two. Kamaraj, Patil, Desai, and Chavan had voted for him; Indira Gandhi had proposed the name of Jagjivan Ram as a unity candidate; he and Nijalingappa abstained from voting, while Ali Ahmed voted with Mrs. Gandhi for her candidate. But this was just the beginning of a new round in a battle of attrition, some elements of which pertain to the issue of nationalization, which we will presently relate. But it needs to be said at this point that the bosses made their move not without apprehension, which is why they held back the announcement and asked Nijalingappa to talk to Mrs. Gandhi before it was announced. If these steps were intended to soften the blow, they failed. It was reported that when the prime minister left the

[24] *The Statesman*, 12 July 1969.

[25] *The Statesman*, 13 July 1969.

[26] *The Statesman*, 14 July 1969.

CPB meeting, she was supposed to have said that those who had foisted a candidate would have to 'face the consequences'.[27]

The shenanigans over the presidential candidature had two consequences, to anticipate the climax. The one that need not detain us was the split in the Congress following the result of the electoral contest, for Giri entered the fray and defeated the official Congress candidate.[28] He could not be faulted given that the Congress bosses had taken the literally unprecedented step of not seeking to elevate the vice-president to the presidential post. The other, which concerns us directly, was, to put it bluntly, the nationalization of the 14 large scheduled banks, sparing a few small banks and the branches of foreign banks. These two stories cannot, to be sure, easily be separated, mainly because the events that led to the nationalization of banks also led, eventually, to the split in the Congress via the outcome of the presidential elections. But the two stories have to be told separately to keep the focus attention on the bank nationalization because of the overall design of the project of which this chapter is just one part.

Within days, reports surfaced that a bill would be prepared on the basis of the prime minister's note to force cabinet colleagues to support measures approved by the CWC and AICC, even if they were not all part of formal resolutions.[29] The very next day, Mrs. Gandhi divested Desai of his finance portfolio. Desai quit, calling it retaliation against the CPB vote. Explaining her action, Mrs. Gandhi wrote a letter to Desai saying that given the party mandate, she would not like to burden him with the implementation of economic policy he did not agree with. What followed were efforts at managing what appeared to be a definitive crisis, with Desai refusing to withdraw his resignation despite a second letter from the prime minister.[30]

Without too much of a fuss, Mrs. Gandhi promulgated an ordinance nationalizing fourteen major banks.[31] The cabinet showed it the green light unanimously. The banks were estimated to have deposits totalling Rs. 2,000 crore. At the end of June, their outstanding credit was Rs. 3,536 crore. Under the ordinance, each bank would be an individual corporate entity managed by government appointees, to which end the existing boards of directors would be dissolved and advisory boards would take over; continuity of banking services would be maintained, however. A banking commission, already formed in January, would look into necessary structural change.[32] Profits, it was later said, would be transferred to the government by

---

[27]*The Statesman*, 13 July 1969.

[28]*The Statesman*, 14 July 1969.

[29]*The Statesman*, 16 July 1969.

[30]*The Statesman*, 18 July 1969.

[31]The banks were Central Bank, Bank of India, United Commercial Bank, Bank of Baroda, Punjab National Bank, Union Bank of India, Dena Bank, United Bank of India, Canara Bank, Syndicate Bank, Indian Overseas Bank, Bank of Maharashtra, and Indian Bank.

[32]*The Statesman*, 20 July 1969.

each individual entity.[33] I shall return to the objectives of bank nationalization, the need for it, if any, and the question of how bank nationalization played out, once I have pursued further the politics surrounding the issue and, briefly, how it survived legal hurdles to become law.

Hurdles on the Road to Nationalization

The ordinance was challenged in the Supreme Court, which stayed some of the provisions of the Banking Companies (Acquisition and Undertakings) Ordinance: it prevented the government from removing chairpersons, who had consequent upon the promulgation of the ordinance been designated custodians, and the provisions relating to compensation. The prime minister told the Rajya Sabha that till the disposal of the petition challenging the ordinance, the RBI would continue to advise the banks in accordance with the existing Banking Laws (Amendment) Act of 1968.[34] A bank nationalization bill was subsequently moved in parliament; amendments for referral to a joint select committee and the inclusion of foreign banks within the ambit of the bill were defeated.[35] The bill which was eventually passed by parliament was voided by the Supreme Court. It was reported that the finance ministry had ready emergency plans if some clauses were struck down, but was wrong footed by the sweep of the verdict.[36] An anomalous situation was created with government already in possession of the banks' assets. Two options were reviewed: an appeal for a stay to introduce fresh legislation, or introduction of another ordinance. Amidst the debacle, the government could take heart from the court's view that parliament had upheld the right of legislation to nationalize, though it had voided the particular act on a number of grounds, chief among which was that the government had been guilty of 'hostile discrimination' in banning the nationalized banks from engaging in any businesses and on the issue of compensation.[37]

There were confabulations between Mrs. Gandhi, senior colleagues, officials, and experts; the conclusion arrived at was that the entire banking industry need not be nationalized, though political pressure to do so would most likely build up, to meet the 'hostile discrimination' objection, the removal of a clause barring the erstwhile banking companies from carrying out non-banking businesses would suffice, and it was felt that compensation was the real issue. There was some palaver as well on whether to take the ordinance route, the law ministry's preference, or draft fresh legislation, the finance ministry's preference.[38] Finally, the ordinance

---

[33] *The Statesman*, 21 July 1969.

[34] *The Statesman*, 23 July 1969.

[35] *The Statesman*, 29/31 July 1969.

[36] *The Statesman*, 11 February 1970.

[37] *The Statesman*, 11 February 1970.

[38] *The Statesman*, 12 February 1970.

route was favoured and an ordinance passed to meet the Supreme Court's strictures as regards compensation, which was generous with provisions being made for payment in cash or in securities or a combination of the two, and ban on carrying out non-banking businesses, which was lifted.[39] The government got leave to introduce fresh legislation, which was eventually passed, bringing the judicial saga to an end.[40]

Politics of Bank Nationalization

In the period of time that elapsed between the first ordinance and the passage of the final bill, bank nationalization became the focus of intense politics. Let me begin with an editorial comment because it will help us shift our focus back on the politics of bank nationalization and subsequently the substance of the policy.

The Statesman had assailed the bill on the standard line that it was an iniquitous attack on property immediately after nationalization.[41] But in a later editorial, it made interesting and connected points about bank nationalization. First, it said, the measure was hasty and legislation badly drafted and unlike the takeover of the Imperial Bank, which became the State Bank of India after nationalization, was not preceded by proper groundwork, and pointed out that even the supporters of the bill had been in favour of referring it to a joint select committee. In fact, it pointed out with some justification that even days before the promulgation there was no indication of how many banks would be taken over, citing Subramaniam's proposal, repeated by Mrs. Gandhi, that five or six banks would be taken over. Second, it cast doubts about the prime minister's statement that 95 % of people supported the bill, referring to what it called the orchestrated rallies outside her residence in favour of the bill after the original ordinance had been promulgated. Third, it asked somewhat rhetorically that if the measure was non-partisan why had it not been brought in earlier and why had the government experimented with social control.[42] In essence, the editorial was saying that this was a partisan measure used by the prime minister in her battle with the party bosses, casting doubts about its relevance to the people and saying it was unnecessary.[43] In fact the last

[39]*The Statesman*, 15 February 1970. The Supreme Court order also rekindled the debate on the right to property. Some of those opposed to the order wanted it removed point blank, while others wanted it removed as a *fundamental* right.

[40]*The Statesman*, 28 February 1970; 25 March 1970. When the Lok Sabha passed this hugely controversial bill, only 80 members were present.

[41]*The Statesman*, 20 July 1969.

[42]*The Statesman*, 12 August 1969.

[43]Quite the contrary opinion was expressed by a correspondent, writing in EPW. In the context of the Congress (R)'s Azadnagar (Bombay) session, the writer said that though for the more sophisticated the effects of bank nationalization might have worn off, for ordinary people it remained a symbol of defiance of big business and held out hopes of change. EPW (1970a, p. 8).

point was explicitly made elsewhere as well, where it was argued that only 45 % of the banking business would be affected, the SBI and its subsidiaries accounting for 30 % and it was the small banks, which had been exempted, that served the small customers 20 %. (There is a 5 % deficit in the arithmetic, which we can assume was in the hands of foreign bank branches.)[44]

The first point made is fair. As our brief tour of legal hurdles has shown, the first set of ordinance and bill was drafted badly and passed in haste. It was, for instance, also reported that the first voided act was put up for the law minister, Govinda Menon, so late that he could not study it properly but nevertheless gave it his imprimatur.

This does suggest that the law was introduced hastily for political gains, as the editorial comment suggests. But it does not logically, or factually, in any way imply that the kind of popular support for nationalization that Mrs. Gandhi claimed for it did not exist and that rallies had to be 'orchestrated' to manufacture support. On the contrary, it does suggest that popular support did exist for the policy measure, which is why Mrs. Gandhi banked on it to give her the upper hand in the battle for control over the party.[45] Factually, it was clear that no major party opposed the move, except the Swatantra Party. The left and communist parties, and some in the Congress party, in fact wanted the measure to be more radical and include in its ambit the entire banking establishment, including foreign banks, and many, both in the ruling party and outside, felt that the compensation was too generous.[46]

M.R. Masani of the Swatantra Party and A.B. Vajpayee of the Jana Sangh had attacked the first bill when it was introduced.[47] Later the Jana Sangh merely asked for its referral to a joint select committee.[48] But the most revealing political position on bank nationalization was that of the Congress (O), the Syndicate wing of the by then split Congress. It was probably par for the course for Kamaraj to call for follow-up action on nationalization, since he had always favoured the move.[49] But it was not just Kamaraj. The parliamentary party of the Congress (O), CPP(O), had officially decided to demand nationalization of foreign banks, after the nationalization move. Though details of the meeting were not divulged, it was reported that Desai was party to the decision. It also decided to move amendments along such lines to the new banking bill. Asoka Mehta, once one of Mrs. Gandhi's inner circle, told the CPP(O) that to navigate the objections of the Supreme Court, all banks with deposits of Rs. 50 lakh and above, or those which could reach that mark, would have to be nationalized. Nijalingappa was also quick to point out that

[44]*The Statesman*, 28 July 1969.

[45]On this 'orchestration', Frankel writes, 'Although the demonstrations were, in part, organized by the CPI, the sentiments they tapped were clearly spontaneous'. See Frankel (1978, p. 420).

[46]*The Statesman*, 15 February 1970; also see EPW (1970a, b, c, d, e, p. 70).

[47]*The Statesman*, 27 July 1969.

[48]*The Statesman*, 30 July 1969.

[49]*The Statesman*, 12 February 1969.

the policy to nationalize banks was that of the undivided Congress, and Mrs. Gandhi was trying to make political capital out of the measure.[50] In a war of letters, preparatory to the great split, he had also accused Mrs. Gandhi of taking personal credit for bank nationalization.[51] Even second-tier leaders Tarakeshwari Sinha and Sucheta Kripalani had written to Mrs. Gandhi seeking nationalization of foreign banks, while Sharda Mukherjee had demanded in the Lok Sabha debate that the bill be referred to a joint select committee.[52]

What I am trying to show here is that bank nationalization was an intensely political and probably emotive affair. If Mrs. Gandhi used it as a political instrument in a political battle to achieve her ends, her immediate opponents spared no effort at denying her this success and trying to steal her thunder, while political parties in the visitors' seats pushed their own rhetorical, political and opportunistic agenda as well.

Bank Nationalization: Progressive or Retrograde?

But whether bank nationalization was used as a political instrument or not surely has no bearing on the merits of the case. An unnecessary and retrograde measure could be completely non-controversial and unanimous, while a necessary and progressive measure could well be a partisan political instrument. The question is that whether in the context of the times bank nationalization was necessary and if it was, did the implementation of the measure in the immediate years following its promulgation achieve its objectives, stated or otherwise.

In her broadcast to the nation on 19 July 1969, the day the fourteen banks were nationalized, Mrs. Gandhi explained that the measure was supposed to accelerate the objectives of social control: removal of control by a few; provision of credit to agriculture, small-scale industry (SSI) and exports (which came to be known as the priority sectors); professionalizing management; encouragement of a new class of entrepreneurs; and provision of adequate training and terms of service to bank staff. Later, in parliament, she emphasized the role of nationalized banks in fostering growth. These were the broad parameters: in operational terms nationalization envisaged a massive programme of branch expansion into unbanked areas to mobilize deposits and the diversification of bank credit to serve the needs of hitherto neglected sectors of the economy (Ghosh 1979, pp. 227–228).

One of the major achievements claimed for nationalization was a rapid expansion of branches, the number of people served on average per branch going down from 69,000 on 19 July 1969 to 26,000 in June 1976. There was geographical spread as well, with the number of districts with a population-to-branch ratio

[50]*The Statesman*, 15 February 1970.

[51]*The Statesman*, 31 October 1969.

[52]*The Statesman*, 1 August 1969.

of over 100,000 going down from 156 at the end of June to 19 at the end of December 1975. Inter-regional disparities did not change substantially, however, with most of the change happening in the first two years after nationalization. Looking at the performance of the nationalized banks from the point of view of not just the opening of rural branches, no significant difference can be noted. For instance, between June 1969 and June 1975, only new rural branches accounted for a substantial increase in terms of both deposits and credit (60.60 and 58.90 %), while in semi-urban, urban, and metropolitan areas, the figures ranged from 20 to 28 %. More significant was the fact that the share of rural branches in total deposits and credit in this period were a mere 11.50 and 8.40 %. Interesting, too, was the fact that in rural and semi-urban areas, the share of agriculture and allied activities in total advances in June 1973 was just 28.70 %, while industry and trade accounted for 50 %. The study of banking policy already cited also found that the licensing policy followed by the RBI was just a little too hands-off, leaving wide powers of discretion to individual banks in choosing locations for new branches. Though immediately after nationalization the RBI issued a circular specifying the number of unbanked areas in which the newly nationalized would have to open branches, indicating a bank-wise distribution, it issued another circular in February 1970 stipulating a ratio for opening new branches in metropolitan/urban areas, on the one hand, and rural/semi-urban areas, on the other; this inevitably brought the idea of the profitability into operation. A combination of these two meant ultimately that the banking system had neither the incentive nor direction to meet the overall developmental needs of the country, especially with regard to addressing the problem of regional imbalances and rural backwardness (Ghosh 1979, pp. 230–244).

Another positive feature has been noted: provision of credit to the priority sectors. D.N. Ghosh notes a sharp increase: in June 1969, public sector banks had borrowable accounts of Rs. 2.6 lakh, rising to Rs. 47.22 lakh in June 1976; in the same period, the quantum of lending rose to Rs. 441 crore to Rs. 2,527 crore. The percentage of lending to the priority sectors rose in the same period from 14.90 to 25.50 %. Within the priority sector, the most striking increase was in agriculture in which the share of direct finance (loans given to the end-user rather than to providers of inputs and services, state electricity boards for example) rose from 9.11 to 28.73 %. The increase in direct finance as compared to indirect finance has been noted, alongside the provision of finance largely to better-off farmers. The thrust was to provide loans for infrastructure development in the form of minor irrigation projects, installation of pump sets, and so on. Of term loans provided, 62.30 % went to those with holdings above 10 acres and 20.8 % to those with 5–10 acres. This pattern of providing credit to large and medium farmers persisted despite RBI guidelines exhorting the nationalized banks to provide credit to small and potentially viable farmers, without any specific direction (Ghosh 1979, pp. 269–302).

Further, Ghosh notes there was a clear sectoral redeployment of credit (evident despite some problems of classification) between June 1968 and June 1976. Large and medium industry found their combined share dropping from 60.60 to 37.99 % (though this statistic is rendered somewhat suspect because of classification issues); SSI found its share up from 6.9 to 11.00 % (after peaking at 12.1 % in June 1972); and agriculture went up from 2.2 to 10.40 %, though the direct finance component within it went up from 4.00 to 5.6 % (Ghosh 1979, pp. 305–308).

Finally, Ghosh notes the RBI's failures in respect of monitoring lending to prevent misuse of credit—commonly, for instance, the use of production loans to build inventories and stocks. He also notes that despite repeated attempts, the central bank failed to curb credit expansion to curb inflationary trends, but attributed that largely to government borrowing, both centre and state, the borrowings by public sector undertakings and entities like state electricity boards and loans for food procurement; in short to government passing expenditures previously met through budgetary resources on to the banking system (Ghosh 1979, pp. 305–330).

If Ghosh was a kind critic of government policy following nationalization, there were unkind ones around as well. And the columns of the *Economic and Political Weekly* gave them hospitable space. Thus, no sooner had the nationalization measure gone through, a correspondent enthused about its possibilities, urged integration of the banking system with the planning process, gave more general advice such as the need for a credit policy, but warned that business as usual would scupper the promise: changes in top personnel, lending policy was necessary; the present boards of the SBI and RBI, the correspondent warned, should not continue in present shape to let management continue in old style (EPW 1969a). In much the same vein of enthusiasm and exhortation, a correspondent warned that since the majority of credit would continue to go to big industry in the near future, credit policy would have to be calibrated against the underlying approach to the monopolies bill then being considered and licensing policy reform. It said credit must be treated as a scarce commodity and rates of interest had to reflect that scarcity (EPW 1969b).

In page after page, issue after issue, correspondents urged one fundamental point: that the derailed planning process had to be restored and within that process a bold, holistic credit policy had to be inscribed to bring out precisely those changes in the Indian economy that Mrs. Gandhi had promised in her post-nationalization broadcast. As the enthusiasm dimmed, the criticism of the government, the RBI, and the nationalized banks started becoming strident and metronomic.

But in the early days, the tone was optimistic. Knowledgeable sources, a report said, had it that it should be possible 'to stretch itself adequately' to open 4,000 new branches in three years in under-banked regions of Uttar Pradesh, Bihar, Madhya Pradesh, Orissa, Assam, and Jammu and Kashmir (EPW 1969c). A report in a national daily, however, put out a much more cautious report: that an RBI committee had envisaged a two-phase plan for under-banked areas: some with 10,000-plus population to be banked by March 1970 and 197 towns with population less than 10,000 in Assam, Bihar, Jammu and Kashmir, Madhya Pradesh, Orissa, Uttar Pradesh, and West Bengal by end 1970.[53]

[53]*The Statesman*, 15 September 1969.

Mrs. Gandhi appeared to mean business when she told the custodians of the nationalized banks, within the stipulations of the Supreme Court order, to open branches, mobilize deposits, and devise credit arrangements through personal investments. She also told them they would get treasury business and public sector accounts, which till then had been SBI's sole preserve and warned them that she had come to hear that some bankers came under extraneous pressures 'traceable to links with big business' (EPW 1969e).

At a session of the All India Congress (R) Committee, a note to the committee said loans to agriculture had risen from Rs. 162 crore to Rs. 250 crore (time period not specified) and 350,000 farmers had been covered. The report on the event pointed out that this could also have been achieved under the social control regime; in fact, it went on to say, it was likely that the momentum created in that period was responsible. It also said that banks were showing little initiative in reaching out to agriculturists, small industrialists, and exporters; what had transpired till then did not amount to a policy, especially since there was no clarity on which segments of agriculturists were to be covered or what the impact would be on production or traditional suppliers of credit (EPW 1969d, p. 958).

The first anniversary of bank nationalization, when the banks' custodians met, passed without fanfare. A commentator said it had done so with good reason; deposit mobilization had slowed down. The writer also noted that the ratio of currency to monetary resources had gone up in a year of unprecedented growth of bank branches and this needed to be inquired into. Conceding the point that most of these branches had been opened in areas with low deposit potential, the columnist pointed out that even in farm-surplus areas, deposit mobilization had not taken off, as in Punjab, even though procurement had put money into farmers' hands (EPW 1970e). But on an optimistic note, another report said 1,067 branches had been opened in the first nine months after nationalization, of which 628 were in unbanked areas (EPW 1970d).

By the middle of 1971, after the Congress (R)—the Mrs. Gandhi faction—won an unprecedented majority in the Lok Sabha, no coherent credit policy had been worked out nor fundamental conceptual issues cleared, though 2 years had passed since the bank nationalization move had been announced. The debate over differential rates of interest made that quite obvious. The report of a committee set up by the RBI had recommended that weaker sections and the priority sector be provided loans at a rate of interest lower than the usual. This finally sparked off a debate, with some commentators pointing out that the rate of interest was not the real issue; the real issue was the availability of credit, given the fact that the bulk of credit available especially in rural areas was from moneylenders, which commanded a much higher rate of interest than any institutional credit anyway. Such were the issues that led critics to berate the government on its failure to implement the bank nationalization policy in any meaningful way (EPW 1971a).

But an official press note struck an obviously optimistic note: deposits up 17.6 % in June 1970–May 1971 as against 15.3 % June 1969–May 1970; 2,934 branches opened between 19 July 1969 and 30 April 1971; advances to 'neglected sector' rose faster in comparison with other banks; thus, while the nationalized banks' contribution had been 14.50 % in June 1969 and 21.20 % in June 1970, it constituted 22.8 % in March 1971. The riposte to this note was: So what? Private banks' deposits had grown in the same period by 16.7 %; as far as new branches went, while the numbers opened had been 1,658 between July 1969 and June 1970, between July 1970 and April 1971, 1,276 branches had been opened, with the monthly average down from 138 to 128. Excluding the SBI group, the figures were 99 and 80. Advances had gone down to Rs. 15.20 crore between July 1970 and March 1971 from Rs. 26.90 crore between July 1969 and June 1970. The statistical war was, however, a sideshow. The point of the riposte was that the nationalized banks seemed to be adrift, functioning without an overall plan. A further suggestion was that with the enthusiasm of the early months ebbing, the policy of bank nationalization was running aground (EPW 1971b, p. 1414).

Let me shift gears a little and fast forward to 1974. The burden of criticism in the early 1970s was that the government and RBI were not moving fast enough to formulate a coherent credit policy, to bring it into line with development goals, and the planning and budgetary process; in other words, it was in the realms of broader ideological and political issues. By the mid-1970s, these were not the main issues anymore. Expectations among the intelligentsia had evaporated. Now the criticism had more to do with technical issues: the nitty-gritty of credit-control mechanisms; persistent criticism of the RBI for sticking to failed formulae; the details of monetary policy as it related to seasonal credit expansion, not adequately compensated by contraction; and other minutiae. To this was added what seems suspiciously valid, if somewhat trenchant, criticism of the RBI (and, at least, by implication of the government) for not being able to force banks to direct credit to the priority sectors and colluding with large corporate houses, the substantial traders and peasants in misusing credit obtained for productive purposes to indulge in hoarding, stock-building, profiteering, and related criminal activity, especially in periods of shortages and spiralling prices.[54]

Six years or so after the bank nationalization law was passed, the eminent economist Datta (1976) took a look at what it had achieved. First, he noted, the former owners were happy; they had not only been generously compensated, but since the compensation had been paid to the companies rather than individuals it could be used for new ventures. Moreover, the former owning groups found their influence with their old banks undiminished and no serious change in operations.

But it would be wrong, Datta argued, to say that no improvements had been made in the directions desired: deposits of public sector banks (including the SBI) had risen from Rs. 3,897 crore at the end of 1958–1969 to Rs. 9,936 crore at the end of 1974–1975 and thence to Rs. 11,500 crore at the end of January 1976. The number of branches had increased from 6,595 at the end of June 1969 to 15,077 at the end of June 1975. Advances, too, had risen from Rs. 2,783 crore in July 1969 to Rs. 6,466 crore in December 1974; advances to the agriculture sector had risen

[54]See for instance, EPW (1974a, b, 1976). This is a small sample of *EPW*'s reportage on these issues.

from Rs. 162 crore to Rs. 706 crore, of which Rs. 478 crore was in the form of direct finance. Advances to the priority sectors combined rose from Rs. 645 crore to Rs. 2,509 crore.

But, Datta showed, deposits of private scheduled banks rose 4.23 times in comparison with the 2.55 times achieved by the nationalized banks in 6 years; the SBI's branches multiplied 2.21 times, those of its subsidiaries 1.95 times, those of the 14 nationalized banks 2.29 times, and those of the private scheduled banks 2.56 times. It could be argued, Datta went on, that the figures flattered the smaller private banks because they began from a low base, but the fact that their deposits rose from Rs. 441 crore to Rs. 1,869 crores and number of branches from 1,320 to 3,385 did not speak highly of the brave new world of nationalized banking. Moreover, if the performance of private banks was a matter of a deliberate licensing policy, it did not explain why, consistent with the objectives of nationalization in the first place, nationalized banks were not given priority; the logical policy would have been to bring all possible bankable assets under government control. As for rural branches, the figures, themselves not impressive, were rigged since most branches labelled rural were actually urban or suburban. Moreover, Datta added it was not just a question of number of branches; at the end of June 1974, rural branches accounted for 7.8 % of deposits and 5.3 % of advances.

Datta concluded by damning the Lead Bank Scheme, the centrepiece of nationalized banking, with no praise, calling it a chaotic failure, not inconsiderably because of unhealthy oligopolistic competition via interest rate wars and competition for deposits (Datta 1976, pp. 781–786).

Conclusion

This brief review of some of the outcomes of the nationalization of fourteen banks leaves us with some propositions: first, though a programme of branch expansion had been successfully undertaken, its early momentum was lost after a couple of years, especially with regard to concentrating on unbanked or under-banked areas; second, there was some success in deposit mobilization; third, redirection of credit to the priority sectors was not conspicuously successful up until the mid-1970s, though some reallocation had happened; fourth, the success in channelling credit to the agrarian sector was vitiated, in terms of stated objectives, by the fact that credit was almost completely monopolized by the rich peasantry, which was not altogether surprising since the first few years of bank nationalization coincided with the new agricultural strategy or green revolution and the political economy of the agrarian sector; fifth, though large industry's share of the credit pie was somewhat reduced, the feeble attempts made by the RBI to impose credit-control measures could not prevent its ability, and the ability of big commercial players and rich agrarian interests, to circumvent these measures to direct credit received to purposes other than those stipulated; such credit was often, in fact, diverted to fund unlawful activities such as hoarding and stockpiling scarce commodities in times of shortages and price rise, exacerbating the endemic economic crises of the time; and, finally, massive year-on-year credit expansion became difficult to control to a significant extent because of government borrowings, both at the centre and in the states, and the demands for credit made of the nationalized banks for purposes such as running public utilities such as state electricity boards, transport corporations, and procuring food grains, earlier funded by the government itself through budgetary support or other means.

So the big gainers from bank nationalization were the rich peasants and government, while credit support for big business and industry was not compromised. The weaker sections and 'small' people had once again been given short shrift.

Yet as political events of the following years showed, at the end of the day, the state could claim that it had come out of a financial crisis that bank nationalization had proved to be a welfare instrument for poverty alleviation goal and for the required task of poverty alleviation government had the money. In the history of the financial strategy of a post-colonial state, this was a novel step. Future history showed that the bank nationalization had proved a critical step towards facilitating capital accumulation through at least stabilizing the society and providing bank credit to various kinds of loan seekers, including the big cat defaulters. With this, also would start the game of the big cats of pressurizing the government to lower the interest rates and get loans and secure exemptions of all kinds. A different crisis would appear down the road. This, however, is a different story.

References

Datta, B. (1976). The banking structure: A Re-appraisal. *Economic and Political Weekly, 11*(21) (22 May), 781–86.

Economic and Political Weekly (henceforth EPW). (1967a). Not a Simple Revolt. *2*(26) (1 July), 1151–1152.

EPW. (1967b). Revolt in the AICC. *2*(26) (1 July), 1160–61.

EPW. (1969a). Budget plus banks. *4*(28–30), Special Number: 1093–1094.

EPW. (1969b). Starting points for a policy leap. *4*(31) (2 August), 1093–94, 1256.

EPW. (1969c). Programme for branch expansion. *4*(32) (9 August), 1292.

EPW. (1969d). Starting points for a policy leap. *4*(37) (13 September).

EPW. (1969e). Modest beginnings. *4*(40) (4 October), 1579.

EPW. (1970a). Azadnagar socialism on tap. *5*(1) (3 January), 8.

EPW. (1970b). Uncertainly poised. *5*(7) (14 February), 70.

EPW. (1970c). Economic post-mortem on the split. *5*(25) (20 June), 958.

EPW. (1970d). One year after: The prospect. *5*(29–31), Special Issue: 1129.

EPW. (1970e). Unfinished business. *5*(29–31), Special Issue: 1107–08.

EPW. (1971a). How cheaply to lend little. *6*(27) (3 July), 1305.

EPW. (1971b). Floundering without a plan. *6*(29) (17 July), 1414.

EPW. (1974a). Credit Policy: Loss of credibility. *9*(17) (27 April), 692–94.

EPW. (1974b). Money delusion. *9*(24) (15 June), 929–30.

EPW. (1976). Uneasy portents. *9*(4) (24 January), 85.

Frankel, F. R. (1978). *India's political economy, 1947–77: The gradual revolution*. Princeton, NJ: Princeton University Press.

Ghosh, D. N. (1979). *Banking policy in India: An evaluation*. Bombay: Allied Publishers.

Malhotra, I. (1969). Congress unable to check its downward drift. *The Statesman*, 14 March.
Malhotra, I. (1989). *Indira Gandhi: A personal and political biography*. London: Hodder & Stoughton.
Sen, S. K. (1998). *The Transitional State: Congress and Government in U.P., c. 1946–1957*. Unpublished Ph.D. dissertation. London.
Singh, S. N. (1969). Choice of presidency exposes pulls within congress. *The Statesman*, 16 May.

Part II
Caste, Gender, Race: Axes of Accumulation

Life, Labour, Recycling: A Study of Waste Management Practices in Contemporary Kolkata

Debarati Bagchi and Iman Kumar Mitra

Abstract This chapter attempts to foreground the question of migrant labour and their survival in contemporary Kolkata with a study of workers in both 'formal' and 'informal' sectors of the solid waste management industry. In the age of ecological awareness and hygienic aesthetics, the image of a solitary woman/man sweeping the city streets in the early mornings, carrying the hazardous waste on her/his shoulders, clearing the overflowing litterbins with sharp dexterity produces a strong and darkly ironical visual effect. Apart from these heart-wrenching stories of exploitation and under-appreciation, there are other aspects of the waste disposal industry which deserve attention—especially the institutional details of their participation in the city workforce. In this chapter, the authors look at these issues by exploring work forms and life stories of conservancy workers who have migrated from different parts of the country and have been employed by the Kolkata Municipal Corporation, and of homeless rag-pickers who participate in the apparently non-official systems of waste management in the city. Closely looking at a group of 'settled migrant' rag-pickers, mostly women, this chapter seeks to understand the time, territory, family structures and the pattern of shifts in occupation taking place in and around a particular dwelling area. Put differently, it explores the relationship between the contingencies of occupation and the question of social reproduction, keeping the question of space alive in the context of a burgeoning rent economy in the city.

Keywords Urbanization · Waste · Recycling · Labour · Caste

D. Bagchi (✉)
Centre for Historical Studies, Jawaharlal Nehru University, New Delhi, India
e-mail: bagchidebarati@gmail.com

I.K. Mitra
Mahanirban Calcutta Research Group, Kolkata, India

I.K. Mitra et al. (eds.), *Accumulation in Post-Colonial Capitalism*,
DOI 10.1007/978-981-10-1037-8_8

Introduction: Waste and Recycling in the Context of Urbanization

There is little doubt about the centrality of the question of labour in discourses of urban development. Most of the time, it revolves around the phenomenon of migration, especially when cities are becoming less a site of production and more a space of circulation and restrictive elitism. This aspect of 'restriction' is particularly important as 'migration' has always been considered by the 'original' residents as a sort of infringement in the socio-economic sovereignty of the city space. At one level, the migrants seem to 'take away' the means of economic sustenance from the locals and, on the other, they are prone to 'violating' the established social and cultural norms of urbanity. The current conceptualization of the city space as a 'gated community', manifested in various strategies of 'gentrification', makes good use of these axes of fear, discomfort and embarrassment, although, in India, migration to the cities has certainly not stopped and, if anything, has increased in absolute numbers (Samaddar 2009).

Taking clues from these observations, we wish to explore the question of labour in contemporary Kolkata by emphasizing the structural relationship between reconfiguration of urban space and labour informality. For that, we take up a specific form of work that becomes vital in the tectonic world of space making and zoning practices in the city, namely solid waste disposal. There are quite a few reasons for choosing this particular work form. Solid waste disposal is one of the most essential components of urban civic infrastructure which is now increasingly being associated with the drive of aestheticization ('beautification') of the city, and ensuing zoning strategies, in the garb of ecological normativity. Secondly, it accommodates a large number of migrant workers from various parts of the country with different linguistic, cultural, and communitarian backgrounds. It is also one of those work forms which are experiencing aggressive informalization of labour following the 'neoliberal' turn of the Indian economy since the early 1990s. Finally, the sector of solid waste disposal emerges today as a crucial site of accumulation in a very material sense of the term. 'Accumulation' attains a technical dimension when discussed in the context of waste disposal. It refers to the process by which 'wasteful' particles pile up during production and consumption of utilities (Plourde 1972; Smith 1972). In that sense, it bears a negative connotation as waste is considered a 'disutility'. It is unavoidable but should be 'managed' efficiently to ensure smooth functioning of the system.

This negative sense had been operative since the colonial time. Vinay Gidwani has argued that one of the foundations of liberal governmentality in British India was the desire to 'transform wasteful forms of moral conduct' (Gidwani 2008, p. 14, emphasis in original). By deploying their knowledge of political economy and security apparatuses, the colonial rulers adopted 'a modality of power that [strove] for an optimal balance between the *internment* and *circulation* of nonhuman flows as well as human bodies with their dispositions and desires' (Gidwani 2008, p. 14, emphasis in original). In the course of this chapter, we shall argue that the modality of power which characterizes post-colonial governmentality is founded on a discourse of recycling that refers to accumulation and disposal of waste as a means of capacitating production of utilities. Gidwani points out that creation of 'value' by transforming moral and material wastes was very much a concern of colonial power (2008). However, the post-colonial mode of accumulation tends to stretch this normative consideration to its limit and posits the urban territory as the most effective site of extraction. Neoliberalism attempts to tackle the crisis of capitalism—a steady falling rate of profit—by exploring and manufacturing sites which are de-regularized and informalized, but not de-institutionalized or ungoverned, like the special economic zones in India. Urban planning with its huge repertoire of zoning practices gives it an opportunity to stage the latest adventures of capitalist accumulation (Brenner and Theodore 2002).

The next sections in the chapter deal with the official system of waste management in Kolkata, mostly performed by the city municipal authority, the Kolkata Municipal Corporation (KMC), along with another network of waste picking by female pavement dwellers in the city. This network may be described as 'informal' as opposed to the 'formal' system adopted by KMC. However, with the progress of the chapter it will be evident that clear demarcation between pristine categories is difficult to achieve in the murky sites of post-colonial accumulation.

The Mechanisms of Waste Disposal in Kolkata

In the age of ecological awareness and hygienic aesthetics, the image of a solitary woman/man sweeping the city streets in the early mornings, carrying the hazardous waste on her/his shoulders, clearing the overflowing litterbins with sharp dexterity produces a strong and darkly ironical visual effect. Apart from these heart-wrenching stories of exploitation and under-appreciation, there are other aspects of the waste disposal industry which deserve our attention, especially the institutional details of their participation in the city workforce and the shared genealogies of their sociopolitical compositions. But before getting into that, let us have a look at the current waste management practices in Kolkata.

Although in most of the 'developed' countries, solid waste management is performed through practices like incineration and sanitary land-filling, a recent study of municipal waste management in Kolkata tells us that here the usual practice is to dump the waste in open spaces (Das and Bhattacharyya 2013, p. 147). All operations of solid waste management in Kolkata are done in four steps: sweeping, collection, transportation and disposal.

> In the city area, street cleaning and collection involves collection of MSW [municipal solid waste] from the streets (road sweeping) and households in handcarts. Thereafter, the waste is dumped at one of the 664 collection points (primary collection). MSW is then loaded into transportation vehicles (trucks) (secondary collection), which transport the waste (transfer) to disposal sites. (Das and Bhattacharyya 2013, p. 148)

The same study informs that the total numbers of waste bins in the city are 664 (Das and Bhattacharyya 2013).[1] The vehicles that are used to transport the waste to the dumping ground are owned by the Kolkata Municipal Corporation. The total amount of waste collected and dumped every day exceeds 5000 metric-tonnes. Although another study accounts the households for contributing more than 50 % of the solid waste in the city (Sarkhel 2006), the study to which we have referred earlier states otherwise: maximum amount of waste is generated from commercial and market areas (36.37 %) and the minimum from institutions and offices (6.32 %). The urban households generate 34.20 % of the solid waste whereas waste gathered from sweeping of the streets is 22.80 % of the total collection (Das and Bhattacharyya 2013, p. 148).

Though they differ on the amount of waste belonging to the households, both studies are in agreement with one point: the existing waste management system in Kolkata is inefficient. The major problem with the current system is the inability to sort and separate various waste items at the source or collection point. Since in most parts of the city, residential, commercial and industrial plots exist next to each other, different sorts of waste including biodegradable kitchen items, inert solid waste sauch as coal and ash, toxic and non-biodegradable items coming from the hospitals and industrial complexes are put in the same cart, transported in the same garbage truck and dumped in the same open ground at the landfills in Dhapa, Noapara and Garden Reach (Das and Bhattacharyya 2013, p. 149; Sarkhel 2006, pp. 2–3). The only household items that are separated at source are the ones which have reuse or resell value—paper, plastic, metal and glass—which are collected and recycled through another system of waste management run by door-to-door vendors and wholesale traders of junk materials. The anxiety about mixing different types of waste emanates not only from the possibility of health hazards caused by reckless handling of toxic materials, but also from the despair at the lost opportunity of recycling biodegradable materials more gainfully into compost manure.[2]

Waste Disposal and the Rent Economy

Evidently, the issue at stake here is not only cleaning the city and making it more hygienic and eco-friendly. The whole discourse of waste management is obsessed with the notion of recycling where management means turning the waste into something profitable. Turning waste into energy and fuel is described as an essential feature of the smart cities in the Mission Statement and Guidelines for Smart Cities published by the Ministry of Urban Development, Government of India (Government of India 2015). The Kolkata Municipal Corporation (KMC) is not

[1]The estimate was done in 2011.

[2]More than 50 % of the solid waste generated in Kolkata is biodegradable (Das and Bhattacharyya 2013, p. 149).

very behind in realizing this wisdom. In its Budget Statement for the year 2014–2015, the Mayor of KMC declares, 'A Vat-free Kolkata is now our motto and we are working towards it. Our SWM [Solid Waste Management] Department has taken initiative to build a Waste to Energy Plant at Rajarhat along with a Bird Sanctuary at Dhapa' (KMC 2014, p. 6). In fact, as the Mayor informs quite proudly, the mission of VAT-free city has already been initiated in Ward No. 85, a bastion of Trinamool Congress,[3] 'by using battery operated vehicles with hydraulic tipping system' (KMC 2014, p. 24). More such vehicles will be introduced in different boroughs or conglomerates of municipal wards in the city very soon, the Mayor adds.

It seems that KMC is quite keen on reorganizing the whole set-up of solid waste management in the coming years where special attention will be given to central business district areas.[4] 'Additional 50 mazdoors and supervisors have been engaged' to perform waste disposal services in these areas (KMC 2014, p. 25). Also six 'modern scientific waste compactor stations have been installed at Kalighat Park Vat, Southern Avenue, opposite to AAEI Club, Gobinda Auddy Road and Samsul Huda Road Vat' (KMC 2014, p. 25)—all so-called posh neighbourhoods in south Kolkata where both house rent and commercial rent are ostensibly higher than those in the rest of the city. Along with introducing pollution-free vehicles for carrying waste, KMC has also been looking for additional landfill sites where the waste would be dumped in case of exhaustion of the current site in Dhapa: 'Fifty-two hectares of land very close to the existing active dump site has been identified for interim waste disposal site' (KMC 2014, p. 25).

If we look closely at these statements, a map of the city becomes apparent—a map of exuberant urbanism characterized by an ever-growing rent economy. Evidently, recycling takes another meaning in this context: reorganization of the city space in terms of production and extraction of urban rent. The vicious cycle of rent continues as areas which produce more rent are adorned with facilities that ensure extraction of even greater amounts of rent. Curiously, in this scenario, the question of labour gets a silent treatment. In the whole budget statement, only once the issue of employment of workers is mentioned, when the Mayor informs about appointing additional *mazdoor*s (labourers) for the central commercial area. The rest of the statement talks only about durable capital in the form of carts, dumpsters and garbage trucks.

---

[3]The All India Trinamool Congress is the party in power in the state of West Bengal at the time of publication of this chapter. It also has the majority of councillors in KMC. The mayor himself is a member of the same party.

[4]The Budget statement mentions areas such as the neighbourhoods of the Writers' Building, Indian Exchange Place, Fairly Place, BB Ganguly Street, BBD Bag, Bankshall Court, and Koilaghat Street. All these places are located in central Kolkata and constitute the business centre of the city which includes the headquarters of the nationalized banks, the state secretariat at the Writers' Building and the main offices of major commercial enterprises.

The Labour in Question

In the academic and governmental discourses on waste management in India, the question of labour appears only in connection with the deplorable practice of manual scavenging: clearing of sewers and septic tanks in households and commercial buildings with manual labour.[5] The whole identity of workers in this industry—scavengers, or '*safai karmachari*'—revolves around the notion of manual scavenging. A National Commission for Safai Karmacharis, for example, was formed to eradicate the practice of manual scavenging soon after the Employment of Manual Scavengers and Construction of Dry Latrines Prohibition Act was passed in 1993.[6] West Bengal has its own set of rules regarding the practice. It is titled the West Bengal Prohibition of Employment as Manual Scavengers and their Rehabilitation Rules, 2015, and to be administered under the jurisdiction of Backward Classed Welfare Department, Government of West Bengal (*The Kolkata Gazette* 2015, p. 1). According to this rule, a *safai karmachari* or 'sanitary worker' is one who is 'engaged in or employed for any sanitation work other than domestic work…'. The rule also specifies a number of safety measurements to be taken by the employer during clearing of sewers and septic tanks. However, apart from manual scavenging, waste disposal in a city involves a lot of other responsibilities.

In a circular dated 12 June 2013, the Government of West Bengal mentions a list of all the workers in waste management.[7] The list is divided into three categories: unskilled, semi-skilled and skilled workers. The list of unskilled workers includes 'Sweeper, Sweeping Labour, Helper, Work Assistant, Door-to-door cleaner, Drain Mazdoor, Tructor Labour [sic], Garbage cleaner/Mazdoor, Conservancy Labour, Scavengers, Latrine cleaner, Drain/Garbage Coolie, Safai Karmachari whose work involves Sweeping, Cleaning and carrying operation'. The list of semi-skilled workers consists of the following: 'Auto Van Driver, Night Soil Cleaner-mechanical, Cesspool labour, Lorry Sardar, Conservancy Supervisor, Ward Sardar'. The list of skilled workers comprises: 'Garbage Tractor Driver, Conservancy-in-charge, Drainage/Sewerage/Engineering Mazdoor, whose work involves skill or competence and who is capable of handling machines and/or chemicals in a modern cleaning process'. The circular also mentions the minimum monthly wage rates for all the three categories according to their 'zones' of employment: Rs. 5,997 and Rs. 5,709 for unskilled workers in

[5]The National Human Rights Commission provides a long list of books and articles on manual scavenging on their website: http://nhrc.nic.in/bib_manual_scavenging.htm; accessed on 14 August 2015.

[6]http://ncsk.nic.in/index2.asp; accessed on 14 August 2015. This Commission works under the Ministry of Urban Employment and Poverty Alleviation, Government of India.

[7]Circular, Government of West Bengal, Office of the Labour Commissioner, Memo No. 756/Stat/RW/108/568/2012/LCS/JLC, dated 12.06.2013.

Zone A and Zone B, respectively; Rs. 6,597 and Rs. 6,279 for semi-skilled workers in Zone A and Zone B, respectively; and Rs. 7,257 and Rs. 6,907 for skilled workers in Zone A and Zone B, respectively. The distinction between Zone A and Zone B is based on the extent of urbanization and, accordingly, workloads in different municipalities in the state. Thus, Zone A includes the entire KMDA area, Siliguri and the industrial township of Asansol, and Zone B, the rest of West Bengal.[8] We also get to know that a normal working day for a worker in the waste disposal industry will consist of eight and half hours of work including interval for half-an-hour for rest.

Although the circular does not mention it explicitly, but there are suggestions that these rules are applicable to all workers employed by either the municipal authorities or private companies.[9] Even with a growing number of private waste management services, KMC still remains the largest employer of *safai karmacharis* in Kolkata. The traditional caste group which used to serve as scavengers in British India were the Bhangis[10] who were deployed by the municipal authorities to clear out the garbage in the cities, including human excreta and dead bodies (Sharma 1995). The practice still continues in post-colonial India where services like sweeping the streets and cleaning sewers and septic tanks are performed by people of specific caste groups like the Bhangis, Mehtars, Balmikis (or Valmikis) and Helas (Human Rights Watch 2014). The Government of West Bengal puts Bhangis, Mehtars, Methars and Haris under the same serial number in its list of Scheduled Castes in the state, indicating that these groups fall under the same category in the caste hierarchy and probably perform similar functions in a caste-based society.[11]

---

[8]The full list of municipalities under Zone A are as follows: 'Areas Notified under Kolkata Metropolitan Development Authority (KMDA), (ii) Asansol Municipal Corporation, (iii) Durgapur Municipal Corporation, (iv) Siliguri Municipal Corporation, (v) Digha-Shankarpur Development Authority, (vi) Thermal Power plant areas including Township areas, (vii) All the Municipal areas in different Districts, (viii) All the Sub-Divisions in the districts of Howrah, Hoogly, Burdwan and 24-Parganas (N) [excluding Barasat and Basirhat], (ix) Alipur Sub-Division and Baruipur Sub-Division in the district of 24-Parganas(S), (x) MidnaporeSadar Sub-Division and Kharagpur Sub-Division in the district of West Midnapore, (xi) Siliguri sub-division in the district of Darjeeling, (xii) Bankura Sub-Division and Bishnupur Sub-division in the district of Bankura, and (xiii) Raghunathpur Sub-Division in the district of Purulia.' See Circular, Government of West Bengal, Office of the Labour Commissioner, Memo No. 756/Stat/RW/108/568/2012/LCS/JLC, dated 12.06.2013.

[9]In one of the paragraphs, the circular states, 'Where the existing rates of wages of any employee based on contract or agreement or otherwise are higher than the rates notified herein, the higher rates shall be protected and treated as minimum rates of wages applicable for the purpose of this notification to such employees' (paragraph (e), Circular, Government of West Bengal, Office of the Labour Commissioner, Memo No. 756/Stat/RW/108/568/2012/LCS/JLC, dated 12.06.2013).

[10]Bhangis are an 'untouchable' low-caste group originally from Punjab whose traditional occupation is scavenging. For details on the Bhangis, see Sharma (1995).

[11]List of Scheduled Castes in West Bengal http://www.wb.gov.in/portal/banglarMukh/CMSPage/BMCMSPortletWindow?action=1&in.gov.wb.portal.MENU_ID_PARAMETER=47&fileId=75&in.gov.wb.portal.MENU_ID_PARAMETER=47; accessed on 14 August 2015.

A study on Hindi-speaking Dalits[12] in West Bengal recounts how people belonging to these castes were brought from Uttar Pradesh, Haryana, Delhi, Bihar and other states to Calcutta during the British raj for conservancy services in the city (Rawat N.D.). 'Bengal does not have its own scavenging community and therefore it imported people from the Hindi heartland', the study continues. Though the semi-skilled and skilled labourers are hired from different caste groups and linguistic communities, most of the unskilled workers still belong to the traditional 'scavenger castes'.

Forms of Informality

The informality of labour in the waste disposal industry does not only indicate absence of job security—a larger section of the workers are hired on a contractual basis with irregular pay (*The Hindu* 2015)[13]—but also other forms of exploitation including cultural bias and lack of social prestige. But all this is surpassed by the everyday realization of insecurity in terms of horrible living and work conditions. Only a few unskilled workers get to live in the labour settlements built and maintained by KMC. The rest of the *safai karmacharis* have to jostle for residence in numerous squatter colonies scattered all over the city. Often, they are not welcome in these slums because of their job description. Even the 'official' residences do not have all the necessary civic amenities required for healthy and comfortable living.[14] This is not the end of the story. As we have noticed earlier, the Government of West Bengal groups all the 'scavenger castes' under one category: 'According to government notification Safai is a profession and not a caste and all those who are involved in this profession should be called as [sic] Mehtars' (Rawat N.D.).

[12]The literary meaning of the term 'Dalit' is oppressed. It is mostly used by political activists to denote the lower caste groups. It was first used by the nineteenth-century Marathi social reformer Jyotirao Phule in the context of caste hierarchies and the system of untouchability in India. 'Although the term is quite widespread, it still has deep roots in a tradition of political radicalism inspired by the figure of B.R. Ambedkar' (Mendelsohn and Vicziany 1998, p. 4). The term, however, does not feature in government policies where the preferred terms are Scheduled Castes and Scheduled Tribes.

[13]Interviews with few sweepers in KMC Ward No. 2 reveal that the contractual system has started in the present generation (last 20 years) while the earlier generations of workers enjoyed some sort of job security, employment benefits like pension and fixed monthly wages from KMC. The KMC officials have, however, stated that most of the workers in the conservancy department still enjoy these benefits whereas the private waste management services do not provide any such facility.

[14]A visit to such an official quarter at Ward No. 11 (between Maniktala and Hatibagan) confirms the complaints often made by the residents of these quarters. Although there are electric and water connections available to the residents, they are infrequent and inadequate. The rooms are small and dingy and shared by more than five occupants oftentimes.

This amalgamation of different castes creates a lot of confusion. A huge number of sweepers in Kolkata belong to the Hela caste. However, to get the Scheduled Caste certificate, they have to apply under the name of Mehtars, which could be difficult in the absence of necessary documents. Hence, even after belonging to the lowest order in the caste hierarchy, many unskilled workers in the waste management industry cannot avail of the benefits of affirmative action.

The study on Hindi-speaking Dalits in West Bengal makes another interesting observation. By the Employment of Manual Scavengers and Construction of Dry Latrine (Prohibition) Act of 1993, the Government of India initiated the process of putting a stop to the practice of manual scavenging. However, this law and subsequent mobilizations against the practice resulted in unemployment of many Dalit workers who had no alternatives presented to them. Also, the drive to 'modernize' waste management services has lessened the importance of unskilled workers in the industry. The study of Hindi-speaking Dalits informs us that people with upper- and middle-caste backgrounds have now started looking for options in this industry. The ghastly picture of carrying pots of night soil over one's head is fading away as a relic from a pre-modern, pre-urban, pre-recycling India. A symbolic realization of this social transformation is captured in the Swachh Bharat Abhiyan where all citizens of India are requested to take up the broom and clean their own neighbourhoods. With the breaking of social taboos about waste disposal, the traditional scavenger castes are being crowded out from the system and their brooms are turning into another instrument of middle-class activism.

A Different Network of Waste Disposal

As we have noted earlier, another system of waste disposal is in operation in the city which involves separation, collection and recycling of waste materials by door-to-door vendors or junk salespeople. In this chapter, however, we shall discuss a different network of waste disposal where the same functions are performed by waste pickers or rag-pickers living and working on the streets of the city. The fact that most of the waste pickers in Kolkata are also pavement dwellers is also endorsed by the city development authorities. In two surveys on pavement dwellers in Kolkata, done in the periods of 1973–1974 and 1986–1987 consecutively, it was maintained that almost 5–17 % of them were involved in waste picking (Mukherjee 1975; Jagannathan and Haldar 2004). If the 'original' employees in the conservancy department of KMC hailed from various other states in the country, the waste pickers, according to both surveys, migrated from the southern districts in West Bengal, especially those closer to Kolkata. The surveyors noted variation in the earnings of waste pickers based in different locations:

> … a waste picker with access to the garbage vat outside a luxury hotel or a fashionable residential complex can be expected to earn much more than another person who has to be content with the pickings from a depressed neighbourhood. (Jagannathan and Haldar 2004, p. 132)

This observation makes the waste pickers part of the same rental economy of recycling where difference in earnings depends on the difference in potential rents to be extracted from a particular location. In the rest of the chapter, we shall have a closer look at the practice of waste picking and its appropriation in the politics of urban space making with reference to one of the present authors' fieldwork among female waste pickers in Kolkata.

One of the complaints about handling of waste in Kolkata focuses on the figure of the waste picker as ignorant and inefficient. Efficient collection of waste from households means an increase in the number of formalized door-to-door waste collectors, either employed by the KMC or by private agencies. An increase in the frequency of collections will surely make the garbage inaccessible to the 'informal' waste pickers. As early as in 1990, the Kagad Kach Patra Kashtakari Panchayat—a trade union of waste pickers based in Pune, Maharashtra—fought for the waste pickers' right to collect scrap segregated at source (households) as that offered better working conditions and allowed the children among the pickers more time for education. They made identity cards for about 30 adult women and observed dramatic improvements in their earnings (Chikarmane and Narayan 2005). This observation is quite pertinent in the case of Kolkata as well. As Supriya Routh's study of waste pickers in Kolkata elucidates, 'with its existing resources and waste management framework, the KMC is able to segregate and recycle solid waste in only seven of the one-hundred-and-forty-one *wards* (administrative units)…' (Routh 2013, pp. 243–44). In the rest of the 134 wards, the waste pickers help in segregating and recycling the waste. Routh's study also mentions that most of the female waste pickers whom he interviewed in Kolkata were 'typically migrant workers' (Routh 2013, p. 244). However, this study, although being one of the very few existing on waste pickers in the country, does not connect the livelihood practice of waste picking with the homelessness of people involved in this sector. The layered spatiality of the waste picker's living and working conditions, as it will be apparent from the following narrative, is instrumental in understanding the accumulative processes of recycling in the context of urban development.

Gulbahari's Story

Gulbahari Purkayit belongs to a three-member rag picking/pavement-dwelling family under the Bijan Setu, a flyover in the Ballygunge-Gariahat area in Ward No. 68 of KMC.[15] The infrastructure of the flyover creates spaces underneath which could potentially turn into shelter for the pavement dwellers. This arrangement is viable

[15]It is the same posh South Kolkata neighbourhood which found a mention in the budget statement of the Municipal Corporation regarding improvement of waste disposal systems in the city. Gulbahari's narrative follows from her conversation with Debarati Bagchi over 1 year (2014–15) as part of her research on the migrant waste pickers in Kolkata.

because it does not impede the movements of the automobiles and pedestrians on an otherwise very busy traffic junction. Under the flyover, two parallel roads meet at a U-turn blockade which has a pay-and-use toilet installed by the municipal authority. There are two floors beneath the bridge and adjacent to the toilet, which are usually rented to shopkeepers, although most of the shops remain closed, as it does not make much economic sense for the shopkeeper to rent a shop by which pedestrians scarcely pass. The waste pickers from this secluded neighbourhood, mostly women, make use of the shaded frontage of the locked shops. They annex these spaces with pieces of tarpaulin sheet, build a notion of privacy and use these spaces as the extension of the inner spaces inside the bridge.

Most of the waste pickers have been living here for the last two or three generations. Gulbahari's is the only Muslim family in this particular area among the largely low-caste population. She lives with her daughter and granddaughter. Now in her early 1970s, she cannot remember the exact year of her migration to the city from the East Mallikpur village near Laxmikantapur in the district of South 24 Parganas near Kolkata, but indicates the time as '*Naxaler somoy*' (at the time of the Naxalite Movement), presumably around the late 1960s or 1970s. Deserted by her husband who also came to the city earlier in search of a job and persuaded by her ailing father-in-law, Gulbahari came to the city along with two daughters and a son. She started as a domestic worker in nine households with a monthly income of 180 rupees. After a few months, she shifted to rag picking. Gulbahari's daughter Putul accompanied her to her job here since she was a child. From the age of 12, Putul started picking waste on her own.

Gulbahari's story is not unique. She used to work with a group of women who came from different villages on the two sides of the rail track running between Sealdah and Laxmikantapur, suggesting strong pre-existing village networks that led to territorialization of this vocation. A large number of female rag-pickers/pavement dwellers in this area migrated with their mothers under different circumstances. Many of them begged for a while, or worked as domestic help and gradually shifted to rag picking like Gulbahari. The waste pickers of adjacent areas have an informal understanding on their territorial jurisdiction; instead of fighting with each other over coverage of waste picking areas, they negotiate and fix the boundaries before they go out to work.

The female waste pickers in the Ballygunge neighbourhood set off for their day's work at around 3 or 4 a.m. and come back before the sweepers start cleaning the roads. Major streets and intersections are always the most lucrative stretches because of the shops and cars throwing out recyclable litter such as empty plastic bottles, paper bags and remnants of metal and glass articles. Also freshness of the litter is a crucial factor, as fresh-looking scrap fetches more money. The segregation is done at the places of dwelling, under the flyover, in tandem with other domestic duties such as cooking and looking after the children. The flexibility of work hours plays an important role in taking the decision of quitting other jobs and joining this profession. It is this kind of a work-time arrangement that seems to have made waste picking a largely female dominated sector, although the work conditions are abjectly stressful. They often get wounded and infected while sorting and picking from all kinds of waste with bare hands. Monsoons are always the worst time with waterlogging in most of the city streets. During heavy rains, they usually sit on some elevated place and wait until the water recedes.

The Underbelly of Recycling

However, defying all difficulties, many women like Gulbahari have stayed back on the pavements, along with their daughters and granddaughters, for the last few decades. One reason for sticking to this particular area is its proximity to their area of scavenging. Their work starts at early hours when no train would take them to their area of work. This is a point of major difference with those who commute everyday to the city to work as domestic help in the middleclass households. Also the second phase of the work, sorting and segregating the collected scraps, is carried out in the places where they live. The collected scraps are piled in front of their dwellings. Then, every object is sorted—plastic of various kinds, glass, aluminium foil, metals, cloth, etc.—and put in separate sacks. Discarded waste turns into recyclable and saleable waste only after it undergoes such processes of segregation.

After segregation, the sacks are carried to a nearby scrap dealer who exists at the lowest rung in the ladder of intermediary traders in the recycling industry. These shops are usually known among the waste pickers as *kabadi dokan* (scrap dealers), *kanch-loha dokan* (glass–iron dealers) or *kagoj dokan* (waste paper dealers). Different objects fetch different rates of payment.[16] There are various categories of plastic. The transparent plastic in which garments are wrapped (known as PP) sells at Rs. 20 per kg if they are clean, and a little less if they are soiled; the bigger plastic bags for Rs. 5 per kg; Mother Dairy[17] plastic containers of milk sell at Rs. 12 per kg; plastic bottles of mineral water sell for Rs. 10 per kg while the bottle caps sell at a doubled price. Everyday fibre items and shoes fetch around Rs. 10 per kg. All kinds of alcohol bottles sell at Re. 1 per kg, whereas beer bottles sell at Re. 1 per piece. Discarded perfume containers are expensive; they earn Rs. 80 per kg. Aluminium foils and beer cans, gathered mostly from the garbage bins of restaurants, fetch Rs. 40 per kg. Scrap tin is priced at Rs. 8 per kg; iron at Rs. 10 per kg, while discarded steel vessels at Rs. 18 per kg. Packing boxes collected from electronic and other shops constitute a chunk of their everyday collection; these are sold for Rs. 7 per kg. Elderly waste pickers like Gulbahari earn around Rs. 300 a week. For the younger ones, the earnings fluctuate between Rs. 100 and 200 a day. However, some of the women living in Gariahat earn some more (around Rs. 800 a month) by cleaning the big shops at the time of their opening. At this rate, at least the young waste pickers earn as much as the contractual employees do in the public sector of waste disposal: Rs. 4,000–6,000 per month.

---

[16]As in August 2015.

[17]Mother Dairy is particular brand of milk products.

Conclusion: Biopolitical Labour

The advent of neoliberalism is often characterized by the notion of 'immaterial labour', a conceptual category introduced by Maurizio Lazzarato (N.D.) and popularized by Hardt and Negri (2000, 2004).[18] Capitalism in the twenty-first century is certainly conducive to proliferation of the service sectors that specialize in production and circulation of knowledge, information and other 'immaterial goods', but, simultaneously, one must be aware of various material labour forms which sustain and realize accumulation through reproduction of a rental economy of space making.

There is no obvious disagreement between material and immaterial labours. In fact, as Hardt and Negri point out, 'the labor involved in all immaterial production…remains material—it involves our bodies and brains as all labor does' (Hardt and Negri 2004, p. 109). They admit that this identity between material and immaterial labours renders the latter term ambiguous and suggests to use the term 'biopolitical labour' instead: 'labor that creates not only material goods but also relationships and ultimately social life itself' (2004, p. 109). Even this definition is too broad and encompasses almost all forms of labour. Hardt and Negri, in the end, want to retain the term 'immaterial labour' with its conceptual shortcomings because, in spite of constituting a minority of the workers at a global scale, 'it has become *hegemonic in qualitative terms* and has imposed a tendency on other forms of labour and society itself' (Hardt and Negri 2004: ibid, emphasis in original). One of the objectives of this chapter has been to investigate this claim, especially keeping in mind that the binary of material and immaterial labour itself is a product of hegemonization of immaterial labour. From the above discussion, we feel that it is better to stick to the term 'biopolitical labour', at least in the context of urban waste management, to intervene in this paradigm and draw attention to its conceptual details.

Workers in the waste disposal industry—both the 'formally' appointed municipal workers and the self-employed waste pickers—can be categorized as 'biopolitical labour'. As we have seen, the discourses and practices of recycling take the issue of social life quite seriously. In many ways, accumulation and disposal of bodily excess (human and non-human excreta) have been at the core of discursive and practical treatment of waste. It has been conceptualized as biopolitical excess which needs to be recycled and effectively put to use for betterment of life in general and urban life in particular. This discourse of life, however, cannot escape a

---

[18]Primarily, in Hardt's and Negri's conception, 'immaterial labour' is defined as 'labor that produces an immaterial good, such as a service, a cultural product, knowledge, or communication' (Hardt and Negri 2000, p. 290). In their later work, they have expanded the definition and included 'a relationship, or an emotional response' in the list of 'immaterial products' (Hardt and Negri 2004, p. 108). In this book, Hardt and Negri make a distinction between the two forms of immaterial labour: the first is 'primarily intellectual or linguistic' and the second is that which produces and manipulates affects such as a feeling of ease, wellbeing, satisfaction, excitement, or passion. They call the second form 'affective labor.' In this context, also see Hardt (1999, pp. 89–100).

notion of risk which is ever-present in the production and consumption of utilities. The various legislations declaring the practice of manual scavenging as potentially harmful for the lives of the workers point to the governmental calculations that skilfully control the risk of biohazards in the name of an ethical–juridical preconception of waste as dangerous excess. At the next level in the paraphernalia of post-colonial accumulation, then, the excess is identified with and transferred to the realm of the informal.

Even though the lines between the formal and the informal are quite blurred in the context of waste disposal, there always remains a gap between the two sites of recyclical extraction. The legislations like the one that prohibits manual scavenging define the formal in such a way that the informal appears as the host of all the excesses (including labour) which cannot be contained in the formal domain. Hence, no legislation saves the waste pickers from the risks of biohazards or accidents at work. Ironically, the so-called formal sector also goes through different sorts of informalization (in the form of contractual employment, displacement from the official settlements, and more generally through invisibilization of labour from the official discourses of development) that broadens the scope of management of the same excess.

Within the description of biopolitical labour, therefore, we discover differences and hierarchies which are internalized as unmanageable, and yet, that unmanageability ensures a perfect, unspoiled mechanism of excess management by segregation and subsumption of the formal by the informal sites of extraction. The discourse of waste in the postcolony works as a model of accumulation where the recycling of excess channelizes the dynamism of social life. This life, especially in the urban context, is not accessible to everyone; and that inaccessibility, concretized in the contradiction between life and urban life, defines the exclusivity of post-colonial capitalism.

References

Brenner, N., & Theodore, N. (2002). Cities and the Geographies of 'Actually Existing Neoliberalism'. *Antipode, 34*(3), 349–379.

Chikarmane, P., & Narayan, L. (2005). *Organising the Unorganised: A case study of the KagadKach Patra Kashtakari Panchayat (Trade Union of Waste Pickers)*. Retrieved August 14, 2015, from http://wiego.org/sites/wiego.org/files/resources/files/Chikarmane_Narayan_case-kkpkp.pdf

Das, S., & Bhattacharyya, B. K. (2013). Municipal solid waste characteristics and management in Kolkata, India. *International Journal of Emerging Technology and Advanced Engineering, 3*(2), 147.

Gidwani, Vinay. (2008). *Capital, interrupted: Agrarian development and the politics of work in India*. Minneapolis and London: University of Minnesota Press.

Government of India. (2015). *Smart cities: Mission statement and guidelines*. Ministry of Urban Development: Government of India.

Hardt, M. (1999). Affective Labour. *Boundary 2*, 26(2), 89–100.

Hardt, M., & Negri, A. (2000). *Empire*. Cambridge, MA, and London: Harvard University Press.

Hardt, M., & Negri, A. (2004). *Multitude: War and democracy in the age of empire*. New York: Penguin.

Human Rights Watch. (2014). *Clearing Human Waste: "Manual Scavenging," Caste and Discrimination in India.*

Jagannathan, N. V. & Halder, A. (2004). Pavement dwellers of Calcutta–1987: A socio-economic study April 1988. In *Metropolitan Calcutta: An Anthology of Socio-Economic Studies and Survey Reports of KMDA 1970–2004*, Vol. 4, 1986–1992. Calcutta Metropolitan Development Authority: Socio-Economic Planning Unit, Directorate of Planning and Development.

Kolkata Municipal Corporation. (2014). *Kolkata Municipal Corporation: Budget Statement by Shri Shovan Chatterjee, Mayor, Kolkata, 2014–15.* Central Municipal Office.

Lazzarato, M. (N. D.) Immaterial labor. Retrieved August 14, 2015, from http://www.generation-online.org/c/fcimmateriallabour3.htm

Mendelsohn, O., & Vicziany, M. (1998). *The untouchables: Subordination, poverty and the state in modern India.* Cambridge: Cambridge University Press.

Mukherjee, S. (1975). Under the shadow of the metropolis: They are citizens too. September 1973-March 1974. A Report on the Survey of 10,000 Pavement-Dwellers in Calcutta. In *Metropolitan Calcutta: An Anthology of Socio-Economic Studies and Survey Reports of KMDA 1970–2004.* Vol. 1, 1970–1979. Calcutta Metropolitan Development Authority: Socio-Economic Planning Unit, Directorate of Planning and Development.

Plourde, C. G. (1972). A model of waste accumulation and disposal. *The Canadian Journal of Economics, 5*(1), 119–125.

Rawat, V. B. (N.D.) *Hindi Speaking Dalits at the Receiving End in West Bengal.* Retrieved August 14, 2015, from www.ambedkar.org/VBRawat/WB_Dalits_Rawat.html

Routh, S. (2013). *Informal Workers in India: Reconceptualizing Labour Law to Promote Capabilities.* Unpublished Dissertation, Victoria University.

Samaddar, Ranabir. (2009). Primitive accumulation and some aspects of work and life in India. *Economic and Political Weekly, 44*(18), 33–42.

Sarkhel, P. (2006). Economics of household waste management in Kolkata: Proposed steps towards improved efficiency. *Contemporary Issues and Ideas in Social Sciences*, March 1.

Sharma, R. (1995). *Bhangi, scavenger in Indian Society: Marginality, identity and politicization of the community.* New Delhi: M. D. Publications.

Smith, V. L. (1972). Dynamics of waste accumulation: Disposal versus recycling. *The Quarterly Journal of Economics, 86*(4), 600–616.

The Hindu. (17 July 2015). Conservancy Workers Demand Regular Wages.

The Kolkata Gazette. (2015). *The Kolkata Gazette*, Extraordinary. 19 February.

Ayurveda Tourism: Issues of Development and Gender in Contemporary Kerala

Rashmi Gopi

Abstract This chapter aims to understand the self-projection of Kerala through Ayurveda tourism and what this is doing to concepts of masculinity and femininity and to the idea of development. The author focuses on actual female and male bodies as producers and consumers of Ayurveda tourism, arguing that the rigidity of what constitutes femininity and masculinity is not questioned, but who possesses it is interchanged. This in turn exposes the construction of the binary opposition between femininity and masculinity as there exist multiple combinations of masculinity and femininity at any given time and space. Touching upon debates around modernity and tradition in Ayurveda tourism, the author argues that the dominant ideas of men as active, and women as passive, are shaped by the discourse of upper caste Hindus and colonial modernity. The predominant trend, throughout world, to understand development as something only related to economic growth has gained momentum in Kerala. What this paper emphasizes is the fact that Ayurveda tourism may have contributed to economic growth of the state at the cost of subaltern communities, but it has not addressed the cause of 'economic justice' in the state. The researcher raises political questions in the field of Ayurveda and development, trying to redefine the political and re-looking at interactions of plural femininity and masculinity.

Keywords Ayurveda · Gender · Biopolitics · Development · Tourism industry

A defined value of life has been pursued by governmental agencies. It is regarded as an essential element of cost–benefit analysis to guide public policy in the areas of regulation and investment in health and safety. Some measure is necessary to ensure prudent management of public and private resources. In Kerala, when government policies and funding is creating a hierarchy between Allopathy and

R. Gopi (✉)
Maitreyi College, University of Delhi, Chanakyapuri, India
e-mail: rashmi.gopi@gmail.com

I.K. Mitra et al. (eds.), *Accumulation in Post-Colonial Capitalism*,
DOI 10.1007/978-981-10-1037-8_9

alternative medical practices such as Ayurveda, Unani, Siddha and Homeopathy on the one hand and erasing many other forms of medical practices on the other hand, it is simultaneously deciding whose life is valuable and how much money should be spent on it and what are the benefits attached to it. Due to this biocapitalist impact, three things are happening (Rose 2008):

1. The practice of medicine has become infused with these ways of thinking about the value of life. Belief in the value of a healthy life and of one's right to control and shape that life has become central to the ethical self-management of many individuals and families and underlay many challenges to the paternalistic power that doctors exercised over their patients. Attempts to 'empower' the recipients of medical care to emphasize active citizenship have transformed 'patient' into a 'consumer'.
2. The practices of medicine have become saturated with issues of financial value. For examples, the growth of private health insurance and the commodification of health it entails, and the regulation of prescriptions and reimbursements.
3. Medical knowledge, indeed medical truth itself, has become subject to intense capitalization. It is evident in the way pharmaceuticals' grip is increasing over the medical practice; by the way, biotech corporate is controlling researches. Biopolitics has become bioeconomics, wherein investment is proportionate to the returns.

History of medicine is a social and cultural history. The present and future of medicine are also entrenched in social and cultural structures in our society. The social conditions produce morbidity and mortality. The ways diseases are seen, the socially accepted ways to treat the sick, how doctors and other health professionals are trained and evaluated and how medicine is practiced in a given society are influenced by the politics of the time. The access and control over material and cultural resources in the society shapes politics of medicine and health care. The intersections between gender understandings and medicine are deep. The women's rights movement, the struggles for the liberalization of contraception and abortion, the homosexual liberation movement and, recently, the activism of intersex people stimulated historian's interest in the ways that science and medicine shaped sexualized bodies in the twentieth century. These studies were partly connected by the uses of sex hormones to control female fertility, to treat a wide range of conditions perceived as pathological or undesirable, to enhance performances of bodies and to deal with atypical bodies such as those of intersex people and those wishing to change their sex/gender. The historians studied biological laboratories, production plants, slaughter houses (a rich source of sex glands used to extract hormones), doctors' offices and hospital wards. They also focused on social movements and political debates, the regulation of medicines and bodies, the routine management of sexualized/gendered bodies and the radical reshaping of identities (Palsson 2009). Through this paper on Ayurveda tourism, the author is looking at the contemporary politics in the state of Kerala that is not only changing nature of Ayurveda in itself but also how sexualized/gendered bodies and identities are constructed.

Tourism is seen as the panacea for all the economic illness of the state of Kerala. The weakness of 'Kerala Model of Development', that is economic illness in spite of social wellbeing saw its remedy in Ayurveda tourism. The government believes that Kerala is a state meant for tourism with its blessed natural geographic features and literate human resources. In the past two decades, the department of tourism in the state has aimed to maintain government tourism projects alongside profit-yielding private players (Sankar 2005). The trump card for Kerala tourism has been its claim to 'authentic Ayurveda'. Kerala's climate and culture both are shown to be ideal for Ayurveda.

Kerala Model of Development

The Kerala model has been defined as:

1. A set of high material quality-of-life indicators coinciding with low per-capita incomes, both distributed across nearly the entire population of Kerala.
2. A set of wealth and resource redistribution programmes that have largely brought about the high material quality-of-life indicators.
3. High levels of political participation and activism among ordinary people along with substantial numbers of dedicated leaders at all levels. Kerala's mass activism and committed cadre were able to function within a largely democratic structure, which their activism has served to reinforce.

This has been ensured by the multiple factors that has shaped the current Kerala. These include forward looking rulers, foreign trade and interactions with outside world, presence of Christian missionary in educational and health sectors, social movements by the backward communities and Communist movement in the state. But lately, this 'Kerala Model' has come under a scanner for excluding and exploiting the communities in the periphery. It has highlighted impoverished state of *Adivasis* (indigenous populations) and Dalits (downtrodden castes) in the state. It has shown the miserable condition of fisher-folk. The claims of education, healthcare has evaded these communities, who are termed as 'outliers' in the development discourse (Oommen 1999). What the present Ayurveda tourism propagated by the state promises to do is to erase this disparity. This chapter highlights the complexities in understanding the impact of Ayurveda tourism.

Contemporary Ayurveda

Practitioners of Ayurveda today concede that it has severed its ties with divinity. In my interviews with practitioners, therapists and patients of Ayurveda, I continuously met with the argument that lack of time is the reason why divinity and spiritual life are ignored. One of the doctors I met said that personally he does not believe in divine interventions in treatment but for the solace of patients he recommends special rituals at temple/church/mosque according to the patient's belief system. One of the therapists belonging to a traditional family of vaidyars said that as a child he has seen his father performing prayers before each treatment at their residence. But now he himself does not follow this due to the large number of patients to whom he has to cater.

Although divinity as such has no role to play anymore, Ayurveda has become closely linked to a particular religion, Hinduism. It is common to see temples in the premises of resorts and treatment centres. The connection of Ayurveda with Hindu religion makes it unchallengeable. It is believed that something which is created by God is infallible and everlasting. It negates the need for context-based adaptations, research and review. Any effort of critical intervention is not encouraged. One of the drawbacks of Ayurveda as a medical system is the lack of a critical eye within the system. What are the sources of its origin? Why is there a complete absence of discussion about female practitioners of Ayurveda? What are the contributions of different castes and religions to Ayurveda? These questions are not critically engaged with by the course of study of Bachelor of Ayurvedic Medicine and Surgery (BAMS). It is seen as a system of treatment given directly by the God Dhanvanthiri, an incarnation of Lord Vishnu. Due to popularization of this view, critical engagement with evolution of Ayurveda is missing.

Today Ayurveda is seen as a modern medicine limiting itself to the period of disease, and to the body. The practitioners of Ayurveda no longer think of it as a way of daily living addressing mind, body and soul. Ayurveda prescribes in detail one's routine: rising and sleeping patterns, cleaning, eating, exercising and meditation. In Ayurveda tourism, however, the emphasis on daily care/lifestyle has been ignored. Majority of the tourists (both domestic and foreign) availing Ayurveda treatment agreed that once out of treatment, sleeping patterns become erratic, food with nutrition is neglected, and exercise and meditation finds no place. Even during the course of the treatment, some patients/tourists find irksome the restrictions on food, sleeping patterns, stress on exercise and meditation. In Ayurveda tourism, the patient/client has become the centre of treatment. Therefore, it is clients who dictate the time and technique of treatment.

Patients/clients have forced Ayurveda to adopt the pharmaceutical form. Now, easy-to-carry, easy-to-eat capsules and tablets have replaced traditional oils, tonics and powders (Banerjee 2009). Along with this, restrictions on food items have been ignored. Today Ayurveda is imitating modern medicines not only in its appearance, but also in its application. The most popular Ayurveda product in the Kerala market is Lavana Thailam. It is an oil claiming slimming benefits without any food restriction or exercise. This product conforms to common and prevalent notions of health and wellbeing and is about display and outward appearance rather than holistic health based on healthy body, mind and soul.

It is agreed across sections of the society, by those supporting and by those opposing Ayurveda tourism that the sudden revival of Ayurveda is due to its popularity among foreigners. When they recognized the benefits of Ayurveda, that locals reclaimed it. With this sudden revival, there has been immense demand on limited herbal resources. A stage will soon come when only big pharmaceuticals and big resorts can afford Ayurvedic medicines. With Ayurveda tourism, Ayurveda has become the medicine of the rich. Poor doctors and poor patients cannot afford its medicines.

Madhulika Banerjee has argued that the trend towards homogenization of Ayurveda can be seen broadly at two levels: in the production of its history and in the standardization of its practice (Banerjee 2009). This trend can be seen in Kerala quite clearly.

Homogenization of Ayurveda's History in Kerala

Ayurveda by its nature is plural. *Darshana*, the Sanskrit word for philosophy, literally means 'seeing'. Philosophy is that which allows one to see things in a certain way. Ayurveda is a philosophy which allows physicians to see patients the way nature sees them. The sages who created Ayurveda were called 'seers' because of their ability to perceive reality clearly. They could see how the world and its parts operate and described their observations in words which allowed those who came later, to see and perceive in similar ways. Since each seer saw things from different viewpoints, there are many systems of Ayurveda. Following this tradition, each of the Ayurvedic physicians has his or her individual system, derived from the experiences of the great seers and augmented by personal experience (Svoboda 2010). These seers were not limited to any religion, any caste or creed.

The history of Ayurveda in Kerala can be studied in three stages: pre-Sanskrit Era, Sanskrit Era and the modern period (Varier 2009). It is believed that Ayurveda reached Kerala with the advent of Sanskrit. However, some features of Ayurveda in Kerala—medicinal species, methods of treatments and peculiarities of advancement—show certain unique characteristics. There is reason to believe that some indigenous system of healing prevailed here before the advent of Sanskrit and Ayurvedic works.

According to some scholars, the most powerful and widespread upsurge of Sanskrit must have been between the fifth- and seventh-century BCE. An examination of the societal structure, family organization, customs, modes of production and other characteristics reveals the inclination of the people of Kerala towards pre-Aryan traditions. Therefore, it would be quite reasonable to think that prior to the propagation of Sanskrit Ayurvedic works in Kerala, there already was in existence a more or less developed system of treatment. Ayurvedic system and Sanskrit literary works came later and only reformed this system and gave it a new form and content. For example, the coconut milk and tender coconut water used in many Kerala Ayurvedic formulations is unique to Kerala. Treatment procedures such as *dhara*, *navarakizhi*, *pizhichil*, *talam*, *tala-political* have been widely accepted as methods of treatment systematized in Kerala.

Scholars believe that priesthood, sorcery and medicines were intermixed in Kerala in the pre-Sanskrit Era. These were not limited to particular castes. The physicians were drawn from different strata of society. Medical practice never remained the monopoly of any class or caste. Along with the Brahmin *ashta vaidyas*[1] who were entitled to study the Veda, there were many traditional Ezhava families (backward caste) who studied Sanskrit works in-depth and practised the science through generations. There were families that had specialized in particular aspects of treatment, such as the Velan and Mannan castes specialized in midwifery (these are presently placed as Scheduled Castes; traditionally, they have been associated with washing of clothes belonging to upper castes), Panikkan (traditionally one who works with wood, iron, gold, etc.) and Ganakan (traditional occupation as astrologer) were specialized in paediatrics, and Kuruppans (traditional occupation as barbers) in massage and *marmacikitsa.*[2] Some families specialized only in one ailment. All these facts indicate that there was a widespread social foundation for medical practice in Kerala prior to the advent of Sanskrit (Varier 2009).

During the Sanskrit Era, Hindu temples became centres for popularizing Vedic knowledge. Here, the study of Sanskrit, grammar, astrology and medicine was encouraged. Medicine, toxicology and sorcery became the traditional professions of Namboodiri (Brahmin) families. Their professions acquired special status and recognition as they belonged to the upper strata of society. Simultaneously, art forms such as *kalarippayattu* (a form of martial art), *kathakali* (classical dance) and *marmacikitsa* contributed towards special treatment of Ayurveda in Kerala.

In the modern age, the traditional *gurukula*[3] system gave way to institutions. The princely families of Thiruvananthapuram (Travancore) and Kochi took special interest in establishing them. A school for Ayurveda was started in the palace of Travancore. A diploma course in Ayurvedic Medicine was set up in 1857. P.S. Varier started the Ayurveda pathasala (school of learning for Ayurveda) in 1917 and an Ayurveda college in Tripunithura was established in 1958. Thus in the modern age, rulers of the state took special care to promote Ayurveda in the face of stiff competition from modern medicine.

One often overlooked aspect is that Ayurveda has both oral and textual history. P.S. Varier, founder of Arya Vaidya Sala, Kottakkal, while tracing history of Ayurveda mentioned that there were continuous contributions to Ayurveda from wandering tribes. But these oral, practice-based contributions to Ayurveda are not given due credit. It was with the unprecedented growth of the caste system by the

---

[1]*Ashtavaidyas*, or eight physicians, are so-called because it is believed that they have studied all eight branches of Ayurveda: general medicine, paediatrics, toxicology, surgery, medico-surgery, promotive therapy, aphrodisiacs and ailments caused by invisible agents. But over the years for different reasons they have concentrated only on one or two branches. The roots of *ashta vaidya* families are traced to following places: Aalyittur, Kannur, Kuttancheri, Taikkad, Vayaskara, Vellod, Chirattaman, Pulamanthole, Olassa and Walajapet.

[2]Marma Chikitsa is a significant aspect of the AYURVEDIC treatments, where specific points are present on the body where the application of pressure induces the flow of vital energy (prana) along a complex system of subtle channels called (nadis).

[3]Traditional system of education.

fifth- and sixth-century BCE against the background of a priest-controlled feudal scheme of authority over land that the gap between thought and action grew larger. Gradually thought and action became hierarchical and stagnant. Those engaging in thought became superior, and thought-based professions were demarcated as hereditary. Those engaging in action or practice/labour were relegated to inferior positions. The oral tradition of Ayurveda started deteriorating. Even in textual traditions, casteist views gained supremacy. P.S. Varier reveals that although there is no support for 'purity of blood' theory in any authoritative Ayurvedic texts, later casteist injunctions can be found. He cites instances such as how the lowest castes were forbidden from studying Ayurveda and if they did, they could not chant the mantras. Varier quotes the strange view found in the *Kashyapa Samhita*[4] which appears to suggest a different duration for the menstrual cycle in respect of women of different castes. He also highlighted that the *samhita*s, though known by the names of individuals, were produced by systematizing the heterogeneous practices of many groups elaborating, compressing and refining them (Varier 2009).

During my fieldwork, one of the therapists emphasized that in recent times we could see attempts to Hinduize Ayurveda. The God of Ayurveda is shown as Dhanvanthiri, an incarnation of Lord Vishnu. In fact, many practitioners oppose this trend by saying that Dhanvanthiri was only one of the seers of Ayurveda. Due to his healing powers, people gave him a status of God but he had nothing to do with Lord Vishnu.[5] In my fieldwork, many practitioners of Ayurveda also pointed out that emphasis on Sanskrit and vegetarianism is a part of project of Hinduism Ayurveda—to be specific, upper caste Hinduization. As mentioned before, Ayurveda has many contributors; different seers have different views. Chicken soups and mutton soups were and are an integral part in increasing immunity of a patient. Likewise, many medicines included animal fats. Only for certain treatments in Ayurveda are the intakes of non-vegetarian food curtailed.

Due to this upper caste Hinduization of Ayurveda, many Ayurvedic resorts promote traditional *kasavumundu* for male and female therapists. This is one of the traditional attires worn by upper caste women and men of Kerala; it is an unstitched piece of cream-coloured cloth with golden brocade along the edges known as *kasavu*. Other features of upper caste Hinduism are also propagated: sandalwood paste on forehead, temples inside the resort and singing of *bhajan*s (devotional songs) as part of treatment. Ayurveda had a link with the divine but it was not religious. However, now Ayurveda is projected as a solely upper caste Hindu practice.

---

[4]An ancient text.

[5]Interaction with the therapist Manoharan. There is a whole debate in Kerala on what constitutes Ayurveda. Some limit it to written Sanskrit texts; some relate it to all treatments derived from nature. This issue was debated in depth in 'Locating the indigenous', an international conference on local, national and global forms of Indian medical practices held by University of Calicut on 21–23 October 2010. My stand is that Ayurveda is plural. There is no single Ayurveda. Traditions can be plural both in its theory and practice. Ayurveda has both written and oral traditions. Simultaneously within each of these exists many voices. Ayurveda of Kerala is a mixture of written Sanskrit texts and local oral and written practices.

The second aspect of homogenization is visible in the way Ayurveda is practised today. In my interaction with Ayurveda doctors teaching in a government Ayurveda medical college, it was highlighted that in the name of standardization, the BAMS course is designed by the government for producing Ayurvedic doctors. Only those with this degree are allowed to practise Ayurveda. The course content is limited. Ideally, an Ayurvedic doctor has to study beyond it. One of the limitations of this course is that preparation of medicines for particular ailments is not taught. Thus, dependency of Ayurvedic doctors on pharmaceuticals is increasing day by day. This in turn is triggering commercialization of Ayurvedic treatment. Once dependence on pharmaceuticals is established, specialized treatment according to the nature of constitution of each person will end. The same medicine will be given to different patients.

When it comes to resorts, in most cases it is the management that decides treatment packages. These packages are applied to all. If a client has a particular need, he/she is charged extra. For example, a client with mental stress will be given the massage package designed for all. Additionally, to deal with stress, counselling and separate treatments are provided on extra charges. Client-based particular packages are rare in resorts. In the process, the message of Ayurveda has been reduced to 'massage'. In Ayurveda, *panchakarma* (five detoxification processes: medicated emesis, medicated purgation, medicated enema, medication through the route of nose and bloodletting) is a time-consuming and very delicate therapy to be used with caution for those fit to take the treatment. But under Ayurveda tourism, *panchakarma* is done to almost everyone, within a short span of time.183[6]

It is not only the producers of Ayurveda who emphasize homogeneity, but also consumers demand it too. In my interview with doctors and therapists, it was revealed how clients, both men and women, demand treatments which their friends, relatives or neighbours have received. They are not bothered about their own particular health. For example, massage is demanded by almost all clients. Medicines prepared by a particular doctor are not trusted. Clients/patients demand pharmaceutical medicines which can be obtained in any chemist shop. Now the trend is to rely on Ayurvedic products targeting beauty and wellness. Thus, the market is flooded with Ayurvedic beauty care products. In the process, the plurality of Ayurvedic traditions has been destroyed and scope of Ayurveda has been reduced to a selected few (Banerjee 2009).

Having brief look at the nature of Ayurveda and its historical development in the state of Kerala, the next section will begin the process of understanding the self-projection of Kerala through 'Ayurveda tourism' and what is it doing to concepts of masculinity and femininity. There are several other debates around Ayurveda tourism—its impact on the environment and its supposed link to sex rackets in the state but these are not the focus of this study. This study draws attention to 'Ayurveda tourism' and its relationship to gender (masculinity and femininity) in the public sphere. The following points may be noted:

---

[6]Interactions with therapists in various Ayurveda resorts in Kerala.

a. The activities and processes involved in 'Ayurveda' tourism are constructed out of gendered societies and, consequently, the masculine and feminine identities articulated by both host and guest societies come into play in the promotion of tourism.
b. 'Ayurveda tourism' involves power relations between groups of people, both within the host society and between host and guest societies. These power relations reflect class, caste, modernity and tradition, which all are gendered in turn.

Female and Male Bodies as Producers and Consumers of Ayurveda Tourism

In this section, I will focus on how doctors, therapists and *vaidyar*s act as producers of Ayurveda tourism and how patients and clients of their services consume Ayurveda tourism.

To understand the ways in which they produce Ayurveda tourism, four points are taken into consideration: their appearance, the language they use, their understanding of knowledge and their assessment of the success of Ayurveda tourism.

Appearance

While interacting with various doctors, therapists, swamis and *vaidyar*s, two distinct voices came up, one emphasizing inner beauty and mental wellbeing and the other, outward beauty. Traditional practitioners of Ayurveda (*vaidyar*s) all emphasized the relationship between traditional art forms and physical/mental appearance.

Raghu Vaidyar is 55 and a second-generation practitioner of Ayurveda. He is also an expert in *kalari.*[7] He learnt *kalari* from his father. He says that *kalari* not only keeps him physically fit but mentally alert. For daily use, he wears white *dhoti/mundu* and shirt.

Similarly, Udyan Namboodiri, aged 65, is a Kathakali performer. He belongs to a Namboodiri family which for generations has specialized in curing mental ailments. He feels art helps him to relax mentally. Kathakali helps him to find his own balance while dealing with mental patients suffering from depression and phobias. His daily clothing is white *dhoti/mundu* and *veshti* (white unstitched cloth). He has also grown a beard.

[7]Traditional martial art from Kerala.

Likewise, Chandu Vaidyar, an Ezhava by birth, is an expert in *kalari*, astrology and palmistry. He can judge the health of people just by looking at them. He eats meat but in moderation. He believes that regular practice of *kalari* and disciplined diet has helped him fight age-related diseases. He wears white *dhoti/mundu*, shirt and walks barefoot. He is above 80 years of age but looks like a 60-year-old.

It appears that knowledge of traditional and popular art forms and adoption of the widespread local dress *dhoti/mundu* have helped practitioners maintain a distinct identity from that of BAMS doctors and Allopathy doctors. This has made them producers of not only Ayurveda, but also of Kerala traditions. They enjoy maintaining this Old World's Charm to add authenticity to their claim to Ayurveda.

BAMS doctors, however, follow modern dressing and grooming styles. Male doctors, without exception, have adopted shirt and trousers as their attire and most of them dye their hair black (as I have been told during my interaction with them) and are clean-shaven. In their clinics, weighing machines, stethoscopes and blood pressure-checking instruments are common. Female BAMS doctors in their appearance have stayed with the traditional *saree*. This trend reflects the predominant trend of seeing women as carriers of tradition. In my interaction with female BAMS doctors in hospitals and resorts, I did not come across a single one wearing trousers or skirts or *salwarkameez* (traditional clothing which is more common in north India). They have the opinion that *saree* is a 'decent' and 'professional' dress as compared to *salwarkameez* or any Western outfits.

Therapists working in hospitals generally have uniforms. For women, there is a choice between *saree* and *salwarkameez* with a coat, and for men shirt and trousers with a coat is the norm. Here special care is taken that the body (both of female and male therapists) is not exposed before patients. Their body is neutralized and asexualized. Their uniforms are of dull colours such as grey, dark blue or white. Uniforms are loosely stitched. No emphasis is laid on good grooming. Therapists in Ayurvedic resorts, however, dress differently, with traditional upper caste Hindu *kasavusaree*s for women and *dhoti*s for men. One can observe that they are extremely soft-spoken and maintain a 'traditional' look. The women put jasmine flowers in their hair. Male therapists are advised to keep trimmed hair and a clean-shaven face. Good grooming of therapists is emphasized.

Thus, we see that Ayurveda tourism has kept the image of traditional woman intact for both female doctors and therapists. Where the men are concerned, they are expected to look 'modern', though male therapists in private resorts are made to look 'traditional'. In government hospitals, both male and female therapists are given uniforms signifying their organized strength and respect. Most of them identified respect for a profession with wearing a uniform.

Ayurveda tourism has redefined the concept of fitness and beauty, emphasized outer grooming, cleanliness, care and softness. One of the questions in my work was whether emphasis on these supposed feminine characteristics has opened up this profession to women. With increasing numbers of male clients/patients for Ayurveda, and with recent restrictions by government on cross-gender treatments, many men have joined this 'service-based' and 'display-based' industry.

What Foucault has called the 'disciplining of the body' (Foucault 1995) is quite evident in this industry. Men and women have been tutored to shave/wax regularly, as the hairy body is seen as a symbol of untidiness. Men have been asked to deal with their clients/patients with utmost care and softness. Some resorts provide pre-service and in-service courses on behaviour and etiquette to their employees. Dr. Veena from a five-star Ayurveda resort pointed out how this disciplining is necessary to add a professional touch to Ayurveda tourism. She further stated that the clients in the five-star resort are mostly white foreigners. They demand fluency in English, submissive and soft body language, and utmost cleanliness in the services provided. To satisfy them, training—both pre- and post-service—is necessary. In my fieldwork I realized that men are comfortable with this kind of tutoring of behaviour, while many women are uncomfortable.

Language—Verbal and of the Body

Most of the BAMS doctors emphasized the need to learn Sanskrit to practise Ayurveda, as they believe that the textual basis of Ayurveda lies in Sanskrit. Similarly, *vaidyar*s also showed expertise in Sanskrit. However, some alternative voices also came up. Manoharan, aged 55, therapist in a government Ayurvedic college emphasized Ayurveda's non-Brahmanical roots. He said one could learn beyond Sanskrit texts from *Adivasi*s who actually practise Ayurveda. It is a highly misplaced understanding that Ayurveda begins and ends with Sanskrit. He also emphasized that it is important for practitioners of Ayurveda to bridge the gap between Sanskrit texts and local language of the people.

All of them—doctors, therapists and *vaidyar*s—agree that language of Ayurveda is that of love and compassion. They believe that any medicine and treatment becomes effective only when it is delivered with love and care. Thus, a feminized body language is practised by all of them.

Understanding of Knowledge

Therapist Manoharan stresses the fact that Ayurveda as knowledge originated on the day life form took shape on earth. It is the knowledge to preserve life. It is of pre-Sanskrit–pre-Aryan origin. Ayurveda has its roots in various groups of people. It is only a later development when Ayurveda came to be equated with Hindu gods and mythology. Ayurveda is divine, it is not religious. It is divine as it connects visible with invisible, this birth with previous birth. It is the knowledge of daily healthy living.

Swamy Radhakrishna, a non-trained Ayurveda practitioner on a beach whose clients include both foreigners and locals, echoes this sentiment. He says that Ayurveda is divine; it is not about limited theory and competitive approach.

Ayurveda is a knowledge based on truth, and on nature. He explains 'Ayurveda is a wife, who is not ready to share her bed for money with anyone. Ayurveda tourism is a prostitute, who is ready to share her bed for money'. This perception of women in the binary—of either a wife or a whore—is deeply rooted in many societies and especially in Kerala. The understanding is that the former has many clients, whereas the latter has one master; a wife seeks shelter and security under a single man, being a wife is not a selfless act and is not devoid of desire and pleasure. However, a prostitute too is not only a prostitute. She is also a daughter, a sister, a wife and a mother, as highlighted in the autobiography of Jameela (2007), an Indian bestselling author, activist and sex worker from Thrissur, Kerala. In any case, while the profit-making aspect is more visible in Ayurveda tourism, even traditional practitioners seek to make a living off it.

According to Raghu Vaidyar, aged 55, a second-generation practitioner of Ayurveda and an expert in *kalarippayattu*, knowledge is one or unitary but there are many ways to reach it. As a practitioner of Ayurveda what he is doing, he believes, is sharing that knowledge, not creating a new one. Raghu Vaidyar believes in unity of all forms of medicines, and that different systems of medicine are different ways to the knowledge.

Many doctors and *vaidyar*s feel that the training in Ayurveda that is imparted today is taking its students away from practical knowledge, because it is purely theoretical. Dr. Murali, aged 55, who teaches in a government Ayurvedic college and belongs to a traditional *vaidyar* family, says he has deep knowledge about herbs used in Ayurveda only because he belongs to a family of *vaidyar*s. But his students who are enrolled in BAMS are at no point given sufficient exposure to various herbs.

Assessment of Ayurveda Tourism by Its Producers

Dr. Murali, who has resisted the uncontrolled mushrooming of Ayurvedic resorts for promoting Ayurveda tourism, highlights three points. (1) He says that Ayurveda tourism is against the ethics of Ayurveda. Ayurveda involves a strict regimen of prohibited and permitted food, timings of intake of medicines and specific methods of treatment for different patients; everything is compromised in Ayurveda tourism. He feels that the tourism aspect has led to 'one-size-fits-all' thinking. It ignores the particular needs of particular bodies. (2) He strongly protests the misuse of valuable and rare medicinal plants for momentary pleasure, when they can be used in life-saving treatments. (3) He points out that Ayurveda tourism is in fact a gross misuse of Ayurveda's human resources—Ayurveda doctors are becoming rubber stamps for the predetermined agenda of the managers of tourist resorts.

Others in the business of Ayurveda tourism do not agree. According to therapist Bindu, aged 35, working in a government Ayurvedic college, it has opened doors of employment to many trained Ayurvedic doctors and therapists. She points out that Ayurveda's human resource is not 'misused' but rather utilized well. She stresses the fact that government hospitals and medical colleges have very few jobs and they prefer their own students. At least with the coming of resorts, many have found jobs to support their families. Dr. Veena feels it is the responsibility of the government to develop more herbal gardens to increase the availability of herbs. Dr. Veena feels ethics is a personal matter and that not all doctors in hospitals follow the ethics of Ayurveda. She maintained that in her resort there is no pre-fixed treatment package for all clients. Treatment package is charted out according to the need of each patient.

On the one hand, therapists working in resorts are thankful to tourism for their employment, but on the other hand, none of them want their children to enter the same profession. They feel that society has not given them respect. They have pointed out that people at large believe they are indulging in sex services rather than in health services. Saba, aged 24, a female therapist in a private hospital from a conservative family in north Kerala, mentioned that her job has given her the opportunity to be the bread winner for her family, but many marriage proposals got cancelled because of the presumed lack of respectability of her profession.

This discussion has opened out the ways in which producers of Ayurveda tourism are tied to both 'tradition' and 'modernity' for survival. Ayurveda tourism uses modern marketing in its promotion but its reliance is on highlighting the upper caste Hindu, traditional face of supposed Kerala femininity based on cleanliness, care and tenderness. In the Kerala Ayurveda tourism brochures by Kerala Tourism Development Council (KTDC), we can see women wearing upper caste traditional dress, the *kasavumundu*, sandalwood paste on the forehead, jasmine flowers in the hair, welcoming tourists in five-star resorts or doing massage on clients in these resorts. The discourse of Ayurveda tourism is silent about the disciplined body and uniform-wearing women working in many of the pharmaceutical companies. It is silent about poor women practising Ayurveda in small shanty huts in various beaches of Kerala and about poor *adivasi* women who supply valuable herbs to many practitioners of Ayurveda in the state. Thus, women belonging to economically weaker sections and lower castes have no representation in the promotional images of Ayurveda.

The other significant point that has emerged during my fieldwork was that the notion of what constitutes 'femininity' and 'masculinity' remains unchanged but who can possess these qualities becomes more fluid. Men can be 'feminine' and women can be 'masculine'.

Although caring and sensitivity are parts of their self-presentation at work, male practitioners understood this in different ways. Some like Arun, for instance, argue that at home he is the same person, a man who has control over his wife and children; this caring/soft side is reserved for his clients. On the other hand, therapist Raju feels he has always been comfortable with his feminine side. At home, he shares household chores with his wife and he feels uncomfortable in social gatherings where there is display of material wealth and alcohol consumption. Most of them feel it is not the nature of work but the structure of the wage that is problematic under conditions of ever increasing inflation.

For girls like Saba, a therapist, it has given her the power to be a 'man'—educating her siblings, moving freely at any time of day or night. At the same time, this successful emulation of 'masculinity' has hampered her chances of getting married.

Therapist Jayan belongs to fourth generation of an Ayurveda Vaidyar family. He emphasized the fact that effectiveness of Ayurveda treatment depends upon the 'caring' attitude of the practitioner of Ayurveda treatment. Producers of Ayurveda can succeed only if they are ready to empathize with their patients/clients. This caring attitude is similar to that of a mother towards her children. It has the elements of both attachment and detachment. Attachment is necessary to understand one's patients/clients real needs, welfare and situation. At the same time, detachment is important. In his years of experience, he has seen many therapists successfully internalizing such feminine role for their patients/clients. He pointed out that in Ayurveda caring attitude is equally important as medicines for curing the mind and body of the patients/clients.

Therapist Raju agrees with this view. He says that when treatment is going on, the therapist whether male or female acts as a primary caregiver to the patient/client. Patient's/client's wellbeing is of utmost importance. Here, the gender of the therapist is immaterial.

In this context, it is relevant to consider the arguments of Partha Chatterjee about the division between the 'home' and the 'world' in nationalist movement in India. The Indian nationalists equated material with the world and spiritual with the home. The world is external. The home represents one's inner spiritual self and one's true identity. The world is a treacherous terrain of the pursuit of material interest where practical considerations reign supreme. It is the domain of the male. The home is the domain of the female. The Indian nationalists took upon themselves the task to protect, preserve and strengthen the inner/spiritual domain. In this, the voice of women got lost. The story of nationalist emancipation was a story of betrayal of women's question (Chatterjee 1994).

The practitioners of Ayurveda, interestingly, locate the practice of Ayurveda entirely in the 'inner domain' of spirituality. Thus, whether male or female, the practitioners of Ayurveda are 'feminized' in terms of how Indian modernity has produced masculinity and femininity.

All these voices reflect the fact that Ayurveda tourism has enabled many men to explore their feminine side and empowered women to 'feel like men' through employment. It has made it possible for many to accept the coexistence of varying degrees of femininity and masculinity within themselves. But an acceptance of these feminine-men and masculine-women in the larger Kerala society is not evident.

Consumers of Ayurveda Tourism

Ayurveda tourism takes shape not only through its producers, but consumers' demand also has an impact on it. Consumers of Ayurveda tourism are diverse, but the demand to see the 'traditional' face of Kerala cuts across consumer categories.

Maria from Germany has a fair degree of knowledge about Ayurveda. She has made many visits to Kerala and interacted with various practitioners of Ayurveda. Over the past two decades, she has noticed the growth of Ayurveda tourism in the state. She feels that in the race to be commercially successful, the quality of medicines has deteriorated. She is concerned also about the ever-decreasing herbal resources in the state. This is also leading to rising prices of Ayurvedic products and medicines, making them more and more inaccessible to common people. She is concerned about the number of untrained and unskilled doctors and therapists entering the field in the rising industry of Ayurveda tourism. She predicts that in the long run, with further development in electronics 'do-it-yourself' demonstrations will be available, thus taking Ayurveda even further away from its roots and social context. However, Maria feels that Ayurveda tourism has undoubtedly revived traditional art forms such as *Kathakali*, *kalarippayattu*, *panchavadyam*,[8] palmistry and astrology, as tourists of Ayurveda treatment simultaneously demand different kinds of entertainments to add to their experience of Kerala.

Michael, a carpenter from Sweden, feels that Ayurveda tourism has definitely helped people outside India to realize its potential. He says it is a misconception that only rich foreigners come for Ayurveda tourism, and that he himself finds prices for goods and services to be highly inflated. He mentioned that it is out of his lifetime savings he has come to Kerala. His aim is to regain his health. He feels that the Ayurveda treatment offered in Kerala is cheaper and yet more effective than other treatments in his own country. Michael points out that promotion of traditional art forms with Ayurveda is a win-win situation for both; it provides livelihood and popularity to practitioners of both art and Ayurveda. For clients, it makes the whole experience more pleasurable. He pointed out that he has enjoyed performance of Kathakali in the Ayurveda resort and he personally prefers traditional attire of therapists rather than a uniform. He asks, what is the harm in promoting one's own culture on a business model? Here, it is to be noted that there is nothing wrong in promoting culture, but it is problematic when a particular culture of a dominant section of the society (in this case, the upper caste–upper class culture) is projected as the culture of the entire state.

We have seen how consumers demand masculinity and femininity rooted in traditional art forms and upper caste attires. This demand has created a homogenized portrayal of men and women in the Ayurveda tourism. Again, we can see fewer restrictions on Ayurveda beauty products as exports to Western countries have increased and Indian Ayurveda pharmaceutical companies are investing more on such products. This demand has a spillover effect in Kerala as Ayurveda is associated by men and women with beauty products rather than with medicines. Another aspect is that better purchasing power of foreign and domestic tourists has inflated the prices of Ayurveda products. This is distancing local women and men from using Ayurveda products and treatments.

---

[8]Panchavadyam literally meaning an orchestra of five instruments is basically a temple art form that has evolved in Kerala.

Sheela, a local resident of Kerala belonging to an economically weaker section of society, recollected that her faith in Ayurveda was established in 2007 when she tried but failed to cure chikungunya fever through Allopathy. Even after weeks of treatment her feet were swollen and she had unbearable knee and back pain. It was Ayurveda that came to her rescue. She feels that more support from the government and media highlighting the benefits of Ayurvedic treatment (not Ayurveda tourism) will help the public at large. She mentions that Ayurveda tourism has adversely increased the cost of medicines, making it difficult for poor people to have access. She looks forward to simple, affordable and traditional treatments of Ayurveda.

Manu, a local resident of Kerala belonging to the upper middle class, also feels that the government has to promote cheap and effective Ayurveda in a better way. Its target should meet people's need rather than profit. He is not negating Ayurveda tourism based on five-star resorts, but calls for a more balanced growth of Ayurveda.

Feminine as Passive: A Brahmanical-Western Concept

The production of Ayurveda in an upper caste Hindu Sanskritized mould must be seen in the context of the general transformation of the heterogeneous cultures of Kerala along the lines of the values of the dominant upper castes and middle classes. The dominant idea of men as active and women as passive is shaped by the discourse of upper caste Hindus and colonial modernity.

Upper caste Hindu mythology is presented as 'Hindu' mythology. Here, we can see that all the main goddesses such as Lakshmi, Saraswati, Sita and Parvati are subjugated as consorts to male gods such as Vishnu, Ram and Shiva (Ilaiah 1996). Only in times of crisis do some of the female deities take the shape of active figures such as Kali, but active/violent form of female energy is seen as a deviation rather than the norm. Even in day-to-day reference, people want their daughters to be like Sita or Parvati but not Kali.

Like Ilaiah, Kerala's *adivasi* leader C.K. Janu also speaks about how tribal deities were ordinary in their character. Their stories reflected deities doing normal everyday tasks such as fighting wild animals or healing wounds. Goddesses were symbolized in rocks or trees. Speaking to them never needed special rituals or language (Janu 2004). The reflection of dominance of upper caste Hinduism on Kerala society is clearly visible in the transformation of the Kodungallur Bharani festival. J.J. Pallath[9] reported for Asian Human Rights Commission in 2002 on how this festival in Kerala is one of the very few festivals which allowed lower caste people to freely express their emotions through sexualized songs. Lower caste people throughout Kerala come together to sing sexually explicit songs with

[9]J.J. Pallath wrote in the Asian Human Rights Commission Report. Retrieved from www.hrsolidarity.net/mainfile.php/2002vol12no06/2251/.

their families or clans. They celebrate freedom, drink and dance. They forget the humiliation they face in the hierarchical Hindu caste order. In this semi-conscious state of being they reach another world of freedom, peace and tranquillity. With widespread English education and the accompanying cultural domination in the last century, this indigenous celebration has been progressively taken over by the high castes, which organized themselves under a swami a decade ago and prohibited sexually explicit songs. Their argument is that it goes against the moral sensitivity of the public and of the 'true devotees'. When the lower caste people fiercely objected, the government handed over the celebration to the police as a law and order issue. Today, the police harass the lower caste devotees who try to revive the past tradition.

Another change over the years in Kodungallur temple is the neglect of *kezhakekkavu* (a shrine under a tree) supposedly established by lower castes. For upper caste Hindus, a humanized idol and temple structures are essential. They refuse to see divinity in a tree. Likewise, we can observe disciplining of language in the temple premises. Lower castes used to address the deity familiarly as *thalla* (colloquial form of 'old lady', a familiar form of address). Now calling the idol *thalla* may invite trouble as *thalla* is seen as a disrespectful term. *Amma* (mother) or *Devi* (goddess), supposedly more civilized words, has replaced *thalla*.

These instances are relevant to our chapter on Ayurveda tourism as the same upper caste forces have played a key role in producing Ayurveda as 'Hindu', based on vegetarianism, Sanskrit, and as originating from an incarnation of Vishnu. This trend has moulded Ayurveda in the style of upper caste femininity as Ayurveda tourism producers are regularly portrayed as passive, homely, traditional and tender. Together with the upper caste discourse of femininity as passive, Western influence in the form of colonial modernity has strengthened this understanding. As Nandy (1983) states, British arrival in India led not only to colonialism of the nation, but also to colonialism of mind. British colonialism led to production of and control of non-West by the West. Even the interpretation of West by the non-West is coloured by Western standards. Nandy highlights how as a result a monolithic picture of the West emerged as masculine, active, aggressive, progressive and civilized, whereas a monolithic non-West came to be counted as feminine, passive, submissive, savage and uncivilized. Modernity through colonialism not only compartmentalized femininity and masculinity into binary oppositions, but also hierarchized the relation between the two, putting masculine above feminine. Masculine was projected as superior on the basis of competitive individual achievements, courage, militarism, efficiency and technologically sound mind. The British justified the rule of a masculine West over a feminine non-West (Nandy 1983).

Emily Martin (1991) has pointed out that Western culture shapes how even biological scientists describe what they discover about the natural world. Dominant modern science reiterates the fact that the sperm (male) is active and egg (female) is passive. For example, textbook descriptions stress that all of the ovarian follicles containing ova are already present at birth. Far from being produced, as sperm are, they merely sit on the shelf, slowly degenerating and ageing 'like an over stocked inventory' (Martin 1991, p. 487). Here, the male is portrayed as active as he is continuously producing sperms, while the female is passive as eggs are already produced at the time of birth. Thus, the dominant language of Western modernity shapes even the language of science (Martin 1991).

Fatima Mernissi (2002) has spoken about the Muslim concept of active female sexuality as opposed to the Western concept of passive female sexuality. She explains how the veil is not an indicator of weakness of female sexuality. Rather, the veil is used to control men, not women, as the assumption is that the power of beauty of women can make men crazy. This will lead to chaos and that is why the veil is needed. Women, on the other hand, can control their sexual desires better even when seeing unveiled men. She quotes Imam Ghazali's interpretation of the Koran which casts the woman as the hunter and the man as the passive victim in the whole process of procreation. Thus, Mernissi views the Islamic notion of female sexuality as active and male sexuality as passive, as opposed to the dominant Western notions (Mernissi 2002).

Like other non-Western knowledge systems, Ayurveda has for centuries had a distinct understanding of male/female that is not compatible with modern, Western understanding of the male being active and the female passive. It is believed that the source of all existence is cosmic consciousness, which manifests as male and female energy, Shiva and Shakti. *Purusha* is the male, while *prakruti* is the female energy. *Purusha* is formless, colourless and beyond attribute and takes no active part in the manifestation of the universe. This energy is choiceless, passive awareness. *Prakruti* has form, colour and attributes: it is awareness with choice. It is Divine Will, the One who desires to become many. The universe is the child born out of the womb of *prakruti*, the Divine Mother. *Prakruti* creates all forms in the universe, while *purusha* is the witness to that creation. It is primordial physical energy containing the three attributes found in all nature, the evolving cosmos. The three attributes are *sattva* (essence), *rajas* (movement) and *tamas* (inertia). These three are the foundations for all existence. They are contained in balance in *prakruti*. When this balance is disturbed, there is an interaction of the attributes which engenders the evolution of the universe (Lad 2005).

'Feminine' Ayurveda Versus 'Masculine' Allopathy?

Through my engagement with Ayurveda practices in Kerala, I have reflected on the nature of Ayurveda itself. One question which has occurred to me during the process is whether Ayurveda is conceptualized as 'feminine'[10] in comparison with allopathy whose hegemonic masculinity needs to be equated with:

[10]Interview with Allopathy doctors on Ayurveda brought out many voices but predominantly they saw Ayurveda as inferior to Allopathy.

i. having access to public policy matters;
ii. having control of finance;
iii. having access to power centres: government–corporate–media;
iv. devoid of emotion, being rational;
v. in binary opposition to masculinity–femininity under contemporary conditions means;
vi. being dependent;
vii. being submissive;
viii. being denied access to finance;
ix. being denied access to power.

Let us consider these aspects in detail.

Access to Finance

In my interviews with Ayurveda professors in a government college, it was highlighted that the access to funds is systematically denied to Ayurveda doctors. For example, under the National Rural Health Mission,[11] funds are controlled by Allopathy doctors. They spend it in their own sphere. As controllers of funds, Allopathy doctors influence policies and the appointments to important health sectors. Today about 80 % of the funds allotted to the health sector is spent on Allopathy, thus curtailing the growth and development of Ayurveda and other systems such as Unani, Siddha and Homeopathy. Under this situation, Ayurveda is in a state of dependency and submissiveness in relation to Allopathy.

Access to Policy Matters

Again in my fieldwork Ayurveda doctors and professors pointed out that as all relevant appointments are controlled by doctors practising Allopathy, all policy matters are in their favour. For example, the hierarchy is established at the entrance examination to medical education itself. In this system, top rankers would be allotted Allopathy courses and others would be allotted other forms of medical practices. It is assumed that better students will study Allopathy. Similarly, branches such as gynaecology in Ayurveda have been systematically ignored. Even when one opts for a specialization in it, there is no hospital allowing practical exposure to Ayurvedic gynaecology treatment. The students are made to observe and learn gynaecological treatment in Allopathy. Thus, further research and development in Ayurveda is curtailed.

[11]The National Rural Health Mission (NRHM) was launched on 12 April 2005, to provide accessible, affordable and quality health care to the rural population, especially the vulnerable groups.

Access to Media

Allopathy has superior control not only over funds, appointments and other policy matters, but it also controls soft power through media. Successful treatments in Ayurveda like for chikungunya fever and skin diseases are under-reported in both print and visual media. Likewise, the effectiveness of Allopathy medicines and publicity of Allopathy hospitals are inflated in the media. The dominance of Allopathy over Ayurveda appears to reflect the authority of husband over wife in a patriarchal society. The aggressiveness of Allopathy and submissiveness of Ayurveda might change in future with change in equations of power structures. But until then it is not incorrect to think of Allopathy as masculine and Ayurveda as feminine.

Ayurveda Tourism and Idea of Development: The Case of Vizhinjam Beach

The idea of development has narrowed down to mean only economic growth. Development as a tool for individual and community ascendency and development as a balance between individual's growth and social justice have been ignored. According to Devika (2007), the concept of development as economic growth, social welfare and socialistic redistribution of resources has been intimately linked to the construction of the idea of a 'Malayalee people' as a distinct sociocultural entity in the post-independence India. Today, this Malayalee identity has been thrown into a crisis as the desire for development still remains unfulfilled; the idea of 'social development' has been put into back-burner, opening up a vacuum (Devika 2007). Ayurveda tourism is one of the efforts to fill the lack but itself falls into the trap of one-sided, economic, growth-based development. For example, the illusions of inclusiveness generated by developmentalism are fading. The hitherto marginalized identity of fisher-folk is asserting political claims to 'beach' as their symbol of culture and existence.[12] Although it has achieved limited success in this endeavour, it has definitely questioned the hegemonic masculinity based on upper caste and upper class power in exploiting resources of the nature. They are questioning 'private beaches' accumulated by big Ayurvedic resorts in collaboration with political elites. In Vizhinjam, there are 80 Ayurveda resorts with private beaches. When the poor fisher-folk residing in nearby slums are facing acute drinking water shortage, the same has been diverted to resorts for their tourism activities. Utilization of resources by the poor will not fill the treasury of the government, but earnings from resorts can do this. Resources are not only diverted but denied to them. Fisher-folk highlight this aspect when they tell stories of the

[12]This aspect has come out when I interacted with members of a fisher-folk union called the Kerala Swantantra Matsya Tozhilali Union.

strengthened bureaucratic arm of the state in forced evictions without adequate compensation or rehabilitation. In the garb of scientific and modern Ayurveda tourism, the inequities of caste and gender are made invisible. The author feels that this might have led to certain job opportunities to displace fisher-folk but this is not what they want at the cost of their culture and identity.

Conclusion

Ayurveda tourism captures the contradictory forces in contemporary Kerala society. Ayurveda tourism stands for, on the one hand, consumerism, homogenization and limited vision and on the other for re-inventing one's lost multiple traditions.

The sudden revival of Ayurveda in the form of 'Ayurveda tourism' has led to mushrooming of Ayurvedic health resorts throughout the state, from *thattukada*s (small make-shift operations) to five-star arrangements. It has touched every strata of society. Girls and boys belonging to poor families serve as therapists in this business. Rich people become customers and consumers of Ayurveda tourism. The middle class has been playing both roles of service providers and receivers. The idea of beauty and wellbeing as something both 'traditional' and 'instant' has been propagated, 'traditional' in the sense of something going back for centuries and 'instant' meaning something that can be attained within 15–30 days of Ayurveda package treatment.

'Being a man' in Kerala is based on the hegemonic masculinity based on consumerism, materialism and disrespect towards women as well as towards men who are different from this dominant masculinity. A man is one who is able to provide his family with all the material comforts. Being a man means to have control over female members of the family. In binary opposition to this 'being a woman' in Kerala is about being educated and well earning but never free from the role of wife and mother. Taking care of husband and children are her divine duties. Any woman who declares freedom from family or any other patriarchal norms of the society has only two identities in Kerala—one that she is 'mad' and the other is that she is a prostitute or 'lesbian'. This is evident in the way politically active women K.R. Gowri, C.K. Janu, writer Kamala Das, and defiant nun Sister Jesme are seen in Kerala.

In the final analysis, the development of Ayurveda tourism reveals complex and multiple interconnectedness between notions of modernity and tradition, as well as the emergence of multiple masculinities. In Ayurveda tourism, the emphasis on being scientific reflects influence of modernity. Ayurveda tourism has made Ayurveda this-worldly, based on 'scientific' quantification. Ayurveda tourism has reinforced the importance of body centric and quick treatments as done in allopathy. Influence of modernity is reflected in the way the Ayurveda pharmaceutical industry is working. Its emphasis is on imitating production quality of Allopathy pharmaceuticals. The way neutrality of technology is promoted, the ways workers in these industries are dressed, disciplined—all reflect admiration for efficiency, cleanliness and impersonal touch.

But at the same time we have seen revival of art forms such as Kathakali and *kalarippayattu* as complementary to Ayurveda tourism. It is re-inventing traditions to capture more tourists. In this, Malayalees are drawn to restore their cultural identity. Many in the process have rediscovered plurality in origin of traditions. In my fieldwork, professors who are teaching BAMS students expressed their unhappiness over the homogenized, limited vision of Ayurveda included in the syllabus. They are asking their students to go beyond this syllabus. They are also asking government to fund research focusing on diverse contributions to Ayurveda. One of the therapists brought to light his experience with Adivasis in Wayanad district of Kerala. He said that through their oral history he learnt from them their traditional ways of treating slipped discs using herbal pastes and unique massages. The idea of masculinity being aggressive has been replaced with soft, submissive masculinity in Ayurveda tourism. The idea of masculinity as always in binary opposition to femininity has been challenged in the way men are comfortable doing supposed feminine roles.

Thus, Ayurveda tourism has succeeded in bringing out multiple masculinities in the post-liberalization Era of Kerala. The coexistence of hegemonic masculinity based on upper caste Hinduism, textual knowledge and consumerism, and subaltern masculinities based on lower caste Hindu and non-Hindu communities, oral traditions and submissiveness. The hegemonic masculinity of upper caste Hindu men has established unequal social relations in the field of Ayurveda. It has monopolized claims over defining what Ayurveda is and in utilizing resources of Ayurveda. This hegemony operates in Ayurveda colleges, hospitals and resorts. This hegemonic masculinity has influenced government policies such as non-inclusion of Ayurvedic gynaecology in government hospitals and funding. However, non-hegemonic masculinities are circulating in the peripheries of Ayurveda practices in the forests inhabited by Adivasis, on roadsides and beaches by non-BAMS practitioners of Ayurveda.

What Ayurveda Tourism has done to the idea of development is that it has made paradigm shift based on the centrality of the market and the subordination of the state. The state is now the contract agent in legitimizing and facilitating market-based globalization (Kunhaman 2002). Here, Kerala has moved from land reforms to land consolidation, from eradication of poverty and food self-sufficiency to maximum foreign exchange receipts through Ayurveda tourism. The need of the hour is that the state indulges in restructuring of its development programmes and their implementation through people's participation wherein fisher-folk are subjects, not objects of development.

References

Banerjee, M. (2009). *Power, knowledge, medicine: Ayurvedic pharmaceuticals at home and in the world*. New Delhi: Orient Blackswan Private Limited.

Chatterjee, P. (1994). *The nation and its fragments: Colonial and postcolonial histories*. New York: Princeton University Press.

Devika, J. (2007). A people united in development. *Working paper*, Series 386. Thiruvananthapuram: CDS.

Foucault, M. (1995). *Discipline and punish: The Birth of the prison*. New York: Vintage.

Ilaiah, K. (1996). *Why I am not a Hindu: A Sudra critique of Hindutva philosophy, culture and political economy*. Calcutta: Samya.

Jameela, N. (2007). *Autobiography of a sex Worker*. Chennai: Wasteland.

Janu, C. K. (2004). *Mother forest: The unfinished story of CK. Janu*. Kali for Women: New Delhi.

Kunhaman, M. (2002). *Globalisation: A subaltern perspective*. Thiruvananthapuram: Centre for Subaltern Studies.

Lad, V. (2005). *Ayurveda: The science of self healing*. Delhi: Motilal Banarsidas Publishers Private Limited.

Martin, E. (1991). The egg and the sperm: How science has constructed a romance based on stereotypical male-female roles. *Signs, 16*(3), 485–501.

Mernissi, F. (2002). *Islam and democracy: Fear of the modern world*. New York: Basic Books.

Nandy, A. (1983). *The intimate enemy: Loss and recovery of self under colonialism*. Delhi: OUP.

Oommen, M.A. (1999). *Rethinking development: Kerala's development experience* (Vol. 1). Institute of Social Sciences. New Delhi: Concept Publishing Company.

Palsson, G. (2009). Biosocial relations of production. *Comparative Studies in Society and History, 51*(2), 288–313.

Rose, N. (2008). The value of life: Somatic ethics and the spirit of bio-capital. *Daedalus, 137*(1), 36–48.

Sankar, S. (2005). *Tourisavum Keralavum*. TVM: Spandanam.

Svoboda, R. (2010). *Prakriti: your ayurvedic constitution*. Delhi: Motilal Banarsidas Publishers Pvt. Ltd.

Varier, K. (2009). *History of ayurveda*. Kottakkal: Arya Vaidya Sala Pustakasala.

Caste and the Frontiers of Post-Colonial Capital Accumulation

Ritajyoti Bandyopadhyay and Ranabir Samaddar

Abstract In this chapter, the authors explore the complex relation between caste and post-colonial capital accumulation in India. Their evidence comes from the state of West Bengal which till date remains in the margins of the caste historiography, particularly economic historiography. The authors closely study the small- and medium-scale engineering industry in Howrah, an industrial city near Calcutta, between the 1940s and 1970s in the context of the participation of a particular middle-caste group—the Mahisyas—in various sectors of the industry in the prolonged boom period (1939–1961). It is often argued that caste works differently in West Bengal. It is argued that caste question in West Bengal appears to be subsumed in the larger issues of class and communalism that accounts for the continued hegemony of the upper caste 'gent' in society, polity and culture. Further, it is said that here exists a neat ethnic separation between the composition of the commercial–industrial elite and the cultural–political elite. Often, scholarly discussions on capital accumulation in West Bengal exclude the caste structure among Bengalis and focus on the management of family and kinship capital of the Gujaratis and Marwaris from western India. While discussing entrepreneurialism among members of religious groups other than the Hindus, scholars tend to look into family and kinship infrastructures without necessarily taking a caste optic. This chapter addresses this research gap through the dialectics of caste and capital in West Bengal.

Keywords Caste · Accumulation · Economies of scale · Industrial organization · Frontier

---

R. Bandyopadhyay (✉)
Indian Institute of Science Education and Research, Mohali, India
e-mail: ritajyoti.csssc@gmail.com

R. Samaddar
Mahanirban Calcutta Research Group, Calcutta, India

I.K. Mitra et al. (eds.), *Accumulation in Post-Colonial Capitalism*,
DOI 10.1007/978-981-10-1037-8_10

Introduction

Historical debates have a quaint air to them. As soon as they lose political relevance, which may or may not necessarily mean any intrinsic worth to a debate, they lose their shine. Thinking of the debate that took place more than 30 years ago in the 1970s continuing to the mid-1980s over mode of production in India, particularly in agriculture—whether India was semi-feudal, or semi-colonial and semi-feudal, or capitalist or retarded capitalist (Patnaik 1990); the scarcity of reference to caste as a particular factor in shaping the mode of production is striking. Yet, today it is not difficult to recognize that caste works as an axis of post-colonial capitalism. Therefore, there is a need to theorize the ways in which capital, particularly capital in the hinterland, is shaped or at least influenced by caste dynamics and influences the latter in turn. Equally, there is now a need to study the overwhelming presence of caste as a predicating factor in shaping the destiny of rural labour as agrarian labour or as surplus population absorbed in various forms of petty production, including artisanal mining, and small-scale and medium-scale industries, or as a reserve army of labour, or simply forming the vast army of footloose labour in the country. The relative absence of caste as a critical factor in a discussion on post-colonial political economy is stunning.

Partly, the reason is with the categories with which researchers were working at that time. With received categories they attempted to work out the implications of the dynamics they were studying: green revolution, mechanization of agriculture, form of rent, form of wage, impact of grain trade on production, mode of investment in agriculture, etc. In this connection, we may advance three tentative reasons for which caste was relatively absent in the analysis of the post-colonial political economy:

First, in this exercise there was little attention to an organizational analysis, in other words, on how the labour market is organized, or for that matter the capital market. We were not attentive to the organizational and structural process of accumulation, though this should not have been so. This is because at the same time when the mode of production debate was on, we were being enriched with studies on the interface of caste and capital formation in trade and production, discussions on merchant castes, bonded castes, or let us say a specific merchant banking caste such as the Chettiar (Rudner 1995). We had studies of the interdependence among Indian business practices, social organizations, religions, impact of colonial rule on indigenous commercial systems and the inextricable links through formal and informal institutions between caste, commerce, production and wealth. Practices crucial to the formation and distribution of capital also formed part of the study of the links, which could include factors, such as marriage alliance, status hierarchy and related rational conduct of business. And, remarkably, these studies suggested ways to study caste and agrarian labour and rural labour in general.

Second, we neglected what Tilly (1999) termed as durable inequality, which would refer to the organizational factors determining patterns of employment, purchase, investment, etc., that reproduce inequality. We can say that race, caste, gender or tribe constitute various aspects of the organization of society in which homogenizing tendencies such as accumulation, and equality have to operate. Inequalities endure, because for instance, civil rights legislation addresses only the situation in which a hiring boss, or committee, employs or promotes one person but not another in a formal system of straight competition. But as Tilly said, if we change the story new possibilities are thrown up. The story would thus be as follows: we have a large grocery store where there are different departments: one of them is meat, the other vegetables. It turns out that women move to the vegetables and the men to the meat. At entry level, they are paid the same. No discrimination. Walking about the store the men go to places where they can talk to other men and swap stories about football. Women go to places where there are other women and they can swap stories about prices of vegetables, or children's school fees, etc. But promotion structures work differentially so that managers mainly come from the meat department. There is no point at which you have two managers, one male and another female. No discrimination at the point of entry, or even promotion. But what you get over time is an invisible structure which is, in effect, discriminatory. Therefore, what is needed is again to learn about linkages between enclaves and ghettos, about networks, trust stocks and about migrations. It is the process—no need to go to the economics professor or to Walmart or Imperial Chemicals to know all these. So if we have to know the particularity of the dynamics in which caste works as a factor in accumulation we have to inquire about the process in which some castes stream into some occupations and some into other. The answer is in the processes of self-reproduction. The phenomenon of 'opportunity hoarding' of which Tilly spoke makes the dynamics of social mobility uneven. Overall social mobility has not changed much, and the possibility of moving from the agrarian sector into urban sectors meanwhile has diminished drastically. What is 'opportunity hoarding'? It operates when members of a categorically bounded network acquires access to a resource that it considers valuable, renewable, supportive of the network and enhanced by the network's modus operandi, and thus subject to monopolistic control. 'Opportunity hoarding' thus makes inequality durable. The concept allows insights into inter-group dynamics, race, ethnicity, identity, which include national units also in this dynamics. Economics rarely combines identity and interest; it takes into account only the latter. History emphasizes mostly the former. Tilly wanted to give us an approach based on a combination. The implications of this approach, we suggest, are deeper. Tilly said that large, significant inequalities in advantages among human beings correspond mainly to categorical differences such as black/white, male/female, citizen/foreigner or Muslim/Jew rather than to individual differences in attributes, propensities or performances. In this case, we have two elementary forms: *types of social relations* and *inequality-generating mechanisms*. We can see how a combination of these two elements leads us to an organizational analysis of inequality, organizational view of heterogeneity-generating mechanisms. Thus, although historical accumulations of institutions, social relations and shared understandings produce differences in the day-to-day operation of various sorts of categories (gender, race, citizenship, and so on) as well as differences in various sorts of outcomes (e.g. landed wealth vs. cash income), ultimately interactions of exploitation and opportunity hoarding explain them all. Grusky (1999) in a review of Tilly's work brought out the significance of 'opportunity hoarding' in undertaking an organizational analysis of economic processes.

Third, to grasp the relation between caste and accumulation, we have to use the notion of frontier in the way Bailey had long back (1957) used the word in his study of caste and the economic frontier. Bailey had analysed changes in the internal organization of a comparatively isolated village in the hilly section of eastern India, as a result of what he termed as the extension of the economic and administrative frontier, producing contacts qualified by caste, government policies, and the fact that the village studied by him consisted mainly of Hindu colonists in a predominantly non-Hindu tribal area. What is interesting in this is not the suggestion of a modernization thesis, which was there and is banal now, but the way the frontier of economy works in society. In thinking of the frontiers of accumulation, one sees how the multiple axes work. Caste is in fact the grease for the accumulation machine. The way low castes had their different destinies in districts and villages of West Bengal and Bihar shows how the accumulation machine works.

Now let us correct a bit to what was said in the first paragraph. It is not that caste was absent in the discussion. The presence of caste was considered as evidence that India was semi-feudal; the erosion of caste evidences that India was capitalist. Nothing of the two castes was simply sublimated in the political economy of post-colonial capitalist accumulation.

In this chapter, we try to explore the complex relation between caste and post-colonial capital accumulation in India. Our evidence comes from the state of West Bengal which till date remains in the margins of the caste historiography, particularly economic historiography. We closely study here the small- and medium-scale engineering industry in Howrah between 1940s and 1970s. It should be mentioned here that the city of Howrah has been, since the 1850s, one of the most industrialized settlements of India. We study a particular middle-caste group—the Mahisyas—that participated in various sectors of the engineering industry in the prolonged boom period (1939–1961). In what follows, the chapter posits caste as a key to understanding the dynamics of post-colonial capital accumulation.

It is often argued that caste works differently in West Bengal. We have been variously told that caste question in West Bengal appears to be subsumed in the larger issues of class and communalism that accounts for the continued hegemony of the upper caste *bhadralok* (gentleman) in society, polity and culture. Further, it is argued that in West Bengal there exists a neat ethnic separation between the composition of the commercial–industrial elite and the cultural–political elite. If the former is dominated by the Marwari and Gujarati houses of central Calcutta, the latter is populated predominantly by the upper caste, urban *bhadralok*. Often, scholarly discussions on capital accumulation in West Bengal exclude the caste structure among Bengalis and focus on the management of family and kinship capital of the Gujaratis and Marwaris (Birla 2009). While discussing entrepreneurialism among members of religious groups other than the Hindus, the scholars tend to look into family and kinship infrastructures without necessarily taking a caste optic. What follows then is that one has very little idea about the dialectics of caste and capital in West Bengal. The chapter attempts to address this research gap.

We have chosen the Mahisya caste in Howrah for an initial exploration of the questions we have just mentioned. The 1931 Census (the last census before the Census of 2011 that enumerated caste) placed the Mahisyas in the middle order in Bengal's caste hierarchy. Between the 1920s and 1970s, they played a prominent role in running several engineering workshops in the city of Howrah. How does one explain the significant presence of a predominantly agricultural caste in a particular urban industrial sector? Some studies in the 1950s and 1960s tried to solve this puzzle (RBI-JU 1964; Owens and Nandy 1977). At least two of these works have left enormous archives of field data that we propose to revisit in the light of some more recent historiographical developments, especially with the publication of Chari's (2004) *Fraternal Capital*. We also add new evidence to frame our argument.

In the next section, we present a rough picture of the enormously heterogeneous engineering industry clustered in a particular neighbourhood of Howrah. The third section considers some of the more plausible research findings in the 1950s and 1960s explaining the connection between caste and the accumulation of capital. Based on this, the fourth section proposes what can be called an agrarian history of the inter-sectoral 'switch' of capital, which is arguably the hallmark of capitalist accumulation. Section 'The Rise of Alamohan Das' presents the case of an exceptionally successful Mahisya entrepreneur who leaves behind a rich autobiography. The last section discusses some of our research findings in the context of a larger historiography.

A History of the Engineering Industry in Howrah

In July 1960, Jadavpur University under the auspices of the Reserve Bank of India (RBI-JU 1964) kicked off a survey of 'small engineering units in Howrah'. The survey continued until March 1961. The objective of the survey was to have an evaluation of the small-scale engineering units at the end of the Second Five-year Plan Period (1956–1961) which gave boost to develop steel plants and facilitated the growth of engineering machinery and tools manufacturing industry in India (Rao 1955). In fact, the Second Plan ended an era in the annals of the engineering enterprise in Howrah that had taken off a little more than a century ago with the coming of the railway age in India. The production of machines, machine parts, nuts, bolts, rivets, railway components, electrical goods (from the early twentieth century), pipes and tubes, non-ferrous products, wire products and scientific apparatus intensified to a significant degree in the inter-war and the post-World War II periods. In addition, there was a significant investment in iron foundries, job work, lathe work, sheet metal processing and re-rolling mills clustering in an area slightly more than ten square miles in two sides of the Grand Trunk Road running north–south through the Howrah Municipal area and in Balilious Road, stemming from the Grand Trunk Road to the West. By the mid-1950s, the roads were already teeming with small workshops in both sides. At that time, it was very common to find a unit hosting more than three precision grinders being choked with smoke and heat of several surrounding units. A stranger's stroller in these streets could be easily baffled by the assemblage of a variety of machines: lathe, capstan, shaping, grinding, punching, slotting, and so on. All such machines could be found stuffed in a dark shed measuring around 200–250 sq. ft., producing a range of tools and complex machines. The workers of these tinny shades knew the secret of complex body modulation to navigate around the machines.

The RBI-JU surveyors noted that by 1961 a little over 1,168 smaller units thrived in the area. The units spread even in lanes branching from the two main thoroughfares in all directions where the trucks could hardly pass. A majority of the units (707) were found to have employed less than 10 persons in each, while in 361 units the number of employees varied between 10 and 49 workers. In 80 units, the size of workers varied between 50 and 200 men. Only in rest of the 20 units did the surveyors find the number 200 mark.

The RBI-JU surveyors could retrieve the record of the value of plant and machinery for 868 units, of which they found that 225 units employed 20 or more workers. The RBI-JU surveyors took 200 'medium-sized units' to be a representative sample for the first round of survey. Most of such units came under the Factories Act and complied with the government's definition of 'small-scale units'. There were only a few units within their sample of 200 units that possessed a fixed asset over Rs. 500,000 (in 1960–1961, the conversion rate between the Indian Rupee and the USD varied between 4.77 and 4.78 Indian Rupees to 1 USD). In the second stage of the survey, they chose 396 'small-sized units' employing less than 20 workers.

Let us now mention some of the features of the engineering units as revealed in the RBI-JU survey. We refer to only those features that are found relevant to frame this chapter's argument.

First, it was found that out of the 200 medium-sized units, 39 units were established between 1865 and 1938. The rest of 161 units sprang up between 1939 and 1959. As one can see, the two decades starting from 1939 saw the war, national independence and much of the first two Five-year Plan periods. Further, the survey tells us that a half of the 396 sample small-sized units were set up between 1956 and 1960 which is precisely the Second Five-year Plan period. Only 32 such units were founded before the Second World War. Another 26 units started journey during the war. In short, then, the glorious period of the engineering industry in Howrah started in the late 1930s. It showed the signs of decline since the late 1960s when Owens and Nandy conducted their in-depth ethnography of these units. By 1980s the tide turned completely. It was a time when a devastating recession coupled with a crumbling electricity infrastructure and an emerging regime of environmental law had already crippled the industrial climate of the Balilious Road.

Second, it was found that the nature of ownership of the sample medium-sized units was of four kinds: proprietorship, partnership, private limited and public limited. It was possible to observe change in the pattern of ownership of units. To cite an instance, it was found that the growth of private limited companies was higher than other kinds of ownership. Forty-four units started as private limited company. At the time of the actual survey in 1960–1961, it was found that there were 64 such concerns. On the other hand, the number of proprietorship companies witnessed a marked decline (from 73 units at the beginning to 56 units at the time of survey). The RBI-JU Report considered the decline in proprietorship units and the swelling in the number of private limited companies as an index of prosperity in the overall industrial climate in the sector. The RBI-JU Report also showed that for proprietary and partnership companies, profits being reinvested to the process of production were estimated to be nearly double the amount of capital invested at the beginning of production. However, for limited companies, 'free reserves' and 'undistributed' profits in conjunction gave about two-thirds of the total paid up capital. In the case of the small-sized units, as many as 277 out of 396 sample units were proprietorship initiatives. Who were the owners of these small units? It was here that the RBI-JU report gives a sense of an important sociocultural process which would attract further ethnographic research. We shall come back to it in the next section.

Third, the RBI-JU Report estimated the value of the gross output of the 200 sample medium-sized units as Rs. 6.18 crores (Rs. 6,1800,000). Each unit then produced an average output of Rs. 3 lakhs (Rs. 300,000). In estimating the output, the Report cautions us that this might be an underestimation since one cannot here quantify the impact of the work done through subcontracting in the value of output. It was often found that the payments (including the workers' wage) made for subcontracting were included in the calculation of cost. Further, these figures did not usually include some spot sales. In contrast, the valuation of output in the case of small-sized units was closer to reality as these units did not usually subcontract their work to other units. During 1960–1961, the total annual output of the 396 small-sized units was Rs. 1.15 crore while the average of per-unit annual output would be close to 0.39 lakh.

Fourth, the RBI-JU Report estimated that total wage and salaries paid by the 200 medium-sized units in 1960–1961 was Rs. 1 crore. Taking the percentage of wages paid to net value added, the Report said that the worker's share in the medium-sized units was 39 % when the worker's share in the small-sized units was just 26 %. The Report concluded

> …thus, 74 percent go to owners of small units against 61 percent for the medium. Such a share of non-wage income in the small units will be considered very high indeed. It was higher than in the medium sized units which itself was high as compared with the share in organized industry elsewhere.

Such an estimate leaves no doubt that in the 1950s and 1960s, the engineering industry remained highly exploitative. The profit margin for the owner was generally higher.

Fifth, the RBI-JU Report gave us a picture of the interdependence and interlocking of production processes among the small- and medium-sized units. In the case of medium-sized units, the major consumers were as follows: big engineering concerns in neighbouring districts, textile mills, railways and local dealers. During the first two Five-year Plan periods, the central government's Directorate General of Supplies and Disposals became one of the major procurers from the medium-sized units. It was observed that raw materials such as pig iron and scraps moved first to the foundries. The foundries then passed the materials to a variety of units including the units that catered to railways and manufacture machines and parts of machines. Further, materials such as mild steel bars, gun metal and so forth entered the manufacturers of machines and machine parts again from the raw materials market. It was often seen that the manufacturers of machines transfer some of their products to the manufacturers of machine parts. Once the latter accomplished a bit of finishing work on the products, they came back to the former as ready to enter the market. This interlocking production process was responsible for the density of the engineering units within a very small geography of the city.

Sixth, it is important to note that in the condition of overall prosperity and high profitability in the climate of the engineering industry in Howrah between the 1940s and the 1960s, the real expansion of production took place in what could be called the 'smallholding and proprietary' form of industrial organization (Chari 2004). The happy coexistence of these two forms along with a few giant units in close proximity could possibly have two important implications for the capitalist: (a) a decentralized system of production organization was generally resistant to working class mobilization; (b) such a dispersed system of the accumulation of capital could easily put a cap on the worker's rights and wages which might be difficult if entire production took place in the formal/contractual sector.

What do these six aspects of the Report have to do with the main thrust of our argument?

First is of course the fact, which we shall show in due course, that a decentralized system of subcontracting can be re-aggregated through caste networks.

Second, these aspects relate to identifying the process of capitalist production, the impact of the colonial economy and the issues of class formation and analysis—not surprisingly, the three issues of mode of production that had vexed the debate.

The third aspect is the most significant. The Report conjures up a picture of the *karkhana* (shed, workshop, at times factory, but not in the sense of mill) with *karigar*s (artisans), *mistri*s (chief craftsmen, foremen), *head-mistri*s (some of them jobbers), some expert-repairing mechanics—the entire set up making sense only when we take into account a particular environ of production marked by proximity, small and closed space (very little space for stock keeping, housing quarters, etc.), caste and clan ties, all that made the *karkhana* of a colonial metropolis.

Yet, we must not forget that all this was possible because of the existence of jute and heavy engineering industry in the same town of Howrah that formed an important part of the production and supply chain of the commodities (tools and small machines such as lathe) there. Without caste, the particular organization of small- and medium-scale production which the Report brings out would have been impossible.

The Mahisya Question

We shall now explicate the above formulations. The RBI-JU Report shows that most of the owners of the small-sized units come from nearby neighbourhoods and semi-urban settlements. Let us quote a passage from the Report:

> About 90 percent of the owners are Hindus, and a surprisingly large number of amongst the Hindus are from one particular caste in West Bengal; 179 out of 423 are *Mahisyas* (italics original). This demonstrates, at least to a certain extent, the pool of family tradition, the force of family example and, perhaps, of financial or other family aid on the decision to start business. The analysis of their fathers' occupation reveals that 117 are sons of people in service with very low incomes, and as many as 46 are sons of factory workers; more than a quarter are sons of businessmen. Very few of them, only 13, are directly descended from families of industrialists…

There are at least two significant implications of this finding by the RBI-JU researchers. First, it shows that only a handful of the small-sized units were inherited. This means that in the majority of cases these units were the outcomes of the entrepreneurs' hard work. Second, it hints that the small entrepreneurs were not freshly released from the agrarian sector. Conspicuously absent was the figure of the peasant father in this narrative. This is especially striking when we know for sure that Mahisyas are known as predominantly a peasant caste in Bengal. Is this then a very specific feature of Howrah where the history of the conversion of agricultural land to industrial use predate most of the districts of Bengal? Third, at another level, the above quote appears to resolve the Mahisya question in vague terms, i.e. 'the pool of family tradition', 'the force of family example' and so forth. This hardly explains the reason that Mahisyas and not other castes could become what Owens and Nandy rather cleverly called the 'new Vaishyas' (1977).

Owens and Nandy conducted a fieldwork in the same area between September 1966 and August 1968. In a series of articles and in a book, they made an attempt to understand the Mahisya takeover of the small engineering units in the post-World War II period. They showed that the Mahisya domination was true at all levels of the small engineering sector—from the working class to the entrepreneurs. Owens and Nandy believed that this was not an abrupt or radical transition. Already in the mid-nineteenth century, Howrah was more urbanized and industrialized than any other district in Bengal. The wage differential between agriculture and industry was considerably high coupled with a sharp differentiation among the agricultural workforce. According to the census of 1921, in Howrah, the share of landless labourer in the total agricultural workforce was 30.05 %, which came only second to Birbhum (35 %) and much higher than other districts of western Bengal where differentiation among peasantry was considerably higher than the jute-producing eastern Bengal that has sustained small tenure holdings and small-scale peasant agriculture for a long time (Bose 1986, p. 31). In 1931, the percentage of the landless labour in Howrah further increased to 44.64 %, keeping pace with the general trend in many western Bengal districts (Chatterjee 1984, p. 39). In 1951, however, the share of landless labour in Howrah declined to 38.2 %. If the presence of the landless workforce amidst wage differential between agriculture and industry meant a growing tendency among the population to change their principal source of earning, the gradual decline in the percentage of landless labourer in agriculture between 1931 and 1951 implied that part of this population was absorbed in the non-agricultural sectors. Additionally, one can observe that between 1911 and 1931 the number of Mahisyas involved in cultivation in Howrah dropped by no less than 20 % while there was an increase in the number of landless labourers in agriculture by 12 and 7 % increase in the number of the 'white-collar' workers. We, then, find little reason to challenge the larger ethnographic finding of Owens and Nandy that the engineering workshops were run by the 'local' Mahisya labour force for two generations.

As next step, Owens and Nandy concluded that the Mahisya entrepreneurs of the 1960s and 1970s had prior knowledge of the operation of the workshops as they emerged from the Mahisya working class. During the boom of the First World War, many of workers of the existing engineering units started their own workshops to respond to the surplus demand created by the war. They appeared to gather initial capital from their petty savings and became millionaires in two decades. The old entrants to the industry, the propertied Brahmins and Kayasthas, gradually started losing ground. Their defeat was reflected in the upward mobility of the Mahisyas in sociocultural world of Ward 39 since the early 1920s. The first Mahisya founder of the engineering firm gradually displaced the two important Brahmin families in terms of controlling the real estate of the said ward and sent his son to a prestigious English medium school. The son, in his mature age, entered into Congress politics and became an MP from the Uluberia parliamentary constituency in 1967. Owens and Nandy argued that the ex-peasant and the ex-working class background of many of the Mahisya entrepreneurs have enabled them to cultivate an ethic of work and self-help that the members of the erstwhile rent-seeking castes crucially lacked. Such a privileged ethic of work became crucial at the time of slump and industrial unrest, as unlike their upper caste counterparts the Mahisya entrepreneurs themselves had the capacity to run the work of production. Thus, in a separate paper, Owens observed the following:

> I recall visiting the factory of one Mahishya entrepreneur in my sample who had come upon very hard times as a result of recession in process. The entrepreneur, who in previous interviews had been very much the 'Babu', dressed in spotless white dhoti-jama and supervising the work of several other labourers, was at our last meeting alone in his workshop, dressed in a workman's greasy T-shirt and lungi and working at a lathe. Wiping the grease off his hands as he sat down for the interview, he observed, 'I used to work at the lathe, and I can still do it when I have to' (1991, p. 244).

In another paper, Nandy (1973) confirmed Owens' observations about the work ethic among the Mahisyas. He argues that the 'positive attitude towards manual work' gave the Mahisyas a 'competitive advantage' over the upper castes that ultimately accounted for their success in industry.

The 'Switch' of Surplus

We hold that one cannot make a general argument about the Mahisya entrepreneurs to the extent saying they stemmed from an erstwhile Mahisya working class without furnishing evidence about the formalized banking infrastructure and other sources of savings and credit available to kick off even a small workshop. The RBI-JU survey has already shown that especially in the case of small-sized units' initial borrowings from family and friends outweigh the existing formal facility. The prevalence of dowry must have been another source of initial finance. However, we do not have any quantitative data to calculate dowry among the Mahisyas in Howrah. Given all this, it is difficult to argue that the workers would own the means of production at a mass scale in a given industry within the capitalist mode of production by means of savings from their wage coupled with some meagre wage subsidy from agriculture in the extended family and the ethic of 'self-cultivation' (whose destiny is to become an entrepreneur one day). The initial source must have come from *outside* the particular circuit of production, i.e. from agriculture, trade, money-lending, and so on. Since we do not have data about banking and credit facilities available to the particular segment of workers in early twentieth-century Howrah, we search for some alternative data from other sectors of economy, particularly from agriculture and the prevailing agrarian structure in western and south-western Bengal. We then frame a conversation between such relatively macro-data with our preliminary exploration of the history of one important Mahisya family in the industry.

Let us first look at the trends in land transfers in Bengal (see Table 1). Here, we have to remember that the reliable data come to us only after the passing of the amendment to the Tenancy Act in 1928 that made the transfer of occupancy holdings a statutory right. Overall, scholars of agrarian change in colonial Bengal agree that transfer of land from the small tenure holders and *ryot*s to the rich peasants increased significantly in the 1920s. The trend was checked significantly in 1929–1930, as the 1928 Amendment made it mandatory to pay 20 % transfer fee to the landlord. However, in the depression years of the 1930s, the rate of transfer augmented considerably.

Between 1930–38, Partha Chatterjee calculated from the tables on 'operations under the Bengal Tenancy Act' that the total sale and mortgage of land in the Mahisya belt of Midnapore (16.86 %), Hooghly (12.72 %) and Howrah (12.25 %) was to the higher limits when compared to the prevailing south and western Bengal standards. In 1930–1931, the total mortgage and sale of land in Howrah (2.38 %) was lower than just three districts in the undivided Bengal—Noakhali (3.25 %), Bogra (2.42 %) and Pabna (2.42 %).

Table 1 Transfer of land, 1930–1942

Year	Number of sales	Number of mortgages
1930	129,184	510,974
1931	105,701	376,422
1932	114,619	338,945
1933	120,492	313,431
1934	147,619	349,400
1935	160,341	357,297
1936	172,956	352,469
1937	164,819	302,529
1938	242,538	164,895
1939	500,224	154,780
1940	502,357	160,152
1941	643,113	151,553
1942	749,495	106,088

Source Registration Department Sources, Binay Chaudhuri, cited in Partha Chatterjee (1984, p. 143)

The data reveal a greater concentration of land in the hands of a few. As the historians of Bengal's agrarian transformation agree, those who benefited from this situation were not the members of the old rentier class, such as *zamindar*s and *patnidar*s, but an upwardly mobile rural *jotedar*s (rich peasantry) representing various middle strata of Bengal's complex caste ladder. It has been well documented by historians of colonial Bengal's agrarian relations that the late inter-war period witnessed the weakening of the control of the upper caste *bhadralok zamindar*s in the villages of south-western Bengal. The power of the agrarian economy came to be decidedly controlled by middle-caste *jotedar*s/moneylenders/traders and peasants having substantial land holdings who were 'partially rooted in production at the village levels', but operated generally as 'a kulak class engaged in a variety of economic activities' such as grain trading, and agricultural processing industries(Chatterjee 1984, p. 178). The upward mobility of the castes of Mahisyas in Midnapore, Aguris in Burdwan, and Sadgops and Tilis all over the south Bengal has been well documented by historians (Ray and Ray 1975). While explaining the growth of nationalist mass movements in south-western Bengal, H. R. Sanyal, for example, tells us how political leadership emerged from the *jotedar*/moneylender/trading classes that substantially challenged the *zamindari* sections on the question of village control through newly established union boards, and then by capturing anti-union board mobilization (Sanyal 1976; see also Chatterjee 1984).

The Mahisyas of Midnapore and Howrah featured the emergence of several landholding families in the 1920s and 1930s who also invested substantially in getting land leases in the Sundarbans (south Bengal delta and mangrove forest area). We interviewed one of the prominent members of the fourth generation of one such enterprising ex-peasant family in Howrah. Already in 1910, the founder of this family, Anukul Mondal, shifted from Bauria to Ward 39 of the city of Howrah. Until that time, as Owens and Nandy documented, the community in the said ward was dominated by two Brahmin gentlemen, Jogin Mukherjee and Keshab Chandra Banerjee, who owned most of the real estate of the area, conducted *panchayat*s (local governments) and a grand, month-long feast at the time of Durga Puja. Between 1885 and 1920, Banerjee won local elections by combining his caste position with the glory of being a revered landlord. The Mahisyas were still far inferior in caste hierarchy and mostly engaged in low-paying industrial jobs. Around the first decade of the twentieth century, Anukul Mondal mortgaged 105 bighas of his agricultural land to buy 17 kotthas of land in Ward 39 from a Suvarnavanik family. Anukul build an impressive residential complex on one part of the land and kept the rest for an engineering workshop which, by 1915, employed no less than 22 workers (18 of whom were from his caste group). In 1921, he bought another prime plot of 10 kotthas from Keshab Banerjee to open a second unit of the same workshop employing an additional 40 workers, 32 of whom came again from the Mahisya caste. By 1920, the economic and political fortune of both Jogin Mukherjee and Keshab Banerjee declined drastically.

Owens and Nandy recorded that while the former invested in a coal mine that produced water, the latter made an unsuccessful investment on a mining project that ultimately compelled him to sell his substantial real estate holdings in the adjoining areas of the Ward 39 to Anukul Mondal who, by 1924, started a modest life insurance agency in Howrah with a branch office at Hazra Road, Kalighat. In 1938–1940, Anukul sold off his possessions in the Sundarbans and invested in a number of medical and departmental stores in the Bhawanipore-Kalighat area. The descendants of his second and third sons still run these shops. Anukul's first son, Jugal Mondal, was sent to the prestigious English medium school named Bishop Westcott Institution. Jugal Mondal, in his mature age, became one of the most influential politicians from the Mahisya caste in Howrah, winning Lok Sabha elections in 1967 with a Congress ticket from Uluberia constituency. Later, in the mid-1970s Jugal Mondal joined the Janata Party and in 1978, lost in a Rajya Sabha seat from West Bengal. He is known to the community as a philanthropist who invested in schools and health centres in different Mahisya-dominated villages. Jugal Mondal was associated with over 300 clubs and societies in Howrah and Calcutta and maintained strong linkages between Mahisya caste associations in rural and urban Bengal.

The evidences of the 'switch' may not be overwhelming, as the origins of the 'first fund' to be invested remain hoary. Yet, from the above description, one can imagine the surplus accruing from non-farm activities of an affluent rich agrarian class. The small- and medium-scale units of Howrah got both capital and labour initially from the same caste–clan source, with the interrelation being bruising and intermittently bloody as the numerous strikes and militant workers' protests in Howrah throughout the decades of the 1950s and 1960s testify. No affinitive tie could satisfy the question of wage or the question of profit as recession began to hit the industrial scene of Howrah from the mid-1960s onwards.

The Rise of Alamohan Das

Alamohan Das is possibly the best known entrepreneur–industrialist among the Mahisyas. He leaves behind a rich legacy, an industrial township near Howrah and an equally illuminating autobiography in which he describes himself becoming a 'truly Bengali' industrialist (Das 1949). His eventful life took shape between 1909–1910 and 1949, precisely during the formative years of many of the promising engineering units in Howrah. There are six clear phases in his life. Barring the last phase in which he could sustain his fortune and switch capital to other fields the rest of his life was full of trials and tribulation. He retrospectively attributed his extraordinary success to his ability to toil incessantly and to his frugal living. Until we reach the climax of his narrative, we are repeatedly told how Das cultivated fortunes and then violently got dissociated from his fraternal, social and cultural resources.

Das's father was a farmer with a decent standard of living in a village near Howrah. When Das was a child, he witnessed a devastating epidemic in his village. The rhythm of life broke down as a result. Most of his clan members left the village for the town in search of alternative jobs. After Das's father recovered from a prolonged illness which lasted for about 2 years, he left the village and went to Calcutta. In the meantime, Das's mother fell ill and took refuge in her parental home. The little boy never agreed to the terms of his grandparents and decided to live in their dilapidated home. He ate whatever he found at hand. Subsequently, he went to the local elementary school and immediately attracted the attention of the head teacher. One day, Das discovered a small underground repository of gold coins which his forefathers might have saved and kept intact. With the news of gold coins, Das's parents returned. The father bought some land and started taking care of the household.

Das moved to Calcutta along with one of his neighbours. He found refuge in the shop of one of his acquaintances in the village. Subsequently, he started street-vending puffed rice. Gradually, he learnt many of the complex tricks of business. He never broke his savings unless he reinvested the same in his business. In a few years, he found that his savings would now allow him to start a new business of similar kind. The shop at Cornwallis Street started fetching him a good amount of money. The four walls of the shop appeared to be a bit claustrophobic to Das. Hence, he continued to work both as a shopkeeper and as a street vendor/hawker. In the meantime, he met one Sekhar Chandra Hazra who identified Das as one of his distant relatives. Hazra was a technical officer in one of the *swadeshi* (nationalist) chemical factories. He encouraged Das to develop an acid-making factory. In the meantime, Das had to relocate his shop to Howrah. Subsequently, Hazra visited his shop and gave him a plan to start an acid factory. Das gathered Rs. 5000–6000 and Hazra employed his expertise and technical brain to establish a new concern that came to be known as the 'Howrah Chemical Works'. Das identified a sprawling wasteland in the western fringe of the town of Howrah known in those days as Shanpur. Das wrote how he was able to provide an identity to Shanpur which was known to the locals as a dangerous and malarial place. In the late 1930s, Shanpur was renamed Dasnagar—a site for a number of Das's factories.

Howrah Chemical Works assumed a good name in the market, especially among Calcutta's Chinese tannery owners. However, the factory's fortune was crucially dependent on the intellectual and technical expertise of Hazra. Unfortunately, Hazra fell ill and took quite a number of years to recover. Das tried to somehow retain the goodwill of the factory, but he failed. Gradually, he switched his capital to jute speculation in which Marwaris had an almost exclusive dominance. Initially, he incurred heavy loss; however, gradually he started making some fortunes in this trade too. But, the more he became experienced in speculation, the more he felt that he should invest a portion of his savings to a more secure enterprise to ensure a steady flow of capital. Subsequently, Das started a small factory to manufacture weighing machines. He met a skilled *mistri*, Rajendranath Mondal, who promised to make perfect weighing machines provided that Das invested the initial capital. While working together in the fledging factory Das came to know that Rajen Mondal was one of his distant cousins. The first machine that Mondal made was a failure. Das found it difficult to market the weighing machine. The new product did not have the same brand value as that of the foreign imports. By now, all of Das's capital was locked in the factory's godown. Two things saved Das from this impasse. First, one of his acquaintances named Rajanikanta Pal agreed to become a partner to this initiative by investing Rs. 20,000. Second, Das and Pal decided to supply the new weighing machines free of cost to willing buyers. They promised that they would accept the price after the user was convinced of the machine's quality. To Das this was a master stroke. Within a few days, they sold weighing machines worth Rs. 50,000. Both Pal and Das then decided to expand the factory. They rented a larger factory space at Balilious Road. The brand name of their factory, B. W. Scales, spread in Bengal. The new fortune enabled him to buy ornaments for the family. Pal, on the other hand, withdrew a portion of his initial capital to reinvest the same to buy agricultural land. Das was also able to buy a motor car in the mid-1920s. To further expand the scope of production in the factory, Das loaned Rs. 50,000 from one of his rich acquaintances. But, again, there was a drastic slump in his business. This time Das'sentire fortunes, including his wife's ornaments, were drained out. He became what he used to be when he had gone to Calcutta nearly two decades ago.

Now a pauper, Das wanted to go to Mumbai to find a means of livelihood, but the chain of circumstances drove him to Rangoon (Yangon) in Myanmar via various towns of eastern Bengal. There was no improvement in his material condition during the initial months in Rangoon. He took a loan of Rs. 25 from one of his acquaintances there and started vending tea leaves at various places in Burma. With this new business, again, Das started saving money. He returned to Calcutta in June 1931. He paid back all his debts to friends and regained respectability among the traders in jute speculation. Within a few months of his return, he reopened B.W. Scales. This time, the factory ran well, giving him enough surplus to buy substantial land plots and factory spaces in Balilious Road. By 1933, he started a number of new engineering units to manufacture textile machines, printing machines, lathes, drills and shaper, and so on. Das was now solvent enough to employ a number of skilled engineers. Within a few years, he established a new jute mill exactly where he first started an acid factory. The wasteland gave birth to a new industrial township—Dasnagar. All the necessary equipment and machinery for the new jute mill came from his engineering units. The jute mill was registered as a private limited company. In this way, however limited and imperfect this might have been, vertical integration of his units gave him an advantage. None other than Acharya P.C. Ray inaugurated the jute mill and gave Das a new title—*karmabir* (roughly, hero as a man of work), which became his identity in subsequent years. In 1938, Das purchased 1,000 bighas of land in the Shanpur (Dasnagar) area to further expand the engineering units. In 1940, he started a new bank, the Das Bank Limited with no less than 60 branches in undivided Bengal. The Howrah Insurance Company Limited started in 1941. In the next year, Das made massive investment in founding the Asia Drug Company Limited. In 1945, he made substantial investment in the Great India Steam Navigation Company.

In short, then, by the end of World War II, Alamohan Das was at the helm of several organizations: Das Brothers (a managing agency), Bharat Jute Mills Limited, the Indian Machinery Company Limited (incorporating the Atlas Weighbridge and Engineering Company, B.W. Scales Company and Pal's Engineering Works Limited), Das Bank Limited, Dasnagar Cotton Mills Limited and the Howrah Insurance Company Limited.

This narrative may not seem to belong to the general trend of connection between caste and the accumulation of capital. Indeed, as one flips through Das's *Amar Jiban* (My Life), one finds how Das assigns a particular history to his toil. He tells us how he toiled hard to make Dasnagar an active site of production and circulation. Right at the beginning, he disavows caste, creed and religion and embraces a Bengali national community identity. He dreamt of uniting the entire Bengali national community through industry and entrepreneurship. Nowhere in the text can one find even a perfunctory mention of the Mahisya social movement. In fact, Nibaran Chandra Mondal who served as his private secretary in the 1960s told us in private conversation that Das was mentally far removed from any social movement caught in the language of ritual purity. The autobiography is marked by the author's periodic dissociation from familial relationships. On several occasions, Das identified himself as primarily as an individual free from fetters of the traditional village ties. His disdain for the rentier class is prominent in the narrative. There is no suggestion in *Amar Jibon* to conclude that Das ever ploughed back his capital to the land market. In a sense, his autobiography is a neat, historicist narrative. He starts as a *pheriwala* (vendor), and then is a shopkeeper for a long while. He then invests some surplus to become an entrepreneur. He also invests in jute speculation. After several trials, short-term success waves and a series of failures, he ultimately became an industrialist. Soon after, he switches some of his surplus capital to banking, waterways navigation and finance sectors. In a little over three decades, Alamohan Das travels from the world of petty commercial capital to the significantly advanced stage of finance capital. Das finds a logical unity in this trajectory of movement. He, for instance, recollects how his participation in jute speculation enabled him after a decade or so to become a successful jute mill owner.

How far is caste implicated in this story of transition? In this context, we have to remember that his narrative indicates at the same time the frontiers of accumulation where caste functions as discrete category. As we have seen, Das talks the role of partnership, friendship and fraternity in his narrative. In doing so, he acknowledges the existence of social ties that get full expression in only one community, the Bengali nation. Therefore, while on the one hand, time and again he informs the reader that even during the stressful days of his childhood he never accepted any fraternal support, and that his rise to prominence was completely a product of toil, self-regimentation, and extreme self-discipline, the narrative also speaks about figures such as Hazra and Rajendranath Mondal who appear in it as relatives, friends, etc., and were quite significant in his life. An examination of their caste location reveals that most of the key figures belonged to the Mahisya community.

The accounts of Jugal Mondal and Alamohan Das open up two important directions to study accumulation of capital as a socio-historical process. It leaves no doubt that in terms of age and establishment, Das preceded and exceeded Mondal, though Mondal came from a much more privileged background. Mondal's rise to prominence exemplifies how the switch from agriculture to trade and industry takes place over two generations. It is structurally difficult and a slow process.

Worlds and Ways of Capital Accumulation

In his book *Fraternal Capital*, Chari (2004) shows with great clarity how behind the emergence of Tirupur's (in Tamil Nadu) garment boom in the 1990s lies a prehistory of peasant entrepreneurialism in which the narrative of toil (as entrepreneurial utopia) plays a crucial role of 'institutional memory' (2004, p. 277). In the background of such works in other parts of India, Mondal's ancestral story sounds common. We have fragmentary evidence to show that these newly mobile, agrarian *kulak* classes started investing in Calcutta's real estate and retail sectors in the early 1940s, taking advantage of the wartime decline in the value of property. Here, one must mention that the impulse to diversify investment from the rice market and rice mills to real estate development and urban retail came in the 1930s, at a time when the price of rice started declining in the depression years and owing to—among others—the government's procurement of cheap Burma rice. More substantial *jotedars* also purchased rent-collecting rights in the bazaars from the old *zamindari* houses in Calcutta. They also set up new wholesale spaces in central Calcutta. The Roy family of Arambagh in Hooghly, for example, started investing heavily in the meat and poultry supply chain in Calcutta, while another, the Koley family from Kotulpur, Bankura district, invested initially in vegetable, fish, poultry wholesale (establishing the Koley market in 1932), and later in the food processing industry. The Koley market near Sealdah station became one of the major wholesale–retail centres for vegetables and fish in Calcutta. The Koley biscuit company in Narkeldanga (a segment of the same Koley family) also heavily invested capital in the city's sports culture, and with all these started claiming legitimacy in the city's *bhadralok* public culture. Some others from the same family participated in active politics since the Subhas Bose-J.M. Sengupta Era (1925–30) in the Calcutta Municipal Corporation. While more substantial middle-caste groups invested in urban provisioning from the 1930s, the less substantial *jotedar* families invested capital in urban retail. However, the *kulak-jotedar* capital remained essentially fragmented across multiple caste lines. In the 1950s, they tried to capture the spaces left vacant by substantial Marwaris who, from the 1930s, started replacing British capital in Bengal's veritable jute industry. However, they were extremely successful in establishing long-lasting ties with political parties through representation and everyday finance and subsequently gained from the abolition of *zamindari*, tenancy reforms, bank nationalization and subsidy.

The Great Bengal Famine in 1943 gave a serious blow to the already-shrinking caste-based, specialized, artisanal retail chains in the city. The newly mobile middle-caste groups started buying these moribund shops, and gradually replaced them with the more heterogeneous departmental and grocery stores. This change is well documented in Calcutta Corporation's property and shop register books. A similar change can be found in less substantial real estate properties too.

During our field research, we came across a large grocery store at Ashutosh Mukherjee Road in Bhawanipore. The store was established in 1944 by one Bimal Choudhury, whose ancestral home, we were told by Choudhury's great grandson, was in Kirnahar in Birbhum district. Bimal's father Nagendra Choudhury belonging to the middle caste Aguri community of the middle-West Bengal region, earned a lot of money and landed property in Kirnahar by lending money to some of the declining segments of the Sircar family of the village who had the rent-collecting right as a major *patnidar* of the Maharaja of Burdwan. In 1932, the Sircar family sacrificed its rent-collecting right. The Chaudhurys earned one-fourth of the rent-collecting right from the Sircars as a part of the repayment of the outstanding loans that the latter had incurred from them. Bimal, as the youngest son of Nagendra, inherited a commercial land plot at Bhawanipore, Calcutta, where he later established a grocery shop, a house in Sovabazaar that his father bought from the Deb family of Sovabazaar back in 1938, and some landed property at Kirnahar. Bimal also bought two stores in Shyambazaar (originally selling copper utensils) in 1948 and converted them to grocery stores. Our evidence from many such families in Calcutta attests to the fact that in the 1930s and 1940s there was a major change in the caste composition in Calcutta's wholesale and retail and real estate control.

The material wealth of *jotedar*s did not only come from their superior land control. They also controlled agricultural labour by participating in credit chains. Sharecroppers lacking capital for procuring seeds and food cultivated for half share of grain with loans advanced by the *jotedars*. Owing to credit compulsions, the poor farmers and sharecroppers sold their produce to the local grain dealer (*byapari*), who was often the *jotedar*, without waiting for a higher market price. The *jotedar* equipped with storage capacity (*gola*) would hoard the grain for months to sell them in the middle of the cultivating season when the grain prices would soar again (Ray and Ray 1975). However, due to the fragmented nature of the middle castes in Bengal, the *jotedar* capital could not establish a monopoly ethnic control over the real estate or the segments of the wholesale trade. Nor could they come up with a formalized caste-based banking network that a number of middle-caste trading communities could achieve in southern India.

In West Bengal, the middle-caste *kulak* interest did not always succeed in forming a powerful political party to safeguard its economic position and frame a distinct political goal. The Bangla Congress could at best be called one such moment in the late 1960s when *kulak* interests converged regionally against a potentially radical food movement. The bloc crumbled within 2 years of its formation in 1967. This is not to deny their strong presence in district committees of all the major political parties in the state. By operating through the long-established and regionally dominant political parties, they became the highest beneficiaries of the nationalization of banks, and they still have some control over the commodity traffic in the complex network of national and state highways connecting different parts of the state with the major wholesale centres of central Calcutta. The story of Jugal Mondal appears to be just one instance of a larger economic and social process in late colonial and early post-colonial Bengal.

By contrast, the story of Alamohan Das presents to some extent a different account of accumulation of capital. From his autobiography, it is difficult to show that the initial capital for him came from any definite external source. The fortunate discovery of gold, though, could not replace the need to take recourse to familial contacts again and again. What is noticeable, however, is the fact that until his return from Burma he needed this initial capital a number of times. One may also say that Das could gather the initial investments because of the prevailing political and cultural ambiance of *swadeshi* and economic nationalism that offered him legitimacy to come back to the field again and again. His reading habit, his close relationship with Acharya P.C. Ray and (later) with the B.C. Roy regime in West Bengal are all well-known facts. Das knew how to turn the prevailing circumstance to his advantage to translate and mobilize cultural resources for the accumulation of capital.

The small story of the Mahisyas in Howrah then is just one instance of a larger economic and social process in late colonial and early post-colonial Bengal. This chapter is thus not a conclusive account of how caste has worked in the dynamics of accumulation in post-colonial capitalism. However, the account certainly suggests which way further research can go.

Table 2 tells of one of the ways in which rural money was being diverted into activities other than agriculture. One will also see the substantial presence of the intermediary castes among the owners. Perhaps the ownership pattern of cinema houses, district bus services, vehicles, small foundries and several trading activities would also show the same. The instance of ownership pattern of rice mills is particularly important because as a site of production and investment the rice

Table 2 Rice mills in undivided 24 Parganas and Burdwan: Identity of owners

District	Area within a district	Name of the rice mill	Name and surname of the owner(s)
A. 24 Parganas	a. Belgachia	Siddheshwar Rice Mill	Bhagabati Charan Sadhukhan
		Dhankuriya Rice Mill	Ballabh & Co. Owner: Unknown
		Srimantdas Rice Mill	Unknown
		Rice Mill of Bholanath Chattopadhyay	Bholanath Chattopadhyay & Sons
		S. K. Basu Rice Mill	S. K. Basu
		P. M. Bagchi Rice Mill	P. M. Bagchi
		Ghatak Rice Mill	Ganesh Chandra Ghatak
	b. Belgachia-Daspara	Sadhukhan Rice Mill	Purna Chandra Sadhukhan
		Ballabh Rice Mill	Ballabh & Co. Owner: Unknown
		Radharani Rice Mill	Pannalal Das & Sitanath Das
		Mondal Rice Mill	Nilmani Mondal
		Kamala Rice Mill	Haripada Ghosal
		Rice Mill of Haricharan Sadhukhan	Shayamacharan Sadhukhan
		Shyama Rice Mill	Jogendra Kumar Chanda
		Rice Mill of Haripada Sen	Haripada Sen
		Bimala Rice Mill	Roy Manmathanath Paul Bahadur
		Shanti Rice Mill	Nibaran Chandra Sarkar
		Annapurna Rice Mill	Beharilal Ghatak
		Sarbamangala Rice Mill	Roy Jodunath Mazumdar Bahadur
		Rice Mill of Jaminikanta Kundu	Jaminikanta Kundu
		Shyamsundar Rice Mill	Jogendranath Saha
		Rice Mill of Jamini Mondal	Mondal and Sons
		Bimala Rice Mill	Unknown
		Baghmari Rice Mill	Lalmohan Pal, Sadhucharan Roy
		Gayen Rice Mill	Sudhansu Gayen
		Gobinda Rice Mills. LTD	Birla Brothers
		Rice Mill of Rampadarak Koiri	Rampadarak Koiri

(continued)

Table 2 (continued)

District	Area within a district	Name of the rice mill	Name and surname of the owner(s)
		Rice Mill of Satyacharan Paul	Satyacharan Paul
		Devisankar Saw Rice Mill	Unknown (surname?)
	c. Chetla	Rice Mill of N. C. Kawaji	Unknown (surname?)
		Progress Rice Mill	Unknown
		Kali Rice Mill	Unknown
		Rice Mill of Kalinath Chakrabarty	Kalinath Chakrabarty
		Choga Rice Mill	Unknown
		Annapurna Rice Mill	Unknown
		Mill of Sitanath and Pannalal Das	Sitanath and Pannalal Das
		Mill of Bhagabatchandra Sadhukhan	Bhagabati Charan Sadhukhan
		Rice Mill of Devi Shaw	Devi Shaw
		Chagmal-Haranaran Rice Mill	Unknown
	d. Alipore (mainly Alipore Road)	Lakshmijanardan Rice Mill	Unknown
		Diamond Rice Mill	Unknown
		Kamala Rice Mill	Unknown
		Gauranga Rice Mill	Unknown
		Durga Rice Mill	Nagendranath Sarkar
	e. Tolleyganj	Rupnaran Rice Mill	Unknown
		Ganji-Saji & Co. Rice Mill	Unknown
		Bibhakar Rice Mill	(Unknown)
		Nanci-Kuvarji Rice Mill	Unknown
		Tribhuvan Rice Mill	Unknown
		Rice Mill of Rajnarayan Roy	Rajnarayan Roy
		Gaur-Bishnupriya Rice Mill	Jogen Mondal
		Satyanarayan Mill	Unknown
		Annapurna Rice Mill	Gopal Chandra Das
	f. Sahapur	Rice Mill of Krishnakali Shib-Krishna Roy	Shibkrishna Roy
		Rice Mill of Mahendranath Gayen	Mahendranath Gayen

(continued)

Table 2 (continued)

District	Area within a district	Name of the rice mill	Name and surname of the owner(s)
		Daktarbabu & Co. Mill	Unknown
		Rice Mill of Taraprasanna Karmakar	Taraprasanna Karmakar
		Rice Mill of Basanta Saha	Basanta Saha
		Khekuria & Co. Rice Mill	Unknown
		Gobinda Das Rice Mill	Gobinda Das
		Rice Mill of Nanda Jana	Nanda Jana
		Rice Mill	Jogin Das
		Rice Mill	Pannalal Das
		Rice Mill	Gopal Das
		Rice Mill	Ramsundar Das
		Rice Mill	Upendra Sarkar
		Rice Mill	Upen Dutta
		Rice Mill	Binoykrishna Das
		Rice Mill	Kunja Ghosh
		Rice Mill	Sudhamadhab Mondal
		Emerald Rice Mill	Unknown
		Union Rice Mill	Unknown
		Rice Mill	Srikrishna Saha
		Gazi Miyazan Rice Mill	Unknown
		Rice Mill	Nagen Das
		Rice Mill	Anadh Basu
		Ramdeo-Rameshwar Rice Mill	Unknown
		Rice Mill	Nibaran Paul
		Rice Mill	Sukomol Marwari
		Rice Mill	Aswhini Hajra
		Rice Mill	Rashik Dula
		Rice Mill	Purna Chandra Dutta
		Rice Mill	Ghosh & Co.
		Rice Mill	Upendranath Ghosh
		Rice Mill	Rajababu & Co.
		Rice Mill	Mahendra Guin
		Rice Mill	Rishi Hajra
		Rice Mill	Md. Yashin
		Rice Mill	Bhutnath Hajra
		Shib Durga Rice Mill	Unknown
		Rice Mill	Basanta Kumar Roy
		Jagatlakshmi Rice Mill	Unknown

(continued)

Table 2 (continued)

District	Area within a district	Name of the rice mill	Name and surname of the owner(s)
B. Burdwan	a. Kalna	Rice Mill	Kartik Chandra Ghosh
		Rice Mill	Das-Seth &C.
		Rice Mill	Rajkrishna Seth-Abinash Chandra Das
		Rice Mill	Krishna Chandra Ghosh
		Rice Mill	De &Seth
		Rice Mill	Kamakshacharan Seth
		Rice Mill	Kalipada Sarkar
		Rice Mill	Bhajagopal Nandy
		Rice Mill	Asutosh Seth
		Rice Mill	Chandicharan Das
		Dharmanaran Rice Mill	Unknown (Marwari, personal source)
		Rice Mill	Panchugopal Das
		Rice Mill	Bholanath Kundu
		Rice Mill	Srish Chandra Malik
		Rice Mill	Tulshi Charan Paul
		Rice Mill	Girindranath Dutta
		Rice Mill	Panchanan Kundu
	b. Katwa	Annapurna Rice Mill	Upendranath Dan-Muchiram Dutta
	c. Bainchi	Annapurna Rice Mill	Gangagobinda Nandy-Panchanan Nandy
		Kamala Rice Mill	Basanta Nandy-Jamini Nandy
		Lakshmi Rice Mill	Radhagobinda Nandy-Nashiram Kundu
	d. Memari	Rice Mill	Girindra Hajra
		Rice Mill	Bijoynaran Kundu
		Rice Mill	Bholanath Mukherjee
		Rice Mill	Sarada Hajra
	e. Purbasthali	Rice Mill	Ramkrishna Seth
		Rice Mill	Krishna Chandra Ghosh
	f. Burdwan town and neighbouring areas	Nityakali Rice Mill	Rajkrishna Dutta
		Rice Mill	Ramdayal De & Bhavataran De
		Rice Mill	Birendranath & Girindranath Nandy
		Radhaballav Rice Mill	Banawarilal Kundu
		Rice Mill	Harinarayan Samanta & Brothers
		Srihari Rice Mill	Haribhushan De

(continued)

Table 2 (continued)

District	Area within a district	Name of the rice mill	Name and surname of the owner(s)
		Sarbamangala Rice Mill	Saratchandra Paul
		New Rice Mill	Unknown
		Rice Mill	Ramnarayan Roy
		Annapurna Rice Mill	Nagendranath Samanta
		Rice Mill	Nilmani Das
		Rice Mill	Banawari Panja
		Rice Mill	Ramratan Chaudhury
		Kalinandalal Rice Mill	Unknown
		Rice Mill	Ramsharan Das

Source Computed from Seth (1332 B.S.) and Department of Commercial Intelligence and Statistics, 1925, Kolkata: Government of India Central Publication Branch

mill stands at the crossroad of several economies: supply chain of an important rural commodity, rural credit and money supply, rural and semi-urban investment, stocking and hoarding, transportation and finally wage labour economy. The rice mills also tell us of the 'switch' earlier referred to in this chapter. Of the 133 rice mills in two districts (undivided 24 Parganas and Burdwan) registered and recorded here, while about 10 do not have their owners' identities mentioned, 5 belong to communities such as the Marwaris, Muslims, and Parsis, at least 35 belong to non-upper castes of Bengal. Equally significant is the fact that some of the rice mills under intermediary caste ownership are in urban areas. In all probability, we can say, the investment source for the industrialization of Howrah marked by massive Mahisya presence came from the rural affluent looking for further investment opportunities. Yet, and as always, capital needed labour. The labour too came again, at least initially, from the Mahisya community, which explains the dominance of the *karkhana* pattern of the production site. It is of course a matter of another inquiry if as a consequence the Mahisya community split wide open into capitalists and workers, or with the decline of the small- and medium-scale industries in Howrah with the overall decline of industries in West Bengal, the stasis in small-scale and medium-scale industries in Howrah deferred the split. And the uneasy compromise between caste as community and capital continues.

Conclusion

In conclusion, then, we can go back to the two comments made at the outset. First, to understand the role of caste in accumulation process we have to go deep into an organizational analysis, which as we have tried to show in this chapter would include analysis of supply chains, networks, property transfers and several allied factors that result in durable (in this case ascribed by specific caste identity) positions. The organizational analysis enables us to grasp what is at stake in the phrase 'frontiers of post-colonial accumulation', by which we indicate a dynamic process of interface between the colonial and post-colonial society and the immanent logic of political economy. Second, the debates in the seventies and eighties of the last century on mode of production, such as all social science discourses, were acts of displacement, for while caste and capital were working in several ways in shaping and re-shaping one another in precisely those decades, caste had been already sublimated in the framework of an academic debate.

If we go back to the Mahisyas at the engineering workshops in the city of Howrah, what appears striking to us is the near-absolute homogeneity of the caste composition of the entrepreneurs and the workers. If we accept Owens' and Nandy's conclusion that the entrepreneurs emerged from the workers, we are left with very little to proceed further. Not only evidences point to the external sources of the initial capital, but they also suggest the need to inquire into the operation of caste-based formal/informal associations in coordinating many extra-economic relations and loyalties in recruiting local labourers and mitigating conflicts between labour and capital. Equally suggestive is the need to study the organization of the production place (as brought out by the RBI-JU Report) to see how affinitive ties and the closed nature of the production place called the *karkhana* made capital accumulation possible in Howrah. It is then that we shall be able to understand the layered relation between caste and capital accumulation. Also then we shall be able to see why the concept of frontier is more appropriate than border for understanding the relation between caste and capital accumulation.

References

Bailey, F. G. (1957). *Caste and the economic frontier: A village in highland orissa*. Manchester: Manchester University Press.

Birla, R. (2009). *Stages of capital: Law, Culture, and market governance in late colonial India*. Durham and London: Duke University Press.

Bose, S. (1986). *Agrarian Bengal: Economy, social structure and politics, 1919–1947*. Cambridge: Cambridge University Press.

Chari, S. (2004). *Fraternal capital: Peasant-workers, self-made men and globalization in provincial India*. Ranikhet: Permanent Black.

Chatterjee, P. (1984). *Bengal 1920–1947: The land question*. Calcutta: K. P. Bagchi & Company.

Das, A. (1949). *Amar jiban*. Kolkata: KalikataPrinting Co.

Grusky, D. (1999). Review of durable inequality. *American Journal of Sociology, 104*, 1823–1825.

Nandy, A. (1973). Need achievement in a Calcutta suburb. In M. Singer (Ed.), *Entrepreneurship and modernization in South Asia* (pp. 167–178). Durham: Duke University Program in Comparative Studies on South Asia.

Owens, R. (1991). Peasant entrepreneurs in an industrial city. In M. S. A. Rao, C. Bhat, & L. N. Kadekar (Eds.), *A reader in urban sociology*. New Delhi: Orient Longman.

Owens, R., & Nandy, A. (1977). *The new vaishyas*. Bombay: Allied Publishers Private Limited.

Patnaik, U. (1990). *Agrarian relations and accumulation: The mode of production debate in India*. New Delhi: Oxford University Press.
Ray, R. K., & Ray, R. (1975). Zaminders and JOTEDARS: A study of rural politics in Bengal. *Modern Asian Studies, 9*(1), 81–102.
Rao, K. S. (1955, November 12). The second five year plan: Some methodological considerations. *Economic and Political Weekly 7, 46*.
Reserve Bank of India-Jadavpur University. (1964). *Survey of small engineering units in howrah, Calcutta*. Calcutta: Sri Saraswati Press.
Rudner, D. (1995). *Caste and capitalism in colonial India: The nattukottai chettiars*. Berkeley and Los Angeles: University of California Press.
Sanyal, H. (1976). Dakshin-Paschim Banglay Jatiyatabadi Andolon, 1. *Chaturanga, 38*, 1–26.
Seth, S. (1332). B.S. Bange Chaltattva. Kolkata: Tara Press.
Tilly, C. (1999). *Durable inequality*. Berkeley and Los Angeles: University of California Press.

Governmentalizing NRI Philanthropy in Andhra Pradesh: A Transregional Approach to India's Development

Sanam Roohi

Abstract This chapter looks at the idea of governmentalization of NRI philanthropy in the state of Andhra Pradesh. In a detailed analysis, the author shows how the dominant community of the Kammas in the coastal Andhra region, having historically benefitted from being part of the anti-Brahmin movement, consolidated their identity as the foremost landowners with a concerted effort towards higher education and already established networks enabling them to pursue careers in the USA. This, and a belief in giving back to the village and caste that has enabled their migration and hence success in life, has encouraged philanthropy in the region, in terms of NRI contribution to the NRI cell of Zilla Parishad and the Janmabhoomi project of the then TDP government. This is crucial because, with the term 'governmentalization', she shows how caste interests influence government policy and shape the direction which philanthropy will take, who will be the recipient of the philanthropic measures, how will the philanthropic projects be spatially located and how the existing structures of hegemony will continue in this curious coming together of public and private capital.

Keywords Caste · Governmentalization · Public and private capital · Philanthropic circuits · Accumulation

---

This paper draws on my Ph.D. research conducted under the 'Provincial Globalisation Programme a collaboration between the Amsterdam Institute for Social Science Research (AISSR) University of Amsterdam the Netherlands and the National Institute of Advanced Studies (NIAS) Bangalore India funded by the WOTRO Science for Global Development programme of the Netherlands Organisation for Scientific Research (NWO). I thank the ProGlo team for their support in my research.

S. Roohi (✉)
National Institute of Advanced Studies, Bengaluru, India
e-mail: sanam.roohi@gmail.com

S. Roohi
Amsterdam Institute for Social Science Research, Amsterdam, The Netherlands

I.K. Mitra et al. (eds.), *Accumulation in Post-Colonial Capitalism*,
DOI 10.1007/978-981-10-1037-8_11

Introduction

On 13 December 2014, Chandrababu Naidu's official Facebook page made an announcement about his plans for making a 'Smart Andhra Pradesh'. Naidu, who had taken office 6 months earlier, was ambitious in his endeavour to make the truncated state of Andhra Pradesh (that had undergone bifurcation in June 2014 from which Telangana was carved out), one of the best three states in India.[1] To this effect, he was keen to launch the Smart Village Smart Ward (SVSW) programme, and he announced the plan to his Facebook followers where he explained:

> To make our state sustainable and smart, it is not only necessary to have smart cities but also smart villages and towns. There are 13 districts, 664 mandals, 111 municipal bodies, 12,950 g panchayats and 16,250 villages, including wards and divisions. If these 16,250 villages can be adopted, the entire state can be transformed into 'Smart Andhra Pradesh'. Just like smart cities, a smart village should be interactive and multi-functional; there should be active participation of people in various activities. A smart village should have power, knowledge, healthcare, technology, entrepreneurship and internet connectivity. Our focus on building smart cities is prudent and timely. Simultaneously, if smart villages are built, apart from the benefits that it will bring to villagers, it would also solve one of the biggest problems cities are facing today—migration. This plan also puts our state in tune with the Central government's *Saansad Adarsh Gram Yojana* (SAGY) to adopt one village and develop that village as a model village. I appeal to NRIs, NGOs, VIPs, Corporates, Philanthropists, Ministers, MLAs, etc. to adopt one village each and develop our state into a 'Smart' Andhra Pradesh.

The central precept of this project was that socially aware individuals or corporates could come forward and adopt a village, build its infrastructure, make it self-sufficient and digitally linked, and in the process arrest migration to cities. SVSW programme on the surface appeared to have integrated two of National Democratic Alliance government's schemes, namely the Smart Cities mission[2] that was still in the stage of ideation then, and the *Saansad Adarsh Gram Yojana* (SAGY) that was launched in October 2014 amidst much fanfare.[3] Since the Telugu Desam Party (TDP) was an ally of the National Democratic Alliance (NDA) government led by the Bharatiya Janata Party at the Centre, the SVSW project received widespread coverage from the national media.

The Smart Village Smart Ward scheme was launched soon after in January 2015. Shortly, many villages and wards were 'adopted' by Telugus, but in the spirit of the *Saansad Adarsh Gram Yojana* where individuals or corporates could adopt any village across India, non-Telugus including celebrities like Sachin

[1] http://apvision.ap.gov.in/about_vision.html; accessed on 9 January 2016.

[2] For the statement about the mission, check the following document http://smartcities.gov.in/writereaddata/SmartCityGuidelines.pdf; accessed on 9 January 2016.

[3] More details about this scheme can be found at http://www.nird.org.in/sagy.aspx, accessed on 9 January 2015.

Tendulkar[4] and corporates like Tata[5] had already come forward to adopt villages in Andhra. But once the SVSW scheme was officially launched, there was another group that had come out in big numbers promising their support for the scheme: the NRIs (non-resident Indians)[6] from Andhra Pradesh residing in the USA. Chandra Babu Naidu's son Nara Lokesh had made an official visit to the USA in May 2015 and personally exhorted the American Telugu NRI community there to adopt villages. With this visit, more than 780 NRIs came forward and pledged their support for the scheme to adopt over 1,000 villages.[7]

Six months later, flushed with its 'success', Naidu updated his Facebook followers about how the SVSW scheme had gained momentum in such a short period of time and became a 'movement'. He was keen on not letting this momentum die and made the following appeal to his followers on Facebook:

> I appreciate all the people, Corporates, NRIs, Non-Resident Villages, bureaucrats and public representatives who have come forward to adopt a village/ward/town/constituency in Andhra Pradesh… I want you to stay motivated and make this work. I have alerted all the District Collectors to follow-up with you individually. We, the Government of Andhra Pradesh, realize that it is not easy to make people understand why you need to care about the future of your villages/towns. The idea of this program is to teach people about their responsibility towards society and work on green and sustainable living. This is a people's movement, a movement through which you can give back to the society.

The two excerpts above from Chandra Babu Naidu's official statements about the SVSW scheme bring to the fore a few assumptions that his government hold: first, about envisaging a model of development where non-government stakeholders become partners, and second, *who* the government imagines as these partners. In both these excerpts, NRIs feature prominently—in the first excerpt as probable partners and in the second excerpt as successful partners in development. Given the novel way in which NRIs are seen as actual partners in a government initiated programme, rather than the usual 'NRIs as investors' outlook (Walton-Roberts 2004), this chapter attempts to unravel how and why NRIs have come to occupy this position of harbingers of development in Andhra. Further, analysing the significance of such a model of development where NRI engagements are institutionalized or governmentalized, this chapter interrogates the nature of such transregional governmentalization efforts that seek to realize the neoliberal aim of self-sufficiency, albeit on a micro-scale—at the level of villages and wards.

---

[4]Tendulkar adopted a village under the SAGY scheme. A report on how he transformed this village in Nellore district can be found here http://www.thehindubusinessline.com/news/how-sachin-transformed-an-andhra-pradesh-village/article7054466.ece, accessed on 9 January 2015.

[5]The involvement of a corporate such as Tata is worthy of a full-fledged investigation. This report talks about Tata's philanthropy and how it was also interested in business opportunities http://www.theweek.in/news/india/ratan-tata-andhra-pradesh-Telangana-hyderabad.html, accessed on 9 January 2015.

[6]NRI or non-resident Indians is a legal category which is widely used to denote any Indian living outside of her country.

[7]http://www.newindianexpress.com/states/andhra_pradesh/780-NRIs-in-New-Jersey-to-Adopt-Villages-in-Andhra/2015/05/11/article2808369.ece, last accessed on 10 January 2015.

Finally, this chapter then goes on to disaggregate the concept of neoliberalism itself to make a point about the highly particularized shape it takes, contingent upon the dynamic political nature, arguing that multiple possibilities including governmentalization of NRI engagements in development practices become possible because of the variegated nature of *neoliberalism in practice* as opposed to neoliberalism as a universalizing ideology (Harvey 2006).

NRIs as Partners in Regional Development

The colonial and post-colonial political economy of Coastal Andhra including the adoption of Green Revolution technologies[8] in agricultural production (Washbrook 1975; Satyanarayana 1991; Upadhya 1988a, b) propelled the growth of caste-based landowning communities who were identified as economic and political dominant castes in the Coastal Andhra (Elliot 1970; Kohli 1990). The prominent among these landholding groups—the Kammas—through their numerical concentration in the districts of Guntur and Krishna and their preponderance in controlling economic resources in this fertile riverine region (prominent among which is land and its yields) emerged as the most powerful caste in the region. Through a multi-pronged strategy whereby they controlled the means of production in the region, and technologies of rule including educational institutions (Kamat 2004), bureaucracy (Mooij 2007) and finally with the formation of the TDP (known as a 'Kamma' party) the government itself, the Kammas succeeded in accruing many forms of social, cultural, symbolic and political capital including becoming a community of successful transnational 'high skilled' migrants (Roohi N.D.a).

Carol Upadhya's work shows us in detail how the Kammas of coastal Andhra diversified their economy from a rural agrarian one to a more urbanized one (Upadhya 1988a, b). Not only did they diversify their economy, with the surplus generated from this, but also Kammas (like other landholding castes in the region) started investing in higher education of their children, first their sons and later their daughters too over time. These educated professionals started migrating abroad since the 1960s and continue to do so till this day.

Guntur district (that was a key site of my 15-month long multi-sited ethnographic research) saw a slow but steady flow of outward migration from the region to the USA from the late 1960s from among the dominant castes, particularly the Kammas. The move coincides with the time when Green Revolution technologies began to deliver gains. Many of these US-bound 'high-skilled migrants' became

[8]The Green Revolution of the late 1960s and early 1970s stimulated the growth of commercial agriculture further, and, according to several scholars, capitalist relations of production, leading to economic diversification into business activities and non-agricultural occupations, as well as urban migration within landholding caste groups.

permanent settlers in the USA. My research points out to two waves of migration emanating from the region. The first wave of migration started in the 1960s and continued till the 1980s. This phase saw the outward movement of doctors, engineers, scientists and pharmacists moving to the USA for residencies or higher studies. A large number of engineers followed, who migrated as part of the second wave in the wake of 'Y2K' boom.[9] These two waves of migration to the USA have produced a 'culture of migration' (Connell 2008; Cohen 2004) whereby in places such as Guntur, migration of the youth from the dominant castes is looked at as a positive and even inevitable process.

Though transnational migration to the west has a few decades old history, a parallel but more recent development in the region has been the philanthropic engagements of these NRIs since the late 1990s. Having become 'well settled' with enough disposable incomes, many of these NRIs started to send some money back to their places of origin for various 'development'-oriented philanthropic projects. These philanthropic engagements were over and above the usual trails of *daan* or charity that ended up in building or improving temple complexes with NRI money. On the other hand, these NRI engagements were targeted towards 'developing' the home regions, much of it directed at improving the rural infrastructure of the migrants' native villages. Yet, the most interesting feature of these projects was the involvement of the state government. Such government–NRI collaboration was done under the aegis of the *Janmabhoomi* (motherland) programme,[10] envisioned by Chandra Babu Naidu during his earlier stint as a chief minister in the mid-1990s.

Naidu was the first chief minister of a state that restructured its economy with International Monetary Fund and World Bank guidelines (Reddy 2002). In accordance with these guidelines, Naidu became a proponent of public–private partnership in Andhra's economy and participatory government in the state's development. The *Janmabhoomi* programme must be seen as part of these neoliberal restructuring measures undertaken by the then government of Andhra Pradesh. The programme attempted to reach out to citizens in Andhra Pradesh and those living outside, asking them to help develop the state's infrastructure and donate for civil works throughout the state. As such, a few NRI citizens became partners in rural infrastructure development through a public–private partnership, or PPP model. Though the programme did not find many takers in the rest of Andhra Pradesh, it did catch the imagination of some NRIs in Guntur, and it perhaps

[9]TheY2K boom started as a 'scare' that all of our computer systems around the world would cease to function on 31 December 1999. Computer memory space was expensive early on, therefore using two digits for the date rather than four saved space. Hence, when the year turned 2000, the fear was that most computers would be unable to distinguish between 2000 and 1900. This scare led many software companies especially in the USA to hire software engineers from developing countries such as India to do the software programming.

[10]The programme envisaged greater public participation in local planning and 'community affairs'. For details, follow the link http://helloap.com/objectives-of-janmabhoomi-programme-in-andhra-pradesh/ (last accessed on 28 July 2015).

remains the only district where the NRIs showed some interest in partnering with the local government through the *Janmabhoomi* initiative. The *Janmabhoomi* programme's appeal was limited in its scope, and though it did find some success in some pockets in Guntur initially, soon its appeal fizzled out.

Such public–private philanthropic endeavour took a new shape and further got an institutional boost when the Guntur Zilla Parishad[11] (ZP) started the NRI Cell in 2002, adopting its framework of partnering with private entities from the *Janmabhoomi* programme where both sides (the government exchequer and the private partners) provided a set amount of money for these projects. Since the cell took off, this kind of village development-oriented diaspora philanthropy gained considerable traction in Guntur during the 2000s whereby many NRI villages (or villages from where NRIs hail) benefited from migrant donations, which routed their money through the NRI Cell to build the village infrastructure of a couple of hundred of villages before fizzling out in recent years. More details about the NRI Cell have been discussed in another forthcoming paper of mine (Roohi N.D.b).

With the chief ministership coming into the hands of Naidu again in 2014, he introduced the SVSW scheme in early 2015. Unlike the media representation of the scheme as something 'new/novel', inspired by the central government scheme, we need to see the public–private partnerships in development projects that started off at the state level with the *Janmabhoomi* programme, localized itself through the Guntur Zilla Parishad NRI Cell, and now have again expanded its scope through the SVSW scheme, as part of a continuum with its roots lying in the region rather than in a central government initiative. These schemes are part of Naidu's neoliberal restructuring measures undertaken by his government at different points in time. What is common to all of these programmes/schemes is the involvement of the NRIs as partners that dates back to late 1990s.

Migrant engagements in Coastal Andhra through these schemes coincide with another development occurring parallel to it: financial flows from migrants garnering attention from economists and policy makers who saw these flows as 'the most tangible and perhaps the least controversial link between migration and development' (Ratha 2007), with migrants seen as 'agents' that usher in development of home regions (Faist 2008). Not just policy makers but migrants themselves realized their 'diaspora advantage' and started to play and increasingly prominent role in policymaking and fund-raising for development (Faist 2000). Scholars however have highlighted that this resurgence of policy-based literature on the 'migrant-development' nexus is due to the neoliberal turn in policymaking (Faist 2008; Portes 2009; Glick Schiller 2012; Bakker 2015).

As with remittances, the subject of diaspora philanthropy too has found a deep resonance in international development circles as having great potential for development (Johnson 2007; Valor 2007). As a result, philanthropy is gradually became an important thrust area in Indian bureaucratic discourse (Sidel 2001) and this

[11]India follows a three tier administrative system with the gram panchayat (village level) as the smallest unit of administration, the mandal parishad or block samiti or panchayat samiti (block level) in the middle, and zilla parishad as the district level administrative unit.

aspect of philanthropy as a policy influencing tactic has been noted by Stone (Stone 2010) too. Though diaspora philanthropy is nascent as an academic field of study, there has been some policy-oriented work on the relation between diaspora philanthropy and development in developing countries (Najam 2006; Merz et al. 2007). Several scholars have examined the role of diaspora philanthropy in bringing about global equity, where financial flows move from the developed north to the developing south, viewing it as a mainly positive phenomenon. A migration, globalization and poverty report[12] explains that diaspora populations are often interested in contributing to the development of their countries of origin, but may choose highly varied forms of engagement, ranging from small-scale community initiatives to major investments and transfers of knowledge.

In neoliberal times, remittance flows including diaspora philanthropy (philanthropy cannot be seen as separate from remittances) is considered a panacea for underdevelopment (De Haas 2014), especially if the remittance (and by extension philanthropy) receiving country takes a positive turn through political and economic reform (De Haas 2010). If we take De Haas' analysis, all the schemes and programmes Naidu initiated over the last 25 years can be considered as a step in the right policy direction to harness development potential through transnational financial flows. What such policy-oriented discourses leave out is how and in what shape and particularities do NRIs make sense of a neoliberal paradigm—private resources including remittances or diaspora philanthropy for public welfare/development purposes. The institutionalization of diaspora philanthropy provides a framework through which one can explore this and a few other related questions: What are the motivations of people to give in such organized ways and what is the impact of such institutionalized giving on the development of the targeted town or region? Moreover, why have NRIs become partners in development and does this trend have precedence? David Ludden argues that with increased political participation and increasing demand for development, post-colonial Indian governments turned to groups/people who had money to invest in development. He proposed:

> While in theory, expanding popular political participation would favour the inclusion of all citizen interests in the development process, in fact and in practice, financial pressures to meet citizen demands made governments more dependent on people with money to invest in development. (Ludden 2005, p. 4046)

The dominant castes of the region became 'development' partners by adopting Green Revolution technologies in the 1960s that also increased their political stakes in the region. In this stage, however, development had a different connotation attached to it—increasing agricultural productivity to ensure self-sufficiency in food was considered the aim of development. The notion of development, however, changed over time, particularly with the liberalization of the Indian economy and a move away from state sponsored development (Corbridge and Harriss 2000)—a point I will explore in further detail below. It was at this moment that the NRIs with

[12]The report can be accessed at http://www.migrationdrc.org/publications/misc/Making_Migration_Work_for_Development.pdf, accessed on 1 October 2015.

availability of surplus capital, and the state chose to enter into partnership for bringing rural development in the region.

For the caste-marked NRIs from the region, migration played a multi-pronged role in bringing development. It transforms the fortune of the individual, the family and the community in the private realm, and the region in the public realm when NRIs institutionalized their engagements with the local or state government. NRI-led development, therefore, has an embodied connotation—the figure of the NRI himself or herself is considered as more 'developed' after spending decades in the USA, learning and earning there. These NRIs are also 'developed morally' in thinking beyond their own 'selfish needs', but focusing on the needs of the larger 'public' or 'community' as many of my interlocutors would explain. The NRIs then were in a proficient position to become partners in regional development. Recognizing that the state identifies them as harbingers of development with their transnational financial resources and global expertise, NRIs not only became willing partners but actively particularize their engagement with the state that also fit well into the larger neoliberal framework as I illustrate this point with the example of Chiluvuru village below.

Governmentalization as Opposed to Governmentality?

The Chiluvuru village in Guntur district is one among thousands of wards and villages that have been adopted by the locals and the NRIs under the SVSW scheme launched in January 2015. However, the village has a much longer history of witnessing public–private partnership for improving the village infrastructure. When I was doing my fieldwork between September 2011 and December 2012, Chiluvuru drew my attention because it was one of the villages that were often cited as an exemplar of NRI munificence and a 'model village'. This distinction of becoming a model village was rendered possible because of generous support from two NRIs who hailed from the village.

Another reason for the fame of the village was that it was touted as the first 'Internet village' of Andhra Pradesh. In 2004, an Internet centre was inaugurated in the village, and the note circulated then spelt out what the centre was suppose to do. The centre would connect the village to the World Wide Web through broadband connection. The centre's ambition was also to produce at least one computer literate in every household in the villages nearby. But this was a short-term goal. The long-term goal was to make Chilavuru a rural 'kiosk' to deliver a 'host of services' that would help 'agriculture, health and education', aid the gram panchayat dispense its duties effectively, and become a centre for e-collection of taxes and tariffs—all this is the spirit of public–private collaboration or partnership. Chilavuru was to serve as a model for future rural development across Andhra Pradesh.[13]

[13]These agendas were spelt out in the press note distributed during the inauguration ceremony.

Eight years after it became the 'Internet village', I made a visit to the centre and found out that it was not performing any of these functions. Reeling under severe power cuts, the Internet centre was trying to resuscitate its 'Aadhar Module' training programme,[14] which had become temporarily defunct due to power cuts. Though the centre may not have served the original purpose spelled out during its inauguration, it however was true to one aspect on this new 'model' of rural development—the spirit of public–private partnership remained. The 'public' was variously represented by the Andhra Pradesh state governments (either the Congress-led government or the Telugu Desam Party-led one), and among the 'private' stakeholders, the Yalamanchali (one of the NRI donor families who continue to look after the centre) continued to be one, with other temporary private stakeholders joining hand as and when required.

Chilavuru's fame as a 'model' village had spread to Guntur town as well, when I heard some of my informants speak about it with respect. One of the reasons was that the senior Yalamanchali, an octogenarian and a returned NRI, had made Guntur his home and was widely regarded as a 'philanthropist' and a community notable in the town. Though there are three important families with NRIs in the USA hailing from this village, and apart from the Yalamanchali, they too had been donating money to their village; it was the Yalamanchali who had over the years collaborated with the local and state government on various projects where they had emerged as a key philanthropist–donor family. Long before one enters Chiluvuru, the name of senior Yalamanchali and his son (a big businessman in the USA) is etched on an arch laying perpendicular to the Buckingham Canal (a freshwater canal built in colonial times to connect the eastern coast of the Madras Presidency) at the beginning of the Tummapudi village, which one needs to cross to enter Chiluvuru village.

The Yalamanchali through their Yalamanchali Charities (a locally registered trust) donated money for various purposes ostensibly to serve the 'public'. One of their biggest philanthropic projects was linking multiple villages by laying cement roads from Tummapudi to Chilavuru via the Nambooru village—a project in which the family had donated more than ten million rupees spent between the late 1990s and early 2000s. Later, I learnt that this amount was only one-third of the total cost; the other two-third of the cost to lay the cement road was borne by the local government. Thus, this road building project was undertaken through a public–private partnership model, where the Yalamanchali were the private party donors, and the public was represented by the NRI Cell.

Chiluvuru has attracted a lot of NRI philanthropic funds because it has been a successful migrant sending village. These NRIs are what is usually termed as the 'high-skilled' migrant pool who have moved to the USA in the 1970s and started to 'give back' to their natal village by late 1990s after the *Janmabhoomi* programme came into effect. Today, a hospital, an Internet centre, a water purification

[14]The centre incharge, a man of 22, explained that youngsters were being trained for data entry job for the Aadhar programme (aimed at giving a biometric identity number to all Indian citizens) at the centre run with the help of a Hyderabad-based IT firm.

plant, complete cement roads, etc., have been built with NRI money. Moreover, it will receive more private funds, with matching grants from the government now because it has been adopted by the recently launched SVSW scheme.

Such 'benign' NRI involvement often makes the locals perceive NRIs or transnational actors as 'agents of development'. The literature on migration and development corroborates such a view. NRIs have been contributing in some pockets of India for social development purposes. In Gujarat, for example, roads, school buildings, libraries, community centres and public health centres have been built with NRI donations (Dekkers and Rutten 2011). Similarly, in Punjab and Kerala, too, NRIs have invested money in improving village infrastructure (Walton-Roberts 2014), but with a basic difference that in Andhra, this development work has been institutionalized by partnering with the local and state governments.

NRIs and NRI-led associations and organizations in the USA have established many local foundations, trusts and societies in Coastal Andhra to donate for various sectors such as building and improving health, education and rural infrastructures. Today, philanthropy can be grouped with civil society organizations, representing the 'third sector' that occupies a space between the state and the market. In recent years, many philanthropists have promoted the ideology of neoliberalism in which private enterprise or the 'third sector' is encouraged to take up the state's responsibilities. Unsurprisingly then, in certain instances, such private funds directed towards developmental goals can actually pave the way for privatization of public goods or institutions (Baru and Nundy 2008). This idea gels well with the neoliberal aim to create 'an informed citizenry that is at once able to make demands of the state (including for employment and oversight of public officials), and which is also required to stand on its own feet (in the sense of taking responsibility for making payments to service providers)' (Corbridge et al. 2005, p. 251).

The *Janmabhoomi* programme, the NRI Cell programme and the SVSW scheme though different in their scales, timings and outcomes had one thing in common. In a pioneering approach, these initiatives were bringing PPP into philanthropy for rural infrastructure development by harnessing transnational capital flows. PPPs are a business model where government bodies and private entities enter into a partnership for various (often developmental or infrastructural) projects, and the parties involved share costs and profits generated through these projects. In the PPP model of philanthropy, however, while costs of building infrastructure are shared in the name of 'public good', no visible profits are generated and the benefits accrued are not monetary. On the surface, these partnerships are not 'guided by enterprise logic', but through the currency of 'care and belonging'.

'Care' and 'belonging', 'owing it to the place' one hails from would fit into the pastoral form of the Foucauldian notion of governmentality, had the 'rural development' been directed to the larger rural population. But as my research suggests, the examples of the *Janmabhoomi* and NRI Cell-led interventions were very narrowly spatialized (money flowing into pockets that already are considered developed) and the newly launched SVSW scheme is also showing this spatial bias with more interest shown in the developed districts of central coastal Andhra. What do these transnational flows then do in effect? These funds are not targeted towards the 'poor', nor do they intend to manage and regulate the rural poor, but, rather, the attempt is to consolidate and perpetuate political and economic control of the rural hinterlands through flexible control of the state transnationally with NRI remittances and philanthropy infusing newer meanings of what constitutes the 'public' and the 'private' in a neoliberal milieu. Institutionalization of diaspora philanthropy can help us grasp the mechanics and motivations behind the collaboration between the state machinery and NRIs from the region.

Since money was routed through the government machinery—whereby donors transferred their share of the money to the government—I call these initiatives the *governmentalization* of philanthropy. By governmentalization, I mean the process of institutionalization of an area hitherto outside the domain of the government, taken within the fold of government. The incorporation of diaspora philanthropy within a government entity is an example of governmentalization of diaspora philanthropy. Governmentalization here is not to be equated with Foucauldian governmentality as the former is not a technology of governing through biopower, but more a mutual process of co-option of a state apparatus by the dominant castes/groups in power to serve their own group interests.

As the example of Chiluvuru shows, governmentalization of diaspora philanthropy is a way in which caste hegemony (a form of Gramscian cultural hegemony) is perpetuated. The locals I talked to in Chiluvuru were generally satisfied with the transnational resource flows into their village. They explained the NRI's keen interest as their 'love' for their *swanthaooru* or village. A hegemonic notion of 'NRIs care for their village' pervaded. Interestingly, apart from the laying of roads, all other philanthropic resources including the Internet centre and the water plant charged money and its services were not free. Indeed, the Internet centre had become a training ground for those who would become fieldworkers to collect biometric data. The younger generation of Yalamanchali had business interests in both the USA and India in diverse sectors including technology and health care. Insiders attuned to the local politics explained how the family had good relations with both the TDP and were keen to expand their business in Andhra. When the Congress government came to power, they still maintained good relations with the government by displaying their commitment to 'development' through philanthropy and the family continued to maintain the upkeep of the Internet centre. Their engagement with their village gradually lulled when the Congress leader Y.S. Rajashekhar Reddy died in an accident in 2009.

Similar cases of uneven interest among NRIs and their philanthropic engagement in their villages were observed across many villages in Guntur district when the TDP lost power, first in the state in 2004 and then in the district level in 2007, leading to a decreasing engagement with the government by these caste- and class-marked NRIs. The close collaboration of NRIs is therefore contingent upon the political developments in Andhra.

As the case of Chiluvuru village suggests, while resource mobilization is informed by neoliberal policies that diasporic civil society groups and the state adopt, however, these policies are highly malleable and prone to be shaped by dominant groups' interests. One needs to unpack what negotiations take place at the micro-level and how these can help us to critically understand neoliberalism itself beyond the projection as an overarching framework (Bhagwati 1993), but looking at how it embeds itself in a pre-existing social and power structures.

Neoliberalism in Practice: Development and Capital Accumulation

In this chapter, I make an argument linking the *Janmabhoomi* programme, the NRI Cell and the Smart Village Smart Ward scheme as being part of a continuum informed by neoliberal market economy that Chandra Babu Naidu adopted. Post the 1990s, India saw the implementation of many pro-market reforms in India, which was reeling under pressure from the International Monetary Fund (IMF) to open its market. This opening up of the Indian economy to forces of globalization in its wake ushered in a neoliberal moment for the country (Corbridge and Harriss 2000). Some argued that the state outsourced its functions to NGOs and other non-state entities (Kamat 2004; Ferguson and Gupta 2002, p. 990). Andhra became a pioneer in that it became the first state to take loans directly from the World Bank in order to structure the state's economy (Mooij 2007). For Naidu, the blueprint for neoliberal economic reforms of his state first surfaced when he embraced the *Vision 2020* document produced by the global consultancy firm McKinsey (Government of Andhra Pradesh 1999). The report categorically envisaged the role of the state as a facilitator and catalyst in bringing development rather than undertaking development projects itself. The only successful way the state could remain a catalyst was to let private entities take over the development agenda. Naidu thus promoted SEZs in Vizak (Cross 2014) and built the famed Cyber Towers in Hyderabad in this spirit of public–private partnerships.

PPPs have been widely recognized as a neoliberal tool for developing Asian countries; it is one of the features of the 'Asian model of development'.[15] In a public–private project that entails public participation, proponents of this kind of neoliberal model say it necessitates greater representation from the public (and in India increasingly also its transnational citizens) and that it includes a wide variety of voices in planning and development, thereby upholding the democratic virtue (Lewis 2000).

Neoliberalism is also understood as an exercise in understanding how political power can be shaped along the principles of market economy (Foucault 2010). Indeed, the early proponents of neoliberal models suggested that the advent of neoliberalism in developing countries would curbing the excess of rent-seeking behaviour that plagued the developing countries' political economy (Krueger 1974). What neoliberalism would stand for instead is free market capitalism and/or

[15]For details of this model, see Steger and Roy (2010, Chap. 4).

minimum government, representing 'a shift in the rationality of government and in the shape and nature of states' (Gupta and Sharma 2006, p. 277). Kamat's work on NGOs shows that the discourse surrounding neoliberalism sees the emergence of civil society 'as fully cognizant rational actors capable of going beyond sectarian interests and acting upon matters of general welfare' (Kamat 2004, p. 158). While the ideology of free market is a universal attribute of neoliberalism, the policies and modes of governance or the tools devised to free up the market are not universal. By paying attention to ethnographic particularities, I hope to prevent the erasure of meanings that critics say a framework of neoliberalism does in many instances (Kipnis 2008). The close cooperation of government and businesses is an Asian attribute of neoliberalism, largely seen as amenable to Asian countries' home-grown 'cultural framework' (Steger and Roy 2010, p. 76). The specific 'cultural framework' within which a policy initiative like the *Janmabhoomi* programme, the NRI Cell or now the SVSW scheme can emerge, speaks about the highly variegated nature of the neoliberal project. The examples of the different schemes and projects/programmes gives however us deep insights into ways in which the state and certain powerful groups reinstate their sectarian interest as public interest (Kamat 2004). To see philanthropy undertaken by rational actors devoid of sectarian interests, as not embedded and working for larger good that needs proper harnessing through policy initiatives, in actual fact disfigures the understanding of highly regionalized and specific social and power relations across India.

Because of this place-specific 'cultural framework', in India, the state does not recuse itself from its twin agenda of development and governance; rather in the name of democracy, it actively encourages private entities to represent the public interest. The neoliberal state need not always shrink as is widely understood; indeed, it pulls newer allies in the name of strengthening democracy while the state becomes the important peg on which such public–private relations hinge. Such observations have already been made, for instance in Kuriyan and Ray's study on PPP in telecentres which found that in the two states of Kerala and Andhra Pradesh, the government remained a key player when it entrusted the private sector, particularly small entrepreneurs, mostly 'ordinary citizens, with the responsibility of delivering public services' (Kuriyan and Ray 2009, p. 1671).

When Naidu made a call to its citizens to come forward and share the responsibility to develop the *motherland*, a new vision of PPP was being imagined—outside the scope of the market and in the domain of public good, public participation and public governance. It was not however constitutive of the non-capitalist 'outside' of capital (Sanyal 2007), a product of welfarist governmentality for the political society (Chatterjee 2004), that incubates and reproduces the political and cultural dominance of those who constitute the civil society. Deeper investigation reveals that welfarist notions of public good, public participation and public governance are core constituents in the processes of capital accumulation. Situating capital accumulation within translocal processes generated by present-day neoliberal policies and financial capitalism, Jean and John Comaroff have presented strong arguments about the emergence of particular forms of translocal economic processes and practices in contemporary post-colonial and post-revolutionary societies (Comaroff and Comaroff 1999). In India, caste emerges as a particular node of capital accumulation, and as I argue, globalization and migration do not weaken the node but transnationalize it.

Neoliberalism was touted as a panacea to cure the ills of rent-seeking (or behaviour in which groups or individuals extract rents to maximize economic gains by exploiting their close relations with the government which control and regulate the economy) in countries such as India (Krueger 1974), and PPP became one of the means to achieve this. Yet, PPP in development-oriented philanthropic engagements become the precise mechanism in Coastal Andhra through which rent-seeking behaviour is reconstructed in the language of philanthropy, welfare and public good.

Transnational capital that flows into Guntur and coastal Andhra, ostensibly for welfare and developmental purpose, actually work to exacerbate pre-existing inequalities that mark the region. Rural welfare and development on close examination become shorthand for the interest of dominant caste groups like the Kammas being served whereby their villages got disproportionately high ZP funds or state funds. The other villages are deprived of resources as a corollary. For instance, under the NRI Cell, the dry poorer upland received limited funds and continued to have poorer infrastructure, while the riverine fertile lowland sent produced most migrants and in turn received more NRI funds and state funds as matching grants. Not only spatial inequalities get reproduced, but also social inequalities proliferate. NRI donors come from a particular caste-class background, and their money flows back to their villages benefitting their 'own people', yet giving legitimacy to it because it is done in the name of philanthropy that is seen as altruistic.

These various schemes and programmes adopted by the Chandra Babu Naidu government as not just neoliberal development tool, they are tools of domination and control. The state is embedded in local structures of power, which in turn are steeped in the politics and economics of caste affiliations in a place such as Andhra Pradesh. The regional clientelist state draws heavily from a network of mutual patronage that is structurally woven around dominant castes like the Kammas and enters into a mutual process of co-option of a state apparatus by the dominant castes/groups in power and vice versa to serve their own and group interests. With processes of globalization taking root, and migration becoming the norm for such groups, we need to scrutinize how neoliberalism becomes a handmaiden in the hands of caste-marked NRIs and what does it say about the ideology itself when it takes shape on the ground. In this neoliberal rendering of transnational development efforts where the state actively recruit partners in development from among its scattered diaspora, Kalyan Sanyal's insightful capital and non-capital need economy help us to sociologically understand how social relations and economic relations of production get created, sustained and legitimized (Sanyal 2007). The NRIs were fearful that with migration to the west their villages would pass into the hands of those caste that they consider below them—particularly the Yadavas. With their philanthropy controlled by their kith and kin who remain in the villages on live in nearby towns, land is kept under the leash of these transnational actors. With the recent announcement that the capital for the newly bifurcated state would be in the Guntur district, land prices had appreciated considerably. Even before this move, the price of both agricultural and non-agricultural land was increasing at a steady pace, with some arguing that it was because of the flow of NRI money into the real estate. As such, village infrastructure development becomes a valid and legitimate way in which control of the land can be maintained.

Transnational philanthropy points to a moment in post-colonial capitalist development that channels non-capital economy to maintain political and economic hegemony of certain groups, and a neoliberal tool such as PPP becomes the perfect guise through which the hegemony of the dominant groups of castes such as Kammas is maintained. Such non-capital economy in neoliberal economy gives direct capital gains to the bourgeois and is therefore not the outside but its inside, constitutive in the reproduction of capital.

Conclusion

In early April 2015, I visited Chiluvuru again for a brief period. The TDP government was back in power, and the NRIs were coming forth once again to 'help' the village. The village, which is a Kamma-dominated one (with many belonging to the Scheduled Castes and Other Backward Classes categories), was showing enthusiasm that development of the village and the region would start again soon. Excitement was palpable now that the village was also part of the Smart Village Smart Ward scheme. The Internet centre was working overtime, seeing lot of enrolments and the lull that I witnessed in 2012 was gone. So what does the story of Chiluvuru tell us about the nature of development in India in general and in Andhra in particular? The genealogy of the term development is understood to have a complex history and varied meanings (Sivaramakrishnan and Agrawal 2003), but it does take particular shape in Andhra Pradesh. The excerpt of Chandra Babu Naidu's Facebook update with which I began this chapter holds a clue to what development means and that the idea has found resonance among the NRIs who form the part of what can be termed as post-civil society (Gudavarthy 2013). Development here is means that the future is imagined as that in which infrastructure gets precedence than humans. This infrastructure can be developed by those who have surplus money and the state will actively facilitate them in developing the same. For big projects like the KG Gas basin, one needs a behemoth like Reliance to step in, but for more mundane rural/village development, it is the transnational post-civil society groups that step in, members of which are class-/caste-marked.

Being a 'dominant' caste in the region, it is not surprising that Kammas are in an advantageous position to step into this role and mobilize state resources for their own community or villages. Public funds can be diverted into Kamma villages, neglecting those villages which have a lesser presence of Kammas. Through the examples of *Janmabhoomi* programme, the NRI Cell and the SVSW initiatives, it becomes clear that dominant caste groups such as the Kammas are further entrenching themselves within state structures to accrue collective benefits for their communities at the expense of others and through philanthropy get legitimate control of village land. Philanthropy is generally viewed as selfless, altruistic and without returns, yet it is clearly not so when we see that philanthropy is implicated in the capital accumulation process. Their 'NRI' status allows them to fudge this manipulation by representing their interventions as 'bringing development' and 'doing philanthropy'. These notions do not go uncontested, however, but these contestations do not hinder the seeping of caste interest and enmeshing it with the supposed interest of the state. Such contestations notwithstanding, the governmentalizing of diaspora philanthropy shows one way in which caste hegemony is perpetuated where private interests are garbed as public good. The question then is what role is philanthropy playing here beyond the Bourdieusian explanation[16] of cultural and social capital accrual?

Neoliberalism demands the withdrawal of state. However, the neoliberal state needs not always 'shrink' as is widely understood; indeed, it pulls newer allies and partners in the name of strengthening democracy. What I argue is that its impacts reverberate on a micro-scale. We need to be alert to the highly particularized shape it takes, contingent upon the dynamic political nature, arguing that multiple possibilities including governmentalization of NRI engagements in development practices becomes possible because of the variegated nature of *neoliberalism in practice* as opposed to neoliberalism as a universalizing ideology. In Coastal Andhra, the promise of altruistic capital flow in villages is believed to make them self-sufficient and arrest migration (of the poor) because it has proper roads, education and health facilities, at the level of villages and wards. Such views are not only held by those who have surplus capital but by those who become beneficiaries of the projects into which this capital is utilized. Neoliberalism has made rent-seeking appear as the outside of capital through a novel public–private philanthropic model, whereas it actually becomes a strategic means for capital accumulation.

References

Bakker, M. (2015). Discursive representations and policy mobility: how migrant remittances became a 'development tool'. *Global Networks, 15*(1), 21–42.

Baru, R. V., & Nundy, M. (2008). Blurring of boundaries: Public-private partnerships in health services in India. *Economic and Political Weekly, 43*(4), 62–71.

Bhagwati, J. N. (1993). *India in transition: Freeing India*. New York: Oxford University Press.

[16]Bourdieu's concept of cultural capital (Bourdieu 1986) though useful to explain the economic or non economic benefits one gains by being a part of a network (in this case, by being a member of a 'dominant caste'), does not fully explicate why and how the state and powerful groups enter into alliances.

Chatterjee, P. (2004). *The politics of the governed: Reflections on popular politics in most of the world*. New York: Columbia University Press.
Cohen, J. H. (2004). *The culture of migration in southern Mexico*. Austin, Texas: University of Texas Press.
Comaroff, J., & Comaroff, J. L. (1999). Occult economies and the violence of abstraction: Notes from the South African postcolony. *American ethnologist, 26*(2), 279–303.
Connell, J. (2008). Niue: Embracing a culture of migration. *Journal of Ethnic and Migration Studies, 34*(6), 1021–1040.
Corbridge, S., & Harriss, J. (2000). *Reinventing India: Liberalization, HinduNationalism and Popular Democracy*. Cambridge: Polity Press.
Corbridge, S., et al. (2005). *Seeing the state: Governance and Governmentality in India* (Vol. 10). Cambridge: Cambridge University Press.
Cross, J. (2014). *Dream zones: Anticipating capitalism and development in India*. London: Pluto Press.
De Haas, H. (2010). Migration and development: a theoretical perspective. *International Migration Review, 44*(1), 227–264.
De Haas, H. (2014). Migration Theory: Quo Vadis. IMI Working Paper Series, No. 100.
Dekkers, N., & Rutten, M. (2011). Diaspora philanthropy from a homeland perspective: Reciprocity and contestation over donations in Central Gujarat, India. *Provincial Globalisation Working Paper No. 2*. Bangalore: National Institute of Advanced Studies and Amsterdam Institute for Social Science Research.
Elliot, C. (1970). Caste and faction among the dominant castes: The Reddies and Kammas of Andhra. *Caste in Indian Politics*. New Delhi: Orient Longman.
Faist, T. (2000). Transnationalisation in international migration: Implications for the study of citizenship and culture. *Ethnic and Racial Studies, 23*(2), 189–222.
Faist, T. (2008). Migrants as transnational development agents: An inquiry into the newest round of the migration–development nexus. *Population, Space and Place, 14*(1), 21–42.
Ferguson, J., & Gupta, A. (2002). Spatializing states: Toward an ethnography of neoliberal governmentality. *American Ethnologist, 29*(4), 981–1002.
Foucault, M. (2010). *The Birth of Biopolitics: Lectures at the Collège de France, 1978-1979*. New York: Palgrave Macmillan.
Glick Schiller, N. (2012). Unravelling the migration and development web: Research and policy implications. *International Migration, 50*(3), 92–97.
Government of Andhra Pradesh. (1999). *Swarna Andhra Pradesh: Vision 2020 Hyderabad.*
Gudavarthy, A. (2013). *Politics of post-civil society: Contemporary history of political movements in India*. New Delhi: Sage.
Gupta, A., & Sharma, A. (2006). Globalization and postcolonial states. *Current Anthropology, 47*(2), 277.
Harvey, D. (2006). Neo-liberalism as creative destruction. *Geografiska Annaler, 88 B*(2), 145–158.
Johnson, P. D. (2007). *Diaspora philanthropy: Influences, initiatives, and issues*. The Philanthropic Initiative and Global Equity Initiative: Harvard University.
Kamat, S. (2004). The privatization of public interest: Theorizing NGOs discourse in a neoliberal era. *Review of International Political Economy, 11*(1), 155–176.
Kipnis, A. P. (2008). Audit cultures: neoliberal governmentality, socialist legacy, or technologies of citizenship? *American Ethnologist, 35*, 275–289.
Kohli, A. (1990). *Democracy and discontent: India's growing crisis of governability*. Cambridge: Cambridge University Press.
Krueger, A. (1974). The political economy of the rent-seeking society. *American Economic Review, 64*, 291–303.
Kuriyan, R., & Ray, I. (2009). Outsourcing the state? Public–private partnerships and information technologies in India. *World Development, 37*(10), 1663–1673.
Lewis, D. (2000). Building active partnerships in aid-recipient countries: Lessons from a rural development project in Bangladesh. In S. Osborne (Ed.), *Public–private Partnerships: Theory and practice in international perspective*. London: Routledge.

Ludden, D. (2005). Development regimes in South Asia: History and the Governance Conundrum. *Economic and Political Weekly*, 4042–4051.

Merz, B. J., Chen, L. C., & Geithner, P. F. (Eds.). (2007). *Diasporas and development*. Cambridge, MA: Harvard University Press.

Mooij, J. (2007). Hype, skill and class: the Politics of reform in Andhra Pradesh, India. *Commonwealth & Comparative Politics, 45*(1), 34–56.

Najam, A. (2006). *Portrait of a Giving Community: Philanthropy by the Pakistani-American Diaspora*. Global Equity Initiative.

Portes, A. (2009). Migration and development: Reconciling opposite views. *Ethnic and Racial Studies, 32*(1), 5–22.

Ratha, D. (2007). *Leveraging Remittances for Development*. MPI Policy Brief, June 2007, Washington.

Reddy, G. K. (2002). New populism and liberalisation: Regime Shift under Chandrababu Naidu in AP. *Economic and Political Weekly, 37*(9), 871–883.

Roohi, S. (N.D.a). Caste Kinship and the realization of 'American Dream': Telugu Diaspora in the United States of America. *Journal of Ethnic and Migration Studies* (forthcoming).

Roohi. S. (N.D.b). Transnationalising State's Responsibility: The case of NRI Cell in Guntur, Coastal Andhra.

Satyanarayana, A. (1991). *Andhra Peasants under British Rule: Agrarian Relations and the Rural Economy 1900–1940*. New Delhi: Manohar.

Sanyal, K. (2007). *Rethinking capitalist development: Primitive accumulation, governmentality and post-colonial capitalism*. New Delhi: Routledge.

Sidel, M. (2001). Review essay: Recent Research on Philanthropy and the Nonprofit Sector in India and South Asia. *Voluntas: International Journal of Voluntary and Nonprofit Organisations, 12*(2), 171–180.

Sivaramakrishnan, K., & Agrawal, A. (2003). *Regional modernities: The cultural politics of development in India*. California: Stanford University Press.

Steger, M. B., & Roy, R. K. (2010). *Neoliberalism: a very short introduction*. Oxford: Oxford University Press.

Stone, D. (2010). Private philanthropy or policy transfer? The Transnational norms of the open society institute. *Politics, 38*(2), 269–287.

Upadhya, C. (1988a). The farmer-capitalists of Coastal Andhra Pradesh. *Economic and Political Weekly, 23*(28), 1376–1382.

Upadhya, C. (1988b). The farmer-capitalists of Coastal Andhra Pradesh. *Economic and Political Weekly, 23*(29), 1433–1442.

Valor, C. (2007). A global strategic plan for corporate philanthropy. *Corporate Communications 12*(30), 280–297.

Walton-Roberts, M. (2004). Globalisation, national autonomy and non-resident Indians. *Contemporary South Asia, 13*(1), 53–69.

Walton-Roberts, M. (2014). Diaspora and Divergent Development in Kerala and Punjab, in S. Sahoo and B. K. Pattanaik (eds.), *Global Diasporas and Development: Socioeconomic, Cultural and Policy Perspectives* (pp. 69–85). New Delhi: Springer.

Washbrook, D. (1975). The Development of Caste Organization in South India, in C. J Baker and d. Washbrook (eds.), *South India: Political institutions and political Change* 1880–1940 (pp. 150–203). Delhi: Macmillan.

The Postcolony and 'Racy' Histories of Accumulation

Atig Ghosh

Abstract In this chapter, the author looks at the recent spate of wilful violence against people from the north-east in Delhi, the national capital. As he points out, there is only one way of describing these assaults and the grass roots reaction they elicit: they are racist. It is crucial to note that capitalist development is not necessarily antithetical to cultural racism. The argument can be further extended to indicate that it is in the very nature of capitalist development to produce its well-demarcated racial categories before primitive accumulation can begin. With the emergence of global finance capital, the modes of reconstituting and redeploying races/ethnicities have morphed in significantly new ways. The author argues that racism in India is not an atavistic survival, but the pith and marrow of the contemporary economic exigencies. But, in what ways does global capital reconstitute and redeploy races/ethnicities? The chapter demonstrates this through a study of the Indian north-east where the emergence of the neoliberal market–state complex has given rise to autonomy movements. Most of these movements make political and economic claims in the name of race or ethnic identities. The very mark of their newly imagined minority identity or subject position is actively utilized to make claims for integration into the majoritarian logic, be it global economic or national statist. While the deployment of these 'new' race identities gives groups in the north-east extra teeth in terms of claims-making, it also opens up these groups to racist attacks elsewhere in the country through economic and cultural revisibilization.

Keywords Race · Violence · Accumulation · Autonomy · Capitalist development

In 2014 alone, the national capital witnessed a string of violent incidents perpetrated against people from the north-eastern states of India. An incident which gained greatest publicity is the case of Nido Taniam, a 20-year-old student from

A. Ghosh (✉)
Visva Bharati University, Santiniketan, West Bengal, India
e-mail: atigghosh@gmail.com

I.K. Mitra et al. (eds.), *Accumulation in Post-Colonial Capitalism*,
DOI 10.1007/978-981-10-1037-8_12

Arunachal Pradesh, bordering China, who was studying in Lovely Professional University, Jalandhar. On 29 January 2014, he died after being beaten up at a marketplace in south Delhi, triggering widespread protests. Nido had reportedly gone to the market with three friends and was looking for an address, when someone at a sweet shop allegedly began mocking him. Nido responded by breaking a glass door at the sweet shop and the incident escalated from there.

Four days before Nido's tragic death, barely 3 km from the spot where he was brutally assaulted, two young women from the north-eastern state of Manipur—Tharmila Jajo and Chonmila—were thrashed in full public view by some local goons, and came face to face with the harsh reality of living in Delhi. Chonmila, who worked at a local mall, had gone to a local shop managed by Tharmila to buy some Manipuri herbs. On spotting them, the goons first hurled racial abuses at them. When they did not react, one of them tied the leash of his pet dog to Chonmila's boots. She got so scared that she started kicking the dog away, afraid that it would bite her. Then the men, as if on cue, attacked them (Akram 2014).

In the same area, a 30-year-old Manipuri man, Shaloni, was allegedly beaten to death by a group of men in July 2014. This man was returning from a friend's place, when a group of 5–6 men arrived at the spot by car and attacked him. He was rushed to the trauma centre of the nearby All India Institute of Medical Sciences where he succumbed to his injuries (*The Indian Express* 2014). Incidentally, Shaloni lived in the Munirka area of south Delhi, where too a series of barbaric acts directed against the people of the north-east have transpired in recent times.

In February 2014, a minor girl from Manipur was raped by her landlord's son in Munirka. The 14-year-old girl, who had stepped out to buy some household items from a shop near her house in Munirka, was abducted and forced into a room nearby and raped (*Zee News* 2014; *India Today* 2014). The reaction to this incident by locals of Munirka, however, was shocking. Binalakshmi Nepram, an activist and founder of Manipur Women Gun Survivors Network, reported that a 'panchayat meeting took place on 9 February after the 14-year-old from Manipur was raped.... At the first meeting, some of the people said that the people from north-east are "*gandey log*" (dirty people). Then another meeting was held on Sunday, where they said they wanted to rid of all "*gandey log*"' (Dhapola 2014).

This grass roots reaction, so to speak, is not dissimilar to that which was brought forth by the vigilante-style 'raid' carried out by Aam Aadmi Party (AAP) minister Somnath Bharti in Khirki Extension (also in south Delhi), targeting African nationals on the suspicion that they were involved in a drug and sex racket. The party was criticized for its policy of encouraging vigilantism by people and for standing by Bharti. Nepram was correct when she pointed out: 'This [the Munirka panchayat diktat] is similar to the Khirki incident, and they have said that north-east girls are loose and of bad character' (Dhapola 2014).

There is only one way of describing these barbaric, sometimes mortal, assaults on people of the north-east, and the grass roots reaction they elicit: this is racism. And this description applies, *mutatis mutandis*, to similar attacks on *Dalit*s (downtrodden and marginalized castes) across the country. My intention here, however, is not to festoon this piece with an inventory of grisly racist attacks, important from the political perspective though they may be, but to look at the reactions at the level of the so-called enlightened circles they bring out. In Left/*marxisant tertulias*, the reaction inevitably is one of horrors provoked by an incident that is quickly labelled atavistic. These are crimes committed by Neanderthals; these are ugly social coelacanths that have somehow mysteriously survived in this age of development, globalization and 'progress'. In arriving at such a conclusion, the well-meaning advocates of 'progress' have missed the wood for the trees.

It is crucial to note that capitalist development is not necessarily antithetical to cultural racism. This, of course, is evident from the feverish xenophobia that Western democracies have been exhibiting over many decades. But the argument can be further extended to indicate that it is in the very nature of capitalist development, be it of the colonial vintage or its finance avatar, to produce its well-demarcated racial categories first, that is before primitive accumulation can begin. In other words, as Kar (2007) had argued in the case of colonial Assam, primitive accumulation necessarily presupposes an accumulation of the primitive. Having said this, it is important to point out that with the emergence of global finance capital, the modes of reconstituting and redeploying races/ethnicities before accumulation takes place (and during accumulation) have morphed in significant new ways. If we understand this, then we will realize that racism in India is not an atavistic survival, but the pith and marrow of the economic exigencies of the time.

But, in what ways does global capital reconstitute and redeploy races/ethnicities? For our present purposes, we will focus on the north-east to track this development. However, this is only a paper in the making; I hope, by the time the work is complete, a second section dealing with the constitution of the Dalits as 'race' would become part of this paper. For now, let us turn to the north-east.

Race/Ethnicity Redeployment Through Global Capital

As pointed out in the Introduction, the theme of state in a post-colonial study of accumulation is not accidental. Also, it is not strange that in Western capitalism, theoretical critiques of capitalist accumulation process have almost done way with the state, as if capitalism unfolded in the long twentieth century without the state machinery and the imperialist order. Politics was once more taken out of political economy. In globally positioned views, the state always appears as a minor factor, while in local revolutionary views the state appears always as a crucial factor facilitating globalization and capitalism. The state facilitates restructuring of capitalist order. It is the site of passive revolution. Owing to this, importantly, the theme of state allows us a sustained engagement with the issue of transition and thus to the specific form of post-colonial capitalism. A salient aspect of the post-colonial situation is the near-permanent condition of primitive accumulation as the other of the most modern form of capital, which one may term as virtual capital. Developmental and conflict-induced migration within the country and to other countries takes place under primitive and precarious conditions, and female labour forms a substantial chunk of this scenario. As more and more virtual capital—in the form of offshore funds, venture business, hedge funds, sovereign wealth funds, Internet-based investment and banking, and forward-trading-based wealth—reaches the post-colonial shores and results in massive property boom, skyrocketing land prices, construction upsurge and a new surge in the prices of raw material such as iron ore, and at times foodstuff, the more people are pushed towards accepting precarious and informal work condition; as a consequence, there is more depeasantization, and appearance of unorganized labour, which can be best described as 'immaterial labour' with flexible work hours, uncertain work profile and conditions of reproduction, and automated technologies and flows of new capital.

This condition constitutes the core predicament of the postcolony. On one hand, the postcolony must depend on the state to come out of this two-pronged attack taking place in the form of a combined appearance of primitive accumulation and virtual accumulation. On the other hand, the state is in a bad shape today, and we do not have yet any other substantive form of national autonomy. The post-colonial aggregate, predictably, finds it increasingly difficult to retain flexibility and prise open its way through the vice-like double bind of primitive work conditions and the reproduction of the advanced form of accumulation, a bind that leaves almost nothing as social surplus for the postcolony to develop. Against this backdrop, finance capital breeds its own batch of autonomies in the form of 'races'/'ethnicities', taking advantage of the evident discerptibility of national sovereignty. The case of the Indian north-east bears this out.

With neoliberalism, the older muscular Indian nation-state has gone into decline. Privatization and economic liberalization have resulted in the contraction and redeployment of the state, shifting the locus of political struggles away from direct contestation for state power and opening new spaces to contestation (by new movements and old) over whether they will be controlled from above or below. The state acts increasingly as broker for global capital as it attempts to re-regulate the conditions for accumulation on a global scale. To be sure, neoliberalism involves not simply a headlong retreat of the state but a renegotiation of state-society relations. As such, the attempted recomposition of capitalist hegemony in the north-east too has included targeted social-composition programmes. The 'neoliberal races' have been spawned. There is almost no ministry in New Delhi that does not have a dedicated north-east window, and then there is the Development of North-East Region (DoNER) ministry itself to coordinate various welfare schemes, development projects and sundry governmental policies[1] and also to guide the decisions

[1]To get an idea of the money and projects involved, see the official site of DoNER: http://mdoner.gov.in/.

of the North Eastern Council.[2] Here, we see the kernel of the idea to recompose and redeploy 'ethnicities' as the new fundamentals of market economy.

Immense quantities of money are being pumped into the region in the name of grants-in-aid, infrastructural development, and so on and so forth, to forge a new clientèle sold on the rationale of the neoliberal market. Yet, paradoxically, for this strategy to work smoothly, the neoliberal state has had to depend more and more heavily upon age-old strong-arm tactics of colonial provenance. For state 'largesse' to have its desired impact, the success of counterinsurgency must be guaranteed. This in turn implies that government officials and counterinsurgency forces must enjoy absolute impunity. In the north-east, the draconian Armed Forces (Special Powers) Act, 1958 or AFSPA, has been the chief instrument for guaranteeing such impunity.[3] However, these somewhat contradictory efforts to create a reformulated clientèle for the neoliberal era—one more selective and flexible than the old muscular corporatist structures had allowed—did not entirely succeed in shielding the dominant state from political challenge from below. These efforts, as shall be argued later in some detail, produced new restive, resistive subjectivities. The shift from state-orchestrated to market mechanisms of distribution overlapped with new forms of social movement-based struggles in which the old autonomy question was merely reformulated, not abandoned.

Before we turn to a discussion of the exact contours of this reformulated autonomy question in the north-east, it merits asserting that this market-driven reorientation of governance—one which makes 'social conflicts disappear or at least manageable, contradictions a matter of imagination or at least temporary, and schisms of society a guide to or at least an occasion for social development'—has been evocatively termed by Ranabir Samaddar as the 'government of peace' (Samaddar 2015, p. 1). Not a peace-ingeminating governance is this, but a mode of effecting 'governed peace' which is a potent cocktail of securitization, on the one hand, and developmentalism, on the other hand. This heady mix is the pith and marrow of the statist counterinsurgency mantra in India in the age of globalization. More prosaically, but no less demonstratively, Samaddar also calls this 'social governance' (ibid). However, here an argument for novelty is not being made, either in terms of the time of occurrence of this type of governance or in terms of its site of occurrence, i.e. the north-east. Even as the Mexican military was attempting to encircle and close the noose around the Lacandón jungle region of Zapatista core

[2]The North Eastern Council (NEC) is the nodal agency for the economic and social development of the north-eastern region which consists of the eight states of Arunachal Pradesh, Assam, Manipur, Meghalaya, Mizoram, Nagaland, Tripura and Sikkim (The North-Eastern Council (Amendment) Act, 2002, *inter alia*, added Sikkim as the eighth member–State of the Council). The NEC was constituted in 1971 by an Act of Parliament. The official NEC site has the following to say by the way of publicity: "Over the last 35 years, NEC has been instrumental in setting in motion a new economic endeavour aimed at removing the basic handicaps that stood in the way of normal development of the region and has ushered in an era of new hope in this backward area full of great potentialities." http://necouncil.nic.in. Accessed on 25 October 2013.

[3]For comprehensive information on the AFSPA, see the Report of the National Campaign Committee against Militarization and Repeal of the Armed Forces (Special Powers) Act (1997) and Banerjee (2008, pp. 257–280).

support in December 1994 (no doubt a security measure), targeted social compensation programmes such as the National Solidarity Programme, or the PRONASOL, were already at work. The hide-bound corporatist and clientelist mechanisms once controlled by the PRI party-state were giving way to a recomposition of capitalist hegemony through social governance.[4] The PRONASOL later segued into PROCAMPO and PROGRESA, the latter reconfigured as the 'Oportunidades' programme by President Vicente Fox Quesada in the twenty-first century. What was true of late twentieth century México was, in the same period, true, *mutatis mutandis*, of Guatemala, Ecuador and many other states of Latin America and also true of the Indian north-east. Again, the market-driven reorientation of governance was already evident in Europe at the end of the Second World War with the initiation of the European Recovery Programme (ERP, April 1948–December 1951), better known as the Marshall Plan after its promulgator George Marshall, war 'hero' and US Secretary of State from 8 January 1947. However, in different geopolitical contexts, the security–development complex of social governance can produce very different consequences. And the Indian north-east is a case in point.

Contours of Autonomy

The market-mandated retraction and redeployment of the state poses a critical Foucauldian aporia: the state becomes 'at once that which exists, but which does not yet exist enough' (Foucault 2008, p. 4). And there is much a slip betwixt the cup and the lip. As the turn to the market leaves state authorities in control of fewer resources for co-optation, newly constituted social subjects confronting neoliberalism throughout the north-east formulate a discourse of rights by simultaneously claiming indigenous and other collective rights that markets deny and the citizenship rights that the neoliberal state pretends to offer equally to all.[5] This double strategy is evident in the recent Bodo-Muslim conflict of Assam, which is non-controversial in its 'race' dimensions. While the Bodos stridently assert their ethnic exclusivity in terms of non-belonging to the mainstream body politic, they can at the same time claim citizenship rights and privileges vis-à-vis Muslim agriculturist neighbours whom they brand as aliens. Simply put, the forces of globalization and concurrent social governance that affect class relations are experienced and resisted through a variety of locally relevant 'identities', including ethnicity, race and gender.[6] In the context of the north-east, let us now look at these 'identities' successively and at how social governance, and the entwined peace building efforts, interacts with them.

[4]For an overview, see the chapters in Otero (2004). Also see, Williams (2001).

[5]The same kind of argument has been made for México and Latin America. See Fox (1997), Eckstein and Wickham-Crowley (2003).

[6]For corroborating experiences from other parts of the world, see Nash (2001), Yashar (2005).

It has been suggested that the neoliberal project implies atomization and loss of control to global market forces, posing dilemmas for movements seeking to reassert community identity and grass roots empowerment—that is, in other words, for autonomy movements. On the one hand, what Hellman terms the 'fetishism of autonomy' (Hellman 1992, pp. 52–61)—eschewing affiliation or engagement with any political structure for fear that it might absorb the newly asserted ethnic identity—can be a *cul-de-sac*. On the other hand, negotiating a share of power with existing political institutions runs the risk of replicating dominant hierarchies (serving global capital) and distancing the 'autonomous' representatives from their social bases. Taking advantage of this dilemma, the state, in India at least, has been seen to set up two interrelated kinds of snares, to use a stern metaphor.

The first is to grant regionally based self-governance to autonomy-demanding groups that would amount to a kind of territorial decentralization negotiated with the state. This strategy in some ways predates the emergence of the neoliberal Indian state, harking back to colonial times, and may be loosely termed as a containment policy. The British began administering the north-east region through a series of acts such as the Scheduled District Act of 1874 and the Frontier Tracts Regulations of 1880. In 1873, the British passed the Inner Line Regulation. According to Joysankar Hazarika, the logic behind this regulation was that the 'unrestricted movements which existed between the British subjects in Assam and the wild tribes living across the frontier frequently led to quarrels and sometimes to serious disturbances' (Hazarika 1996, p. 74). However, an equally important reason was that the British administration also wanted to control the rubber trade that was still in the hands of the hill people and that caused frequent skirmishes between the groups. It must be understood that the inner line did not in any way give sovereignty to the hill people; rather, it was a means by which administrative zones of the hills and the plains were separated ostensibly because the 'civilized' faced problems cohabiting with the 'wild'. The Government of India Act, 1935, classified the hill areas of Assam into excluded and partially excluded areas. The excluded areas were not demarcated to protect regional autonomy. This was done mainly to exclude hill areas of Assam from the jurisdiction of the Reformed Provincial Government that included the Brahmaputra plains and the Barak valley. These successive administrative measures, however, had somewhat unpremeditated consequences. Firstly, it resulted in a separate political evolution of the hills and the plains, thereby paving the way for autonomy movements. For the Nagas, for instance, identity claims consolidated into a powerful secessionist movement. The Naga National Council (NNC) was formed in 1946 under the leadership of Angami Zapu Phizo. Under its banner, the Nagas declared their independence on 14 August 1947. The Indian state, of course, quashed this claim brutally with military action, whereafter it adopted the two-track policy of securitization by clamping on the Armed Forces (Special Powers) Act, on the one hand, and initiating a dialogue-based peace process, on the other hand. This dual process has continued till date. 'Dialogues and wars in the north-east with alternative regularity', observes Ranabir Samaddar, 'demonstrate in this way the governmental logic of treating war and peace as a continuum' (Samaddar 2015, p. 10)—a series, if you will.

The second consequence of the British administrative measure is evident from, and flows out of, the above discussion. Territorial demarcation/reorganization became a dominant template of social governance in post-independence India and more so in postliberalization India (Datta Ray and Agrawal 1996). Territorial reorganization, grant of statehood and the introduction of the model of peace accords went hand-in-hand with military operations. Here we can see the processes of the accumulation of the primitive—the recomposition of 'races'—as a precursor to accumulation. Each major military operation was followed by major administrative measures of territorial reorganization and regrouping of villages. There is the example of the creation of Nagaland in December 1963 as the sixteenth state of India; there is also the North-Eastern Areas (Reorganization) Act of 1971 (Datta Ray and Agrawal 1996).[7] Sajal Nag has written about the regrouping of villages in Mizoram (Nag 2011). In Tripura, too, villages were regrouped, though the formal justification in this case was economic: 'cluster villages' were being formed to improve the condition of the indigenous population.[8] Recently, there has been the deliberate policy of introducing rural decentralization in the form of the *panchayati raj* (Dutta Hazarika 2012, pp. 211–244; Dutta Hazarika 2005). More importantly, territorial autonomies along ethnic lines have been created throughout the last 20 years within the states of the region (Barbora 2005; Bhaumik and Bhattacharya 2005, pp. 196–241). Today, the autonomous arrangements have reorganized the states internally while the North-Eastern Areas (Reorganization) Act of 1971 has externally reorganized the states. Of greater importance has been the introduction of autonomy as a result of the many successive peace accords.[9] These autonomous arrangements have been part of the governance structure in the north-eastern states of Assam, Mizoram, Tripura and Meghalaya. They influence the patterns of conflict; they give an idea of the governmental resources to be available for cornering and sharing (an aspect we shall return to later in this essay), the size of the territory to control and the volume of population to govern. As such, they form a major dimension of the 'government of peace'.

Territorial decentralization/reorganization along ethic/race lines may be called a parochial interpretation of autonomy. One of the pitfalls of this interpretation of autonomy from the people's point of view is that it bottles up the actors in a spatial location precisely in an era when their subsistence and cultural identity depend on mobility.[10] This formulation of autonomy may therefore not represent for the struggling groups a real alternative to neoliberal globalization but rather replicate the top-down structure of existing political institutions without developing new leadership capacity at the local community level. At a further level, autonomy-as-decentralization in effect

---

[7]Also find the text of the Act at http://indiankanoon.org/doc/318384/. Accessed 25 October 2013.

[8]On the miserable condition of these 'cluster villages' planned by the Tripura Police Chief, B.L. Vohra, see *The Telegraph*, 1 October 2005 and Prasad (2004–2005).

[9]For a discussion on peace accords and their socio-political function, see Samaddar (2004), Das (2001, pp. 231–252); for a brief account, see Samaddar (2015, pp. 6–11).

[10]A similar argument for Ecuador has been made by Colloredo-Mansfeld (2002, pp. 173–195).

creates a new fourth level of government (alongside the federal, state and municipal institutions) and actively constructs a new, dominant race identity among the various indigenous groups that had formed part of the migrant stream settling in the region in question. The recognition of the benefits of being a member of the dominant group then advances faster among its leadership than the creation of consensus within its diverse base. On the one hand, it therefore suffers from tendencies towards 'boss' politics (or *cacicazgo*, as it is termed in Latin America) and creates resentment among the less privileged elements of the autonomy movement. The charges of 'selling out' to the Indian state that have been periodically raised within an autonomy movement against the dominant group by more 'radical' elements—be it in the case of the United Liberation Front of Assam (ULFA) or the NNC and later the Nationalist Socialist Council of Nagaland (NSCN)—bear testimony to this. On the other hand, it enables the state to affirm its dubious axiom that struggles for autonomy and justice are in essence intergroup struggles for parity and accordingly the state can then play up the resentment within an autonomous region and without (between two autonomous councils, say). This has recently been evident in the slightly removed but intimately related context of the Gorkhaland movement in Darjeeling, West Bengal. Mamata Bandyopadhyay, Chief Minister of West Bengal, in an attempt to put down the wave of Gorkha agitation for autonomy and separate statehood, shrewdly played up the less populous Lepcha and Tamang identity questions within the Gorkhaland Territorial Administration. She also threatened strong-arm action to ensure that the Gorkhaland leaders did not stall 'development' in the Darjeeling Hills and disrupt the lives of the 'people'.[11]

The second snare that the neoliberal state sets up for autonomy movements relates to resource allocation. The same neoliberal ideology that 'frees' individuals to fend for themselves in the market can also spin off unprofitable state functions and services that used to be part of the citizenship compact. The market paradigm privatizes gains while socializing costs and risks. Thus, social sectors and regions may be cut loose as newly autonomous without any hold on state resources, free to compete with each other for a share of the shrinking pie. As a result, *recognition of autonomous spaces in the polity turns out to be a new mechanism for division and co-optation.*[12] As a wider range of groups compete for scarcer state resources, they become vulnerable to clientelistic local politicians and, for that matter, to paternalistic NGOs moving into the breach. In the scramble for resources, in the northeast, it has been seen that when a state government can step in, establish firm control expressed through political will and try to guide the market forces to some extent, the territorial autonomy model works. Tripura is a case in point (*Zee News* 2014; *India Today* 2014). However, where it cannot (that is to say, the rest of the

[11]See the entire 'Ei Muhurte' (This Moment) page of *Ei Samay* (Bangla edition of The Times of India), 27 October 2013 and especially the article on the same page by Sarkar (2013). The Gorkhaland Territorial Administration is a semi-autonomous administrative body of the Nepali-speaking Gorkha ethnic group of the Darjeeling hills that was created in 2011.

[12]Again to get a non-Indian perspective, see Collier (1994, pp. 1–44).

north-east) market, forces wreak havoc on autonomy movements. Developed basically in recent history as what can be called an economy of 'a market along the foothills', which bears the characteristics of an extraction economy around coal and limestone, and a plantation economy around tea and timber, the entire scenario in the north-east represents today what Ranabir Samaddar has termed following Dietmar Rothermund as 'an enclave economy' (Samaddar 2015, p. 14; Rothermund 1993/1988). The neoliberal strategy is designed to pry open this 'enclave' and integrate it with world market. As such, one important mode of social governance in the north-east has been to encourage what can be called at best 'marketization of economic relations' and at worst 'crony capitalism' in the region. There are three more developments strengthening this economic thrust: first, the strategy of opening up the north-east to the greater commercial interests that connect India to Southeast Asia, a strategy known as the 'Look East' policy (Baruah 2004; Das 2010, pp. 343–358); second, the opening of villages and far-flung areas through new institutions, namely schools, colleges, banks, offices and communications networks; and third, the already-alluded policy of encouraging homelands resulting in communal strife, antimigrant measures and ethnic policing. The neoliberal model recognizes the pluralism of race identities as long as those identities do not become the basis for collective organization around substantive rights. Paradoxically, this divisive policy has had the positive impact of ending the insularity of the north-east somewhat (and thereby, negatively, heightened the exposure and concomitant conflict of a person from the north-east with, say, the 'Neanderthals of New Delhi'). However, the situation is also marked by a tense apprehension that unrest may erupt again, for, as Samaddar says, 'While peace has returned, governance has failed to ensure justice' (Samaddar 2015, p. 13). The situation is nonetheless not unremittingly hopeless. To quote Samaddar at length,

> If it is true that what we face here [the Northeast] is a situation of aporia, a cycle of production of nativity-linkages-marketization-immigration-nationalism-ethnicity-violence-law-linkages-marketization-immigration-nativity-nationalism… it is also true that it is contention [and not market forces alone] that prises open the situation again and again. Precisely the collective politics that in its moments of frenzy makes immigration the most contentious issue in the life of a nation, also exhibits factors or aspects that make the dialogic quest for justice continue (ibid).

In other words, what Hale for a different context has termed 'managed neoliberal multiculturalism' (Hale 2002, p. 485) may have worked so far in the north-east—and seems to be working well too. The same state that oversees economic liberalization and privatization is establishing itself as the arbiter of the boundary between individual and race-group rights, carefully circumscribing the latter to exclude challenges to class-based inequalities. Autonomy defined as mere disengagement has left autonomous communities cut off from resources and unprotected from the forces of the global market, and further, autonomy defined as simply cultural pluralism has fallen into the neoliberal 'multiculturalism trap' of atomizing communities, substituting formal 'equality' for the power to establish collective identities and demand substantive rights and in many cases engendering xenophobia. Yet, it is in this tenebrous situation (of collective politics as xenophobic outburst against perceived 'immigrants') that new linkages are being forged which, in Samaddar's powerful enunciation, in time would overcome the ignominious circumstances of its birth and spearhead the 'dialogic quest for justice' (Samaddar 2015, p. 38).

Gendered Dimensions of Autonomy

The forces of globalization and concurrent social governance that affect class relations are experienced and resisted through at least another locally relevant 'identity' than race—gender. The argument here, predictably, is not that women are resplendent symbols of peace who stay away from supporting the male members of their communities when they are embroiled in violent actions. In her book *Battle Cries and Lullabies*, DePauw (2000) has powerfully depicted the various roles women play in situations of conflict. Covering millennia and spanning the globe in its scope, DePauw's study depicts women both and equally as victims and as warriors; as nurses, spies, sex workers, and wives and mothers of soldiers; as warrior queens leading armies into battle; and as baggage carriers marching in the rear. However, it may be argued that such participation does not in any way diminish the marginalization of women. In fact, oftentimes such participation in enforced by patriarchal injunction: women of the Bantu-speaking Kisii tribe in south-western Kenya, for instance, are enjoined by patriarchal requirements to scream to announce the beginning of a war with, say, the Kipsigis, the Maasai or any other hostile Nilotic community. Failure to do this is punished by divorce by their husbands. However, the 'double marginalization of women in conflict situation', as Banerjee (2005, p. 305) terms it[13]—firstly because they are willy-nilly party to the insurgent group claiming autonomy and secondly because they are under the cosh of the same group's patriarchy—does not entirely extinguish their agency. At least in the case of Nagaland in the north-east, appeals have been made with some degree of success to favour political, dialogic and non-military solutions. In other words, the neoliberal state has been able to enlist the support of Naga women to work for peace with some amount of success. In spite of their cooperation with the state as peace builders, however, women have often been able to dodge the governmental 'snares' that were discussed in the previous section and have paved the way for dynamic collective political action of the non-belligerent kind.

[13]Speaking about displaced women, Paula Banerjee writes, 'displaced women are often doubly marginalized since state policies are weighted against them both because they are women and also because often they are members of minority ethnic, religious and linguistic groups' (Banerjee 2005, p. 305). This argument neatly fits the case of women in conflict too. More relevant to our present context is the following statement she makes: 'In situations where the state is not an actor, the majority group imitates state behaviour thereby victimizing women as in the massacres by Bodo militants' (ibid).

To quote at length from the work of Paula Banerjee and Ishita Dey who finished their fieldwork in Nagaland in early 2012:

> [W]omen… through lived experiences of conflict started working for peace [in the Northeast]. In their activism for peace they acquired a legitimacy to enter the space for political decision-making that was denied to them. In their commitment for peace, they motivated their society to observe a ceasefire. The state found in them an unusual ally and could see their far-reaching influence in society. When the state decided to move away from their mode of conflict with the Naga people it reinvented its indispensability by championing the cause of women. It was around the same time that women's activism was going through a generational change. Younger women leaders decided to innovate with new agenda for women and brought in the question of women's rights. In this they found much of the traditional leadership allied against them. They found the state keen to ally with their cause in its role as an arbiter. (Banerjee and Dey 2012, p. 23)

The mutual coming together of Naga women and the Government of Nagaland, Banerjee and Dey argue, is reflected in the activism for a Women's Reservation Bill. The women used all government institutions to further the cause for peace, justice and equity.[14] However, the authors are apprehensive:

> This coming together was timely although the alliance is bound to be fragile. Both the sides are giving lip service to this alliance to further their own interest. However, for now this alliance has proved transformative for gender roles in society, helping the cause of peace, stability and justice. (Banerjee and Dey 2012, p. 23)

They conclude their collaborative study, with the following penetrating *aperçu*: 'It remains to be seen whether this alliance can in any way be liberating for Naga society as a whole; otherwise it will soon become redundant' (Banerjee and Dey 2012, p. 23).

Women in autonomy movements present a peculiar conundrum. On the one hand, they have to identify with the 'autonomous' identity the group promotes and fights for. On the other hand, they are all the time acutely faced with the fact that 'autonomy' after all has long been coded as masculine and is associated with masculine ideal. This is true, despite autonomy being something which women have often called for in their own rights. As Jessica Benjamin argues, while we are formally committed to equality, 'gender polarity underlies such familiar dualisms as autonomy and dependency' (Benjamin 1988, p. 7). In claiming autonomy, therefore, female agents collapse this dubious binary between autonomy and dependency because, as Gilligan persuasively argues, 'for women, identity has as much to do with intimacy as with separation' (1982, p. 98). The trajectory is thus less about individualization and independence than towards ultimately balancing and harmonizing an agent's interests with those of others. This movement towards harmonization is most effectively mediated by women actors. Nagaland is, Banerjee and Dey (2012) may concur, a case in point. At another level, it also announces the arrival of a 'new' subject—whose 'newness' does not consist in merely having a different biological sex, but in the performance of gender roles in a way that

[14]For the activism around the Bill, see *The Morung Express* (2012).

rearticulates the standard modes of interacting with (and counteracting) the market and state's racist agenda.

The role played by women, in Nagaland at least, poses the issue of a certain kind of public ethics of self-government growing out of the dynamics of subject formation through conflict governance. That is to say that conflict can be analysed as a historically singular mode of experience, whereby the 'objects' of conflict governance are transformed into 'subjects' through certain specific procedures, such as the procedure of building peace, or the attempts at peace at microlevels, and through the contradictory process of securitization. Yet, we must understand that subject formation is not a one-sided process. Each phase of 'conflict resolution', so to speak, produces in turn another phase, precisely because the governmental policies of suppression not only stoke fear and loathing but also produce a revised subjectivity that takes stock of the strengths and weaknesses of the 'adversary'. Besides the women in Nagaland, there are also the instances of the recent peasant mobilizations in Assam by Krishak Mukti Sangram Samiti led by Akhil Gogoi and others and the environmental movements in the entire region that we must take note of. These new movements, Sanjay Barbora insists, gives us a picture, however indistinct, of that new kind of subjectivity (Barbora 2011, pp. 19–22; also, Misra 2011, pp. 16–18). Therefore, the result of the operation of new governing techniques is not one that produces passive, depoliticized 'race' subjects—Foucauldian docile bodies, if you will—although such indeed may be the original purpose of social governance. The subject of conflict is, in this sense, irreducibly obstreperous. It can only partially be made the economic subject, and it is important to bear in mind that the economic subject and the subject of rights have different relationships with political power. Their autonomies are of different, often incompatible natures. The problem of 'government of peace', like any other self-styled mode of good governance, is that it will have to deal with different subjects.

The situation that presents itself in the north-east bears the hopeful mark of this dynamic principle of heterogeneity.

References

Akram, M. (2014). Goons assault two Manipuri Women in Delhi, cops go slow on case. *Times of India*. Retrieved July 30, 2014, from http://timesofindia.indiatimes.com/city/delhi/Goons-assault-two-Manipuri-women-in-Delhi-cops-go-slow-on-case/articleshow/29733863.cms

Banerjee, P., & Dey, I. (2012). Women, conflict and governance in Nagaland. *Policies and practices* (Vol. 51, pp. 4–28). Kolkata: Mahanirban Calcutta Research Group.

Banerjee, P. (2005). Resisting erasure: Women IDPs in South Asia. In P. Banerjee, S. Babu Ray Chaudhury, S. K. Das & B. Adhikari (Eds.), *Internal displacement in South Asia: The relevance of the UN's guiding principles* (pp. 280–315). New Delhi: Sage Publications.

Banerjee, P. (2008). Communities, gender and the border: A legal narrative on India's Northeast. In K. Kannabiran & R. Singh (Eds.), *Challenging the rules of law: Colonialism, criminology and human rights in India* (pp. 257–280). New Delhi: Sage.

Barbora, S. (2005). Autonomy in the Northeast: The frontiers of centralized politics. In R. Samaddar (Ed.), *The politics of autonomy: Indian experiences*. New Delhi: Sage.

Barbora, S. (2011). Assam's new voice of dissent. *Economic and Political Weekly, 46*(28), 19–22.

Baruah, S. (2004). Between South and Southeast Asia: Northeast India and the look east policy. *CENISEAS* Paper 4, Guwahati Centre for Northeast India, South and Southeast Asia Studies.

Benjamin, J. (1988). *The bonds of love: Psychoanalysis, feminism, and the problem of domination*. New York: Pantheon Books.

Bhaumik, S., & Bhattacharya, J. (2005). Autonomy in the Northeast: The Hills of Tripura and Mizoram. In R. Samaddar (Ed.), *The politics of autonomy: Indian experiences* (pp. 196–241).

Collier, G. A. (1994). The new politics of exclusion: Antecedents to the rebellion in Mexico. *Dialectical Anthropology, 19*(1), 1–44.

Colloredo-Mansfeld, R. (2002). Autonomy and interdependence in native movements: Towards a pragmatic politics in the Ecuadorian Andes. *Identities: Global Studies in Culture and Power, 9*(2), 173–195.

Das, S. K. (2001). Nobody's Communiqué: Ethnic Accords in Northeastern India. In R. Samaddar & H. Reifeld (Eds.), *Peace as process: Reconciliation and conflict resolution in South Asia* (pp. 231–252). New Delhi: Manohar.

Das, S. K. (2010). India's Look East Policy: Imagining a New Geography of India's Northeast. *India Quarterly, 66*(4), 343–358.

Datta Ray, B., & Agrawal, S. P. (Eds.). (1996). *Reorganization of Northeast India since 1947*. New Delhi: Concept Publishing.

DePauw, L. G. (2000). *Battle cries and lullabies: Women in war from prehistory to the present*. Norman: University of Oklahoma Press.

Dhapola, S. (2014). Delhi: Munirka's campaign against 'gandey log' of Northeast. *Firstpost*, 19 February. Retrieved July 30, 2014, from http://www.firstpost.com/india/delhi-munirkas-campaign-against-gandey-log-of-northeast-1396833.html

Dutta Hazarika, S. (2005). Examining autonomy: The 73rd Constitutional Amendment in Assam. *Policies and Practices 8*. Kolkata: Mahanirban Calcutta Research Group.

Dutta Hazarika, S. (2012). Conflict and development: Implications for democracy and governance. In R. Samaddar & S. K. Sen (Eds.), *New subjects and new governance in India* (pp. 211–244). New Delhi: Routledge.

Eckstein, S. E., & Wickham-Crowley, T. P. (2003). *Struggles for social rights in Latin America*. New York: Routledge.

Foucault, M. (2008). *Birth of Biopolitics: Lectures at the Collège de France, 1978–79*, M. Sennelart (Ed.). (Trans. Graham Burchell). General editors, F. Ewald and A. Fontana; English series editor, Arnold I. Davidson. Picador/Palgrave Macmillan: New York.

Fox, J. (1997). The difficult transition from clientelism to citizenship: Lessons from Mexico. In D. A. Chalmers, C. M. Vilas, K. Hite, S. B. Martin, K. Piester, & M. Segarra (Eds.), *The new politics of inequality in Latin America: Rethinking participation and representation*. New York: Oxford University Press.

Gilligan, C. (1982). *In a different voice: Psychological theory and women's development*. Cambridge, Mass.: Harvard University Press.

Hale, C. R. (2002). Does multiculturalism menace? governance, cultural rights, and the politics of identity in Guatemala. *Journal of Latin American Studies, 34*(3), 485–524.

Hazarika, J. (1996). *Geopolitics of North East India: A Strategical Study*. New Delhi: Gyan Publishing House.

Hellman, J. A. (1992). The study of new social movements in Latin America and the question of autonomy. In A. Escobar & S. E. Alvarez (Eds.), *The making of social movements in Latin America: Identity, strategy and democracy* (pp. 52–61). Boulder: Westview Press. Hazarika, Joysankar. 1996. *Geopolitics of North-East India: A Strategical Study*. New Delhi: Gyan Publishing House.

India Today. (2014). 14-year-old Northeast girl raped by landlord's son in Delhi. Retrieved July 30, 2014, from http://indiatoday.intoday.in/video/manipuri-girl-raped-munirka-south-delhi-vicky-safdarjung-hospital/1/342562.html

Kar, B. (2007). *Framing Assam: Plantation capital, metropolitan knowledge, and a regime of identities, 1790s–1930s*. Unpublished PhD Thesis, Centre For Historical Studies, Jawaharlal Nehru University, New Delhi.

Misra, U. (2011). A new edge to people's protest in Assam. *Economic and Political Weekly, 46*(28), 16–18.

Nag, S. (2011). A gigantic panopticon: Counter-insurgency and modes of disciplining and punishment in Northeast India. Paper presented at *Development, Logistics, and Governance: Fourth Critical Studies Conference*, Kolkata.

Nash, J. C. (2001). *Mayan visions: The quest for autonomy in an age of globalization*. New York: Routledge.

Otero, G. (Ed.). (2004). *Mexico in transition: Neoliberal globalism, the state, and civil society*. London: Zed Books.

Prasad, A. (2004–2005). Forestry and Tribal Development: A Background Note for Tripura State Human Development Report. Retrieved October 25, 2013, from http://planningtripura.nic.in/THDR/backgroundreport/Forestry%20&%20Tribal%20Development.pdf/

Report of the National Campaign Committee against Militarization and Repeal of the Armed Forces (Special Powers) Act. 1997. Where Peacekeepers have Declared War: Report on Violations of Democratic Rights by Security Forces and the Impact of the Armed Forces (Special Powers) Act on Civilian Life in the Seven States of the Northeast. New Delhi.

Rothermund, D. (1993/1988). *An Economic History of India: from Pre-Colonial Times to 1991*. New York: Routledge.

Samaddar, R. (2004). Governing through peace accords. In *The Politics of Dialogue: Geopolitical Histories of War and Peace in South Asia*. Chap. 6. Aldershot: Ashgate.

Samaddar, R. (2015). Government of peace. In R. Samaddar (Ed.), *Government of peace: Social governance, security and the problematic of peace* (pp. 19–56). Surry: Ashgate.

Sarkar, A. (2013). 'Meghmukto Paharh' [Cloudless Hills], *Ei Somoy* (Bangla Edition of The Times of India), 27 October.

The Indian Express. (2014). Manipuri man beaten to death in Delhi. Retrieved July 30, 2014, from http://indianexpress.com/article/cities/delhi/manipuri-man-beaten-to-death-in-delhi/

The Morung Express. (2012). SC directs Nagaland Govt. to respond on 33 % women quota. 20 November. Retrieved October 26, 2013, from http://www.morungexpress.com/frontpage/88603.html

The Telegraph. (2005). Tripura Tribal Rehab Plan goes Awry. 1 October. Retrieved October 25, from http://www.telegraphindia.com/1051001/asp/northeast/story_5304499.asp

Williams, H. L. (2001). *Social movements and economic transition: Markets and distributive conflict in Mexico*. New York: Cambridge University Press.

Yashar, D. J. (2005). *Contesting citizenship in Latin America: The rise of indigenous movements and the post-liberal challenge*. Cambridge: Cambridge University Press.

Zee News. (2014). Manipuri girl allegedly raped by landlord's son in Delhi, North East students stage protest. Retrieved July 30, 2014, from http://zeenews.india.com/news/delhi/manipuri-girl-allegedly-raped-by-landlord-s-son-in-delhi-north-east-students-stage-protest_909992.html

Bibliography

Akram, M. (2014). Goons assault two Manipuri Women in Delhi, cops go slow on case. *Times of India*. Retrieved July 30, 2014, from http://timesofindia.indiatimes.com/city/delhi/Goons-assault-two-Manipuri-women-in-Delhi-cops-go-slow-on-case/articleshow/29733863.cms

Arrighi, G. (2010). *The long twentieth century: Money, power, and the origins of our times*. London: Verso.

Bailey, F. G. (1957). *Caste and the economic frontier: A village in highland orissa*. Manchester: Manchester University Press.

Baker, C., & Washbrook, D. A. (1975). *South India: Political Institutions and Political Change, 1880–1940*. Delhi: Macmillan Company of India.

Bandyopadhyay, R. (2011). Politics of archiving: Hawkers and pavement dwellers in Calcutta. *Dialectical Anthropology 35*(3), 295–316. Retrieved from http://www.scopus.com/inward/record.url?eid=2-s2.0-80053319302partnerID=40md5=3e3d9db51d9b4299b4b61375f7e8933a

Banerjee, M. (2009). *Power, knowledge, medicine: Ayurvedic pharmaceuticals at home and in the world*. New Delhi: Orient Blackswan Private Limited.

Banerjee, P., & Dey, I. (2012). Women, conflict and governance in nagaland. *Policies and Practices* (Vol. 51, p. 23). Kolkata: Mahanirban Calcutta Research Group.

Banerjee, P. (2005). Resisting erasure: Women IDPs in South Asia. In P. Banerjee, S. Basu Ray Chaudhury, S. K. Das & B. Adhikari (Eds.), *Internal Displacement in South Asia: The relevance of the UN's Guiding Principles* (p. 305). New Delhi: Sage Publications.

Banerjee, P. (2008). Communities, Gender and the Border: A Legal Narrative on India's Northeast. In K. Kannabiran & R. Singh (Eds.), *Challenging the Rules of Law: Colonialism, Criminology and Human Rights in India* (pp. 257–280). New Delhi: Sage.

Banerjee-Guha, S. (2009). Neoliberalising the 'Urban': New geographies of power and injustice in Indian cities. *Economic and Political Weekly, 44*(22), 95–107.

Banerjee-Guha, S. (2010). Introduction. In S. Banerjee-Guha (Ed.), *Accumulation by dispossession* (pp. 1–16). Delhi: Sage.

Banerjee-Guha, S. (2013). Accumulation and dispossession: Contradictions of growth and development in contemporary India. *South Asia: Journal of South Asian Studies, 36*(2), 165–179. doi:10.1080/00856401.2013.804026.

Barbora, S. (2005). Autonomy in the Northeast: The frontiers of centralized politics. In R. Samaddar (Ed.), *The politics of autonomy: Indian experiences*. New Delhi: Sage.

Barbora, S. (2011). Assam's new voice of dissent. *Economic and Political Weekly, 46*(28), 19–22.

Baruah, S. (2004). Between South and Southeast Asia: Northeast India and the look east policy. *CENISEAS* Paper 4, Guwahati Centre for Northeast India, South and Southeast Asia Studies.

Benjamin, J. (1988). *The bonds of love: Psychoanalysis, feminism, and the problem of domination*. New York: Pantheon Books.

I.K. Mitra et al. (eds.), *Accumulation in Post-Colonial Capitalism*,
DOI 10.1007/978-981-10-1037-8

Bhattacharya, R., & Sanyal, K. (2011). Bypassing the squalor: New towns, immaterial labour and exclusion in post-colonial urbanisation. *Economic and Political Weekly, 46*(31), 41–48.

Bhaumik, S., & Bhattacharya, J. (2005). Autonomy in the Northeast: The Hills of Tripura and Mizoram. In R. Samaddar (Ed.), *The politics of autonomy: Indian experiences* (pp. 196–241).

Birla, R. 2008. *Stages of capital: Law, culture, and market governance in late colonial India*. Duke University Press.

Birla, R. (2009). *Stages of capital: Law, culture, and market governance in late colonial India*. Durham and London: Duke University Press.

Bose, S. (1986). *Agrarian bengal: Economy, social structure and politics, 1919–1947*. Cambridge: Cambridge University Press.

Bourdieu, P. (1986). The forms of capital. In J. G. Richardson (Ed.), *Handbook of theory and research for the sociology of capital* (pp. 241–58). New York: Greenwood Press.

Bovaird, T. (2011). A brief intellectual history of the public-private partnership movement. In Hodge et al. (Eds.), *International handbook on public private partnerships* (pp. 43–67).

Brass, P. R. (2004). Patel, vallabhbhai jhaverbhai (1875/6–1950). In *Oxford Dictionary of National Biography*. Oxford University Press. Retrieved October 25, 2013, from http://www.oxforddnb.com/view/article/35403.

Brenner, N., & Theodore, N. (2002). Cities and the geographies of 'actually existing neoliberalism'. *Antipode, 34*(3), 349–379.

Buzan, B., Weaver, O., & De Wilde, J. (1998). *Security: A new framework for analysis*. Boulder: Lynne Rienner.

Callinicos, A. (2010). The limits of passive revolution. *Capital and Class, 34*(3), 491–507.

Carruthers, A. (2002). The accumulation of national belonging in transnational fields: ways of being at home in Vietnam. *Identities, 9*, 423–444.

Census. (1971). *Primary census abstract*. Series 21, Part X-B, Uttar Pradesh: District Census Handbook.

Chari, S. (2004). *Fraternal capital: peasant-workers, self-made men, and globalization in provincial India*. Delhi: Orient Blackswan.

Chari, S. (2004). *Fraternal capital: Peasant-workers, self-made men and globalization in provincial India*. Ranikhet: Permanent Black.

Chatterjee, P. (2012). *The black hole of empire: History of a global practice of power*. Princeton: Princeton University Press.

Chatterjee, P. (1984). *Bengal 1920-1947: The land question*. Calcutta: K. P. Bagchi & Company.

Chatterjee, P. (1994). *The nation and its fragments: Colonial and postcolonial histories*. New York: Princeton University Press.

Chatterjee, S. K. (2008). *Personal management and industrial relations*. Delhi: Surjeet Publications.

Chattopadhyay, S. (2005). *Representing calcutta: Modernity, nationalism and the colonial uncanny* (Vol. 2). London and New York: Routledge.

Chibber, V. (2006). *Locked in place: State-building and late industrialization in India*. Princeton: Princeton University Press.

Chibber, V. (2013). *Postcolonial theory and the spectre of capital*. London: Verso.

Chikarmane, P., & Narayan, L. (2005). *Organising the Unorganised: A case study of the KagadKach Patra Kashtakari Panchayat (Trade Union of Waste Pickers)*. Retrieved August 14, 2015, from http://wiego.org/sites/wiego.org/files/resources/files/Chikarmane_Narayan_case-kkpkp.pdf

Collier, G. A. (1994). The new politics of exclusion: Antecedents to the rebellion in Mexico. *Dialectical Anthropology, 19*(1), 1–44.

Colloredo-Mansfeld, R. (2002). Autonomy and interdependence in native movements: Towards a pragmatic politics in the ecuadorian andes. *Identities: Global Studies in Culture and Power, 9*(2), 173–195.

Comaroff, J., & Comaroff, J. L. (1999). Occult economies and the violence of abstraction: notes from the South African Postcolony. *American Ethnologist, 26*(2), 279–303.

Connell, J. (2008). Niue: Embracing a culture of migration. *Journal of Ethnic and Migration Studies, 34*.

Conservancy Workers Demand Regular Wages. *The Hindu*, 17 July 2015.

Crouch, H. (1966). *Trade unions and politics in India*. Bombay: Manaktals.

Das, A. (1949). *Amar jiban*. Kolkata: Kalikata Printing Co.

Das, S. K. (2001). Nobody's communiqué: Ethnic accords in northeastern India. In R. Samaddar & H. Reifeld (Eds.), *Peace as process: Reconciliation and conflict resolution in South Asia* (pp. 231–252). New Delhi: Manohar.

Das, S. K. (2010). India's look east policy: Imagining a new geography of India's Northeast. *India Quarterly, 66*(4), 343–358.

Das, S., & Bhattacharyya, B. K. (2013). Municipal solid waste characteristics and management in Kolkata, India. *International Journal of Emerging Technology and Advanced Engineering, 3*(2), 147.

Datta Ray, B., & Agrawal, S. P. (Eds.). (1996). *Reorganization of northeast India since 1947*. New Delhi: Concept Publishing.

Datta, A. (2009). Public-private partnership in India: A case for reform? *Economic and Political Weekly, 44*(33), 73–78.

Datta, B. (1976). The banking structure: A Re-appraisal. *EPW, 11*(21) (22 May), 781–86.

DePauw, L. G. (2000). *Battle cries and lullabies: Women in war from prehistory to the present*. Norman: University of Oklahoma Press.

Deshpande, A. (2011). Deshpande: The grammar of caste-economic discrimination in contemporary India. *OUP Catalogue*.

Devika, J. (2007). A people united in development. *Working paper*, Series 386, Thiruvananthapuram: CDS.

Dey, I., Samaddar, R., & Sen, S. K. (2013). *Beyond Kolkata: Rajarhat and the Dystopia of Urban Imagination*. New Delhi: Routledge India.

Dhapola, S. (2014). Delhi: Munirka's campaign against gandey log of North East. *Firstpost*. 19 February. http://www.firstpost.com/india/delhi-munirkas-campaign-against-gandey-log-of-northeast-1396833.html?utm_source=ref_article

Dhapola, S. (2014). Delhi: Munirka's campaign against 'gandey log' of Northeast. *Firstpost*, 19 February. Retrieved July 30, 2014, from http://www.firstpost.com/india/delhi-munirkas-campaign-against-gandey-log-of-northeast-1396833.html

District Census Handbook. (1981). *Village and Town Directory*. Series 22, Part XIII A, Uttar Pradesh.

District Census Handbook. (1991). *Primary Census Abstract*. Series 25, Part XII-B, Uttar Pradesh.

District Census Handbook. (2001). *Primary Census Abstract*. Ghaziabad District. Uttar Pradesh. Accessed from Census Data Centre, Jawaharlal Nehru University, New Delhi on 10 September 2013.

Dupont, V. (2011). The dream of Delhi as a global city. *International Journal of Urban and Regional Research, 35*(3), 533–554. doi:10.1111/j.1468-2427.2010.01027.x.

Dutt, R. (2008). Emerging trends in trade union movement. *Mainstream, 46* (20) (3 May).

Dutta Hazarika, S. (2005). Examining autonomy: The 73rd constitutional amendment in Assam. *Policies and Practices 8*. Kolkata: Mahanirban Calcutta Research Group.

Dutta Hazarika, S. (2012). Conflict and development: Implications for democracy and governance. In R. Samaddar & S. K. Sen (Eds.), *New subjects and new governance in India* (pp. 211–244). New Delhi: Routledge.

Eckstein, S. E., & Wickham-Crowley, T. P. (2003). *Struggles for Social Rights in Latin America*. New York: Routledge.

Economic and Political Weekly (henceforth EPW). (1967). Not a Simple Revolt. *2* (26) (1 July), 1151–1152.

EPW. (1967). Revolt in the AICC. *2*(26) (1 July), 1160–61.

EPW. (1969a). Budget plus banks. *4*(28–30), Special Number: 1093–1094.

EPW. (1969b). Modest beginnings. *4*(40) (4 October), 1579.

EPW. (1969c). Programme for branch expansion. *4*(32) (9 August), 1292.

EPW. (1969d). Starting points for a policy leap. *4*(31) (2 August), 1093–1094, 1256.

EPW. (1969e). Starting points for a policy leap. *4*(37) (13 September).

EPW. (1970a). Azadnagar socialism on tap. *5*(1) (3 January), 8.

EPW. (1970b). Economic post-mortem on the split. *5*(25) (20 June), 958.

EPW. (1970c). One year after: The prospect. *5*(29–31), Special Issue: 1129.

EPW. (1970d). Unfinished business. *5*(29–31), Special Issue: 1107–08.

EPW. (1970e). Uncertainly poised. *5*(7) (14 February), 70.

EPW. (1971a). Floundering without a plan. *6*(29) (17 July), 1414.

EPW. (1971b). How cheaply to lend little. *6*(27) (3 July), 1305.

EPW. (1974). Credit policy: Loss of credibility. *9*(17) (27 April): 692–694.

Evelyn Nakano Glenn. (1992). From servitude to service work: Historical continuities in the racial division of paid reproductive labor. *Signs, 18*(1) (Autumn), 1–43.

Flinders, M. (2011). Splintered logic and political debate. In Hodge et al (Eds.), *International handbook on public private partnerships* (pp. 115–131).

Foucault, M., Senellart, M., Ewald, F., Fontana, A., & Burchell, G. (2010). *The birth of biopolitics: lectures at the Collège de France, 1978-1979*. New York: Palgrave Macmillan.

Foucault, M. (2008). *Birth of Biopolitics: Lectures at the Collège de France, 1978–79*, M. Sennelart (Ed.). (Trans. Graham Burchell). General editors, F. Ewald and A. Fontana; English series editor, Arnold I. Davidson. Picador/Palgrave Macmillan: New York.

Fox, J. (1997). The difficult transition from clientelism to citizenship: Lessons from Mexico. In D. A. Chalmers, C. M. Vilas, K. Hite, S. B. Martin, K. Piester, & M. Segarra (Eds.), *The new politics of inequality in Latin America: Rethinking participation and representation*. New York: Oxford University Press.

Frankel, F. R. (1978). *India's political economy, 1947–77: The gradual revolution*. Princeton, NJ: Princeton University Press.

Gaddis, J. L. (1989). *The long peace: Inquiries into the history of the cold war*. New York: Oxford University Press.

Ghosh, D. N. (1979). *Banking policy in India: An evaluation*. Bombay: Allied Publishers.

Ghosh, P., & Geetika. (2007). Unionisation: A feasibility study for the indian software industry. *Russian Management Journal, 2*, 45–56.

Ghosh, P., Nandan, S., & Gupta, A. (2009). The changing roles of trade unions in India: A case study of national thermal power corporation (NTPC). *Unchahar. Asian Academy of Management Journal, 14*(1), 37–57.

Gidwani, V. (2008). *Capital, interrupted: Agrarian development and the politics of work in India*. Minneapolis and London: University of Minnesota Press.

Gilligan, C. (1982). *In a different voice: Psychological theory and women's development*. Cambridge, Mass.: Harvard University Press.

Gooptu, N. (2013). Servile sentinels of the city: Private security guards, organized informality, and labour in interactive services in Globalized India. *International Review of Social History, 58*(1), 9–38.

Government of India. (1929). *Report of the Royal Commission on Labour in India* (30 September 1929), 322.

Government of India. (1963). *Report of National Commission on Labour*.

Government of India. (2007–2008). *Labour Bureau*. Retrieved from www.labourbureau.nic.in

Government of India. (2015). *Smart cities: Mission statement and guidelines*. Ministry of Urban Development: Government of India.

Graham, S., & Marvin, S. (2001). *Splintering Urbanism. Networked Infrastructures, Technological Mobilities and the Urban Condition*. London: Routledge.

Grusky, D. (1999). Review of durable inequality. *American Journal of Sociology, 104*, 1823–1825.

Hale, C. R. (2002). Does multiculturalism menace? Governance, cultural rights, and the politics of identity in Guatemala. *Journal of Latin American Studies, 34*(3), 485–524.

Hardt, M. (1999). Affective Labour. *Boundary 2,* 26(2), 89–100.

Hardt, M., & Negri, A. (2000). *Empire*. Cambridge, MA, and London: Harvard University Press.

Hardt, M., & Negri, A. (2004). *Multitude: War and democracy in the age of empire*. New York: Penguin.

Harijan. (1946). 21 July, 229.

Harvey, D. (2003). *The new imperialism*. Oxford: Oxford University Press.

Harvey, D. (2004). *The new imperialism*. Socialist Register: Accumulation by Dispossession. 40.

Harvey, D. (2005). *The new imperialism* (Paperback ed.). New York: Oxford University Press.

Harvey, D. (2006). *Spaces of global capitalism*. London, New York: Verso.

Harvey, D. (2007). *A brief history of neoliberalism* (Paperback ed.). New York: Oxford University Press.

Harvey, D. (2010). The right to the city: From capital surplus to accumulation by dispossession. In S. Banerjee-Guha (Ed.), *Accumulation by dispossession* (pp. 17–32). Delhi: Sage.

Hellman, J. A. (1992). The study of new social movements in Latin America and the question of autonomy. In A. Escobar & S. E. Alvarez (Eds.), *The making of social movements in Latin America: Identity, strategy and democracy* (pp. 52–61). Boulder: Westview Press. Hazarika, Joysankar. 1996. *Geopolitics of North-East India: A Strategical Study*. New Delhi: Gyan Publishng House.

Hodge, G. A., Greve, C., & Boardman, A. E. (Eds.). (2011). *International handbook on public private partnerships*. Cheltenham: Edward Elgar.

Human Rights Watch. (2014). *Clearing Human Waste: "Manual Scavenging," Caste and Discrimination in India*.

Ilaiah, K. (1996). *Why I am not a Hindu: A sudra critique of hindutva philosophy, culture and political economy*. Calcutta: Samya.

India Today. (2014). 14-year-old Northeast girl raped by landlord's son in Delhi. Retrieved July 30, 2014, from http://indiatoday.intoday.in/video/manipuri-girl-raped-munirka-south-delhi-vicky-safdarjung-hospital/1/342562.html

Jagannathan, N. V. & Halder, A. (2004). Pavement dwellers of Calcutta–1987: A socio-economic study April 1988. In *Metropolitan Calcutta: An Anthology of Socio-Economic Studies and Survey Reports of KMDA 1970–2004*, Vol. 4, 1986–1992. Calcutta Metropolitan Development Authority: Socio-Economic Planning Unit, Directorate of Planning and Development.

Jain and Polmen. (2003). *A handbook for trainers on participatory local development*. Bangkok: Regional Office for Asia and the Pacific, Food and Agriculture Organization of the United Nations.

Jameela, N. (2007). *Autobiography of a sex worker*. Chennai: Wasteland.

Janu, C. K. (2004). *Mother forest: The unfinished story of C*. Kali for Women: K. Janu. New Delhi.

Jeffrey, C. (2001). 'A fist is stronger than five fingers': caste and dominance in rural North India. *Transactions of the Institute of British Geographers, 26*(2), 217–236.

Johnson, E. (1978). Labour as Risk-bearer. *Cambridge Journal of Economics, 2*, 373–380.

Karnik, V. B. (1998). *Indian trade unions: A survey*. Bombay: P.C. Manekalal & Sons.

Kennedy, L. (2007). Regional industrial policies driving peri urban dynamics in Hyderabad. *India. Cities, 24*(2), 95–109.

Kennedy, V. D. (1966). *Unions, employers and government*. Bombay: Manaktals.

Knowels, K. G. J. C. (1952). *Strikes*. Oxford: Basil Blackwell.

Kolkata Municipal Corporation. (2014). *Kolkata municipal corporation: Budget statement by Shri Shovan Chatterjee, Mayor, Kolkata, 2014–15*. Central Municipal Office, 6.

Kothari, R. (Ed.). (1995). *Caste in Indian politics*. New Delhi: Orient Blackswan.

Kumar, S. N. (2000). On the janmabhoomi roller coaster. *Frontline, 17*(2) (22 January–4 February).

Kunhaman, M. (2002). *Globalisation: A subaltern perspective*. Thiruvananthapuram: Centre for Subaltern Studies.

Lad, V. (2005). *Ayurveda: The science of self healing*. Delhi: Motilal Banarsidas Publishers Private Limited.
Lazzarato, M. N. D. Immaterial labor. Retrieved August 14, 2015, from http://www.generation-online.org/c/fcimmateriallabour3.htm
Leander, A. (2005). The market for force and public security: the destabilizing consequences of private military companies. *Journal of Peace Research, 42*(5), 605–622. doi:10.1177/0022343305056237.
Lenin, V. I. (1964a/1915). Karl Marx: A brief biographical sketch with an exposition of Marxism. *Collected Works* (Vol. 21, pp. 43–91). Moscow: Progress Publishers.
Lenin, V.I. (1964b/1916). The junius pamphlet. *Collected Works* (Vol. 22, pp. 305–319). Moscow: Progress Publishers.
Levien, M. (2012). The land question: special economic zones and the political economy of dispossession in India. *The Journal of Peasant Studies, 39*(3–4), 933–969. doi:10.1080/03066150.2012.656268.
Luxemburg, R. (2014a/1915). *Accumulation of Capital*. Section 3, Chapter 26. Retrieved January 20, 2014, from http://www.marxists.org/archive/luxemburg/1913/accumulation-capital/ch26.htm#doc-2
Luxemburg, R. (2014b/1915). *The Junius Pamphlet*. Retrieved February 10, 2014, from http://www.marxists.org/archive/luxemburg/1915/junius/ch01.htm#n3
Malhotra, I. (1969). Congress unable to check its downward drift. *The Statesman*, 14 March.
Malhotra, I. (1989). *Indira Gandhi: A personal and political biography*. London: Hodder & Stoughton.
Martin, E. (1991). The egg and the sperm: How science has constructed a romance based on stereotypical male-female roles. *Signs, 16*(3), 485–501.
Marx, K. (1976). *Capital* (Vol. 1). London: Penguin classics in association with new left review.
Marx, K. (2014a/1867). *Capital* (Vol. 1). Retrieved February 2, 2014, from https://www.marxists.org/archive/marx/works/1867-c1/
Marx, K. (2014b/1939). *Grundrisse*. Retrieved February 2, 2014, from https://www.marxists.org/subject/dialectics/marx-engels/grundisse.htm
Mernissi, F. (2002). *Islam and democracy: Fear of the modern world*. New York: Basic Books.
Mezzadra, S. (2011). How many histories of labour? Towards a theory of postcolonial capitalism. *Postcolonial Studies, 14*(2), 151–170. doi:10.1080/13688790.2011.563458.
Mezzadra, S., & Neilson, B. (2015). Operations of capital. *South Atlantic Quarterly, 114*(1), 11. doi:10.1215/00382876-2831246 y1–2015.
Mezzadra, S., & Neilson, B. (2013). *Border as method or the multiplication of labour*. Durham: Duke University Press.
Mezzadra, S., & Neilson, B. (2013). *Border as method, or, the multiplication of labor*. Durham: Duke University Press.
Mezzadra, S., & Neilson, B. (2014). The state of capitalist globalization. *Viewpoint Magazine*, 4 September. Retrieved November 10, 2014 from https://viewpointmag.com/2014/09/04/the-state-of-capitalist-globalization
Misra, U. (2011). A new edge to people's protest in Assam. *Economic and Political Weekly, 46*(28), 16–18.
Moulier-Boutang, Y. (2012). *Cognitive capitalism*. Trans. E. Emery: Wiley.
Mukerjee, R. (1945). *Indian working class*. Bombay: Asia Public House.
Mukherjee, S. (1975). Under the shadow of the metropolis: They are citizens too. September 1973-March 1974. A Report on the Survey of 10,000 Pavement-Dwellers in Calcutta. In *Metropolitan Calcutta: An Anthology of Socio-Economic Studies and Survey Reports of KMDA 1970-2004*. Vol. 1, 1970–1979. Calcutta Metropolitan Development Authority: Socio-Economic Planning Unit, Directorate of Planning and Development.
Nag, S. (2011). A gigantic panopticon: Counter-insurgency and modes of disciplining and punishment in Northeast India. Paper presented at *Development, Logistics, and Governance: Fourth Critical Studies Conference*, Kolkata.

Nandi, J., & Somreet, B. (2014). Anti-North East Fiat in Munirka, Cops Step In. *The Times of India*, 18 February.

Nandy, A. (1973). Need achievement in a Calcutta Suburb. In M. Singer (Ed.), *Entrepreneurship and modernization in South Asia* (pp. 167–178). Durham: Duke University Program in Comparative Studies on South Asia.

Nandy, A. (1983). *The intimate enemy: Loss and recovery of self under colonialism*. Delhi: OUP.

Nash, J. C. (2001). *Mayan visions: The quest for autonomy in an age of globalization*. New York: Routledge.

Neilson, B. (2014). Zones: beyond the logic of exception? *Concentric: Literary and Cultural Studies*, *40*(2), 11–28.

Neocleous, M. (2008). *Critique of security*. Edinburgh: Edinburgh University Press.

NOIDA. (1983). *Draft Master Plan Noida 2001*. Retrieved September 10, 2013 from http://www.noidaauthorityonline.com/MasterPlanNew/MASTER-PLAN-2001.pdf

Ong, A. (2006). *Neoliberalism as exception: Mutations in citizenship and sovereignty*. Durham: Duke University Press.

Oommen, M. A. (1999). *Rethinking development: Kerala's development experience* (Vol. 1). Institute of Social Sciences. New Delhi: Concept Publishing Company.

Otero, G. (Ed.). (2004). *Mexico in transition: Neoliberal globalism, the state, and civil society*. London: Zed Books.

Owens, R., & Nandy, A. (1977). *The new vaishyas*. Bombay: Allied Publishers Private Limited.

Owens, R. (1991). Peasant Entrepreneurs in an Industrial City. In M. S. A. Rao, C. Bhat, & L. N. Kadekar (Eds.), *A reader in Urban sociology*. New Delhi: Orient Longman.

Palsson, G. (2009). Biosocial relations of production. *Comparative Studies in Society and History, 51*(2), 288–313.

Patnaik, U. (1990). *Agrarian relations and accumulation: The mode of production debate in India*. New Delhi: Oxford University Press.

Planning Commission. (2008). *Approach to Regulation of Infrastructure*. New Delhi: Planning Commission.

Plourde, C. G. (1972). A model of waste accumulation and disposal. *The Canadian Journal of Economics, 5*(1), 119–125.

Policante, A. (2012). *I nuovi mercenari: mercato mondiale e privatizzazione della Guerra*. Ombre corte.

Portes, A., & Landolt, P. (2000). Social capital: promise and pitfalls of its role in development. *Journal of Latin American Studies, 32*(2), 529–547.

Prasad, Archana. 2004–2005. Forestry and Tribal Development: A Background Note for Tripura State Human Development Report. Retrieved October 25, 2013, from http://planningtripura.nic.in/THDR/backgroundreport/Forestry%20&%20Tribal%20Development.pdf/

Ramaswamy, U. (1978). The belief system of the non-Brahmin movement in India: the Andhra case. *Asian Survey, 18*(3), 290–300.

Rao, K. S. (1955). The second five year plan: Some methodological considerations. *Economic and Political Weekly, 7*(46) (12 November).

Rawat, V. B. N. D. *Hindi Speaking Dalits at the Receiving End in West Bengal*. Retrieved August 14, 2015, from www.ambedkar.org/VBRawat/WB_Dalits_Rawat.html

Ray, R. K., & Ray, R. (1975). Zaminders and Jotedars: A Study of Rural Politics in Bengal. *Modern Asian Studies, 9*(1), 81–102.

Report of the National Campaign Committee against Militarization and Repeal of the Armed Forces (Special Powers) Act. 1997. Where Peacekeepers have Declared War: Report on Violations of Democratic Rights by Security Forces and the Impact of the Armed Forces (Special Powers) Act on Civilian Life in the Seven States of the Northeast. New Delhi.

Reserve Bank of India-Jadavpur University. (1964). *Survey of small engineering units in Howrah, Calcutta*. Calcutta: Sri Saraswati Press.

Robinson, J. 2013. Ordinary cities: between modernity and development. Retrieved from http://UWSAU.eblib.com.au/patron/FullRecord.aspx?p=200247

Rose, N. (2008). The value of life: Somatic ethics and the spirit of bio-capital. *Daedalus, 137*(1), 36–48.

Rothermund, D. (1993/1988). *An Economic History of India: from Pre-Colonial Times to 1991*. New York: Routledge.

Routh, S. (2013). *Informal Workers in India: Reconceptualizing Labour Law to Promote Capabilities*. Unpublished Dissertation, Victoria University, 243–244.

Rudner, D. W. (1994). *Caste and capitalism in colonial India: the Nattukottai Chettiars*. Berkeley: University of California Press.

Rudner, D. (1995). *Caste and capitalism in Colonial India: The Nattukottai Chettiars*. Berkeley and Los Angeles: University of California Press.

Samaddar, R. (2004). Governing through peace accords. In *The Politics of Dialogue: Geopolitical Histories of War and Peace in South Asia*. Chap. 6. Aldershot: Ashgate.

Samaddar, R. (Ed.). (2005). *The politics of autonomy: Indian experiences*. New Delhi: Sage.

Samaddar, R. (2009). Primitive accumulation and some aspects of work and life in India. *Economic and Political Weekly, 44*(18), 33–42.

Samaddar, R. (2010). *Emergence of the political subject*. New Delhi: Sage.

Samaddar, R. (2012). What Is postcolonial predicament? *Economic and Political Weekly*, *47*(9).

Samaddar, R. (2013). Michel foucault and our postcolonial time. In S. Mezzadra, J. Reid, & R. Samaddar (Eds.), *The biopolitics of development: Reading Michel foucault in the postcolonial present* (pp. 25–44). Dordrecht: Springer.

Samaddar, R. (2014). A post-colonial critique of capital accumulation today. *Policies and Practices, 64*.

Samaddar, R. (2015a). Government of peace. In Ranabir, S. (Ed.), *Government of Peace. Social Governance, Security and the Problematic of Peace.* Surry: Ashgate.

Samaddar, R. (2015). *The postcolonial bind of Greece*. Retrieved September 9, 2015, from https://viewpointmag.com/2015/08/20/the-postcolonial-bind-of-greece/

Sandhu, A. (2006). Why unions fail in organising India's BPO-ITES Industry? *Economic and Political Weekly*, 14 October.

Sangari, K. (2015). *Solid: Liquid, a (Trans)national reproductive formation*. New Delhi: Tulika.

Sankar, S. (2005). *Tourisavum keralavum*. TVM: Spandanam.

Sanyal, H. (1976). Dakshin-paschim banglay jatiyatabadi andolon, 1. *Chaturanga, 38*, 1–26.

Sanyal, K. (2007). *Rethinking capitalist development: Primitive accumulation, governmentality and post-colonial capitalism*. New Delhi: Routledge.

Sanyal, K. (2013). *Rethinking capitalist development: Primitive accumulation, governmentality, and post-colonial capitalism*. Delhi: Routledge.

Sarkhel, P. (2006). Economics of household waste management in Kolkata: Proposed steps towards improved efficiency. *Contemporary Issues and Ideas in Social Sciences*, March: 1.

Sassen, S. (1991). *The global city: New York, London, Tokyo*. Princeton, N.J: Princeton University Press.

Satyanarayana, A. (1991). *Andhra Peasants under British Rule: Agrarian Relations and the Rural Economy 1900-1940*. South Asia Books.

Sen, S. K. (1998). *The transitional state: Congress and government in U.P., c. 1946–1957*. Unpublished Ph.D. dissertation. London.

Sen, S. (2007). *Globalisation and development*. New Delhi: National Book Trust.

Sen, S., & Dasgupta, B. (2006). Labour in India's manufacturing sector. *Indian Journal of Labour Economics, 49*(1), 79–101.

Sen, S., & Dasgupta, B. (2009). *Unfreedom and waged work—Labour in India's manufacturing industry*. New Delhi: Sage.

Seth, S. 1332 B.S. *Bange Chaltattva*. Kolkata: Tara Press.

Setty, E. D. (2000). *A model for securing people's participation in Janmabhoomi rural development*. Dr. MCR Human Resource Development Institute of Andhra Pradesh.

Sharma, R. (1995). *Bhangi, scavenger in Indian society: Marginality, identity and politicization of the community*. New Delhi: M. D. Publications.

Singh, S. N. (1969). Choice of presidency exposes pulls within congress. *The Statesman*, 16 May.
Sinha, P., & Friedrich, E. S. (2013). *Issues before the Indian Trade Union Movement*. Retrieved September 9, 2015, from http://www.google.co.in/url?sa=t&rct=j&q=&esrc=s&source=web&cd=2&sqi=2&ved=0CDkQFjAB&url=http%3A%2F%2Flibrary.fes.de%2Fpdf-files%2Fiez%2F01963.pdf&ei=US_CUOKBIMrUrQeZyYGYAw&usg=AFQjCNEOnBOq7zrG6aFs02R0o1ufzFla8g&sig2=OQ429fu9ScsA0mnEBOp0mw
Smith, N. (2008). *Uneven development: Nature, capital and the production of space*. Georgia: University of Georgia Press.
Smith, V. L. (1972). Dynamics of waste accumulation: Disposal versus recycling. *The Quarterly Journal of Economics, 86*(4), 600–616.
Solow, R. M. (1990). *Labour market as social institution*. Oxford: Basil Blackwell.
Somayaji, S., & Talwar, S. (Eds.). (2011). *Development-induced displacement, rehabilitation and resettlement in India: Current issues and challenges*. London and New York: Routlege.
Spivak, G. C. (1985). Scattered speculations on the question of value. *Diacritics* (Winter), 73–93.
Srinivas, M. N. (1962). Changing institutions and values in modern India. *Economic Weekly, 14*(4–6), 131–137.
Standing, G. (1999). *Global labour flexibility—Seeking distributive justice*. London: Macmillan Press Limited.
Standing, G. (2002). *Beyond new paternalism—Basic security as equality*. New York: Verso.
Svoboda, R. (2010). *Prakriti: Your ayurvedic constitution*. Delhi: Motilal Banarsidas Publishers Pvt. Ltd.
The Indian Express. (2014). Manipuri man beaten to death in Delhi. Retrieved July 30, 2014, from http://indianexpress.com/article/cities/delhi/manipuri-man-beaten-to-death-in-delhi/
The Kolkata Gazette. (2015). *The Kolkata Gazette*, Extraordinary. 19 February.
The Morung Express. (2012). SC directs Nagaland Govt. to respond on 33 % women quota. 20 November. Retrieved October 26, 2013, from http://www.morungexpress.com/frontpage/88603.html
The Telegraph. (2005). Tripura Tribal Rehab Plan goes Awry. 1 October. Retrieved October 25, from http://www.telegraphindia.com/1051001/asp/northeast/story_5304499.asp
Tilly, C. (1999). *Durable inequality*. Berkeley and Los Angeles: University of California Press.
Tiwari, M. (2003). *Ayurveda: Secrets of healing*. Delhi: Motilal Banarsidas Publishers Pvt. Ltd.
Tse Tung, M. (1956). *Selected Works* (Vol. 5). Retrieved February 6, 2014, from https://www.marxists.org/reference/archive/mao/selected-works/volume-5/mswv5_51.htm
Tse-Tung, M. (1975). *Selected works of Mao Tse-Tung* (Vol. 2). Peking: Foreign Language Press.
Tvarno, C. D. (2011). Law and regulatory aspects of public-private partnerships: Contract law and public procurement law. In G. A. Hodge, C. Greve, & A. E. Boardman (Eds.), *International handbook on public private partnerships* (pp. 216–236). Cheltenham: Edward Elgar.
Upadhya, C. (1988). The farmer-capitalists of coastal Andhra Pradesh. *Economic and Political Weekly, 23*(28), 1376–1382.
Upadhya, C. (1988). The farmer-capitalists of coastal Andhra Pradesh. *Economic and Political Weekly, 23*(28), 1433–1442.
Upadhya, C. (1997). Social and cultural strategies of class formation in coastal Andhra Pradesh. *Contributions to Indian Sociology, 31*(2), 169–193.
Vargeese, M. (2010). *Historical background of trade unionism in India*. Retrieved September 9, 2015, from http://www.google.co.in/url?sa=t&rct=j&q=&esrc=s&source=web&cd=22&ved=0CDYQFjABOBQ&url=http%3A%2F%2Fshodhganga.inflibnet.ac.in%2Fbitstream%2F10603%2F610%2F11%2F11_chapter3.pdf&ei=nxTCUNsnxPetB6q3gIgO&usg=AFQjCNHsrVE8EaGV76WYZFBA27mkVh8aYA&sig2=hddDrVshF2gUEJ3Q_cZdgg
Varier, K. (2009). *History of ayurveda*. Kottakkal: Arya Vaidya Sala Pustakasala.
Wettenhall, R. (2011). Mixes and partnerships through time. In Hodge et al. (Eds.), *International handbook on public private partnerships* (pp. 17–42).
White, A. (2012). The new political economy of private security. *Theoretical Criminology 16*(1), 85–101. Retrieved from http://www.scopus.com/inward/record.url?eid=2-s2.0-84857775244partnerID=40md5=2dfadf6228db4812d42f72bbcd6afd8f

Williams, H. L. (2001). *Social movements and economic transition: Markets and distributive conflict in Mexico*. New York: Cambridge University Press.

Wolff, R. D., & Resnick, S. A. (1987). *Economics: marxian versus neoclassical*. Baltimore, London: The John Hopkins University Press.

Wolff, R. N. D. Capitalism hits the fan. Retrieved September 9, 2015, from http://www.rdwolff.net/sites/default/files/attachment/4/03Wolff.pdf

Xiang, B. (2007). *Global 'body shopping': An indian labour system in the information technology industry*. Princeton University Press.

Yashar, D. J. (2005). *Contesting citizenship in Latin America: The rise of indigenous movements and the post-liberal challenge*. Cambridge: Cambridge University Press.

Zee News. (2014). Manipuri girl allegedly raped by landlord's son in Delhi, North East students stage protest. Retrieved July 30, 2014, from http://zeenews.india.com/news/delhi/manipuri-girl-allegedly-raped-by-landlord-s-son-in-delhi-north-east-students-stage-protest_909992.html

Index

I.K. Mitra et al. (eds.), *Accumulation in Post-Colonial Capitalism*,
DOI 10.1007/978-981-10-1037-8